ROUND TABLE
Viewpoints

# EDUCATIONAL
# LEADERSHIP

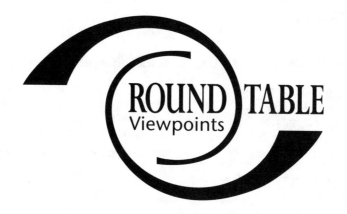

# EDUCATIONAL LEADERSHIP

Selected, Edited, and with Introductions and Summaries by

**Joyce Huth Munro**
*Chestnut Hill College*

 **Higher Education**

Boston   Burr Ridge, IL   Dubuque, IA   New York   San Francisco   St. Louis
Bangkok   Bogotá   Caracas   Kuala Lumpur   Lisbon   London   Madrid   Mexico City
Milan   Montreal   New Delhi   Santiago   Seoul   Singapore   Sydney   Taipei   Toronto

## Higher Education

ROUNDTABLE VIEWPOINTS: EDUCATIONAL LEADERSHIP, FIRST EDITION

✪ This book is printed on recycled, acid-free paper containing 10% postconsumer waste.

1 2 3 4 5 6 7 8 9 0 DOC/DOC 0 9 8 7

MHID: 0-07-337975-1
ISBN: 978-0-07-337975-3
ISSN: 1937-1187

Managing Editor: *Larry Loeppke*
Production Manager: *Beth Kundert*
Senior Developmental Editor: *Susan Brusch*
Editorial Assistant: *Nancy Meissner*
Production Service Assistant: *Rita Hingtgen*
Permissions Coordinator: *Lori Church*
Senior Marketing Manager: *Julie Keck*
Marketing Communications Specialist: *Mary Klein*
Marketing Coordinator: *Alice Link*
Project Manager: *Jane Mohr*
Design Specialist: *Tara McDermott*
Senior Administrative Assistant: *DeAnna Dausener*
Senior Operations Manager: *Pat Koch Krieger*
Cover Graphics: *Maggie Lytle*

Compositor: Hurix Systems
Cover Image: Siede Preis/Getty Images

www.mhhe.com

# CONTENTS IN BRIEF

# CONTENTS

# PREFACE

This book is about some of the most pressing issues that educational leaders face today. They are thorny, complex issues—the kind of problems that do not come with simple answers.

As the title of the series indicates, this book is meant to be more than a collection of readings—it offers varying perspectives that can stimulate deeper thought and wiser action. So expect no magic formulas or absolutes in this book. Instead, expect to find multiple viewpoints on each issue that enlarge your perspective and assist you in examining ways leadership is carried out in schools and institutions. A roundtable discussion is different from traditional debate, where an issue is polarized into two positions. By taking one side of an issue, the debater's goal is to win the argument by appealing to logic and emotions. Nothing is wrong with debate, but a roundtable discussion sets in motion other goals than winning an argument. Think of sitting at a conference table with a group of people who are sharing their perceptions about an important issue facing them. You are there to learn as much as possible from these experts. Civility prevails, even though there's definitely partisanship in the group. Everyone at the table participates in the discussion—demonstrating that this group is committed to "thinking systemically." Consider this book a virtual roundtable discussion. The multiple viewpoints in these pages enable you to learn more about the issues, make connections, and relate the author's statements to yourself in the role of educational leader.

All of the readings have been selected because they are relevant and current. More importantly, they align with latest theoretical developments and best practices. Issues such as accountability and local autonomy are incredibly volatile, eliciting strong responses. Other issues like strategic planning or performance evaluation, while not as controversial, still need to be considered from a variety of angles.

An underlying theme of the book is the importance and benefit of considering educational issues from a systems perspective. Systems has been a traditional way to analyze the mechanical components of an organization, like a production line, but recently the approach has been adapted to managing emotional, relational systems. Because an organization is more than the sum of its parts, problem analysis is more effective if it incorporates relationships and networks and the larger environment. Systems thinking is becoming the foundation on which school leaders analyze issues and build enduring change. This approach to leadership is presented in the introductory essay and reinforced throughout the book.

The purpose of roundtable viewpoints is to enable potential educational leaders to be sensitive to issues in order to be better guides in a chaotic world and into the future. With a systems approach in mind, read and analyze each issue and consider how you would lead if you were in a key leadership position right now.

## STRUCTURE OF ROUNDTABLE VIEWPOINTS: EDUCATIONAL LEADERSHIP

The thirty-nine readings in this volume address ten incisive issues that are organized in three sections: Perspectives on Educational Leadership (Unit 1), Context of Educational Leadership (Unit 2), and Challenges of Educational Leaders (Unit 3). Among the perspective issues are emerging leadership approaches, planning strategies, and balance of central authority and site-based autonomy. The contextual issues include performance assessment, systems approach, culture, and school reform. In the final part, the issues are sustaining diversity, impact of accountability legislation, and educational leadership in the future.

Each issue is addressed through three to five readings that provide a range of viewpoints. The issues and accompanying readings can be thought of as chapters; each chapter begins with an introduction that frames the readings in a larger context and ends with a summary that ties the viewpoints together. The summary is accompanied by several features that extend learning. These features are *Issue Highlights, Critical Thinking,* and *Additional Reading Resources.* These end-of-chapter resources are opportunities for application and skill development. The book concludes with *Contributors*—a listing of authors of the readings and their biographical sketches. The authors are an interesting variety of professionals, including organizational leaders, scholars, reporters, and consultants.

# ACKNOWLEDGEMENTS

My work on this book began with a conversation with Larry Loeppke on another topic altogether. But as he talked about his idea of a new series that would tackle educational leadership issues from multiple perspectives, my writing began to take a different direction. So I am grateful to Larry for introducing me to the Roundtable Viewpoints series and to Susan Brusch for shepherding the drafts and permissions and other vagaries of writing for a new series. My appreciation also goes to Karen Menke Paciorek, with whom I learned what editing actually involves. For over a decade we coedited volumes in other McGraw-Hill (and earlier Dushkin) series. Karen is a multitasker who gets things done—an invaluable combination for any leader in any educational institution.

My first venture in educational leadership was directing an early childhood education program in a community center. Eventually I shifted to higher education, with stops at two national professional associations. Despite differences in formal structure of organizations where I have worked, the nature of leadership problems I have faced has been remarkably steady. What has changed is that I have learned tools for better understanding the system. For that I am indebted to Eleanor Duff and Earline Kendall, great higher education leaders and excellent mentors.

I am also grateful to James Munro, a seasoned organizational leader, who allowed himself to be a sounding board throughout the writing process. Jamie is not only knowledgeable about the field of leadership; he is a good systems thinker who knows how to help organizations get unstuck.

Finally, I deeply appreciate the opportunity for ongoing conversations about many of the issues in this book with the Deanery at Chestnut Hill College.

# GUIDED TOUR

UNIT 3

### Challenges of Educational Leaders

Education is a task that always embodies utopias, looks toward the future, and requires the exercise of our full imaginations.

—Adriana Puiggros

Despite our attempts to cast education as utopia, some matters are persistent challenges for educational leaders. Two of these challenges have been selected for this unit: sustaining diverse and socially just organizations and the impact of accountability legislation. But one challenge is ever-new—the specter of the future and the leader's role in it. Systems theory is germane to challenges addressed in Unit 3. In systems terms, leaders who understand an educational organization's adaptive skill, its commitments, and its response to external demands will be better able to handle challenges like diversity, compliance with legislation, and the future.

We live in an era when schools and institutions are more diverse than ever. And the need to close the achievement gaps among diverse students is more pressing than ever. America's school leaders can ill afford to ignore the challenges that have arisen because of changing demographics. In such a high-stakes environment it could be tempting to treat diversity as a problem instead of an asset. The readings look at diversity issues from several angles—creating cultural competency, complying with law, managing age-diverse faculty and staff, and designing diversity initiatives.

## UNIT OPENER

Designed to outline related issues and capture student interest, each unit opener provides general information for the upcoming issues. The unit openers conclude with a list of issue questions covered in each unit.

ISSUE 2

### What Planning Strategies Work Best in Educational Organizations?

Historically, strategic planning has been one of the main activities of educational leaders. It is a task that occupies many work hours. In its simplest form, strategic planning enables administrators to answer three questions: Where are we going? How will we get there? How do we know we've gotten there? Essentially the purpose of strategic planning is to get everyone—faculty, staff, parents, board—on the same page with their answers to these three questions. Ideally, once in place, a strategic plan should make daily decision making easier.

Approaches to strategic planning vary, depending on the institution's mission and purpose, size, and culture. Institutions can take a goal-oriented, issue-oriented, or program-oriented approach, with goal-oriented being the typical model. Resources for strategic planning are abundant and many organizations are now able to turn to software for planning. (Googling will yield 6000 sources of strategic planning software.) So what are the best strategies for decision making in educational settings?

In truth, the answer to the question varies widely. For some institutions and agencies, strategic planning for a five to ten year period has fallen out of favor. For others, strategic planning as top-down, general-to-specific is passé. And for still others, the three classic planning questions are not even relevant. The problem is that many traditional strategy plans are obsolete instantly. While they are being circulated, educational standards, federal regulations, the neighborhood, and the world have all changed.

Strategic planning continues to be a major activity, but it is taking new shapes. This transformation is driven by much more than technology and resources. It is also due to an ever-increasing need for improvement and sustainability and supported by a mindset that embraces complexity. New planning strategies are more robust, allowing educational leaders to ask the why questions in addition to where and how. Sophisticated approaches like resource mapping, scenarios, and simulations enable leaders to do "what-if" analysis. No longer is strategic planning limited to corporate America and solely about profitability, margin, and performance. Now, as never before, schools and institutions have excellent resources for planning that focus on student achievement, sustainability, school climate, and adaptive systems.

## ISSUE INTRODUCTIONS

Designed to introduce the issue to the reader, the issue introduction states an issue question, provides history, current events, a list of the upcoming article selections for the issue, and relevant information about the issue to help facilitate discussion.

### Fostering Relationships and Systems and Modes of Communication

*How does a Complex Adaptive System approach to planning differ from the learning organization approach as outlined by Rowden in reading 3?*

A Complex Adaptive System approach to Strategic planning is an opportunity to reconstruct relationships and construct possibilities through dialogue and networking among both internal and external groups. This means a shift in emphasis. As in traditional and emerging strategic planning approaches, meetings among stakeholders still have a role in generating information for decision-making, but they have a larger role in nurturing the relationships that contribute to constructing possibilities and encouraging self-organization. Instead of a traditional organizational and environmental SWOT analysis, the agency may use Appreciative Inquiry and other ways to look for the changes already happening or about to happen. There may be a series of large (whole system) and small group meetings of both internal staff and external

## CHALLENGE QUESTIONS

Each issue contains challenge questions, in the form of marginal notes, designed to stimulate critical thinking and discussion. The challenge questions are thought-provoking and relevant to the issue and its selections.

## ISSUE SUMMARIES

Issue summaries appear at the end of each issue text. The summary brings the readings together, offers concluding observations, and suggests new directions for the student to take to further explore the issue.

## ISSUE HIGHLIGHTS

Highlights appear at the end of each issue and help to identify important information and details about the issue. The main points covered in the readings are recapped in the issue highlights.

## CRITICAL THINKING

Found at the end of each issue, this essential feature provides key strategies for using critical thinking skills in discussing the issues and forming an educated and well-thought-out opinion.

## ADDITIONAL READING RESOURCES

This feature encourages further research relevant to each issue. Many perspectives frame each issue, and these resources provide additional material related to the topic being discussed.

# INTRODUCTION

## A SYSTEMS APPROACH TO ISSUES IN EDUCATIONAL LEADERSHIP

This book of roundtable viewpoints on leadership is tied tightly to educational organizations. The readings are about leadership as it is practiced in an educational organization. The location could be a primary or high school, community college, university, professional school, or corporate learning center. In effect, the educational organization is the lens for examining a set of issues that affects how leadership is practiced. The thirty-nine readings in this volume address ten of these issues. They are grouped in three parts: *Perspectives on Educational Leadership* (Unit 1), *Context of Educational Leadership* (Unit 2), and *Challenges of Educational Leaders* (Unit 3). The first set of readings in *Perspectives* deals with the newest approaches to leadership in educational settings. The next readings examine an important function of educational leadership—decision making. Unit 1 ends with multiple perspectives on the critical issue of how much autonomy a school leader is given. Among the contextual issues in Unit 2 are supervision, systems approach, and school culture and reform. The third unit of the book introduces differing views on challenges for educational leaders. Three challenges currently debated in the educational community have been selected: diversity, accountability, and leadership in the future.

It is important to keep in mind that the authors of these readings speak with a variety of voices from different settings. Reading their divergent views on an issue is like sitting down with a group of experts for vigorous discussion. At some point in the conversation, ideas and philosophies will clash and people will disagree. This is an opportunity for critical thinking. By considering different viewpoints on the practice of leadership in educational settings you develop a deeper understanding.

While other leadership books and articles focus solely on the person as leader, this book is about the interface of person-as-leader, place, and participants. Some scholars and researchers refer to this interface as situated leadership. The readings selected for this book deal with the mix of leader, setting, and people, and taken together, they clearly demonstrate that there is no single correct answer to any of the issues. From the perspective of situated leadership, the best answer is "it depends." Firm and fast rules or tried and true principles become less reliable when the focus shifts from solitary leader to interaction of key leadership factors.

### The Changing Nature of Educational Leadership

Although many experts and scholars decry shallow (but popular) depictions of leadership as a bag of tricks or a quick fix, the search continues for a wholly new way to conceive of the leader in today's educational community. It may be tempting to pick up separate pieces and cobble together a picture of how an educational leader should deal with issues. To counter the temptation, this introduction explores concepts of leadership over time and examines the direction educational leadership is taking today. The introduction ends with an explanation of the systems approach, a useful way for leaders to think about organizational issues of schools and institutions. While the tendency is to return to time-honored notions of leadership, systems thinking is certainly changing our need to keep looking backward for answers.

Since the late 1800s when Max Weber first explained the hierarchical structure of bureaucracies, many scholars have explored the nature of organizational leadership. For awhile, researchers were preoccupied with traits of leaders, a school of thought that continues to be accepted. The problem with the traits perspective (a psychological construct) is it narrowly categorizes leadership as the personality of an individual. Moreover, there are as many lists of "most desirable traits" as there are leadership experts and consultants. This is not to denigrate traits of leaders; in fact, exploration of essential personality factors is reappearing in current organizational literature. But leadership in today's schools and institutions is far more complex than a certain set of traits displayed by an individual.

Parallel to the traits perspective in leadership literature runs the concept of control. During the late nineteenth century and into the early twentieth, small family-owned companies were replaced by large-scale organizations—America had entered the age of bureaucratic operations. As the economy grew, so did industry, business, and government. For some time, the leadership model was the "big man," an appropriate match to big business, big industry, and big government. The suggestion behind the image was that only a few leaders knew the "big picture." It wasn't long before the same control concepts permeated educational leadership.

For some people, it is impossible to conceive of leadership without thinking of authority, order, and power. The notion that leadership is about control is ubiquitous.

> The word "management" with its connotations of control is no longer restricted to a technical or indeed political function *within* organizations. It is currently used to encompass areas as diverse and grandiose as the management of the environment, the management of the economy, the management of the African elephant, the management of emotion, or still more ambitiously the management of the planet. . . . For practicing managers, the issue has become one of technique and search for efficiency—how best to control people, information and other resources in the light of continuous change and uncertainty. (Gabriel, 1998, p. 257)

Classic leadership literature is replete with examples of leaders' attempts to predict, categorize, classify, and control for every variable imaginable within organizations. In the age of No Child Left Behind, the stiffest challenges for educational leaders are in the area of academic accountability. But is any aspect of schools and institutions predictable and possible to control?

More and more, organizational scholars are saying no—predictability and control are not an exact science. Scholars are looking to newer theoretical constructs that paint a picture of leadership as fluid, emergent, or connected. Concepts of chaos theory and complexity science are edging out prediction and control in organizational leadership literature. These new sciences cast leadership in a setting that is more like an ecosystem than a machine. Keith Morrison, a well-published expert on organizational leadership, has set the tone for thinking about leadership in an adaptive environment.

... the matter is not simply a structural one for school leaders, i.e., setting up structures and watching them "roll out" to a prefigured future. Rather, complexity theory sees the future as uncertain and emergent, and the school as a tangle of micropolitics which affect the directions of development. The leadership task becomes the management of the micropolitics and of moving the members of the school from a competitive, secretive, isolationist and procedures-driven mentality to a collaborative, interdependent, group- and team-based network, with devolved decision making and its accompanying responsibility and accountability. (2002, p. 35)

Exactly what it means for leaders to deal with the tangle of micropolitics is currently under debate. Leadership experts and think tanks are delving into the nature of leadership in an unpredictable world. At one of these think tanks, The Center for Creative Leadership (CCL), research is giving direction for a new conception of leadership that is more suitable for settings where discontinuity and uncertainty are key features. "Leadership is changing and approaches focusing on flexibility, collaboration crossing boundaries and collective leadership are expected to become a high priority" (2005, p. 3). One of the questions addressed in the CCL study is whether there is a move away from *leader* development toward *leadership* development, which would indicate that attention is shifting from the person to the process. The answer is yes—it makes sense to consider educational leadership as a process.

Embedded leadership—leadership that is influenced and shaped by the organization where it is practiced—is an appropriate phrase for this new view of leadership. In recognition that organization and leadership are interdependent, current research is framing leadership as a set of qualities, imperatives, or elements. Devoid of a location, leadership can be boiled down to "tips" or "points," but in practice, leader work is highly complex, with many crucial areas of organizational life that must be addressed for a school or institution to be successful. Pervasive and escalating change has shaken our ability to think about effective leadership without thinking about its settings and circumstances.

To correct the tendency to study leadership in the abstract, Zaccaro and Klimoski (2001) have formed a set of defining elements of leadership embedded in organizations. Taken together, these elements provide a robust definition of organizational leadership in a world that new sciences are showing us is turbulent and chaotic.

- Organizational leadership involves processes and proximal outcomes that contribute to the development and achievement of organizational purpose.
- Organizational leadership is identified by the application of nonroutine influence on organizational life.
- Leader influence is grounded in cognitive, social, and political processes.
- Organizational leadership is inherently bounded by system characteristics and dynamics, that is, leadership is contextually defined and caused (pp. 2–3).

Out of these elements comes a more holistic view of the true nature of organizational leadership. Look again at the essence of these elements—achieving organizational purpose, problem solving, relationship building, sense-making, contextualizing. This is very sophisticated work. The good news is leadership work is being reconceptualized as work done together over time. The other news is that organizational leadership-as-process has a feel and momentum unique to a particular setting. How leadership is conducted in one school will not look the same as another school. This fact creates another dilemma; it is difficult to examine new leadership work without relying on past theories. While some leadership work is grounded in ancient practices, other work takes new forms as the system adapts to the people in it. So exactly how does systems thinking apply to educational leadership?

## How Systems Thinking Applies to Educational Leadership

To understand systems thinking, we first need to acknowledge the essential role of systems in our lives. Systems are all around us and we are part of various systems. Our bodies are composed of several systems, one of which is the respiratory system. The earth is part of a solar system (which has recently seen its number of planets reduced). We talk of the earth's systems—ecosystems, weather systems. Organizations are also systems, in this case theoretical or conceptual rather than natural. Essentially, systems are self-organizing and evolving. They are not merely the sum or even the product of parts.

Historically, organizational systems have been cast in linear terms—input, feedback, output. When such terms are used for work, it is easy to see why organizations have been viewed as machines. The settings were manufacturing or industry and assembly line problems were fairly well defined. Linear systems were appropriate for the industrial age because the science of industry naturally led to the need for efficiency, error-free production, and quality control. By the 1940s, this approach to systems, referred to as a hard approach, spilled over into other endeavors, particularly information science.

The journey from industry to the information era has not been easy and organizational systems have not always kept pace with new work or education realities. People still tend to think of organizations as stable systems that operate by set rules and formulas. Many have been reluctant to change their ways of thinking about schools and institutions, preferring to cling to age-old ideas like the dichotomy of leaders and followers, the preoccupation with personality enhancement, and the power and control model of leadership. It has taken some effort to recast systems as "open" (inclusive of external forces and factors) and densely interdependent. Thinking about systems as "open" means avoiding the tendency to dichotomize, which people do when they frame situations as either/or or cause and effect. Instead, systems thinkers look for connections, patterns, relationships, spirals, and dynamics. These concepts help educational leaders move away from nineteenth-century mechanics ideas about schools.

In recent decades, chaos theory and complexity sciences have influenced systems thinking and led to terms like sensitivity to conditions, equilibrium, and homeostasis. Discoveries in natural and biological sciences and quantum physics have also helped to increase our awareness of patterns in the midst of confusion and of order despite irregularity.

New ways of thinking about educational leadership are now challenging traditional bureaucratic models of organizations characterized by standardized procedures, division of labor, and expert leaders. Complexity sciences contradict Max Weber's concepts of bureaucracy—impersonalizing of the system, goal orientation rather than values orientation, and vertical hierarchy of authority. The question remains: How useful are new complexity theories if leaders are never sure what the outcome of an action will be?

On the surface, it seems that chaos is simply randomness and that is risky business for any organization. But experts in the new sciences would caution against equating chaos with organizational anarchy.

> Chaos theory does not leave us in a position of powerlessness and confusion: it enables us to observe and analyze such systems, unravel patterns, establish boundaries (e.g., no snowstorms in the Sahara), note similarities, identify areas of tranquility and make short-term forecasts. (Gabriel, 1998, p. 261)

Chaos theory comes into play as a way for leaders to deal with ambiguity while unraveling patterns and establishing boundaries within educational organizations. What we are coming to understand is that it is not the rational, settled organization that will thrive but the innovative, emergent system. This is because the need for homeostasis (stability and identity) actually interferes with attempts to learn, change, and innovate. In combination, systems thinking and chaos theory can help a school or institution keep a sense of security while moving in new directions.

The current and pressing challenge is to find standards of excellence for educational leadership that is embedded, holistic, contextualized. The Interstate School Leaders Licensure Consortium (ISLLC) has crafted model standards that attempt to capture new notions of leadership. Twenty-four states have adopted ISLLC standards, which is encouraging. The fact remains that licensure standards, by their nature, have a limited purpose: public safety, health, and welfare. The encouraging news is that elements of embedded leadership can be captured through systems thinking so they can be learned and practiced. And eventually systems approaches will make their way into standards.

## Emotional Systems in Educational Organizations

One of the striking findings of recent research done by The Center for Creative Leadership is the increasing importance of leader skill in building and mending relationships. Historically, this "soft skill" has ranked low in surveys. But our ideas about necessary leader skills are changing and relationship building is currently the second most important skill (behind another soft skill: leading employees). The high ranking of relationships indicates that the days of casting a private vision, acting unilaterally, and making decisions in isolation are on the wane. It also says that treating faculty and staff as problems is no longer valid; rather, employees are a wealth that has been undervalued.

Attention to relationships becomes even more important due to the changing nature of teaching and learning. Today teachers and staff move across functional boundaries to solve problems or implement new programs or collaborate with community partners. This is quite different from a traditional grade- or discipline-based group led by a single person who is responsible for getting the job done. In a networked institution, the assignment is shared, leadership is shared, and problems and decisions are shared.

Shared work is a practice that fits well in a "complex, no-one-in-charge, shared-power world" (Crosby & Bryson, 2005, p. 4). This paradigm could lead to the idea that sharing power preempts leadership—a troubling notion—until it is placed in perspective.

All this does not mean that the in-charge leadership image has disappeared or completely lost its usefulness. The connective or quiet leader sometimes has to make a decision and implement it using whatever powers and controls he or she has. Similarly, leaders who are formally in charge know they often must consult and compromise with other powerful people before acting. In a shared-power situation, however, leadership that encourages the participation of others must be emphasized because only it has the power to inspire and mobilize those others. In the effort to tackle public problems, leadership and power must be consciously shared with a view to eventually creating power-sharing institutions within a regime of mutual gain. (p. 32)

Work that is shared heightens the importance of relationships in organizations and makes relationship building a central skill for leaders. Interaction skills like consultation, negotiation, compromise, and conflict management are an integral part of daily life for leaders in organizations that operate by sharing power and distributing leadership. Shared work and shared power also mean more investment in team building, group learning, and culture formation.

## Leadership as an Emotional Process (from a Systems Point of View)

Shared work has other unforeseen effects that must be dealt with. One of these is the emotional nature of work, an attribute of work that has been ignored. (Keep in mind that emotional is more than feelings—it is the instinctual response of humans to change, tension, and threat). Teamwork in particular is emotion-filled work. Individuals in teams are in vulnerable positions because their knowledge and expertise are on display in front of others. Every aspect of shared work is done publicly and constant interaction is difficult for some individuals. Stress and anxiety are bound to be present in teams and there are no quick fixes for relationships that are stressful and anxious.

The emotional side of organizational life is a hot topic these days in both popular and academic literature. One practitioner whose work has broken ground on the connections between emotional process at home and at work is Edwin Friedman. His premise (carried forward by Beal and Treadwell) is that emotional processes in society negatively impact American leadership. These processes are so powerful that tinkering with the personnel structure or trying harder does not help.

Administrative, technical, and managerial solutions (such as centralizing, de-centralizing, re-centralizing, deconstructing, downsizing, right-sizing, or otherwise re-engineering) may often alleviate the symptoms of an organization. But they rarely modify the malignant chronic anxiety that could have been part of that institution's "corporate culture" for generations, and that will, if left unmodified, resurface periodically in different shapes and forms. (Beal & Treadwell, 1999, p. 80)

Psychological or sociological theories are not sufficient to support leaders in a "leadership-toxic climate." Climate change begins by recognizing that negative or regressive emotional processes at work are systemic and must be dealt with throughout the school.

An intentional approach to relationship-building means an administrator first understands that teaching is emotion-filled and then knows how to address negative emotions, particularly anxiety. Relationship systems can be thought of in ways similar to the natural systems of biology and physics (open, fluid, interactive, and adaptive). Rather than viewing an organization as a collection of individuals acting out emotional, relational processes, culture is the medium for these processes played out. This focus on relationship processes rather than on the individuals lends itself to applying emotional systems thinking in the workplace.

The paradox of emotional systems theory is that instead of trying to fix relationships or motivate people, educational leaders deliberately shift attention away from others to their own ways of relating and communicating. The chief goal of leaders is to focus on their own integrity and capacity for dealing with the emotional processes of the organization (Beal & Treadwell, 1999, p. 11). Leaders do this by taking well-defined stands, treating conflict as natural, and determining the limits of consensus for good decision making. By dealing with the organization as an emotional system, leaders are less likely to become enmeshed in anxious, risk-averse processes in the organization. Having gained some amount of autonomy (self-differentiation), leaders are better able to connect with teacher or staff teams, without reverting to the tendency to blame or correct. In some ways, this leadership approach to relationship systems is the same as a strengths approach. By looking for and supporting strengths, leaders move the organization in a positive direction rather than enabling it to be reactive or regressive.

Fundamental in the systems approach is a nonlinear view of organizational relationships. Instead of dyadic or two-person interaction, relationships are conceived as emotional triangles, with the third element being an unseen person, an issue, or another relationship. Emotional triangles have both positive and negative effects in the workplace. By analyzing triangles, leaders can be more objective in understanding what is happening and can influence the climate and effectiveness of the entire institution. Perhaps the most important effect of leaders who employ a systems approach to organizational relationships is the increase in opportunities for growth and learning.

Poorly defined leaders unwittingly compromise learning and achievement by avoiding the emotional processes within their schools. The best way to lead is "by taking the kind of stands that set limits to the invasiveness of those who lack self-regulation" (Beal & Treadwell, 1999, p. 11). In other words, leadership must be decisive in dealing with negative processes in the institution.

In shared work settings, leadership "increasingly depends upon the power of creative relationships and all that is required in establishing, sustaining, nurturing, and bearing the anxiety involved in working through the medium of creative relationships" (Krantz, 1998, p. 11). The job of educational leaders in dealing with issues that schools face is to be courageous, take a stand and stick to it, and then stay connected to those who are charged with carrying out the mission. This is a matter of finding the right balance, not finding a quick fix. Friedman portrays the balance a leader needs to find in an emotional system as a continuum.

On the left side of the continuum are behaviors that Friedman calls weak leadership and on the right side are strong leadership behaviors. A leader may be weak in one and strong in another, but through training and practice the pattern of behavior can be strengthened. The goal is to stay balanced in order to effectively lead emotional work systems.

It is important to emphasize that taking a systems approach is not the same as a systematic search for more data or the right technique. The more leaders try to help people by fixing the

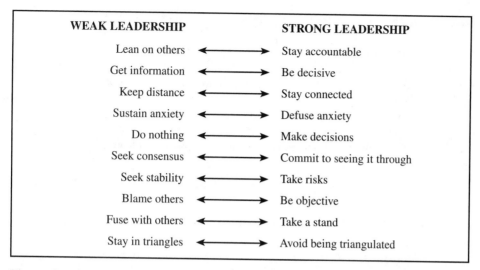

WEAK LEADERSHIP                    STRONG LEADERSHIP

Lean on others  ⟷  Stay accountable

Get information  ⟷  Be decisive

Keep distance  ⟷  Stay connected

Sustain anxiety  ⟷  Defuse anxiety

Do nothing  ⟷  Make decisions

Seek consensus  ⟷  Commit to seeing it through

Seek stability  ⟷  Take risks

Blame others  ⟷  Be objective

Fuse with others  ⟷  Take a stand

Stay in triangles  ⟷  Avoid being triangulated

Figure 1    Continuum of Leadership Functioning in Emotional Systems.
Adapted from Beal & Treadwell, 1999, p. 303.

situation, the less likely the organization is to grow and improve. If educational leaders these days are to be successful, they must find ways of living within the system while remaining steadfast in defense of the common good for the institution.

> The twin problems confronting leadership in our society today, the failure of nerve and the desire for a quick fix, are not the result of overly strong self but of weak or no self. There certainly is reason to guard against capricious, irrational, autocratic, vainglorious leadership in any form of organized life. But democratic institutions have far more to fear from lack of self in their leaders and the license this gives to factionalism (which is not the same as dissent) than from too much strength in the executive power. (Beal & Treadwell, 1999, p. 217)

Ronald Heifetz, a leadership expert at Harvard University, takes a compatible approach to leadership of emotional systems in institutions. Adaptive leadership for today's schools requires leaders who have courage to "interrogate reality." As he describes it, the leader's role in an emotional/social system is twofold: to help people face reality and conflict and to mobilize them to make change. In doing so, a leader must be a diagnostician and, when resistance starts, avoid taking things personally:

> It's dangerous to challenge people in a way that will require changes in their priorities, their values, their habits. It's dangerous to try to persuade people to take more responsibility than they feel comfortable with. And that's why so many leaders get marginalized, diverted, attacked, seduced. You want to be able to stir the pot without letting it boil over. You want to regulate disequilibrium, to keep people in a productive discomfort zone.

Courage . . . diagnosis . . . adaptive work . . . relationship. These are the main functions of educational leaders for our day and time. Leading today is not just about making adequate yearly progress or achieving standards or meeting goals, it is also about bringing value and change to an institution. With so much at stake for educational organizations in the age of the quick fix, leaders must first find a sense of self that is capable of guiding an institution through the long haul.

The purpose of roundtable viewpoints is to enable potential educational leaders to be sensitive to issues so they can be better guides in a chaotic world and into the future. With a systems approach in mind, read and analyze each issue and consider how you would lead if you were in a key leadership position right now.

## Resources

Edward W. Beal & Margaret M. Treadwell, *A Failure of Nerve: Leadership in the Age of the Quick Fix.* Edwin Friedman Estate/Trust, 1999.

Barbara C. Crosby & John M. Bryson, *Leadership for the Common Good: Tackling Public Problems in a Shared-Power World.* Jossey-Bass, 2005.

Yiannis Gabriel, "The Hubris of Management." *Administrative Theory and Praxis,* 1998.

Ronald Heifetz, *Leadership Without Easy Answers.* Harvard University Press, 1994.

Kristina Jaskyte, "Transformational Leadership, Organizational Culture, and Innovativeness in Nonprofit Organizations." *Nonprofit Management & Leadership,* Winter 2004.

James Krantz, "Anxiety & the New Order." *Leadership in the 21st Century,* International Universities, 1998.

Andre Martin, *The Changing Nature of Leadership.* The Center for Creative Leadership, 2005.

Keith Morrison, *School Leadership and Complexity Theory.* Routledge Falmer, 2002.

Warren Smith, "Chaos Theory and Postmodern Organization." *International Journal of Organizational Theory and Behavior,* 2001.

Daniel J. Svyantek & Richard P. DeShon, "Organizational Attractors: A Chaos Theory Explanation of Why Cultural Change Efforts Often Fail." *Public Administration Quarterly,* 1993.

William C. Taylor, "The Leader of the Future: Harvard's Ronald Heifetz Offers a Short Course on the Future of Leadership," Fast Company, May 1999. www.fastcompany.com/online/25/heifetz.html

Stephen J. Zaccaro & Richard J Klimoski, *The Nature of Organizational Leadership: Understanding the Performance Imperatives Confronting Today's Leaders.* Jossey-Bass, 2001.

For more information on systems approach to issues in educational leadership check these sites:

AASA Center for System Leadership, www.aasa.org/AASACenter

Center for Creative Leadership, www.ccl.org

Center for Leadership Studies, www.situational.com

MIT Systems Dynamics in Education, http://sysdyn.clexchange.org

Pegasus Communications, www.pegasuscom.com

The Sustainability Institute, www.sustainabilityinstitute.org

# U N I T 1

# Perspectives on Educational Leadership

I used to think that running an organization was equivalent to conducting a symphony orchestra. But I don't think that's quite it; it's more like jazz . . . more improvisation.

—Warren Bennis

A lot of leaders are attempting to define leadership these days. Place any five high-profile leaders at a roundtable and you'll probably hear five different metaphors woven into the discussion. Conductor of an orchestra, quarterback of a football team, servant of the people, herder of cats. The five readings selected for the issue of *newest approaches to leadership* present divergent perspectives, although none of these metaphors are included. The first viewpoint is an examination of a pattern of behavior that many leaders fall prey to—essentially it is cover-up behavior for times a leader doesn't know what to do. But there is another approach to leading during times of confusion or conflict that can catalyze change. The author outlines a nuanced manner of dealing honestly with confusion. The second approach is "flexible" leadership, a term that acknowledges the practice of leadership cannot be rigid or controlling. The third approach calls for leaders to apply their mental and emotional resources to creating a more positive working atmosphere. The fourth approach is another form of flexible leadership that moves leadership in the direction of a group process. And the final approach focuses even more on process by intentionally distributing leadership throughout the institution.

Four viewpoints are expressed in the roundtable on *strategies* educational organizations use in the planning enterprise. Each author makes a different argument about the best approach for strategy development. One reading calls for the end to traditional strategic planning and another calls for educational organizations to become settings for continuous learning. According to another reading, strategic planning itself isn't the problem; it's whether the process has been collaborative and geared toward problem solving. The final reading outlines a completely different approach to strategic planning—futuring—an alternative form that is appropriate to adaptive organizations like schools.

The readings selected for the third issue on the right balance of *central authority and site-based autonomy* confirm that the matter of governance is causing a rift in the educational community these days. Some experts warn that centralized decision making is crucial for districtwide improvement and others argue that improvement can only happen with buy-in of those who are implementing the programs and teaching the students. Another rift concerns the appropriate role of the school leader—should a leader be more of a business leader or more of an instructional leader. This debate comes to a head in a reading about nontraditional school leaders whose approach is "gunslinging."

**Issue 1:** What Are the Newest Approaches to Educational Leadership?

**Issue 2:** What Planning Strategies Work Best in Educational Organizations?

**Issue 3:** What Is the Right Balance of Central Authority and Site-Based Autonomy?

Quote: National Association of Secondary School Principals, *Interview with: Dr. Warren Bennis.* National Association of Secondary School Principals Audio Education, February 1994.

# What Are the Newest Approaches to Educational Leadership?

There is no question that effective leadership is vital to the success of schools and institutions. What *is* in question is whether one approach is better than another. Should a leader be in charge, authoritative, a celebrity? Or should a leader be a facilitator, empowering, a coach? Is leadership a matter of temperament or talent or training or practice? Should a leader focus on data and regulations or on people and processes?

These crucial questions are dealt with in the readings for this section. But first a caveat is necessary. The roundtable question does not deal with the leader/administrator controversy prevalent in leadership studies today. Administrative work is certainly the responsibility of leaders and leadership is certainly called for in administrators. It is the second side of this equation that is central to the roundtable question, so the readings selected for this issue are theory-based and deal with social influence, process, and characteristics rather than administrative tasks per se. The first reading calls for us to reconsider a leadership pattern once regarded as negative. In two of the readings, new approaches are built on previous practices. One reading introduces a trait that contrasts vividly with time-honored lists of leadership traits. And the final reading tackles an approach unique to educational institutions: distributed leadership. Taken together, the readings provide a multi-perspective look at the question of what defines educational leadership today. Here are the viewpoints discussed by the roundtable.

"Embracing Confusion: What Leaders Do When They Don't Know What to Do" is an intriguing look at how confusion can actually be an asset for leaders. Jentz and Murphy have identified a pattern of behavior they call "lost leader syndrome" that will debilitate leaders unless they learn how to use their confusion effectively. The authors provide a clear description of how leaders can transform confusion into a resource. This reading is a good place to start the roundtable discussion because new leaders—whether new in their career or new in a location—inevitably have to admit they simply don't know what to do.

In "Improving Performance Through Flexible Leadership," two scholars provide a model of leadership that deals with a current and pressing question: Does a leader focus on data and regulations or on people and processes? For Yukl and Lepsinger, leadership quality comes down to how well a leader influences three factors that determine an organization's effectiveness—efficiency, adaptation, and human resources. Although these three factors are typically used in the business world, given today's emphasis on high performance, they certainly apply to schools and institutions. The authors contend that the essential leader characteristic is flexibility. They identify three guidelines for flexible leadership: understanding both the external and internal processes, using systems thinking, and bringing people together in support of a shared purpose. Understanding one factor but ignoring the others is inflexible leadership, which can cripple an educational organization.

"The Socially Intelligent Leader" deals with the temperament question, but with the addition of information from the new field of social neuroscience. Goleman posits that it is not sufficient for a leader to have business savvy—people savvy is also necessary. While this area of leadership has always been intriguing, it is only recently that theorists and researchers have begun a systematic investigation into the underlying factor—emotional intelligence. Goleman defines how social intelligence can change the emotional climate of schools. By creating a positive working atmosphere, leaders can energize staff and impact student outcomes.

The next viewpoint is a bold new perspective on leadership that is inclusive and collective, making the tasks of leading more compatible with current educational, social, and political realities. In "Leading Together: Complex Challenges Require a New Approach," Drath identifies several dynamics that institutions like schools have never faced before. Today's problems are far more complex and are spread across traditional boundaries. Work teams share responsibility and no one person may be in charge. What is called for is a new approach—connected leadership—where shared sense-making leads to shared understanding, where structures are flexible, and where the strategies, as well as the outcomes, are emergent.

The perspective on leadership provided by James Spillane is a relatively new practice in schools. "Distributed Leadership" is about a form of shared leadership that involves a group of individuals and fluid governance structures. The vital difference between traditional forms and the distributed form is an emphasis on practice rather than roles, titles, and lines of authority. Spillane explains: "Rather than viewing leadership practice as a product of a leader's knowledge and skill, the distributed perspective defines it as the interactions between people and their situation."

Will the questions posed at the beginning of this introduction ever be answered once and for all? Consider what Pierce and Newstrom (Jon L. Pierce and John W. Newstrom, *Leaders and the Leadership Process.* McGraw-Hill/ Irwin, 2006) say is happening to leadership:

> Increasingly, organizations are modifying the role of yesterday's manager, changing the role to that of a leader charged with the responsibility to gain follower recognition and acceptance and become a facilitator and orchestrator of group activity, while also serving as coach and cheerleader. It is feasible that many of these roles (e.g., servant, teacher, coach, cheerleader) will become a common

part of the conceptualization of leader and leadership as the twenty-first century continues to unfold (p. 11).

It is evident that the meaning of leadership changes as schools and institutions change. Because educational organizations will continue to vary in purpose, size, and structure, undoubtedly leadership approaches will continue to evolve.

## SOURCES

Barry C. Jentz and Jerome T. Murphy, Embracing confusion: What leaders do when they don't know what to do. *Phi Delta Kappan*, January 2005.

Gary Yukl and Richard Lepsinger, Improving performance through flexible leadership. *Leadership in Action*, September/October 2005.

Daniel Goleman, The socially intelligent leader. *Educational Leadership*, September 2006.

Wilfred H. Drath, Leading together: Complex challenges require a new approach. *Leadership in Action*, March/April 2003.

James P. Spillane, Distributed leadership. *The Educational Forum*, Winter 2005.

# ARTICLE 1.1

# Embracing Confusion: What Leaders Do When They Don't Know What to Do

## Barry C. Jentz and Jerome T. Murphy

While we didn't know it at the time, the seed for this article was planted some 20 years ago when Jerome Murphy became the new—and often confused—associate dean of the Harvard Graduate School of Education. Blind-sided by unexpected problems and baffled by daunting institutional challenges, Murphy often lost his sense of direction and simply didn't know what to do. To make matters worse, he felt like a phony. "For God's sake," he said to himself, "isn't a Harvard dean supposed to have the answers?"

Enter Barry Jentz, an organizational consultant who helped Murphy learn that confusion is not a weakness to be ashamed of but a regular and inevitable condition of leadership. By learning to embrace their confusion, managers are able to set in motion a constructive process for addressing baffling organizational issues. In fact, confusion turns out to be a fruitful environment in which the best managers thrive by using the instability around them to open up better lines of communication, test their old assumptions and values against changing realities, and develop more creative approaches to problem solving.

## THE LOST LEADER SYNDROME

The two of us were recently reminded of our early encounters with confusion when we had the opportunity to work on issues of leadership with a distinguished group of urban school superintendents. Given the challenge of getting to their present positions, all of these superintendents had long since mastered the skill of presenting a confident, take-charge demeanor. But after developing enough trust to talk frankly with one another, these seasoned superintendents admitted that they were often confused and sometimes simply didn't know what they were doing—not that they could ever admit that in public.

This candid discussion revealed a pattern of behavior that we have come to call the Lost Leader Syndrome. The standard pathology may look familiar. No matter how capable or well prepared, managers regularly find themselves confronting bewildering events, perplexing information, or baffling situations that steal their time and hijack their carefully planned agendas. Disoriented by developments that just don't make sense and by challenges that don't yield to easy solutions, these managers become confused—sometimes even lost—and don't know what to do.

*What are some current pressures in public education that can result in "lost leader syndrome"?*

**6**

Many managers inevitably will respond to these symptoms by simply denying that they are confused. Others will hide their confusion—their search for
sense—because they see it as a liability, telling themselves, "I'll lose authority
if I acknowledge that I can't provide direction—I'm supposed to know the
answers!" Acting as if they are in control while really not knowing what to do,
these managers reflexively and unilaterally attempt to impose quick fixes to
restore their equilibrium.

*When leaders hide their confusion, how are faculty and staff affected?*

Sometimes, these managerial responses may even succeed in making the
immediate symptoms of problems go away, but they rarely address underlying causes. More often, they lead to bad decision making, undermine crucial
communication with colleagues and subordinates, and make managers seem
distant and out of touch. In the long run, managers who hide their confusion
also damage their organizations' ability to learn from experience and grow. Yet,
despite these drawbacks, few managers can resist hiding their confusion.

We have observed this dysfunctional pattern hundreds of times in the public, private, and nonprofit sectors—in government agencies, corporations, universities, and foundations—and believe that it is becoming more common as
the pace of change accelerates.

Our recent discussions with school superintendents suggest that this pattern of confusion and hiding or covering up is particularly prevalent in the
pressure-cooker world of public education. Parents, taxpayers, and political
and business leaders expect educators to address issues for which there are
no ready answers. Tony Wagner maintains that "the overwhelming majority
of school and district leaders do not know how to help teachers better prepare
all students for the higher learning standards."[1] Similarly, Richard Elmore
argues that "knowing the right thing to do is the central problem of school
improvement."[2]

In these pages, we will look at a method by which managers can transform
their confusion from a liability into a resource and describe how this resource
can be used to promote learning, new ideas, and the ability to take effective
action. We call this method Reflective Inquiry and Action (RIA), a five-step
process through which managers can assert their need to make sense and enlist
individuals and teams without sacrificing their goals, values, or judgment. We
believe that in the all too frequent situation of not knowing *what* to do, managers can make progress and maintain their authority by knowing *how* to move
forward.

The RIA process is designed primarily for "micro" work, such as that
in private meetings between individuals and small groups. But, as we shall
see, several of the guiding principles behind RIA—embracing your confusion, structuring a process for moving forward, listening reflectively—can
be quite useful on a larger scale and even in public venues. Significantly,
these ideas can help leaders make headway while struggling with the daunting "macro" challenge of educating all children in every school, often a
cause of confusion.[3]

## THE TALE OF THE TAPE

Is "confusion" even the best term for that sense of disorientation caused by having the rug pulled out from under one's feet or by being baffled in the face of an unyielding challenge? It is certainly a loaded word in management circles, and to suggest that an educator should acknowledge confusion, even to close and trusted colleagues, is risky. When a New York City teacher recently posted on her weblog: "I have no idea how to teach these kids, and I'm not sure I ever will," her principal called her in to assess her emotional state.[4]

Even if managers can privately bring themselves to accept their confusion, can they truly use it as a resource for effective management? Many managers dismiss this idea as suspiciously touchy-feely. After all, phrases such as "embracing your confusion" sound too much like "getting in touch with your inner child"—hardly the basis for making progress in a rough-and-tumble world. Some managers may be unsettled by what they see as the "soft" nature of RIA, even if deep down they know that there is truth in the old cliché that real men never ask for directions—instead they end up driving around in circles.[5] (In the RIA model, real managers accept that they are lost and metaphorically ask for directions.)

Nowhere is this skepticism more evident than in RIA workshops. To overcome it and to get managers to take these ideas seriously, we have learned to put participants in front of a video camera and ask them to respond to difficult scenarios that thrust them into confusion. When the tape is played back, participants are surprised to see the discrepancy between how they behave and how they *think* they behave. They watch how their retreat into hiding produces interpersonal dynamics characterized by posturing, guessing, arguing, and accusing—when the truth is that everyone is equally confused.[6]

By contrast, when one of the participants is able to acknowledge her confusion without fear or shame—and to invoke the rigor of a structured inquiry—the videotape reveals a palpable change in the participants' sense of energy, competence, and confidence. For a manager who is capable of creating the conditions necessary for interpersonal learning and for those who have witnessed these methods at work, this moment of discovery raises hope that the RIA process can be the foundation for shared progress. For advocates of RIA, these revelations are a powerful argument against dismissing these ideas as too soft for a tough world.

## THE "OH, NO!" MOMENT

Imagine being the head of a team charged with preventing deadly radiation leaks at a nuclear power plant. You hear an alarm sound. Based on years of experience and training—and a quick review of the data—you make an educated guess about what the problem might be. Suddenly, one of your team members reports that a key piece of information from the reactor systems doesn't fit your hypothesis. In fact, it's the exact opposite of what it should be. You have encountered what we refer to as an "Oh, No!" moment. You can't make sense of what is going on. As you sit stunned in front of your reactor-systems console, your team stares at you, waiting for a decision.

Now imagine that you are a member of the team, looking nervously to your leader. The last thing the situation requires is someone who:

- instinctively blames circumstances or other people when things go wrong;
- says he is open to input but regards any feedback as criticism and doesn't listen to others;
- hates uncertainty and opts for action even when totally confused; or
- takes a polarized view of leadership in which anything less than take-charge decision making shows abject weakness.

We all understand that a manager who neither listens to nor learns from others can quickly turn a messy problem into a nightmare. "Oh, No!" moments are familiar to all of us. They are caused not only by emergencies but also by a wide variety of everyday situations that regularly arise out of the blue and call into question our fundamental assumptions. We just can't make sense of what's going on. Taken aback by these situations, managers become distracted from their strategic agenda and reflexively respond to "Oh, No!" moments like the following:

- A change in technology renders a valued program obsolete.
- A promotion that everyone knows to be "ours" goes to a rival.
- A key administrator resigns without warning, offering an explanation that we simply do not believe.
- After repeated efforts to address a strategic challenge, we get feedback that our latest attempt is a failure.
- The long hours that produce triumph at work also produce trouble at home.

In moments like these—and in many situations that are more mundane but no less challenging—our minds begin to teem with questions. Our stomachs churn with emotion. Our old bearings no longer keep us on course. We struggle to reorient ourselves because the assumptions that gave meaning to our daily lives are suddenly rendered inadequate. We grope for new information that can help us make sense of this new situation and its impact. Often this initial investigation fails to reconcile our old assumptions with our new reality, and we find ourselves confused or even lost.

One of the ironies of these disorienting situations (and the "Oh, No!" moments that signal them) is that we often forget how much we rely on our world to make sense until our world is turned upside down by new information or changing circumstances.

# GOING INTO HIDING

In the face of an "Oh, No!" moment, few of us are willing to reveal our confusion or our sense that maybe we are lost. To admit such a possibility opens the door not only to the fear of losing authority but also to a host of other troubling emotions and thoughts:

- Shame and loss of face: "You'll look like a fool!"
- Panic and loss of control: "You've let this get out of hand!"
- Incompetence and incapacitation: "You don't know what you're doing!"

At the gut level, many managers believe that saying " I'm at a loss here" is tantamount to declaring "I am not fit to lead."

So, when faced with disorienting situations, most managers deny, hide, or opt for the quick fix, rather than openly acknowledge that they feel confused.[7] Denial takes the form of blaming themselves or others, usually the person who delivers the counterintuitive information. Hiding leads to keeping their mouths shut in self-protection, not wanting to risk exposure as anything other than completely composed and confident. (One former school principal calls this the "art of the bluff.") Many managers unilaterally go for the quick fix, often making the wrong choice or dealing with a symptom rather than a root cause. In time, their unwillingness to consult with others and reluctance to seek out new information isolates these managers even further—having earned a reputation for not getting it, they are offered less and less candid information by their colleagues and staff.

Managers who hide their confusion are also sending out a strong signal that open acknowledgment of confusion is not acceptable behavior. Everyone else learns to hide as well. Organizations can spend thousands of dollars every year on development seminars that teach the power of becoming a "learning organization" that grows and improves over time, but managers who hide their own difficulties send the opposite message. They ensure that no growth occurs, that coworkers have no incentive to communicate openly, and that the organization drives around in circles, making the same mistakes again and again.

# THE HIGH COST OF HIDING: A CASE IN POINT

Hiding is not only the natural managerial response to the confusion created by dramatic "Oh, No!" moments but also a common reaction to many mundane, everyday interactions, as illustrated in the following case of a meeting of a school district project team that went disastrously awry.

The superintendent was starting a reform effort with a tight and aggressive timetable. The changes had been long discussed, but never in detail, and now it was time to make definite plans. In her personal kickoff meeting with her business manager, chief deputy, and a senior aide, the superintendent said, "We haven't had much time to talk about the approach, but I'm really not so concerned about that because the problem here is really straightforward." The deputy superintendent was confused. " 'Not much time' is an understatement!" he thought to himself.

He wanted to say, "I don't want to appear stupid, but I need more clarification. I'm not at all sure of the approach you expect." Instead, he chose to hide his confusion, saying, "I think I understand your perspective, but can we talk about the approach a little bit more ?" To which the superintendent responded, "I'm afraid I'm overdue for a meeting. If you get stuck, give me a call. I've got full confidence in the team. We should reconvene in two weeks."

As the superintendent left the room, the deputy thought, "This looks about as clear as mud—but I can't let the others think that I'm not on top of things. They'll lose confidence." Deciding once again to withhold his confusion, the deputy said to the business manager, "It's too bad we didn't have more time with the superintendent, but I think we've got enough to go on. Let's flesh out the work plan." Meanwhile, the business manager was thinking, "Boy, I'm glad I'm not the one who has to make sense of this—but it looks like the deputy is clear. It'll probably work out all right."

When the superintendent saw the draft plan prepared by her team, she was completely caught off guard. "They're only about 60% on target here," she thought to herself. "What the hell is the problem? These are my top people! How could they miss the mark on a plan that should have been as easy as falling off a log?" And what did she do with her confusion? She buried it and admonished the group for not finding the right "focus." Crucial weeks and many hundreds of staff hours had been wasted.

In a project post mortem, the superintendent admitted that she had withheld her confusion after reading the team's first draft and asked why her people had not voiced their own confusion during the first project meeting. Team members gradually acknowledged that they had concealed their confusion because they were afraid of looking stupid, making her angry, disappointing her, and being judged as not up to the job.

*What could have happened if this superintendent had not admitted confusion and jumped to implement a remedial reading program and had then issued a "shape up" memo?*

## THE RIA MODEL

To succeed, managers must learn to embrace a new approach—one that is deceptively easy to describe but remarkably hard to practice. Yet this method can be applied to a wide range of unexpected problems, from time-sensitive emergencies to long-term projects.

Here are five steps for you to consider when you are confused and uncertain about how to get from Point A to Point B (or even unsure of what or where Point B might be). By putting into place an overt and orderly process, you not only maintain your authority but also contain the confusion, avoid premature closure (caused by internal or external pressure to act too quickly), and enlist your team in finding the best way to move forward. You turn your confusion into a resource.

These steps are presented as a sequence, but in practice their implementation should be seen as flexible and opportunistic. They should also be seen as a process within a larger framework: you may need to use them in multiple cycles or multiple venues in order to achieve the best effect.

Because going public with your confusion runs counter to conventional thinking, we suggest care in doing so in circles that go beyond trusted team members, advisors, and confidants. RIA should be tried out initially in limited but critical venues (e.g., with those who report to you directly), and even then you should lay the groundwork carefully by discussing the anticipated change in your problem-solving approach. Schedule a special meeting, distribute this article for discussion, and be open about the potential pros and perceived cons of RIA.

*Step 1. Embrace your confusion.* When confronted with disorienting problems, you need to do the one thing you least want to do—acknowledge to yourself that you are confused *and* that you see this condition as a weakness. Indeed, the biggest hurdle in getting from Point A to Point B is first getting to Point A—that is, acknowledging your true starting point.

Getting to Point A is extremely difficult because disorienting situations typically produce a painful split between feeling confused and listening to the loud voice that says that "real" leaders are not supposed to feel this way. In the grip of this ambivalence, managers will typically respond in primitive fight-or-flight terms, saying to themselves, "What's wrong with me for getting into this mess?" or "How do I get rid of this awful confusion?" Neither of these predictable responses offers a way to get beyond your inner conflict.

Rather than fight or flee, you need both to recognize and accept your tacit, yet firmly held, assumption that confusion means weakness.[8] You might take a deep breath and say to yourself, "I'm confused and that makes me feel weak." Paradoxically, fully embracing where you start will not lead you to wallow in your confusion, but rather frees you to move beyond your inner conflict.

You can then do what you most need to do—question your assumption that confusion is a weakness that needs to be banished and entertain a new assumption that confusion can be embraced as a resource for leadership. Because changing a firmly held belief is so difficult, it helps to develop a personal mantra. Here are some examples:

- "Confusion is not weakness, but the strength to take in new information at the risk of challenging my basic assumptions."
- "Leadership is being out in front where I have no choice but to encounter situations that make no sense to me."
- "Leadership is not about pretending to have all the answers but about having the courage to search with others to discover solutions."

*Step 2. Assert your need to make sense.* Having prepared yourself mentally, you now need to engage in dialogue. This face-to-face interaction will normally take the form of a meeting in which you describe your confusion so that others will know the point you (and they) are starting from. You might say any one of the following:

- "This new information just doesn't make sense to me."
- "I have a few thoughts about this, but I'll be the first to say we don't have enough information to suggest a definitive course of action."
- "Before I can make a decision, I need help in understanding this situation and our options for dealing with it."

Unless you come to recognize that being confused is a normal—even necessary—consequence of leadership, it will be difficult for you to state firmly that you are at a loss. How you deliver this message is as important as the words you use. Unless you unambiguously assert, with conviction and without apology, your sense of being confused, others will fulfill your worst expectations—concluding that you *are* weak—and they will be less willing to engage in a shared process of interpersonal learning.

At the same time, publicly asserting your confusion helps others to do the same—to claim their own confusion and begin trying to make sense out of a disorienting situation. By taking the lead, you make it easier for others to follow. Together you and your team will often discover that you share a common problem: how best to structure a process that can turn confusion into a productive, shared search for innovative solutions.

*Step 3. Structure the interaction.* Publicly acknowledging that you are confused is important, but it is only a beginning. Without skipping a beat, you must next provide a structure for the search for new bearings that both asserts your authority and creates the conditions for others to join you. You provide such a structure by stating the purpose of the joint inquiry, offering a set of specific steps or procedures to fulfill that purpose, providing the timetable, and identifying the criteria and methods by which decisions will be made. By doing so, you will tacitly send the message, "To be confused is not incapacitating. I may not know what course to take, but I know the next step. I know how to structure a process that we can go through together to make sense of our new situation and move forward." In other words, you announce that you are metaphorically asking for directions but that you are still in charge of a process that will produce a clear outcome.

As an example, let's return to our story of the nuclear power plant executive and recall that after hearing the alarm he receives a report telling him the exact opposite of what he expected. Stunned, he is thrown into a state of confusion. While it will not be easy for him, he must acknowledge his confusion in a spirit of inquiry so that others might question his theories or offer explanations for the discrepancy between the expected and the actual report. To establish a good structure for this discussion, the manager might say, "Listen up! We've got two minutes, and then you'll get my decision. Between then and now, I'm going to talk about what's got me confused, and you are going to give me new information, feedback, or explanations for what is going on."

As in this example, it normally makes sense to start a meeting by revealing your state of mind, describing how you propose to structure the interaction, and then offering suggestions about the type of data you need to clarify and resolve the problem.[9]

*Step 4. Listen reflectively and learn.* You now need to listen reflectively as others respond to you. In the context of the RIA model, "reflective" carries both of its common meanings: you reflect thoughtfully on what other people have to say, and you consciously attempt to reflect your understanding of what was said back to the speaker.[10]

Reflective listening is not normal listening. Ordinarily, most of us listen from a reflexive mindset that automatically judges the other person. This mindset is embodied in the question: "What's right or wrong with what was just said and what am I going to do about it?" In effect, your first mental act is to judge the worth of what was said, and your first verbal act is to agree or disagree. This typically leads to a confrontation, not a joint inquiry.

By contrast, reflective listening requires you to put yourself in the other person's shoes and, with an open mind, reflect upon her words, tone, demeanor, and nonverbal behavior. You then test what you have heard by reflecting back in your own words the essence of what she was trying to express. Finally, you come to a full stop and allow the other person the time to confirm, retract, or modify what she originally said. Here's the sound of reflective listening:

- "You seem to be saying that $x$ caused $y$. Do I have that right?"
- "You're torn between two explanations. On one hand, you think $x$ accounts for $z$; on the other hand, you think $y$ does?"
- "So you're angry because I am saying one thing and yet doing quite another?"

Reflective listening sounds simple but is actually an acquired skill that requires repeated practice, like hitting a backhand in a fast-paced tennis match. And even after you have learned how to do it, you will still encounter major challenges in applying it to real-world situations. One such challenge is dealing with people who typically are not very good listeners themselves. In conversation with them, it will be only natural to respond to their reflexive style by falling back into the same pattern. Indeed, our habit of responding in kind is such a powerful force that it has a name: the Norm of Reciprocity. ("If you don't listen to me, I'll be damned if I'll listen to you.")

To make matters worse, reflective listening is especially difficult when you most need to do it—in situations where new information threatens to undercut your cherished assumptions. Because you are inside your frame of reference, you tend to be blind to what may seem obvious to those around you; to you, their perceptions sound stupid, wrong, and intentionally hurtful.

For all these reasons, surprisingly little reflective listening goes on in most organizations. Yet, as hard as reflective listening may be, it is an essential tool for checking the depth and accuracy of your understanding and thereby avoiding action based on untested inferences. Reflective listening also ensures that the other people in the discussion feel that they have been heard and understood, thus increasing their inclination to trust and collaborate with you. By mastering and using this skill, you produce conditions for joint inquiry rather than confrontation.

*Step 5. Openly process your effort to make sense.* Once you have taken in what others are saying—some of which will probably be puzzling and may be upsetting—you need to process your responses out loud. You must suppress the automatic instinct to process internally and simply announce the products of your private search for new bearings. When you find the courage to externalize your intellectual process, you invite others to engage in interpersonal learning. Working together, you can discover the limitations of one another's thinking—limitations that you cannot know as long as you process privately. Here are three examples:

- "That's news to me. I haven't heard that before."
- "That really throws me. How do you get to that from what you were saying?"
- "That helps me a lot by pointing out *x*."

If you end up using all of the available time without coming to a clear resolution, bring closure by explicitly summarizing where you are in the learning and decision-making process and describing next steps. You can say something like, "Clearly, we have a disagreement here. Let's state it and put it aside for now. We should move on and get next steps in place, including agreement on when and how this will be finally decided."

# ANOTHER CASE IN POINT: RIA ON A LARGER SCALE

This case illustrates one way that the techniques of RIA apply not only to isolated and limited interactions and meetings but also to larger-scale initiatives.

Two months into a new job, a school superintendent received the results of a statewide literacy assessment: 25% of his district's eighth-graders couldn't read! A flash flood of dismay, blame, and calls for immediate action stormed in from the community, the media, and the schools. Behind the scenes, the school board demanded that the superintendent institute an emergency remedial reading program in all elementary schools and issue a strong "shape up" memo to the entire teaching staff. The teacher union made it clear that teachers were not going to be scapegoats.

Confronted on all sides with demands for action, the superintendent used RIA to interrupt the blame game, gain time for analysis, and avoid a rush to a quick fix, which he thought would exacerbate factional divisions without solving the problem. He was also confident that he could deal with his confusion without appearing weak or out of control.

Meeting privately with each board member, with small groups of the district's administrative staff, and with the head of the teacher union, he asserted his confusion about the test scores; he listened reflectively to accusations, demands, and explanations for the poor results; and he argued that action should follow a better understanding of the problems. He used a similar approach, with only slightly less candor, with business and community leaders, parent groups, and the local media. By listening carefully to everyone's concerns, the superintendent was able to garner support for a period of structured inquiry.

After these initial meetings, the superintendent created an inquiry group of teachers and administrators, charging it to analyze existing student data to evaluate the competing explanations for the poor results. As the group examined the data and tested hypotheses, everyone realized that they were all in the same boat—deeply confused. None of their assumptions or preconceptions seemed to account for the low test scores. That shared recognition freed them to work in concert.

Within weeks, the inquiry group came up with three significant findings: most of the nonreaders had entered the district after the third grade and so had missed the district's exemplary phonics program; the nonreaders were clustered in several schools in disadvantaged neighborhoods; and the transfers of students from one grade to the next were uncoordinated, so that those who needed long-term remedial assistance were not getting it.

On the basis of this new, shared understanding of the problems, targeted programs were implemented to address them, which led to an improvement in test scores the following year. More over, the superintendent gained widespread credibility because his more measured and informed approach avoided an ill-considered quick fix and produced results.

"So what?" a skeptic might say. "So the superintendent did his job—big deal." The fact remains that, every day, managers in similar situations don't do their jobs because they are afraid of their own confusion. Instead of acting on it with some version of the steps described in this article, they insist on denying it, hiding it from others, or trying to banish it with a quick fix. And, all too often, the problems get worse.

## CONFUSION AS A RESOURCE

In the 21st century, as rapid change makes confusion a defining characteristic of management, the competence of managers will be measured not only by *what they know* but increasingly by *how they behave* when they lose their sense of direction and become confused. Organizational cultures that cling to the ideal of an all-knowing, omnicompetent executive will pay a high cost in time, resources, and progress, and will be sending the message to managers that it is better to hide their confusion than to address it openly and constructively.

Being confused, however, does not mean being incapacitated. Indeed, one of the most liberating truths of leadership is that confusion is not quicksand from which to escape but rather the potter's clay of leadership—the very stuff with which managers work. Managers can be confused yet still be able to exercise competent leadership by structuring a process of reflective inquiry and action. The RIA process can help address the maddening "Oh, No!" moments that can hijack managerial agendas. Equally important, the central principles of RIA can be quite useful on a larger stage (as seen in the school superintendent case) and can help managers make progress when taking on longer-term, strategic challenges, such as meeting the public expectation that all children learn.

The RIA process provides an orderly way for managers to move forward when they don't know what to do, to stay "in charge" when confused and even lost, to contain shared confusion and work on it, and to avoid premature closure. It enlists the manager's team in finding the best way to make progress and promotes honesty, trust, and mutual respect. It turns a perceived weakness—confusion—into a resource for learning and effective action.

Armed with confusion and the RIA process, leaders can take timely, constructive action—even when they don't yet know what to do.

# ENDNOTES

1. Tony Wagner, "Beyond Testing: The 7 Disciplines for Strengthening Instruction," *Education Week,* 12 November 2003, pp. 28, 30.
2. Richard F. Elmore, "Knowing the Right Thing to Do: School Improvement and Performance-Based Accountability," NGA Center for BEST PRACTICES, August 2003, p. 9, available at www.nga.org/center. Click on the center's logo, and search on the author's name.
3. When applied to these "macro" agendas, RIA may be seen as one of many methodologies available to managers to pursue the larger-scale challenges of long-term "adaptive" leadership, as described by Ronald A. Heifetz in *Leadership Without Easy Answers* (Cambridge, Mass.: Harvard University Press, 1994).
4. Mark Toner, "'Blogs' Help Educators Share Ideas, Air Frustrations," *Education Week,* 14 January 2004, p. 8. For many leaders, it's easier and safer to employ humor or euphemism. After a long lifetime of blazing trails on the American frontier, the octogenarian Daniel Boone was asked by a friend if he'd ever been lost. "No, I can't say as ever I was lost," Boone replied, "but I was bewildered once for three days."
5. One of the lessons of our work in leadership and management training is that this pattern of reluctance to seek assistance from others when lost and confused is not limited to male executives. It may be that many female leaders respond to the pressure of gender bias by cultivating a style even more self-contained than that of their male colleagues.

6. The discrepancies between the way managers behave and the way they *think* they behave has been extensively reviewed in the literature on leadership theory. See Chris Argyris and Donald Schön, *Theory in Practice: Increasing Professional Effectiveness* (San Francisco: Jossey-Bass, 1974).

7. Some managers may take their confusion "off-line," revealing it to only one or two trusted confidants. As one veteran executive told us, "I could never say something like that in public. It would be suicide. But there are people I can call on to talk things through with and then say, 'This conversation never happened.'" Unfortunately, while this safety valve provides a valuable sense of relief for managers wrestling with confusion, it doesn't help others in the organization to open up and engage in productive conversation.

8. For a similar argument about the power of basic assumptions, see Robert Kegan and Lisa Laskow Lahey, "The Real Reason People Won't Change," *Harvard Business Review*, November 2001, pp. 85–92.

9. The joint inquiry model can be used on as small a scale as a one-on-one meeting but has obvious applications in larger situations as well. At the macro level, one of the best situations in which to use this model is when a manager starts a new job. Obviously, entering a new workplace is bound to throw a manager into a state of confusion, since historical explanations of key events will vary from source to source and there will be little initial guidance about which sources are reliable (i.e., whom to trust). For a detailed account of "structuring the interaction" at the beginning of a new job, see Barry Jentz et al., *Entry* (McGraw-Hill, 1982; reprint, Leadership & Learning, Inc., available from www.entrybook.com).

10. The definitive article on listening remains Carl R. Rogers and F. J. Roethlisberger, "Barriers and Gateways to Communication," *Harvard Business Review*, November/December 1991, pp. 105–11. (Originally published in 1952.)

# Improving Performance Through Flexible Leadership

## Gary Yukl and Richard Lepsinger

In most industries there are companies that consistently outperform competitors that have similar business strategies and operating models and must deal with the same economic conditions. Examples include Southwest Airlines versus America West, Dell versus Gateway, and Wal-Mart versus Kmart. The key factor in explaining the difference in long-term performance for these firms is the quality of leadership.

Leaders of successful companies are able to influence three key determinants of company performance—efficiency, adaptation, and human resources. A business organization is more likely to prosper and survive when it has efficient and reliable operations, when it is adaptable and innovative in providing the products and services that customers want at prices they are willing to pay, and when it has people with a high level of skill, commitment, and mutual trust. There are two basic approaches for influencing these performance determinants.

One is the use of specific leadership behaviors. Efficiency can be improved through task-oriented behaviors such as short-term planning, clarifying work roles and task objectives, and monitoring operations and employee performance. Adaptation to the external environment can be improved through change-oriented behaviors such as identifying external threats and opportunities, explaining the need for change, articulating a vision for the future, and encouraging innovative thinking. And human relations and resources can be improved through relations-oriented behaviors such as empowering employees and providing support, recognition, and coaching.

The second approach that leaders can take to influence the performance determinants is the use of management programs, systems, structural forms, and external initiatives. Efficiency can be improved through process-improvement and cost-reduction programs and standardization and functional specialization in the design of work processes and sub-units. Adaptation can be improved through programs to learn about customer preferences and competitor actions, programs to encourage and facilitate innovation, structural forms to facilitate innovation, and external initiatives to enhance growth and diversification. Human resources and relations can be improved through quality-of-work-life programs; employee benefit, development, and empowerment programs; and talent management programs. The authority to initiate or modify management programs and systems is usually reserved for top management, but a new program

**19**

or system is unlikely to be successful without the support and cooperation of managers at all levels of the organization.

## WORKING TOGETHER

These two different approaches for influencing performance determinants are complementary rather than mutually exclusive, and they can be used together in a mutually supportive way. Some leadership behaviors can be used to facilitate the implementation of new programs or systems and help make them successful. Some management programs and systems can enhance the effects of the leadership behaviors or reduce the need for them.

Efforts by leaders to influence improvements in efficiency, adaptation, and human resources are complicated by the complex relationships and potential trade-offs among these performance determinants and by changing conditions that can alter their relative importance. There is no simple formula to guarantee success in dealing with these leadership challenges, but flexibility is an essential ingredient. Here are several useful guidelines for flexible leadership:

*Maintain situational awareness.* Situational awareness involves knowledge about external and internal processes that affect a leader's organization or team. It is difficult to diagnose the causes of a problem and identify good solutions without a clear understanding of the prior events and decisions that determined how the organization got to where it is, the attitudes of people who will be affected by major change, and the political processes that determine how strategic decisions are approved. To obtain up-to-date information about relevant events and trends, it is usually necessary for leaders to develop an extensive network of contacts inside and outside the organization. These contacts can provide information that is not available from formal communications or from the regular information systems. Even when the company has a good information system, leaders can improve their understanding of organizational processes and problems by visiting facilities, observing operations firsthand, and meeting with employees, customers, and suppliers.

*Embrace systems thinking.* Systems thinking is needed to understand the complex interdependencies among performance determinants and the short- and long-term effects of attempts to influence them. In large organizations, actions invariably have multiple outcomes, including unintended side effects. Complex problems often have multiple causes, which may include actions taken earlier to solve other problems. Changes often have delayed effects. A change in one part of a system will eventually affect other parts of it, and any short-term benefits may be lost as effects of the change eventually ripple through the system. Unless a new program or initiative is compatible with the competitive strategy, the organizational culture, and other programs and systems, the potential benefits will not be attained. It is essential to identify trade-offs and consider potential consequences in preparing for a change or new initiative, and leaders should look for ways to achieve synergy among different programs, systems, and structures.

*How is "managing by walking around" different from maintaining situational awareness?*

*Build commitment to a core ideology.* To achieve sustained high performance in a large organization, the actions of the various leaders must be compatible with one another and with the competitive strategy. It is difficult to achieve the necessary level of cooperation and coordination unless each leader's decisions and actions are guided by a core organizational ideology. This ideology usually includes shared values and beliefs about the mission and purpose of the organization, the quality of products and services, and the rights and obligations of individuals.

A primary responsibility of leadership at the top is to help members come together in support of a shared purpose or mission for the organization. A primary responsibility of the leadership at the middle and lower levels is to build support for the core ideology by ensuring that it is clear and by explicitly using it to guide decisions and actions. When decisions are made, the ideals and values should be emphasized more than the policies and procedures that supposedly reflect them. In other words, the "spirit of the law" should be emphasized more than the "letter of the law" when the two are inconsistent.

*How does building commitment to a core ideology differ from the traditional notion that a leader casts the vision?*

The core ideology also provides a mental compass to help leaders identify appropriate forms of adaptation. Successful adaptation requires a good understanding of customer needs, but it is not appropriate to do anything that customers want just to increase sales. For example, clients of auditing, consulting, and financial firms may prefer to get rosy reports that overlook or minimize serious problems. However, a biased report designed to ensure future business from a client is inconsistent with the ideal of providing accurate and objective appraisals and recommendations.

*Lead by example.* Setting an example through one's own behavior is an important form of influencing that can be used to emphasize any of the performance determinants. When top executives act in highly visible ways that emphasize the importance of efficiency, innovation, or human relations, the effects can cascade down through the organization. For example, selling the corporate jet and the limousines used by executives is a way to communicate the importance of reducing costs. Setting a bad example can be as powerful as setting a good example, and it is essential to keep decisions and actions consistent with espoused values and the core ideology. Unethical behavior and decisions based primarily on the leader's self-interest can undermine the trust and commitment of employees.

## A HELPFUL MODEL

The importance of efficiency, adaptation, and human resources may seem obvious, but many business failures and derailed management careers are largely a result of a lack of understanding and appreciation of the complex relationships among the performance determinants and their joint effects on the long-term performance of an organization. Even though there is no simple formula for success, it is helpful to have this model as a reminder that the combined effects of all three determinants should be considered when planning improvements in organizational effectiveness.

# ARTICLE 1.3

# The Socially Intelligent Leader

## Daniel Goleman

**M**s. Smith, a seasoned middle school principal, prided herself on acclimating new teachers to her school's practices. She modeled lessons for teachers and made herself available to answer their questions. She remained frustrated, however, when three of her newly hired teachers were slow to use strategies that she knew would help their students.

So Ms. Smith[1] tried something different. One day, she got substitute coverage for the three teachers and took them to another school to watch two master teachers instruct their classes. Afterward, she took them out to lunch as her guests and spent the rest of the day talking over what they had observed. Within two weeks, she was seeing the changes in their classrooms that she had hoped for.

Taking time to forge that human connection gave this leader more leverage than she had thought possible. The new field of social neuroscience suggests why a personable leadership style makes sense. The person-to-person climate created by positive interactions can make principals more effective leaders—which in turn helps both teachers and students learn better. The improvement touches all students, from gifted youth to those most at risk of dropping out. A rising tide, an old saying goes, lifts all boats.

## THE SOCIAL BRAIN AND LEARNING

The existence of neural wiring between the thinking and emotional centers of the brain suggests that emotions can either enhance or inhibit the brain's ability to learn (Ashcroft & Kirk, 2001). And recent findings about neural mechanisms known as *mirror neurons* have shown that humans have the ability to create an internal simulation of what is going on in the minds of other people. When two people interact, their emotional centers influence each other, for better or for worse.

These findings have direct implications for creating school climates that boost students' ability to learn. The best climate for learning comes when students, teachers, and school leaders each take steps to become more emotionally self-aware and *socially intelligent*. Social intelligence, as I define it, encompasses both interpersonal awareness and social facility (Goleman, 2006).

### Brains at Their Best

First, the neuroscience. Psychologists have known for a century that people do their best when they experience both high motivation and manageable stress; when people are undermotivated or overstressed, their performance suffers. At a quickening pace since the 1990s, brain studies have clarified the link between emotions and the capacity to think and learn. The hormones mobilized by the human body to meet an emergency flow freely when we are stressed. One neural side effect is that the brain shunts energy to emotional centers, diminishing our ability to think at our best. The more intense the pressure, the weaker our ability to focus, remember, pay attention, and use what we know to solve problems. High anxiety shrinks the brain's systems for learning, whereas boredom underactivates these systems. Even gifted students can fail while gripped by anxiety (Beilock & Carr, 2005).

In contrast, during inspired moments of learning, students experience a potent mix of attention, interest, and good feelings. Neuroscientist Antonio Damasio (2003) argues that upbeat moments signify a neurological state of maximal cognitive efficiency—a brain ready to learn at its best.

## Mirror Neurons and Emotional Contagion

New discoveries in social neuroscience reveal an even more subtle power of emotions: Emotional states are contagious, brain-to-brain. What's now called "the social brain" attunes itself to the state of the person with whom we are interacting and adjusts our own feelings and actions to get into sync with the other person (Winkleman & Harmon-Jones, 2006). Mirror neurons facilitate this automatic attunement.

Mirror neurons create, within a person's brain, a replica of the brain state of whomever that person is with. When an individual sees someone with an angry, hurt, or happy expression, that individual's mirror neurons activate circuits in the brain for anger, hurt, or happiness. Neuroscientists believe that empathy and recognition of another person's intended response to a given state of mind, among many kinds of interpersonal understanding, stem largely from mirror neuron activity. When a teacher quiets a noisy group of students with a stern warning glance, the mirror neuron circuits of these students presumably sense the teacher's irritation and her intention to quiet them. They change their behavior to placate her.

During any interaction, these neurons set up a conduit for passing emotions back and forth between parties. Whatever the supposed business at hand, we continually transmit emotions, making one another feel better or worse.

# IMPLICATIONS FOR SHAPING SCHOOL CULTURE

Such discoveries in social neuroscience hold great significance for the emotional climate of schools. Sociologists know that in any group, emotions ripple outward, with the strongest concentration of emotion coming from the most powerful person in the room (Barsade, 2002). In the classroom, this is generally the

*Think of a school situation you have experienced where the person in charge created a negative emotional climate. What effect did it have on your learning?*

teacher; in a staff meeting, it's the principal. Best practices for learning include having teachers, school staff, and leaders all contribute to a positive school environment typified by trust and caring relationships. That's where school leaders make a crucial difference. If a principal wants to create an emotional climate that "lifts all boats," he or she must lead the group toward positive, empathetic social interactions.

A school's climate is the summation of all the positive and negative interactions among all people at the school in a given day. The tone of those interactions is largely shaped by the school's *culture*—the unspoken norms, habits, and traditions that influence how people behave. To shape a socially intelligent culture, school leaders may need to change norms, starting with their own behavior. What we now know about how humans' brains mirror the emotional states of others—particularly others in power—reinforces the need for leaders to be emotionally grounded and skilled in personal interaction, both as a model and as the source of an emotional ripple effect.

## A Principal's Progress

New York City Schools operates a pilot program called Star Factor Coaching that aids school leaders in this kind of emotional growth. Designed by Janet Patti, codirector of the Leadership Center at Hunter College, and Robin Stern, a social-emotional learning specialist at Columbia University's Teachers College, the program coaches principals and aspiring school leaders to become more emotionally and socially intelligent (Patti & Tobin, 2006). Ms. Smith, mentioned at the beginning of this article, was one of the principals in this coaching program.

Consider another principal in the program, who had an in-your-face style that intimidated her teachers and assistants. This principal, Dr. Lee, would routinely talk over others' voices and ask questions without hearing the answers or, too often, without even waiting for an answer. In staff meetings, her listeners responded in various ways, from sullen silence to outright confrontation.

Even a leisurely session meant to encourage staff members to share their concerns became tense because of this principal's leadership style. When one assistant principal did speak up, Dr. Lee made a remark after every sentence. At the sound of the period bell, everyone bolted out of the room. Afterward, exasperated with how things had gone, she asked her coach, "I'm still doing it, aren't I?"

After a series of coaching sessions, Dr. Lee had a breakthrough. One Friday, she accompanied the district's regional instructional supervisor on a walkthrough of the school's English Language Arts classrooms. Afterward, she was furious that the teachers had been unable to adequately explain the objectives of their lessons to this district official. So at 2:00 p.m. on a Friday, Dr. Lee called a 3:30 p.m. emergency meeting of the teachers involved.

Suddenly she realized that the timing of the meeting would seem punitive—and that her sense of urgency was fueled by her own anger. After pausing to

## Six Common Leadership Styles

**Visionary.** Inspires by articulating a heartfelt, shared goal; routinely gives performance feedback and suggestions for improvement in terms of that goal.

**Coaching.** Takes people aside for a talk to learn their personal aspirations; routinely gives feedback in those terms and stretches assignments to move toward those goals.

**Democratic.** Knows when to listen and ask for input; gets buy-in and draws on what others know to make better decisions.

**Affiliative.** Realizes that having fun together is not a waste of time, but builds emotional capital and harmony.

**Pacesetting.** Leads by hard-driving example and expects others to meet the same pace and high performance standards; tends to give *F*s, not *A*s.

**Commanding.** Gives orders and demands immediate compliance; tends to be coercive.

Source: Goleman, Boyatzis, & McKee, 2004. Reprinted with permission. This material also appeared in "Primal Leadership" in *Harvard Business Review* (December 2001).

reflect, she arranged to have the meeting the following week. As Dr. Lee told her coach, she recognized for the first time that her anger was propelling her response, and instead she pursued a more effective option.

## Intelligent Leadership Styles

Dr. Lee's rescheduling may seem like a trivial change, but it showed a shift in style. A leader's habitual style of interacting can either energize or demotivate people. Goleman, Boyatzis, and McKee (2004) have identified six common leadership styles and determined how each style affects an organization's climate (see "Six Common Leadership Styles"). Four of these styles—visionary, coaching, democratic, and affiliative—help create a positive climate in which people feel energized to do their best. But two styles of leadership tend to sap motivation: the command-style chief who leads simply by issuing fiats and demanding compliance; and the pacesetting type who criticizes but never praises and sets a frantic pace.

*How would a school board discover emotion/ social qualities of candidates for school administrator?*

The best leaders can deploy four or more of these leadership styles as needed; the poorest leaders tend to overuse the last two. Each style can be useful in a specific situation—for instance, the command style works in an emergency (if combined with other styles), but otherwise alienates people. On the other hand, someone who relies heavily on "being nice" (the affiliative style) may fail to articulate a motivating vision or confront simmering problems.

For example, a study of headteachers (principals) in Great Britain found that each leader's personal style strongly affected both the climate for teachers and, in turn, students' academic achievement (Hay Group, 2000). Teachers did their best job and felt most satisfied when they perceived that the school head

- Led flexibly rather than sticking to needless rules.
- Let them teach in their own way, holding them accountable for the results.
- Set challenging but realistic goals for excellence.
- Valued their efforts, recognizing a job well done.

In the atmosphere set by school heads who exhibited these kinds of actions, teachers sensed that they contributed to a larger goal and shared a common purpose that made them proud. The headteachers, data analysis found, could best create such a climate when they were firm but fair and had a "people first, task second" attitude, addressing teachers' personal needs as well as their collective goals. The best leaders also invited teachers to take part in making decisions and generating new ideas. They understood the importance of making a long-term investment in a teacher and helped teachers develop their skills even at a short-term cost to the school.

The British study found that the more of these leadership styles a school leader could exhibit as needed, the better the achievement scores of the schools they led. The results were so striking that England's national training center for headteachers has built part of its curriculum around boosting these key skills of leadership.

A report funded by the Ontario, Canada, Ministry of Education found that principals in Ontario who were rated by their staff and supervisors as being in the top 20 percent of school leaders shared a similar cluster of personal abilities (Stone, Parker, & Wood, 2005). They were empathetic, attentive, and understanding of others' feelings. These principals flexibly adjusted their own responses to colleagues and openly and effectively solved problems that otherwise might fester. They nurtured mutually satisfying relationships. In short, they demonstrated both emotional and social intelligence.

The report concluded by recommending that school boards should recruit and promote school administrators who exhibited these qualities, rather than simply looking at their job histories, as is often the case.

# SOCIAL INTELLIGENCE AND STUDENTS

Effective leaders will extend the strengthening of a school community's social intelligence to the interactions of students themselves, using any of the well-validated programs in social-emotional learning. Such programs teach students essential personal skills: self-awareness, stress and anger management, empathy, strategies for working out disagreements constructively, and decision making.

Roger Weissberg, president of the Collaborative for Academic, Social, and Emotional Learning, recently conducted a meta-analysis of hundreds of studies of social-emotional learning programs (Durlak & Weissberg, 2005). He found that effective programs lead to significant drops in problems like violence and substance abuse and, on the upside, to better attendance and a classroom atmosphere that enables teachers to spend less time disciplining and more time teaching. The strongest programs fit seamlessly into the standard academic curriculum (Devaney, O'Brien, Resnik, Keister, & Weissberg, 2006). Best of all, students learn better in a more positive emotional climate. Students who participated in social-emotional learning, compared with matched peers who did not participate, had higher grade point averages and ranked 12 percentile points higher on academic achievement tests (Durlak & Weissberg, 2005).

## DOING OUR BEST

The essential task of a school leader comes down to helping people get into and stay in an optimal state in which they can work to their best ability. This typically means creating an atmosphere of warmth and trust—of global rapport—in which people feel good about themselves, energized about their mission, and committed to giving their finest.

Understanding the power of the social brain expands the range of tools we have available for staying in that optimal state. Other people become part of our neural tool kit for doing our best, just as we become part of theirs. Leading a school to create a warmer and more connected school culture need not mean sacrificing academic rigor. Instead, socially intelligent leaders help schools better fulfill their main mission: teaching.

## REFERENCES

Ashcroft, M., & Kirk, E. (2001). The relationship among working memory, math anxiety, and performance. *Journal of Experimental Psychology, 130,* 224–227.

Barsade, S. (2002). The ripple effect: Emotional contagion and its influence on group behavior. *Administrative Science Quarterly,* 47, 644–675.

Beilock, S., & Carr, T. (2005). When high-powered people fail: Working memory and "choking under pressure" in math. *Psychological Science, 16,* 101–105.

Damasio, A. (2003). *Looking for Spinoza: Joy, sorrow, and the feeling brain.* New York: Harcourt.

Devaney, E., O'Brien, M. U., Resnik, H., Keister, S., & Weissberg, R. P. (2006). *Sustainable schoolwide social and emotional learning: Implementation guide and toolkit.* Chicago: Collaborative for Academic, Social, and Emotional Learning.

Durlak J., & Weissberg, R. (2005, August). *A major meta-analysis of positive youth development programs.* Presentation at the Annual Meeting of the American Psychological Association, Washington, DC.

Goleman, D., Boyatzis, R., & McKee, A. (2004). *Primal leadership: Learning to lead with emotional intelligence.* Boston: Harvard Business School Press.

Hay Group. (2000). *Raising achievement in our schools: Models of excellence for headteachers in different settings.* Available: www.ncsl.org.uk/media/F7B/52/kpool-hay-models-of-excellence-parts-1-2.pdf.

Patti, J., & Tobin, J. (2006). *Smart school leaders: Leading with emotional intelligence.* Dubuque, IA: Kendall-Hunt.

Stone, H., Parker, J. D., & Wood, L. M. (2005). *Report on the Ontario Principals' Council Leadership Study.* Available: www.eiconsortium.org/research/opc_leadership_study_final_report.htm.

Winkleman, P., & Harmon-Jones, E. (2006). *Social neuroscience.* New York: Oxford University Press.

## ENDNOTE

1. Names in this article are pseudonyms.

# Leading Together: Complex Challenges Require a New Approach

Wilfred H. Drath

*Leadership has become more difficult because of challenges that are not just complicated but also unpredictable. Such challenges demand that people and organizations fundamentally change, and make it virtually impossible for an individual leader to accomplish the work of leadership. What is needed is a more inclusive and collective leadership, a prospect that although difficult to achieve holds much potential.*

People in organizations want and need to work together effectively and productively. Individuals long to be part of a bigger picture that connects them to a larger purpose. This is what they expect leadership to accomplish. They expect leadership to create the direction, alignment, and commitment that will enable them, working together, to achieve organizational success.

The trouble is, it's getting harder and harder to make this happen. Creating direction, alignment, and commitment—the work of leadership—is becoming more difficult than ever.

There are a number of reasons for this. As organizations break down functional silos and develop greater global reach, people more often work with others who are not like them. It's harder to get people who don't share a common set of values and perspectives to get behind a common direction, to align, and to commit to one another.

Adding to this difficulty, people don't work side by side as much anymore. People working together might be scattered over several regions and time zones, even over different countries. Subtle and not-so-subtle barriers to communication and trust are created by the lack of simply being in the same room together. It's harder to shape a common purpose and get people aligned, and it's more difficult for people who don't see each other face to face to commit effectively to one another.

It's also getting harder to make leadership work because of changes in the attitude toward traditional ways of practicing leadership. Increasingly people without formal authority want to be involved in setting their own direction and in designing their own work and how they will coordinate with others. They are less willing to commit themselves to work in which they have had no say.

Yet people may not be prepared to participate effectively in leadership this way. They may knock on the door demanding to be let in on leadership without actually knowing how to enter into it. It's harder to create direction, alignment, and commitment when there are different and sometimes competing ideas of how to best accomplish this leadership work and when people have differing levels of readiness for participating in leadership.

# FACING THE UNKNOWN

In general, leadership is more difficult today because of what Ronald A. Heifetz, in his book *Leadership Without Easy Answers*, calls *adaptive challenges*, which can also be thought of as complex challenges. A complex challenge is more than just a very complicated problem. Complexity implies a lack of predictability. Complex challenges confront people with the unknown and often result in unintended consequences.

This unpredictability also means that a complex challenge is quite different from a technical problem. Technical problems are predictable and solvable. Using assumptions, methods, and tools that already exist, people can readily define the nature of a technical problem and prepare a solution with some confidence in the results. So, for example, if a key supplier changes the pricing on critical components, and such changes are expected to happen from time to time (the problem is already understood), and there are established ways of responding (tools for solving the problem already exist), then this is a technical problem. A technical problem arises and is solved *without any fundamental change* in assumptions, methods, or tools. Also, the people who solve a technical problem don't themselves have to change.

A complex challenge cannot be dealt with like this. Existing assumptions, methods, or tools are no good in the face of a complex challenge and may even get in the way. To be faced successfully, complex challenges require altered assumptions, different methods, and new tools not yet invented. Complex challenges require people and organizations to change, often in profound and fundamental ways. This is where things get unpredictable. Some examples of current complex challenges are the need for companies that have merged to bring about culture change, for the health care industry to address the nursing shortage, for many companies to make the transformation from product push to customer pull, and for social agencies to get diverse constituents with differing perspectives to work together on such deep-rooted issues as reducing the number of youthful offenders.

Complex challenges are made even more difficult by the fact that no one can say with any authority or accuracy just how things need to change. This is where leadership starts to get a lot harder. Because the complex challenge lies beyond the scope of existing assumptions, the frameworks that people use to try to understand the nature of the challenge itself are not adequate. So, for example, it's not just that people in an organization that needs to undergo a culture change don't know how to make the change happen. It's worse than that. They have no way of being sure what sort of new culture is needed. No one who is part of the existing organization has any kind of especially gifted insight into the needs of the new, changed, still-unknown organization of the future. Everyone has ideas, of course, and everyone has a point of view and may be quite attached to it. Only by virtue of position and authority are anyone's ideas given special status. Unfortunately, although having a lot of authority may make it possible for a person to make sure his or her views hold sway, that doesn't guarantee the effectiveness of those views.

If all of this makes it sound as though a complex challenge requires a lot of talk and reflection among a lot of people in an organization, it does. And all that talk and reflection takes a lot of time. Because the complex challenge is not only complex but also a challenge, however, it demands a response now, not someday. So facing a complex challenge puts people in a bind and ensures that they will experience some stress as they try to think and reflect together without letting analysis lead to paralysis.

*What can a leader do to ease stress when a school or institution faces a complex challenge?*

## NO GOING IT ALONE

In the face of complex challenges, a leader, no matter how skilled and otherwise effective, cannot simply step into the breach, articulate a new vision, make some clarifying decisions, and proclaim success. Because a complex challenge requires a whole system and all the people in it to change, it lies beyond the scope of any individual person to confront. Complex challenges make it virtually impossible for an individual leader to accomplish the work of leadership, and individual leadership therefore reaches a distinct limit in the face of complex challenges.

Since about the 1920s (in the writings of Mary Parker Follett) there has been talk of the possibility of distributing or sharing leadership and making leadership more inclusive and collective. If leadership is still needed (and who can deny that it is), and if no individual alone can provide leadership in the face of a complex challenge, then perhaps what is needed is the collective action of many people. It's conceivable, even compelling, that everyone in an organization could contribute in some way to facing a complex challenge. The possibility that a more inclusive and collective way of leadership could help organizations meet complex challenges and be more effective is promising.

The problem has always been—and remains today—*how* to get more people involved in leadership, and *how* to make leadership more inclusive and collective.

Two critical problems continuously block the way. The first could be called the *too-many-chefs* problem: the effort to make more people into leaders seems doomed to collapse in a cacophony of differing visions and values as too many individuals exhibit leadership. The second could be called the *diffused accountability* problem: when people share leadership, it seems inevitable that accountability will also get shared until, as everyone becomes accountable, no one is really accountable at all.

Both of these problems are real. Attempts to make leadership more inclusive and collective have often—if not always—foundered on just these obstacles. Such failures have made many people realistically pessimistic about the utility of a more inclusive and collective approach to leadership. Yet the promise of such leadership grows brighter as complex challenges surpass the ability of the individual leader to respond.

The problem is how to develop more inclusive and collective ways of making leadership happen without running afoul of the twin problems of too many chefs and diffused accountability. Somehow we need to develop the whole process by which direction, alignment, and commitment are created—not just develop individual leaders. We at CCL call the development of individual leaders *leader development*; the development of the whole process for creating direction, alignment, and commitment we call *leadership development*. Both leader development and leadership development are needed. But even though leadership development is becoming more critically important every day, it lags far behind leader development in most organizations.

*What possible barriers could an individual leader face in making the leadership process more collective?*

## DEFINING THE TASKS

A good place to start developing a more inclusive and collective leadership is to think of leadership (both individual and collective) as a process that is used to accomplish a set of *leadership tasks*. This makes it possible to focus not on the way leadership is practiced but rather on what people hope to *accomplish* with leadership. A useful question is, What work is leadership expected to get done? As already suggested, leadership is expected to set direction, create alignment, and generate commitment—or some similar list of desired outcomes.

The too-many-chefs problem that often comes up in trying to share leadership is created when organizations try to get more people to act as leaders and exhibit leadership. This is subtly but importantly different from getting more people involved in the process of accomplishing the leadership tasks.

Getting more people to act like leaders does little more than multiply the individual leader approach. In the face of a complex challenge, simply having more people trying to say what should be done is unlikely to be effective.

In the same way, the diffused accountability problem is created when organizations make more people accountable by designating more people as leaders. This is also little more than a way to multiply individual leaders. Many ways of trying to share leadership in order to make it more inclusive and collective are actually still firmly rooted in the tradition of the individual leader—designating more leaders can just add to the difficulty of accomplishing the leadership tasks in the face of complex challenges.

So having more leaders is not the answer. Instead the answer is to create richer and more complex processes of accomplishing the leadership tasks. Focus on how to create direction, alignment, and commitment in the face of complex challenges, and forget about how many people are, or are not, leaders.

Putting the accomplishment of the leadership tasks at the heart of leadership frames different and more useful questions: What are the obstacles to clear direction, effective alignment, and solid commitment? What resources exist in the organization for creating direction, alignment, and commitment as a complex challenge is being confronted? What different approaches to accomplishing the leadership tasks are possible for the organization? How might people act in new and different ways to accomplish the leadership tasks?

Answering questions like these can help organizations avoid the traditional problems of shared leadership by getting them past the idea that more inclusive and collective approaches require making more people individual leaders.

# THREE CAPABILITIES

Complex challenges require richer and more complex ways of creating direction, alignment, and commitment. The ways people talk, think, and act together—the culture of the organization along with its systems and structures—are what need to become richer and more complex.

At first this may seem to be a bad idea. When facing a complex challenge, surely the last thing needed is more complexity. Yet the very complexity of the challenge calls for an equally complex capacity to respond. A complex capacity to respond means something different from just a more complicated process. It means a more varied, less predictable, more layered process capable of greater subtlety. At CCL we believe that making the leadership process more collective, pushing the process beyond one that depends primarily on individuals, enriches the process of leadership to the level of sensitivity and responsiveness required by a complex challenge. Continuing to depend on individual leaders (no matter how many) to lead people through basic and profound changes is risky. This is because any individual leader, no matter how capable, may be unable to make such changes personally. Getting more people working together in more ways increases the likelihood that people who are able to make the needed changes themselves will become influential in the leadership process. We call this *connected leadership*.

Three collective capabilities can be useful for organizations needing to achieve connected leadership: shared sense-making, connection, and navigation.

**Shared sense-making** • Complex challenges do not come wrapped with an explanation. By their nature they cause confusion, ambiguity, conflict, and stress. They are immediate, so they press for a solution now. But they also force people to change toward the unknown, so they also require reflection. Moving too fast can make things worse. What seems to be required is the capability to engage in shared sense-making.

This is not problem solving; it's not even problem defining. It's a process that must come before a challenge can even be thought of as a problem with solutions. The outcome of this sense-making is shared understanding. It involves people in paying attention to both the parts and the whole of the challenge. It requires people to experience multiple perspectives and to hold conflicting views in productive tension. It answers the persistent question about difficult change: Why change? Without an understanding of why change is required, people are rightly suspicious of it.

**Connection •** The process of leadership is realized in the connections between people, groups, teams, functions, and whole organizations. Complex challenges threaten existing connections. Think of what happens in an organization seeking to become more customer focused. The existing structures and boundaries that differentiate and coordinate such entities as production, marketing, sales, and finance begin to be more like impediments than workable ways of organizing. Facing complex challenges requires people and organizations to develop and enrich their forms of connection.

The outcome is relationships made to work in new ways both within and between groups and communities. Getting relationships to work in new ways requires people to see patterns of connection (and disconnection) in order to explore the root causes of the complex challenge and clarify differing and sometimes conflicting values. Often, new language emerges.

**Navigation •** Because a complex challenge is not a familiar problem to be solved but a reality to be faced through change and development, the process is one of learning from shared experiments, small wins, innovations, and emergent strategies. No one can set a goal whose achievement will resolve the complex challenge. It is a journey whose destination is unpredictable and unknown. A key to success is the ability to be keenly sensitive to the forces of change as they happen, like mariners who sail a ship by making minute, mutual adjustments to one another and to the elements of wind and current.

These capabilities cannot be taken on by individuals. They can be developed only between individuals and between groups, functions, and whole organizations. Too often the move to more inclusive and collective approaches to leadership is attempted without making this move into the space in between. More inclusive approaches to leadership have often been expected to flow from a change in the competencies of individual leaders, such as when leaders are called on to be more empowering and inclusive and to share leadership. The persistence of the obstacles to more inclusive and collective leadership comes from the failure to let go of long-held and long-valued assumptions about the individual nature of leadership.

## MAKING GAINS

In facing complex challenges, people, organizations, and communities can develop ways of accomplishing the leadership tasks that give more people a sense of being responsible for setting direction, creating alignment, and generating commitment. Successfully facing complex challenges will support a sense of shared power and collective competence.

It will also create the possibility for leadership strategy. Because strategy means making choices among alternatives, no strategy is possible without alternatives to consider. So if the development of connected leadership, of a more inclusive and collective leadership process, adds to the alternative ways that leadership can be carried out, it also creates the possibility that choices can be made about leadership. Leadership then would no longer be a matter of making a single kind of practice work for every context. Instead of seeing leadership as simply a natural force to which humans are subject and that comes in only one naturally determined version (such as the forceful leader taking charge), people would come to see leadership as a process that humans control and that can be shaped to human needs through intentional choices.

# ARTICLE 1.5

# Distributed Leadership

## James P. Spillane

*Stories of leadership successes follow a familiar structure: A charismatic leader, often the CEO or school principal, takes over a struggling school, establishing new goals and expectations and challenging business as usual within the organization. This leader creates new organizational routines and structures that with time transform the school's culture, contributing in turn to greater teacher satisfaction, higher teacher expectations for students, and improved student achievement.*

Stories in the "heroics of leadership" genre, however, are problematic for at least two reasons. First, these epics equate school leadership chiefly with an individual leader—typically the school principal. This is inaccurate because school principals, or any other leader for that matter, do not single-handedly lead schools to greatness; leadership involves an array of individuals with various tools and structures. Though scholars have long argued for moving beyond those at the top of organizations in studies of leadership (Barnard 1938), the "heroics of leadership" genre persists. The second problem with these accounts is their inattention to leadership practice. They dwell mostly on the "what" of leadership—structures, functions, routines, and roles—rather than the "how" of school leadership—the daily performance of leadership routines, functions, and structures (Hallinger and Heck 1996). Leadership practice centers not only on what people do, but how and why they do it. Understanding leadership practice is imperative if research is to generate usable knowledge about and for school leadership. Distributed leadership is a recent antidote, or more correctly a series of antidotes, to the work in the heroics of leadership.

*What is the significance of the term "distributed" when applied to leadership?*

Distributed leadership has garnered considerable attention in the United States and abroad. It often is used interchangeably with "shared leadership," "team leadership," and "democratic leadership." Some use distributed leadership to indicate that school leadership involves multiple leaders; others argue that leadership is an organizational quality, rather than an individual attribute. Still others use distributed leadership to define a way of thinking about the *practice* of school leadership (Gronn 2002; Spillane, Halverson, and Diamond 2001, 2004). Distributed leadership's popularity likely has to do with how easily people can use it to relabel familiar approaches. It is little wonder that many observers are perplexed about the meaning of distributed leadership and whether it is anything new. Perhaps distributed leadership is just another case of old wine in new bottles.

My understanding of distributed leadership, based on *The Distributed Leadership Study* (School of Education and Social Policy at Northwestern University 2004), an elementary school leadership research study, is outlined. The following question is addressed: What does it mean to take a distributed perspective on school leadership? My intent is not to provide a comprehensive review of different perspectives or identify the "one best" definition, but to lay out my own definition of distributed leadership. An overview of distributed leadership, in which key terms and ideas are introduced and defined, is provided. I next address how leadership is distributed over an interactive web of people and situations, examining how leadership is spread over both leaders and followers given key aspects of their situation, including organizational routines, structures, and tools. I then illustrate how this definition of distributed leadership is a case of new wine—not new bottles for old wine—and consider its implications for research, practice, and leadership development.

# PUTTING LEADERSHIP PRACTICE CENTER STAGE

Distributed leadership is first and foremost about leadership practice rather than leaders or their roles, functions, routines, and structures. Though they are important considerations, leadership practice is still the starting point. A distributed perspective frames leadership practice in a particular way; leadership *practice* is viewed as a product of the interactions of school leaders, followers, and their situation. This point is especially important, and one that is frequently glossed over in discussions of distributed leadership. Rather than viewing leadership practice as a product of a leader's knowledge and skill, the distributed perspective defines it as the interactions between people and their situation. These interactions, rather than any particular action, are critical in understanding leadership practice. Too frequently, discussions of distributed leadership end prematurely with an acknowledgment that multiple individuals take responsibility for leadership in schools. This "leader plus" view, however, is just the tip of the iceberg because, from a distributed perspective, leadership practice that results from *interactions* among leaders, followers, and their situation is critical.

Some educators might argue that this is merely semantics, pointing out that leadership scholars have long recognized the importance of these interactions and acknowledged that leadership typically involves more people than those at the top of the organizational hierarchy. My argument is not simply that situation is important to leadership practice, but that it actually constitutes leadership practice—situation defines leadership practice in interaction with leaders and followers. This way of thinking about situation differs substantially from prior work.

# PEOPLE AND PRACTICE

Equating leadership with the actions of those in leadership positions is inadequate for three reasons. First, leadership practice typically involves multiple leaders, some with and some without formal leadership positions. It is essential, therefore, to move beyond viewing leadership in terms of superhuman actions. Second, leadership practice is not something done to followers. From a distributed perspective, followers are one of the three constituting elements of leadership practice. Third, it is not the actions of individuals, but the interactions among them, that are critical in leadership practice.

Existing scholarship shows that responsibility for leadership functions can be distributed in various ways. Studies have shown how this responsibility can involve multiple leaders—not just principals or coprincipals—who work in a coordinated manner at times and in parallel at others (Heller and Firestone 1995). Recent work in more than 100 U.S. schools showed that responsibility for leadership functions typically was distributed among three to seven people, including administrators and specialists (Camburn, Rowan, and Taylor 2003).

*The Distributed Leadership Study* also showed that responsibility for leadership routines involves multiple leaders, though the number involved depends upon the routine and subject area. Some routines, such as monitoring and evaluating teaching practice, involve fewer leaders (typically the principal and assistant principal), compared with routines such as teacher development in literacy, which often involve the principal, curricular specialists, and lead teachers. The extent to which responsibility for leadership routines was distributed differed by school subject, with fewer leaders involved in leadership routines for mathematics than for literacy. For example, at Adams Elementary School, the principal, literacy coordinator, curriculum specialist, and lead teachers were frequent and active participants in executing leadership routines for literacy. Conversely, leadership routines for mathematics instruction were typically defined by one of four lead mathematics teachers (Spillane, Diamond, and Jita 2003).

*Is distributed leadership more appropriate for elementary schools than high schools or universities?*

Leaders act in situations that are defined by others' actions. From a distributed perspective, it is in these interactions that leadership practice is constructed. *The Distributed Leadership Study's* analysis of leadership performance documents how leadership practice is defined through the interactions of two or more leaders. When observing leadership routines for literacy instruction at Adams Elementary School, one immediately notices how leadership practice becomes defined in the interactions of leaders and followers. These leadership routines often involve some combination of four leaders: the principal, the school's literacy coordinator, the African-American Heritage coordinator, and a teacher leader. At times, these leaders' actions parallel or overlap one another; at other times, they do not. The principal emphasizes goals and standards, keeps the meetings moving, summarizes comments, and reminds participants of what is expected in their classrooms. The literacy coordinator identifies problems with literacy instruction, suggests solutions and resources, and encourages teachers to present their ideas. The teacher leader describes his or her efforts to implement a teaching strategy that the literacy coordinator shared. The actions of followers (in this case, primarily classroom teachers) also contribute to defining leadership practice. They provide knowledge about a particular teaching strategy—knowledge that sometimes is used by leaders to illustrate a point about improving literacy instruction.

Leadership practice takes form in the interactions between leaders and followers, rather than as a function of one or more leaders' actions (Spillane et al. in press). Individuals play off one another, creating a reciprocal interdependency between their actions. The Distributed Leadership Study identified interdependency as the primary characteristic of interactions among leaders. This theory has been informed by the work of organizational theorists (Thompson 1967; Malone et al. 1999). Three types of interdependencies identified by Thompson (1967)—reciprocal, pooled, and sequential—served as the basis.

Leadership practice can be spread across two or more leaders who work separately yet interdependently. The leadership practice used in monitoring and evaluating teaching at Ellis Elementary is illustrative. The principal believes that biannual visits are inadequate to evaluate a teacher's practice. She and the assistant principal developed a comprehensive routine for monitoring and evaluating teaching practice. The assistant principal, who has a good rapport with teachers, visits classrooms frequently to conduct formative evaluations and give regular feedback to teachers. The principal engages in summative evaluations through her biannual visits to classrooms. Through formal and informal meetings, the principal and assistant principal pool their information to develop an understanding of teachers' practices. Through this "pooled" interdependency, these two leaders' separate actions interact to define a collective practice for monitoring and evaluating teaching.

Sometimes separate leadership practices are spread over the actions of two or more leaders and must be performed in a particular sequence. In these cases, multiple interdependent tasks, arranged sequentially, are critical to the performance of a leadership routine. For example, the five-week assessment at Adams School illustrates how leadership practice can be stretched over leaders over time. This assessment involves seven stages performed in a specific order:

- The literacy coordinator creates the student assessment instruction.
- Teachers administer the assessment.
- The literacy coordinator and her assistant score and analyze the results.
- The principal and literacy coordinator meet to discuss the assessment results, using information from classroom observations to diagnose problems.
- The literacy coordinator compiles resources and strategies that might enable teachers to address the problems identified through the analysis of assessment data.

- The literacy coordinator reports assessment results to teachers during literacy committee meetings.
- The literacy coordinator, principal, and teachers interpret assessment results and identify instructional strategies to address problem areas.

This sequence illustrates coordinated leadership. The term "coordinated" is used to emphasize that leadership practice that involves a sequential interdependency must be performed in a particular sequence.

## PEOPLE, PLACE, AND PRACTICE

Leaders typically have interaction with others. They also have interaction with aspects of the situation including a variety of tools, routines, and structures. Tools include everything from student assessment data to protocols for evaluating teachers. The five-week assessment described here is an example of a routine. Structures include routines such as grade-level meetings and the scheduling of teachers' prep periods. From a distributed perspective, these routines, tools, and structures define leadership practice; the situation both enables and constrains leadership practice.

Aspects of the situation define and are defined by leadership practice in interaction with leaders and followers. Structures, routines, and tools are the means through which people act. Yet, these same structures, routines, and tools are created and remade through leadership practice. The distinction between the ostensive and performative aspects of organizational routines (Feldman and Pentland 2003) is helpful.

The ostensive aspect refers to the "routine in principle," while the idealized version of the performative aspect refers to the routine in practice in particular places and at particular times. For example, the seven stages of the five-week assessment represent the ostensive aspect of this routine, while reporting student assessment results to teachers in a literacy committee meeting is the performative aspect of the routine. The ostensive aspect frames practice—both enabling and constraining it. Practice creates and recreates the ostensive aspect. Though Feldman and Pentland (2003) confined their discussion to organizational routines, ostensive and performative distinctions can be applied to other aspects of the situation, including structures and tools.

Student assessment data, a widely used leadership tool by all schools in *The Distributed Leadership Study*, is a good example. In an effort to reflect the district's policy of holding schools accountable for student achievement, the student assessment data tool framed leadership practice in a particular way across all schools by focusing leadership practice on curriculum content coverage. The student assessment data tool, however, was transformed differently in and through leadership practice at each school. In some schools, assessment data were reported, problem areas were identified, and specific topics on which teachers should focus were presented at faculty meetings. In other schools, assessment data were used differently. At Baxter School, for example, assessment data were disaggregated and used as the basis for ongoing conversations about instructional improvement and curricular priorities.

Sometimes tools designed for other purposes are appropriated for leadership. At Hillside School, students' "writing folders"—designed for classroom writing instruction—have become a core leadership tool. The key leadership routine is the monthly review of these folders by the school principal. Every teacher submits a folder containing one composition written by each student in his or her class. The principal reads each student's work and provides teachers and students with written feedback. The leadership practice in this example is defined in the interactions of the principal and the writing folders, as well as those between teachers and students. Through this monthly routine, writing folders have been redesigned as a leadership tool. In turn, the writing folder fundamentally shapes a leadership practice grounded in what students are learning about writing and engaging teachers and students in improving writing instruction.

Is this perspective on situation new? After all, contingency theorists have long maintained the importance of situation to leadership. Leadership circumstances influence leaders' actions, as well as their effect on followers (Bossert et al. 1982; Murphy 1991). From a contingency perspective, situation works independently to influence a leader's behavior or mediate its effects. A distributed perspective differs in at least two respects. First, situation does not simply affect what school leaders do as an independent, external variable. Rather it defines leadership practice in interaction with leaders and followers. Second, there is a two-way relationship between situation and practice. Aspects of the situation can either enable or constrain practice, while practice can transform the situation.

# A CASE OF OLD WINE IN NEW BOTTLES?

The answer to this question depends on the particular definition of distributed leadership being considered. Distributed leadership often is cast as some sort of monolithic construct when, in fact, it is merely an emerging set of ideas that frequently diverge from one another.

The distributed perspective on leadership in this paper gives center stage to leadership practice. Though scholars have viewed leadership as a behavior or act for some time (Fiedler 1973), this work equates leadership practice with the acts of individual leaders. From a distributed perspective, leadership practice takes shape in the interactions of leaders, followers, and their situation, thus breaking new ground rather than simply relabeling old ideas.

Shared leadership, team leadership, and democratic leadership are not synonyms for distributed leadership. Depending on the situation, a distributed perspective allows for shared leadership. A team leadership approach does not necessarily involve subscribing to a distributed perspective in which

*Distributed leadership implies more involvement by more people. Does distributed leadership also take more time and effort?*

leadership practice is viewed as the interaction of leaders, followers, and situation. Similarly, a distributed perspective allows for leadership that can be democratic or autocratic. From a distributed perspective, leadership can be stretched over leaders in a school but is not necessarily democratic.

Distributed leadership is considered by some educators as a cure-all for all that ails schools—an opinion to which I do not subscribe. Distributed leadership is a perspective—a conceptual or diagnostic tool for thinking about school leadership. It is not a blueprint for effective leadership nor a prescription for how school leadership should be practiced.

The lack of empirical evidence on the effectiveness of distributed leadership in promoting instructional improvement and increasing student achievement is considered a weakness. While this concern is understandable, it is not crucial. What matters for instructional improvement and student achievement is *not* that leadership is distributed, but *how* it is distributed. Descriptive theory building is essential before causal links between distributed leadership, instructional improvement, and student outcomes can be established.

From a distributed perspective, leadership is a system of practice comprised of a collection of interacting components: leaders, followers, and situation. These interacting components must be understood together because the system is more than the sum of the component parts or practices.

# REFERENCES

Barnard, C. I. 1938. *The functions of the executive.* Cambridge, MA: Harvard University Press.

Bossert, S. T., D. C. Dwyer, B. Rowan, and G. V. Lee. 1982. The instructional management role of the principal. *Educational Administration Quarterly* 18(3): 34–64.

Camburn, E. M., B. Rowan, and J. Taylor. 2003. Distributed leadership in schools: The case of elementary schools adopting comprehensive school reform models. *Educational Evaluation and Policy Analysis* 25(4): 347–73.

Feldman, M. S., and B. T. Pentland. 2003. Reconceptualizing organizational routines as a source of flexibility and change. *Administrative Science Quarterly* 48(1): 94–118.

Fiedler, F. E. 1973. The contingency model: A reply to Ashour. *Organizational Behavior and Human Decision Processes* 9(3): 356–68.

Gronn, P. 2002. Distributed leadership as a unit of analysis. *Leadership Quarterly* 13(4): 423–51.

Hallinger, P., and R. H. Heck. 1996. Reassessing the principal's role in school effectiveness. *Educational Administration Quarterly* 32(1): 5–44.

Heller, M. F., and W. A. Firestone. 1995. Who's in charge here? Sources of leadership for change in eight schools. *Elementary School Journal* 96(1): 65–86.

Malone, T. W., G. Herman, M. Klein, E. O'Donnell, K. Crowston, J. Lee, B. Pentland, C. Dellarocas, G. Wyner, J. Quimby, C. S. Osborn, and A. Bernstein. 1999. Tools for inventing organizations: Toward a handbook of organizational processes. *Management Science* 45(3): 425–43.

Murphy, J. 1991. Restructuring schools: *Capturing and assessing the phenomena.* New York: Teachers College Press.

School of Education and Social Policy. 2004. *The Distributed Leadership Study.* Chicago: Northwestern University. Available at: *http://dls.sesp. northwestern.edu.*

Spillane, J. P., J. B. Diamond, and L. Jita. 2003. Leading instruction: The distribution of leadership for instruction. *Journal of Curriculum Studies* 35(5): 533–43.

Spillane, J. P., R. Halverson, and J. B. Diamond. 2001. Investigating school leadership practice: A distributed perspective. *Educational Researcher* 30(3): 23–28.

Spillane, J. P., R. Halverson, and J. B. Diamond. 2004. Towards a theory of leadership practice: A distributed perspective. *Journal of Curriculum Studies* 36(1): 3–34.

Spillane, J. P., J. B. Diamond, J. Sherer, and A. Coldren. in press. Distributing leadership. In *Developing leadership: Creating the schools of tomorrow,* ed. M. Coles and G. Southworth. Milton Keyes: Open University Press.

Thompson, J. D. 1967. *Organizations in action: Social science bases of administrative theory.* New York: McGraw Hill.

# ISSUE SUMMARY

————————————————————————————●

Taken together, these readings on the newest approaches to leadership may best be understood by the larger question: What is educational leadership today? Foremost, the readings indicate that leadership is a group process, not a set of traits or skills embodied in a single person. If this premise is true, educational leadership involves more than personality, influence, power, or role. Its context is broader, involving actions of all participants, accountability of all participants, and success or failure of all participants.

Having considered the readings, now reflect on this contemporary definition of organizational leadership:

> A social process in which a member or members of a group influence the interpretation of events, choice of goals/outcomes, organization of work activities, motivation, abilities, power relations, and shared orientations. (Hoy, 2003)

If you give credence to this definition, these concepts or models may be less important:

- Traits model of leadership
- Leadership tasks
- Position power
- Transactional leadership
- Followership

All of the authors make the case for situating leadership in a specific context of time and place. But beyond the situation, educational leadership is a relational phenomenon. We are left with the notion that leadership happens because of the relationship that exists between leader and participants. Leadership has psychological, sociological, and demographic characteristics that are not just interesting—they are vital to understanding the nature of the process. The future of educational leadership lies in how we will advance leadership as a resource.

## ISSUE HIGHLIGHTS

- The key factor in organizational success is leadership quality and flexibility.
- The success of an organization does not depend on a single leader.
- Leadership today is more difficult because of unpredictable challenges.
- One emerging approach to leadership involves adapting to changing situations, maintaining efficiency, and using a systems approach.
- Complex challenges require leadership that is more inclusive, yet decisive.
- An approach, labeled "connected leadership," occurs through shared sense-making, relationships, and emergent strategizing.

- The "socially intelligent" leader has a people first, task second attitude and leads the group toward positive, empathetic interactions.
- "Distributed leadership" focuses on the interactions and interdependency of multiple individuals in leading an organization.

# CRITICAL THINKING

Compelling evidence shows educational leadership is undergoing fundamental changes in perspective and approach. But the proliferation of books, Web sites, and resources on leadership, intended to be helpful, can actually make it more difficult to sort out the nature and direction of the changes. The sheer quantity of resources shows that effective leadership looks different to different people.

One way to sort out the essentials for yourself is to adopt a definition of leadership that takes into account multiple perspectives of the readings. Rather than choosing one specific approach over another (flexible leadership versus situational leadership), a definition can include elements of several approaches. Obviously, not all definitions will suffice. Start by comparing the following definitions of leadership:

> Leadership is an influence relationship among leaders and followers who intend real changes that reflect their mutual purposes. (Rost, 1993, p. 102)
>
> Leadership is: knowing what to do next, knowing why it is important, and knowing how to bring appropriate resources to bear on the need at hand. (Biehl, nd)
>
> Leadership is a dynamic and working relationship, built over time, involving an exchange between leader and follower in which leadership is a resource embedded in the situation, providing direction for goal attainment. (Pierce & Newstrom, 2006, p. 6)

On the surface, these contemporary descriptions of leadership emphasize similar elements. First, leadership is understood as a process that places the emphasis on the interaction, not on the individual. Second, the process of leading is one of influence. Third, the context is a group or community. But take a closer look at the way "resources" is used in the second and third definitions. Resources are understood in very different ways. In one definition, resources are external to the interaction and must be supplied by the leader and in the other definition, leadership itself is a resource. Also take a look at the use of the terms *purposes* and goal *attainment* in definitions one and three. These terms differ in their level of complexity and in extent. Any of these definitions may be useful, but questions like these help determine whether they are equally valid for capturing the direction of new approaches in educational leadership.

Finally, using the three definitions as reference, overlay the clusters of concepts described in the readings. In reading one the concepts are perplexing information, making sense, structuring interactions. In reading two the concepts are situational awareness, systems thinking, commitment to core ideology.

In reading three the concepts are empathy, emotional groundedness, personal interaction skill. In reading four the concepts are shared sense-making, patterns of connection, navigating complex challenges. And in the final reading, the concepts are interactions, interdependency, situations. At this point, the fundamental question is whether one of these definitions is sufficient to capture the particular concepts you value most or whether you will need to look elsewhere for a better definition.

This process of aligning a definition with clusters of concepts provides a framework for organizing your understanding of new approaches to educational leadership. Essentially, you come to understand that no single definition or theory or model is sufficient because so many variables impact leader behavior and practice.

## ADDITIONAL READING RESOURCES

Katy Anthes, *What's Happening in School and District Leadership?* Education Commission of the States, 2005.

Bernard M. Bass and Ronald E. Riggio, *Transformation Leadership*. Lawrence Erlbaum, 2005.

Barbara C. Crosby and John M. Bryson, *Leadership for the Common Good: Tackling Public Problems in a Shared-Power World*. Jossey-Bass, 2005.

Ronald Heifetz, *Leadership Without Easy Answers*. Harvard University Press, 1994.

Wayne K. Hoy, *Educational Administration: Theory, Research, and Practice*. PowerPoint presentation at *http://www.coe.ohio-state.edu/whoy/new_page_1.htm*

Wayne K. Hoy and Cecil G. Miskel, *Educational Administration: Theory, Research, and Practice* (7th ed.). McGraw-Hill, 2005.

Jon L. Pierce and John W. Newstrom, Introduction to leadership. In *Leaders and the Leadership Process*. McGraw-Hill/Irwin, 2006.

Joseph C. Rost, *Leadership for the Twenty-First Century*. Praeger, 1993.

Gary Yukl, *Leadership in Organizations*. Prentice Hall, 2006.

For more information on approaches to educational leadership, check these sites:

The Center for Creative Leadership *www.ccl.org*
Leadership and Learning, Inc. *www.entrybook.com*
weLEAD Leadership Development *www.leadingtoday.org*
Center for Leadership Studies *www.situational.com*
The Conference Board *www.conference-board.org*
Leader to Leader Institute *www.leadertoleader.org*

# What Planning Strategies Work Best in Educational Organizations?

Historically, strategic planning has been one of the main activities of educational leaders. It is a task that occupies many work hours. In its simplest form, strategic planning enables administrators to answer three questions: Where are we going? How will we get there? How do we know we've gotten there? Essentially the purpose of strategic planning is to get everyone—faculty, staff, parents, board—on the same page with their answers to these three questions. Ideally, once in place, a strategic plan should make daily decision making easier.

Approaches to strategic planning vary, depending on the institution's mission and purpose, size, and culture. Institutions can take a goal-oriented, issue-oriented, or program-oriented approach, with goal-oriented being the typical model. Resources for strategic planning are abundant and many organizations are now able to turn to software for planning. (Googling will yield 6000 sources of strategic planning software.) So what are the best strategies for decision making in educational settings?

In truth, the answer to the question varies widely. For some institutions and agencies, strategic planning for a five to ten year period has fallen out of favor. For others, strategic planning as top-down, general-to-specific is passé. And for still others, the three classic planning questions are not even relevant. The problem is that many traditional strategy plans are obsolete instantly: While they are being circulated, educational standards, federal regulations, the neighborhood, and the world have all changed.

Strategic planning continues to be a major activity, but it is taking new shapes. This transformation is driven by much more than technology and resources. It is also due to an ever-increasing need for improvement and sustainability and supported by a mindset that embraces complexity. New planning strategies are more robust, allowing educational leaders to ask the *why* questions in addition to *where* and *how*. Sophisticated approaches like resource mapping, scenarios, and simulations enable leaders to do "what-if" analysis. No longer is strategic planning limited to corporate America and solely about profitability, margin, and performance. Now, as never before, schools and institutions have excellent resources for planning that focus on student achievement, sustainability, school climate, and adaptive systems.

A chronic complaint about strategic planning is that the most important decisions are not in the plan. Another complaint is that strategies do not translate into performance. Mankins and Steele, the authors of the first reading, have discovered several reasons for misguided strategic plans. Chief among the reasons are bad timing and an ineffective planning process. Mankins and Steele's survey of 156 large companies shows that although many of the organizations continue to use strategic planning, the traditional process may not be worthwhile. There is a disconnect between planning and decision making, largely because leaders make decisions continually yet they plan periodically. Mankins and Steele believe strategic planning can be done right by moving to a continuous decision-oriented process.

Imagine high-performing schools that do not measure up on comprehensive improvement plans. Does this mean these schools aren't doing any planning? Actually the reverse is true. Craig Jerald, the author of the second reading, explains how some schools are using continuous forms of planning that involve deep collaboration and intensive problem solving. While it would seem apparent that high-performing schools are problem-solving schools, this is not always the case. Jerald outlines problem solving that is strategic and collaborative in an important policy brief from the Center for Comprehensive School Reform and Improvement.

The third reading, "The Learning Organization and Strategic Change," is based on the premise that organizational learning is not about a separate type of organization but learning as a model of strategic change. The author explains four versions of strategic planning and shows how each is a variation of the learning process. From the conventional "predict and plan" model to a focus on implementation, to a focus on readiness, each version is limited in its ability to help organizations "plan and execute significant organizational change amid rapidly changing business conditions." The fourth version—continual learning organization—is one of constant readiness and continual planning, and according to the author is the best way to introduce fundamental changes.

"You can't create the future in a structure designed to repeat the past," according to Rosabeth Moss Kanter (2002, p. 78). Kanter, along with other organizational leadership experts, has been influencing organizations to use new models for strategic planning—models that rely less on predictability and control, more on changeableness and alternatives. John Vogelsang, from the Support Center for Nonprofit Management, is also a proponent of new models for strategic planning. In "Futuring: A Complex Adaptive Systems Approach to Strategic Planning," Vogelsang presents a thorough comparison of traditional approaches and emerging approaches. Behind the newest approaches are theoretical constructs from the fields of chaos theory, complexity sciences, and quantum physics. When these constructs are incorporated, planning is vastly different from traditional strategies.

Traditional strategic planning is about actions and results—all of which lead to increased knowledge. Notice that knowing is at the end of the formula.

For many educational leaders today, this formula begins at the wrong place. Instead of actions, the process should begin with knowledge, and then move to actions and results. The assumption is that knowledge management and integration will enable organizations to deal with emerging events and opportunities, not just solve immediate problems. Making knowledge management a key component of strategic planning means an organization must replace traditional techniques with those that can accommodate unpredictable conditions, globalization, and an unforeseeable future (Akhter, 2003).

# SOURCES

Michael C. Mankins and Richard Steele, Stop making plans: Start making decisions. *Harvard Business Review*, January 2006.

Craig Jerald, Planning that matters: Helping schools engage in collaborative, strategic problem solving. *The Center for Comprehensive School Reform and Improvement*, April 2005.

Robert W. Rowden, The learning organization and strategic change. *SAM Advanced Management Journal*, Summer 2001.

John Vogelsang, Futuring: A complex adaptive systems approach to strategic planning. *Support Center for Nonprofit Management*, March/April 2004.

# ARTICLE 2.1

# Stop Making Plans: Start Making Decisions

## Michael C. Mankins and Richard Steele

Is strategic planning completely useless? That was the question the CEO of a global manufacturer recently asked himself. Two years earlier, he had launched an ambitious overhaul of the company's planning process. The old approach, which required business-unit heads to make regular presentations to the firm's executive committee, had broken down entirely. The ExCom members—the CEO, COO, CFO, CTO, and head of HR—had grown tired of sitting through endless PowerPoint presentations that provided them few opportunities to challenge the business units' assumptions or influence their strategies. And the unit heads had complained that the ExCom reviews were long on exhortation but short on executable advice. Worse, the reviews led to very few worthwhile decisions.

The revamped process incorporated state-of-the-art thinking about strategic planning. To avoid information overload, it limited each business to 15 "high-impact" exhibits describing the unit's strategy. To ensure thoughtful discussions, it required that all presentations and supporting materials be distributed to the ExCom at least a week in advance. The review sessions themselves were restructured to allow ample time for give-and-take between the corporate team and the business-unit executives. And rather than force the unit heads to traipse off to headquarters for meetings, the ExCom agreed to spend an unprecedented six weeks each spring visiting all 22 units for daylong sessions. The intent was to make the strategy reviews longer, more focused, and more consequential.

It didn't work. After using the new process for two planning cycles, the CEO gathered feedback from the participants through an anonymous survey. To his dismay, the report contained a litany of complaints: "It takes too much time." "It's at too high a level." "It's disconnected from the way we run the business."And so on. Most damning of all, however, was the respondents' near-universal view that the new approach produced very few real decisions. The CEO was dumbfounded. How could the company's cutting-edge planning process still be so badly broken? More important, what should he do to make strategic planning drive more, better, and faster decisions?

Like this CEO, many executives have grown skeptical of strategic planning. Is it any wonder? Despite all the time and energy most companies put into strategic planning, the process is most often a barrier to good decision making, our research indicates. As a result, strategic planning doesn't really influence most companies' strategy.

**50**

In the following pages, we will demonstrate that the failure of most strategic planning is due to two factors: It is typically an annual process, and it is most often focused on individual business units. As such, the process is completely at odds with the way executives actually make important strategy decisions, which are neither constrained by the calendar nor defined by unit boundaries. Not surprisingly, then, senior executives routinely sidestep the planning process. They make the decisions that really shape their company's strategy and determine its future—decisions about mergers and acquisitions, product launches, corporate restructurings, and the like—outside the planning process, typically in an ad hoc fashion, without rigorous analysis or productive debate. Critical decisions are made incorrectly or not at all. More than anything else, this disconnect—between the way planning works and the way decision making happens—explains the frustration, if not outright antipathy, most executives feel toward strategic planning.

*What are some of the "disconnects" between the way planning works and the way decision making happens in schools and institutions?*

But companies can fix the process if they attack its root problems. A small number of forward-looking companies have thrown out their calendar-driven, business-unit-focused planning processes and replaced them with continuous, issues-focused decision making. By changing the timing and focus of strategic planning, they've also changed the nature of top management's discussions about strategy—from "review and approve" to "debate and decide," meaning that senior executives seriously think through every major decision and its implications for the company's performance and value. Indeed, these companies use the strategy development process to drive decision making. As a consequence, they make more than twice as many important strategic decisions each year as companies that follow the traditional planning model. (See the exhibit "Who Makes More Decisions?") These companies have stopped making plans and started making decisions.

## WHERE PLANNING GOES WRONG

In the fall of 2005, Marakon Associates, in collaboration with the Economist Intelligence Unit, surveyed senior executives from 156 large companies worldwide, all with sales of $1 billion or more (40% of them had revenues over $10 billion). We asked these executives how their companies developed long-range plans and how effectively they thought their planning processes drove strategic decisions.

The results of the survey confirmed what we have observed over many years of consulting: The timing and structure of strategic planning are obstacles to good decision making. Specifically, we found that companies with standard planning processes and practices make only 2.5 major strategic decisions each year, on average (by "major," we mean they have the potential to increase company profits by 10% or more over the long term). It's hard to imagine that with so few strategic decisions driving growth, these companies can keep moving forward and deliver the financial performance that investors expect.

Even worse, we suspect that the few decisions companies do reach are made in spite of the strategic planning process, not because of it. Indeed, the traditional planning model is so cumbersome and out of sync with the way executives want and need to make decisions that top managers all too often sidestep the process when making their biggest strategic choices.

With the big decisions being made outside the planning process, strategic planning becomes merely a codification of judgments top management has already made, rather than a vehicle for identifying and debating the critical decisions that the company needs to make to produce superior performance. Over time, managers begin to question the value of strategic planning, withdraw from it, and come to rely on other processes for setting company strategy.

**The calendar effect** • At 66% of the companies in our survey, planning is a periodic event, often conducted as a precursor to the yearly budgeting and capital-approval processes. In fact, linking strategic planning to these other management processes is often cited as a best practice. But forcing strategic planning into an annual cycle risks making it irrelevant to executives, who must make many important decisions throughout the year.

There are two major drawbacks to such a rigid schedule. The first might be called the *time* problem. A once-a-year planning schedule simply does not give executives sufficient time to address the issues that most affect performance. According to our survey, companies that follow an annual planning calendar devote less than nine weeks per year to strategy development. That's barely

---

## Who Makes More Decisions?

Companies see a dramatic increase in the quality of their decision making once they abandon the traditional planning model, which is calendar driven and focused on the business units. In our survey, the companies that broke most completely with the past made more than twice as many strategic decisions each year as companies wedded to tradition. What's more, the new structure of the planning process ensures that the decisions are probably the best that could have been made, given the information available to managers at the time.

Here are the average numbers of major strategic decisions reached per year in companies that take the following approaches to strategic planning:

**Annual review:** focused on business units: **2.5** Decisions Per Year
**Annual review:** focused on issues: **3.5** Decisions Per Year
**Continuous review:** focused on business units: **4.1** Decisions Per Year
**Continuous review:** focused on issues: **6.1** Decisions Per Year

*Source:* Marakon Associates and the Economist Intelligence Unit

two months to collect relevant facts, set strategic priorities, weigh competing alternatives, and make important strategic choices. Many issues—particularly those spanning multiple businesses, crossing geographic boundaries, or involving entire value chains—cannot be resolved effectively in such a short time. It took Boeing, for example, almost two years to decide to outsource major activities such as wing manufacturing.

Constrained by the planning calendar, corporate executives face two choices: They can either not address these complex issues—in effect, throwing them in the "too-hard" bucket—or they can address them through some process other than strategic planning. In both cases, strategic planning is marginalized and separated from strategic decision making.

Then there's the *timing* problem. Even when executives allot sufficient time in strategy development to address tough issues, the timing of the process can create problems. At most companies, strategic planning is a batch process in which managers analyze market and competitor information, identify threats and opportunities, and then define a multiyear plan. But in the real world, managers make strategic decisions continuously, often motivated by an immediate need for action (or reaction). When a new competitor enters a market, for instance, or a rival introduces a new technology, executives must act quickly and decisively to safeguard the company's performance. But very few companies (less than 10%, according to our survey) have any sort of rigorous or disciplined process for responding to changes in the external environment. Instead, managers rely on ad hoc processes to correct course or make opportunistic moves. Once again, strategic planning is sidelined, and executives risk making poor decisions that have not been carefully thought through.

M&A decisions provide a particularly egregious example of the timing problem. Acquisition opportunities tend to emerge spontaneously, the result of changes in management at a target company, the actions of a competitor, or some other unpredictable event. Faced with a promising opportunity and limited time in which to act, executives can't wait until the opportunity is evaluated as part of the next annual planning cycle, so they assess the deal and make a quick decision. But because there's often no proper review process, the softer customer- and people-related issues so critical to effective integration of an acquired company can get shortchanged. It is no coincidence that failure to plan for integration is often cited as the primary cause of deal failure.

**The business-unit effect** • The organizational focus of the typical planning process compounds its calendar effects—or, perhaps more aptly, defects. Two-thirds of the executives we surveyed indicated that strategic planning at their companies is conducted business by business—that is, it is focused on units or groups of units. But 70% of the senior executives who responded to our survey stated they make decisions issue by issue. For example, should we enter China? Should we outsource manufacturing? Should we acquire our distributor? Given this mismatch between the way planning is organized and the way big decisions are made, it's hardly surprising that, once again, corporate leaders look elsewhere for guidance and inspiration. In fact, only 11% of the executives we surveyed believed strongly that planning was worth the effort.

The organizational focus of traditional strategic planning also creates distance, even antagonism, between corporate executives and business-unit managers. Consider, for example, the way most companies conduct strategy reviews—as formal meetings between senior managers and the heads of each business unit. While these reviews are intended to produce a fact-based dialogue, they often amount to little more than business tourism. The executive committee flies in for a day, sees the sights, meets the natives, and flies out. The business unit, for its part, puts in a lot of work preparing for this royal visit and is keen to make it smooth and trouble free. The unit hopes to escape with few unanswered questions and an approved plan. Accordingly, local managers control the flow of information upward, and senior managers are presented only with information that shows each unit in the best possible light. Opportunities are highlighted; threats are downplayed or omitted.

Even if there's no subterfuge, senior corporate managers still have trouble engaging in constructive dialogue and debate because of what might be called information asymmetry. They just don't have the information they need to be helpful in guiding business units. So when they're presented with a strategic plan that's too good to be believed, they have only two real options: either reject it—a move that's all but unheard-of at most large companies—or play along and impose stretch targets to secure at least the promise that the unit will improve performance. In both cases, the review does little to drive decisions on issues. It's hardly surprising that only 13% of the executives we surveyed felt that top managers were effectively engaged in all aspects of strategy development at their companies—from target setting to debating alternatives to approving strategies and allocating resources.

*What kinds of "information asymmetry" can occur between the instructional or grade level and school level?*

# DECISION-FOCUSED STRATEGIC PLANNING

Strategic planning can't have impact if it doesn't drive decision making. And it can't drive decision making as long as it remains focused on individual business units and limited by the calendar. Over the past several years, we have observed that many of the best-performing companies have abandoned the traditional approach and are focusing explicitly on reaching decisions through the continuous identification and systematic resolution of strategic issues. (The sidebar "Continuous, Decision-Oriented Planning" presents a detailed example of the issues-oriented approach.) Although these companies have found different specific solutions, all have made essentially the same fundamental changes to their planning and strategy development processes in order to produce more, better, and faster decisions.

**They separate—but integrate—decision making and plan making** • First and most important, a company must take decisions out of the traditional planning process and create a different, parallel process for developing strategy that helps executives identify the decisions they *need to make* to create more shareholder value over time. The output of this new process isn't a plan at all—it's a set of concrete decisions that management can codify into future business plans through the existing planning process, which remains in place. Identifying and making decisions is distinct from creating, monitoring, and updating a strategic plan, and the two sets of tasks require very different, but integrated, processes.

Boeing Commercial Airplanes (BCA) is a case in point. This business unit, Boeing's largest, has had a long-range business plan (LRBP) process for many years. The protracted cycles of commercial aircraft production require the unit's CEO, Alan Mulally, and his leadership team to take a long-term view of the business. Accordingly, the unit's LRBP contains a ten-year financial forecast, including projected revenues, backlogs, operating margins, and capital investments. BCA's leadership team reviews the business plan weekly to track the division's performance relative to the plan and to keep the organization focused on execution.

The weekly reviews were invaluable as a performance-monitoring tool at BCA, but they were not particularly effective at bringing new issues to the surface or driving strategic decision making. So in 2001, the unit's leadership team introduced a Strategy Integration Process focused on uncovering and addressing the business's most important strategic issues (such as determining the best go-to-market strategy for the business, driving the evolution of BCA's product strategy, or fueling growth in services). The team assigned to this process holds strategy integration meetings every Monday to track BCA's progress

---

## The Disconnect Between Planning and Decision Making

**How Executives Plan**
66% Periodically
Percentage of surveyed executives saying their companies conduct strategic planning only at prescribed times
67% Unit By Unit
Percentage saying planning is done unit by unit

**How Executives Decide**
100% Continuously
Percentage of executives saying strategic decisions are made without regard to the calendar
70% Issue By Issue
Percentage saying decisions are made issue by issue
No wonder only **11%** of executives are highly satisfied that strategic planning is worth the effort.

in resolving these long-term issues. Once a specific course of action is agreed upon and approved by BCA's leadership team, the long-range business plan is updated at the next weekly review to reflect the projected change in financial performance.

The time invested in the new decision-making process is more than compensated for by the time saved in the LRBP process, which is now solely focused on strategy execution. The company gets the best of both worlds—disciplined decision making and superior execution. BCA has maintained the value of the LRBP as an execution tool even as it has increased the quality and quantity of important decisions. Managers believe that the new process is at least partially responsible for the sharp turnaround in Boeing's performance since 2001.

*What key themes might be the focus of strategy discussions at an elementary school . . . a middle school . . . a high school . . . a university . . . a corporate learning center?*

**They focus on a few key themes** • High-performing companies typically focus their strategy discussions on a limited number of important issues or themes, many of which span multiple businesses. Moving away from a business-by-business planning model in this way has proved particularly helpful for large, complex organizations, where strategy discussions can quickly get bogged down as each division manager attempts to cover every aspect of the unit's strategy. Business-unit managers should remain involved in corporate-level strategy planning that affects their units. But a focus on issues rather than business units better aligns strategy development with decision making and investment.

Consider Microsoft. The world's leading software maker is a highly matrixed organization. No strategy can be effectively executed at the company without careful coordination across multiple functions and across two or more of Microsoft's seven business units, or, as executives refer to them, "P&Ls"—Client; Server and Tools; Information Worker; MSN; Microsoft Business Solutions; Mobile and Embedded Devices; and Home and Entertainment. In late 2004, faced with a perceived shortage of good investment ideas, CEO Steve Ballmer asked Robert Uhlaner, Microsoft's corporate vice president of strategy, planning, and analysis, to devise a new strategic planning process for the company. Uhlaner put in place a Growth and Performance Planning Process that starts with agreement by Ballmer's leadership team on a set of strategic themes—major issues like PC market growth, the entertainment market, and security—that cross business-unit boundaries. These themes not only frame the dialogue for Microsoft's annual strategy review, they also guide the units in fleshing out investment alternatives to fuel the company's growth. Dialogues between the P&L leaders and Ballmer's team focus on what the company can do to address each strategic theme, rather than on individual unit strategies. The early results of this new process are promising. "You have to be careful what you wish for," Uhlaner says. "Our new process has surfaced countless new opportunities for growth. We no longer worry about a dearth of investment ideas, but how best to fund them."

Like Microsoft, Diageo North America—a division of the international beer, wine, and spirits marketer—has recently changed the way it conducts strategic planning to allocate resources across its diverse portfolio. Diageo historically focused its planning efforts on individual brands. Brand managers were allowed to make the case for additional investment, no matter what the size of the brand or its strategic role in the portfolio. As a result, resource allocation was bedeviled by endless negotiations between the brands and corporate management. This political wrangling made it extremely difficult for Diageo's senior managers to establish a consistent approach to growth, because a lack of transparency prevented them from discerning, from the many requests for additional funding, which brands really deserved more resources and which did not.

Starting in 2001, Diageo overhauled its approach to strategy development. A crucial change was to focus planning on the factors that the company believed would most drive market growth—for example, an increase in the U.S. Hispanic population. By modeling the impact of these factors on the brand portfolio, Diageo has been better able to match its resources with the brands that have the most growth potential so that it can specify the strategies and investments each brand manager should develop, says Jim Moseley, senior vice president of consumer planning and research for Diageo North America. For example, the division now identifies certain brands for growth and earmarks specific resources for investment in these units. This focused approach has enabled the company to shorten the brand planning process and reduce the time spent on negotiations between the brands and division management. It has also given senior management greater confidence in each brand's ability to contribute to Diageo's growth.

**They make strategy development continuous** • Effective strategy planners spread strategy reviews throughout the year rather than squeeze them into a two- or three-month window. This allows senior executives to focus on one issue at a time until they reach a decision or set of decisions. Moreover, managers can add issues to the agenda as market and competitive conditions change, so there's no need for ad hoc processes. Senior executives can thus rely on a single strategic planning process—or, perhaps more aptly, a single strategic decision-making model—to drive decision making across the company.

Textron, a $10 billion multi-industry company, has implemented a new, continuous strategy-development process built around a prioritized "decision agenda" comprising the company's most important issues and opportunities. Until 2004, Textron had a fairly traditional strategic planning process. Each spring, the company's operating units—businesses as diverse as Bell Helicopter, E-Z-Go golf cars, and Jacobsen turf maintenance equipment—would develop a five-year strategic plan based on standard templates. Unit managers would then review their strategic plans with Textron's management committee (the company's top five executives) during daylong sessions at each unit. Once the strategy reviews were complete, the units incorporated the results, as best they could, into their annual operating plans and capital budgets.

In June 2004, dissatisfied with the quality and pace of the decision making that resulted from the company's strategy reviews, CEO Lewis Campbell asked

## Traditional Planning

Companies that follow the traditional strategic planning model develop a strategy plan for each business unit at some point during the year. A cross-functional team dedicates less than nine weeks to developing the unit's plan. The executive committee reviews each plan—typically in daylong, on-site meetings—and rubber-stamps the results. The plans are consolidated to produce a company-wide strategic plan for review by the board of directors.

Once the strategic-planning cycle is complete, the units dedicate another eight to nine weeks to budgeting and capital planning (in most companies, these processes are not explicitly linked to strategic planning).

The executive committee then holds another round of meetings with each of the business units to negotiate performance targets, resource commitments, and (in many cases) compensation for managers.

The results: an approved but potentially unrealistic strategic plan for each business unit and a separate budget for each unit that is decoupled from the unit's strategic plan.

Stuart Grief, Textron's vice president for strategy and business development, to rethink the company's strategic planning process. After carefully reviewing the company's practices and gathering feedback from its 30 top executives, Grief and his team designed a new Textron Strategy Process.

There were two important changes. First, rather than concentrate all of the operating-unit strategy reviews in the second quarter of each year, the company now spreads strategy dialogues throughout the year—two to three units are reviewed per quarter. Second, rather than organize the management committee dialogues around business-unit plans, Textron now holds continuous reviews that are designed to address each strategic issue on the company's decision agenda. Both changes have enabled Textron's management committee to be much more effectively engaged in business-unit strategy development. The changes have also ensured that there's a forum in which cross-unit issues can be raised and addressed by top management, with input from relevant business-unit managers. The process has significantly increased the number of strategic decisions the company makes each year. As a result, Textron has gone from being an also-ran among its multi-industrial peers to a top-quartile performer over the past 18 months.

John Cullivan, the director of strategy at Cardinal Health, one of the world's leading health-care products and services companies, reports similar benefits from shifting to a continuous planning model. "Continuous decision

## Continuous, Decision-Oriented Planning

Once the company as a whole has identified its most important strategic priorities (typically in an annual strategy update), executive committee dialogues, spread throughout the year, are set up to reach decisions on as many issues as possible. Since issues frequently span multiple business units, task forces are established to prepare the strategic and financial information that's needed to uncover and evaluate strategy alternatives for each issue. Preparation time may exceed nine weeks. The executive committee engages in two dialogues for each issue at three to four hours each.

The first dialogue focuses on reaching agreement on the facts surrounding the issue and on a set of viable alternatives. The second focuses on the evaluation of those alternatives and the selection of the best course of action. Once an issue is resolved, a new one is added to the agenda. Critical issues can be inserted into the planning process at any time as market and competitive conditions change.

Once a decision has been reached, the budgets and capital plans for the affected business units are updated to reflect the selected option. Consequently, the strategic-planning process and the capital and budgeting processes are integrated. This significantly reduces the need for lengthy negotiations between the executive committee and unit management over the budget and capital plan.

The results: a concrete plan for addressing each key issue; for each business unit, a continuously updated budget and capital plan that is linked directly to the resolution of critical strategic issues; and more, faster, better decisions per year.

making is tough to establish because it requires the reallocation of management time at the top levels of the company," he says. "But the process has enabled us to get sharper focus on the short-term performance of our vertical businesses and make faster progress on our longer-term priorities, some of which are horizontal opportunities that cut across businesses and thus are difficult to manage."

To facilitate continuous strategic decision making, Cardinal has made a series of important changes to its traditional planning process. At the corporate level, for example, the company has put in place a rolling six-month agenda for its executive committee dialogues, a practice that allows everyone inside Cardinal to know what issues management is working on and when decisions will be reached. Similar decision agendas are used at the business-unit and functional levels, ensuring that common standards are applied to all important decisions at the company. And to support continuous decision making at

Cardinal, the company has trained "black belts" in new analytical tools and processes and deployed them throughout the organization. This provides each of the company's businesses and functions with the resources needed to address strategic priorities that emerge over time.

**They structure strategy reviews to produce real decisions** • The most common obstacles to decision making at large companies are disagreements among executives over past decisions, current alternatives, and even the facts presented to support strategic plans. Leading companies structure their strategy review sessions to overcome these problems.

*What are potential difficulties with continuous strategic decision making for a school or institution?*

At Textron, for example, strategic-issue reviews are organized around "facts, alternatives, and choices." Each issue is addressed in two half-day sessions with the company's management committee, allowing for eight to ten issues to be resolved throughout the year. In the first session, the management committee debates and reaches agreement on the relevant facts—information on the profitability of key markets, the actions of competitors, the purchase behavior of customers, and so on—and a limited set of viable strategy alternatives. The purpose of this first meeting is not to reach agreement on a specific course of action; rather, the meeting ensures that the group has the best possible information and a robust set of alternatives to consider. The second session is focused on evaluating these alternatives from a strategic and financial perspective and selecting the best course of action. By separating the dialogue around facts and alternatives from the debate over choices, Textron's management committee avoids many of the bottlenecks that plague strategic decision making at most companies and reaches many more decisions than it otherwise would.

Like Textron, Cadbury Schweppes has changed the structure of its strategy dialogues to focus top managers more explicitly on decision making. In 2002, after acquiring and integrating gum-maker Adams—a move that significantly expanded Cadbury's product and geographic reach—the company realized it needed to rethink how it was conducting dialogues about strategy between the corporate center and the businesses. The company made two important changes. First, strategy dialogues were redesigned to incorporate a standard set of facts and metrics about consumers, customers, and competitors. This information helped get critical commercial choices in front of top managers, so that the choices were no longer buried in the business units. Second, senior executives' time was reallocated so they could pay more attention to markets that were crucial to realizing Cadbury's ten-year vision and to making important decisions.

Cadbury's top team now spends one full week per year in each of the countries that are most critical to driving the company's performance, so that important decisions can be informed by direct observation as well as through indirect analysis. Strategy dialogues are now based on a much deeper understanding of the markets. Cadbury's strategic reviews no longer merely consist of reviews of and approval of a strategic plan, and they produce many more important decisions.

Done right, strategic planning can have an enormous impact on a company's performance and long-term value. By creating a planning process that enables managers to discover great numbers of hidden strategic issues and make more decisions, companies will open the door to many more opportunities for long-term growth and profitability. By embracing decision-focused planning, companies will almost certainly find that the quantity and quality of their decisions will improve. And—no coincidence they will discover an improvement in the quality of the dialogue between senior corporate managers and unit managers. Corporate executives will gain a better understanding of the challenges their companies face, and unit managers will benefit fully from the experience and insights of the company's leaders. As Mark Reckitt, a director of group strategy at Cadbury Schweppes, puts it: "Continuous, decision-focused strategic planning has helped our top management team to streamline its agenda and work with business units and functional management to make far better business-strategy and commercial decisions."

## ARTICLE 2.2

# Planning That Matters: Helping Schools Engage in Collaborative, Strategic Problem Solving

Craig Jerald

## PROBLEMS WITH THE PLANNING PROCESS

Earlier this year, the Prichard Committee for Academic Excellence released a report highlighting practices in Kentucky's high-performing, high-poverty schools. Researchers collected information using the same audit tool that the Kentucky Department of Education uses to diagnose problems in schools identified for improvement, then compared those results with similar information amassed by state-conducted audits of low-performing schools.

The analysis yielded some unanticipated results. While the successful schools scored well on some areas of the audit, they did not score well on indicators related to comprehensive planning. Indeed, the data revealed no significant difference between high- and low-performing schools on any of 16 indicators measuring how well schools had followed the recommended process for creating Comprehensive School Improvement Plans.[1]

What can this mean? Do high-performing schools really not bother to engage in systematic planning? Is there no real relationship between good planning and measurable school improvement?

The answer, of course, is no. The same study revealed that high-performing schools engage in more collaborative decision making, work harder to connect professional development to student achievement data, and make more efficient use of time and resources. None of those activities is possible, or at least possible to do well, without serious and thoughtful planning.

When asked to comment about this apparent paradox, an audit team member said of one school, "Their [Comprehensive School Improvement Plan] was not exemplary, but their school was. They are planning, but it did not get captured in that document, not formally." Another recalled having seen the reverse situation when participating in state audits of schools needing improvement. Some low-performing schools had crafted "model" plans and documentation, this team member said, but "did not appear to be doing much of it in the classrooms."[2]

Instead of dismissing this finding as a bizarre anomaly, policymakers and assistance providers would do well to ponder its implications. Too often the formal planning process required by state and federal policy is perceived as a bureaucratic exercise resulting in written plans that do not drive real change efforts for the day-to-day work of schools. And too often it is disconnected from the kind of planning that can lead to significant, measurable improvement. . . .

The real problem is that schools can follow all of the recommended steps for formal planning, engage in all of the activities and meetings suggested, and even craft excellently written plans, yet—even with hands-on assistance—*still* not engage in the kind of deliberate activities that propel real change and drive professional work in effective schools.

# PROBLEM SOLVING THAT IS STRATEGIC AND COLLABORATIVE

Formal planning and documentation are important responsibilities under state and federal law, and we certainly want schools to approach them seriously and conscientiously. However, if we are to realize success in helping all of our low-performing schools get onto a path leading toward sustained improvement in student outcomes, we also must find ways to isolate and understand the kind of real-life planning that matters most, provide compelling examples of it, and deliberately build the capacity of all schools to engage in it.

A glimpse into that kind of planning can be gleaned from the full findings of the Kentucky study as well as other recent research on high-improving schools elsewhere in the United States. The picture that emerges is one that *sometimes* has to do with the formal planning process with which we all are familiar, but almost *always* has to do with a deeper layer of planning that can best be called *collaborative, strategic problem solving*.[3]

## What Do We Mean by "Problem Solving?"

Problem-solving schools:

- Establish a results-based orientation focused on tangible student outcomes. First, staff members firmly believe that whatever other functions schools might perform in a community, they are *at least* and *primarily* responsible for making sure that students learn. Second, they take direct responsibility for student achievement. They do not get mired in the belief that family and social problems present insurmountable obstacles to learning. Instead, they believe that what children experience within schools and classrooms can have a decisive impact on whether and how much they learn.
- Relentlessly analyze data and other empirical evidence at all levels—student, grade, subject, and schoolwide—to identify problems. Then they gather additional evidence to identify internal weaknesses that are causing or abetting low outcomes and obstructing improvement.
- Identify possible solutions to problems and opportunities for making changes that will lead to greater success. They use common sense,

*What is missing from traditional planning that occurs through collaborative problem solving?*

creativity, and extensive investigation of research- and evidence-based practices to decide among those possible solutions.

To understand how these three things might work together, consider a hypothetical example based on a challenge all too common in U.S. high schools.

A high school improvement team identifies a problem with particularly low achievement and high retention rates in the ninth grade. Rather than simply assuming that most 14-year-olds naturally struggle because of "hormones," they collect additional information that might explain the problem and find that high ninth-grade failure is partly due to low literacy levels among entering freshmen.

Although the problem at first seems "outside their control," team members take responsibility and seek solutions. After examining the research and seeking examples of schools that have addressed the problem, they consider working with a handful of feeder middle schools to craft "transition standards." The standards could include implementing diagnostic assessments as part of an "early warning system," creating a "fast track" literacy program to provide immediate and intensive help for students who need it, and changing the master schedule to reduce class sizes and assign more experienced teachers to ninth-grade classrooms. . . .

Of course, all schools that go through a formal planning process engage in a similar set of steps as part of a required needs assessment. But problem-solving schools approach the task from a more powerful perspective—one that confronts problems more openly and deals with them more aggressively in the following ways:

- They diagnose problems and solutions from an "inside-out" orientation that first considers classroom instruction, schoolwide policies and arrangements, and finally external family, community, and social factors—instead of "blaming" nonschool factors first (e.g., "parents are uninvolved, so students don't do homework and can't learn").
- They "dig deeper," examining a full range of internal practices and conditions that might be causing low achievement and impeding improvement, including areas that often are ignored or glossed over because it is uncomfortable to talk about them. For example, these schools examine "opportunity gaps" within the school to determine if poor, minority, and low-achieving children are less likely to have access to qualified teachers, demanding classwork, and rigorous curricula. . . .
- They treat practices, policies, and arrangements as "variables rather than givens" and are much less likely to believe something cannot change simply because "that's the way we've always done it." Because they have less respect for the inflexible traditions and sacred cows of the past, they benefit from an expanded sense of what can be discarded, adapted, or changed within their schools.

To illustrate why this notion of strategic problem solving is different from traditional needs assessments and planning—as such *activities often play out*—consider a discrete, concrete example: the vexing issue of teacher quality and classroom assignments.

A number of recent studies have confirmed that novice teaches are far less effective at raising student achievement over the course of a school year than their more experienced colleagues.[4] Yet low-achieving, high-poverty, and high-minority students all are more likely to be assigned to inexperienced teachers. The fault does not lie only with forces outside a school's or district's control, either. Researchers in North Carolina recently found that nearly two thirds of the statewide black-white gap in exposure of elementary school students to novice teachers is due to the inequitable assignment of students to teachers within districts, with between one quarter and one third exclusively due to inequitable assignments *across classrooms within the same school.*[5]

Such patterns persist at the high school level, too, where the strongest, most experienced teachers are often assigned to teach Advanced Placement (AP) and honors subjects to "the best" juniors and seniors, while novice teachers assigned to ninth-grade classes struggle to help low-achieving freshmen get caught up.

Yet teacher-quality gaps are seldom, if ever, documented in formal needs assessments or addressed in written plans. Even though most schools and districts have ready access to information that could easily be used to analyze staffing patterns, these inequities largely have remained hidden from view, in part because schools take student assignment for granted and have not traditionally considered it related to student performance and school improvement. Some schools ignore it because they do not want to upset middle-class parents who often push administrators to assign their children to more experienced teachers.

However, some problem-solving schools and districts are finding ways to *intentionally match their strongest teachers with their weakest students.*

In Hamilton County, Tennessee, teachers who demonstrate high effectiveness in raising student achievement are eligible for significant bonuses and other incentives if they transfer to one of nine persistently underperforming elementary schools in Chattanooga, Tennessee. The district also has worked with local foundations to improve leadership, provide intensive teacher support, and reward success in those schools, making them better able to retain excellent teachers in the long run. Some of the nine schools have gone a step further and have begun to use achievement data to match students who are weak in a particular mathematics or reading skill to teachers who are especially adept at teaching that skill.[6] Together, these efforts are paying off. Last year, the state of Tennessee judged all nine schools to be achieving at above-average or exceptional rates of annual growth in student learning.[7] . . .

## What Do We Mean by "Strategic?"

Problem-solving schools do not simply write, sign, seal, and deliver an improvement plan once problems have been candidly identified, strengths and weaknesses have been assessed, goals have been prioritized, and solutions have been chosen. They shape their solutions into a coordinated and thoughtful strategy to be implemented over a given period of time.

Problem-solving schools:

- Consider internal alignment. Do their proposed solutions (i.e., the changes they intend to make and new practices and programs they intend to implement) align with one another? Or do they conflict in such a way that one will undermine another? Do they add up to a coherent package? Do they offer the best fit for a school's particular culture and context? What additional variables, if left unaddressed, will offer roadblocks to any or all of the solutions?
- Consider external alignment. How well do their solutions align with district and state goals, policies, and reform efforts?
- Decide how to line up existing resources to support their solutions, including budgets, time, and available staff, as well as where they might obtain additional resources if necessary.
- Proceed from an assumption that problem solving and improvement is an ongoing process rather than a once-a-year exercise. They plan ahead to examine data and other hard evidence on whether a solution or set of solutions is working, and they commit to adapt solutions or change course entirely whenever necessary. Of course, the nature of the solution and the availability of evidence both determine whether it is possible to establish a formal timeline or final deadline for such review, though both can help ensure it happens.

Equally important, though, is the attitude behind the commitment. As one principal told the author of a recent study comparing California schools that had sustained improvement with schools that had not, "You can't feel sorry that something doesn't work; you just have to try something different."[8]

*Can strategic planning succeed without being collaborative?*

## What Do We Mean by "Collaborative?"

The research is very clear that sustained improvement requires shared responsibility for problem solving and coordinated effort among staff members.

Problem-solving schools:

- Distribute responsibility for analyzing data, brainstorming solutions, and developing improvement strategies among teachers, administrators, and support staff.
- Ensure broad-based involvement of stakeholders, including parents, community members, and secondary-level students, in the problem-solving process and strategic implementation of solutions.
- Have school leaders who share all data openly so problems, obstacles, and opportunities are transparent and everyone knows what is at stake.

A long-term study of Washington schools achieving and sustaining significant improvement found that a major factor differentiating those schools from schools "on the slow track" was that improvement efforts were carried out by a "schoolwide team rather than random associations of individuals." About 70 percent of high-improving schools implemented shared, schoolwide strategies as opposed to about 20 percent of comparison schools. Nonimproving schools were four times as likely to have implemented individual strategies instead of schoolwide reforms.[9]

Surprisingly, given the popular notion that it takes high-profile "superstar" principals to turn around low-performing schools, *every one of the eight* high-performing schools in the Kentucky Prichard Committee study were found to have a culture of shared decision making rather than an authoritarian leader.[10]

On the other hand, some researchers have sounded a cautionary note about waiting too long to achieve buy-in from everybody on staff before committing to a reform strategy. A study examining *slow-improving* schools in Washington found that some schools had "an excessively consensus-oriented approach to change" that can act as "a major impediment to having reform take hold and move forward."[11] Clearly, schools need help finding the appropriate balance.

Many schools treat requirements for parent, community, and student involvement in the planning process as merely a meaningless courtesy or an empty nod to political correctness. That is unfortunate because such "external" involvement can help put a healthy pressure on educators to grapple with sensitive issues and candidly address crucial weaknesses. . . .

# BUILDING CAPACITY FOR PROBLEM SOLVING

Policymakers, education officials, and school assistance providers must take the lead in helping schools become better strategic problem solvers. That means more than simply outlining a few additional steps in the formal planning process or offering a supplemental tool (although neither of those things would hurt). Good problem solving works best as a continuous process, and we must learn how to help educators develop the mindset and skills necessary to candidly identify and actively solve problems as a regular part of their everyday work.

Here are a few additional recommendations for building the problem-solving capacity of public schools:

1. *Provide schools with the latest research showing the effect of in-school factors on student achievement and attainment.*

Many teachers and administrators continue to place excessive emphasis on family and social factors in explaining educational outcomes because they are not familiar with recent research revealing the power of schools and classrooms to significantly influence student achievement. This includes the growing body of "value-added" research demonstrating that effective classroom teaching is the strongest variable of all in determining how much students learn from year to year. During the coming year, The Center will offer valuable tools for communicating about this research with educators.

2. *Give schools the resources they need to effectively examine data and other kinds of evidence.*

Schools generally need three things before they can engage in the analytical work at the heart of problem solving: (1) data and other kinds of telling evidence to examine; (2) adequate time to examine them; and (3) the expertise to examine them thoughtfully.

State and local leaders should commit to providing schools with timely data and help them find the time required to analyze the data thoroughly. When asked how their state could help them continue to improve, principals in one study of high-improving schools "said they could target their efforts much more effectively if they had better information. They also pointed to having little time to undertake the kind of ongoing, thoughtful analysis of their needs, which they believe necessary to make major improvement."[12]

Of course, problem-solving schools examine many kinds of evidence, only some of which gets delivered to the schoolhouse door through official channels. Sometimes schools must actively "harvest" additional data from the following kinds of sources:

- Reports or Web sites published by federal, state, or local agencies (an often overlooked resource mined very effectively by North High School's *Jovenes Unidos*).
- Files or databases maintained by state or district agencies.
- Artifacts that can be found within the school itself (e.g., some high schools are learning to analyze their master schedules to identify inefficiencies in how they distribute learning opportunities, allocate time, and deploy staff).

Finally, of course, educators and external partners need to know how to analyze such evidence, especially how to cross-tabulate information to look for telling patterns. While "data-driven decision making" has become the latest buzzword in the school improvement arena, few educators know where to look to find the best practical assistance on how to do it.

3. *Encourage schools to ask hard questions about their outcomes, policies, and practices, and provide incentives that reward them for doing so.*

Unfortunately, school administrators traditionally have been rewarded for hiding problems rather than publicly revealing and dealing with them. As a result, the data and other evidence presented in too many school improvement plans are shaped either to make the school look good or to make a preconceived improvement strategy look good. Effective problem-solving schools dig deeper to analyze all kinds of data and evidence, no matter how uncomfortable, and they use those hard facts to drive solutions rather than the other way around. Educators who "dig and dish" difficult truths about their schools should receive praise, and principals in such schools should be held up as examples among their peers.

4. *Provide training in how to use available research to craft solutions to identified problems and weaknesses.*

Hugh Burkett, director of The Center, recalls working in one district where "we got very good at using data to define problems, but not very good at using data and the research base to identify solutions." Identifying weaknesses is important, but only if doing so leads to effective solutions.

5. *Help schools transition from writing multiple plans that are meaningless to one strategic plan that can drive change.*

Even well-intentioned laws and regulations can push schools to adopt a "paper chase" approach to planning rather than an organic, problem-solving orientation. States should consider accepting a single unified plan for federal programs and provide a template to help schools craft it.

6. *Help schools find ways to develop a truly broad-based, collaborative approach to problem solving.*

Problem solving and planning must be "staffwide work" rather than simply "committee work." In larger schools where a team must guide the process for practical purposes, principals can rotate team members regularly and establish formal mechanisms for involving a wide range of other staff members in analyzing data and proposing solutions to problems.

Schools often need help thinking about how to involve parents and community members, especially when it comes to inviting collaboration based on honest data about the need for change. But good examples can be found: Norview High School in Norfolk, Virginia, began experiencing significant support from parents after showing hundreds of them a slide presentation about low test scores.[13]

## CONCLUSION

Collaborative, strategic problem solving is not just another "activity" that educators must somehow learn how to perform on top of their already busy work lives. In our most effective schools, it is a *deeply ingrained way of perceiving and approaching day-to-day work*—one that is fundamentally different from the fatalism too often encouraged by the traditional culture of American education.

It requires the conviction that what happens within school buildings can make a profound difference in the learning of disadvantaged students; the willingness to accept responsibility for student achievement; the courage to zealously identify and publicly expose areas of weakness in deeply entrenched traditions and practices; a determined ingenuity in the face of finite resources; and the desire to do whatever it takes to increase learning.

*How can leaders structure collaborative problem solving so it becomes a normal process?*

Most educators want desperately to improve educational outcomes for their students—many are ready for such a change—but they will need considerable help from policymakers, leaders, and assistance providers to make it happen.

# ENDNOTES

1. Kannapel, P. J., & Clements, S. K. (2005). *Inside the black box of high-performing, high-poverty schools.* Lexington, KY: The Prichard Committee for Academic Excellence. (page 23)

2. Kannapel, P. J., & Clements, S. K. (2005). *Inside the black box of high-performing, high-poverty schools.* Lexington, KY: The Prichard Committee for Academic Excellence. (page 23)

3. Jerald, C. (2003). Beyond the rock and the hard place. *Educational Leadership, 61*(3), 15–16. See also: Hillman, L. S. (2004). *Breakthrough high schools: You can do it, too! Vol. 1.* Reston, VA: National Association of Secondary School Principals. (pages 3–4)

4. Viadero, D. (2005). Teacher turnover tracked in city district. *Education Week, 24*(24), 16. One recent study found that an otherwise highly effective teacher capable of improving student achievement by nine points annually would only be able to raise achievement by five points if he or she were a first-year teacher. See also: Hanushek, E. A., Kain, J. F., O'Brien, D. M., & Rivkin, S. G. (2005). *The market for teacher quality* (Working Paper No. 11154). Cambridge, MA: National Bureau of Economic Research. (page 29)

5. Clotfelter, C., Ladd, H. F., & Vigdor, J. (2004). *Teacher quality and minority achievement gaps.* Durham, NC: Terry Sanford Institute of Public Policy, Duke University. (pages 9–12)

6. Carey, K. (2004). The real value of teachers: If good teachers matter, why don't we act like it? *Thinking K-16, 8*(1), 7. Washington, DC: The Education Trust.

7. Tennessee Department of Education. (2004). *Report card 2004.* Retrieved March 28, 2005, from http://www.k-12.state.tn.us/rptcrd04/

8. Chrisman, V. (2005). How schools sustain success. *Educational Leadership, 62*(5), 16–21.

9. Lake, R. J., Hill, P. T., O'Toole, L., & Celio, M. B. (1999). *Making standards work: Active voices, focused learning.* Seattle, WA: Center on Reinventing Public Education, University of Washington.

10. Kannapel, P. J., & Clements, S. K. (2005). *Inside the black box of high-performing, high-poverty schools.* Lexington, KY: The Prichard Committee for Academic Excellence. (page 18)

11. McCarthy, S., & Celio, M. B. (2001). *Washington elementary schools on the slow track under standards-based reform.* Seattle, WA: Center on Reinventing Public Education, University of Washington. (page 26)

12. Lake, R., McCarthy, M., Taggart, S., & Celio, M. B. (2000). *Making standards stick: A follow-up look at Washington State's school improvement efforts in 1999–2000.* Seattle, WA: Center for the Reinvention of Public Education, University of Washington. (page 29)

13. Gewertz, C. (2005). One subject at a time. *Education Week, 24*(21), 34–37.

# ARTICLE 2.3

# The Learning Organization and Strategic Change

Robert W. Rowden

## INTRODUCTION

Imagine that you are taking a journey into the mountains. The nature of the experience will vary considerably from one mountain range to another. There are two kinds of mountain ranges. One type, like the North American Rockies, is dominated by prominent peaks, their majestic summits rising silently and austerely above the landscape. The foothills and smaller mountains, dwarfed in the foreground, dramatize the formidable scale of the highest peaks. On a trip, the summit dominates the horizon, an endpoint against which progress can be easily gauged.

But there is another type of mountain range, such as the Cascades in the Pacific Northwestern United States, composed of gradually rising peaks, the size of one peak not revealing itself until the last one has been conquered, the summit being but one final stage in the gradual ascent.

Aesthetically, each has an elegance and beauty—the first, awesome and inspiring, the second, mysterious and surprising.

Organizations also take journeys in their attempts to mount significant strategic change. Examples of these journeys include entering international markets, downsizing, forming strategic alliances, improving customer satisfaction, achieving quality improvements, pioneering new technical innovations, and introducing new products. Increasingly, a company's viability is being determined by its ability to make such systemic, organization-wide change happen, and happen fast.

Traditionally, firms have approached these journeys as if the business landscape resembled a mountain range like the Rockies. At the outset of the journey, the organization would scan the horizon and spot the summit. With the presumption of clear vision, it would set a goal and develop a precise roadmap to achieve its end target. Clouds of resistance, fog banks of shortsightedness, or storms of crisis might obscure the final destination now and then. However, the summit would still be reached if only the organization maintained momentum and stayed on course.

In the highly uncertain business conditions emerging in the early 21st century, the topography of the business environment might be more like the mysterious Cascades than the majestic Rockies. Clouds of swirling technological,

72

competitive, marketplace, social, economic, and political changes obscure the final destinations. Until an organization takes some action and mounts the first hill, the size and scope of the next peak cannot be foreseen. Business environments are too chaotic and organizational change too complex to establish firm objectives, fixed plans, and concrete programs of change.

Amid sometimes unpredictable, always uncertain, and highly turbulent business conditions, an organization's capacity to learn as it goes may be the only true source of competitive advantage. No longer able to forecast the future, many leading organizations are constructing arks comprised of their inherent capacity to adapt to unforeseen situations, to learn from their own experiences, to shift their shared mindsets, and to change more quickly, broadly, and deeply than ever before. In other words, to become learning organizations. According to Kiechel, the notion of the learning organization is . . . a very big conceptual catchall to help us make sense of a set of values and ideas we've been wrestling with, everything from customer service to corporate responsiveness and speed (1990, p. 133).

The idea of the learning organization has been around quite some time. It derives from Argyris' work in organizational learning (Argyris & Schon, 1978) and is indebted to Revans' (1983) studies of action learning. It has roots in organization development (especially action research methodology) and organizational theory (most notably, Burns and Stalker's work on organic organizations). Its conceptual foundations are firmly based on systems theory (Senge, 1990a) and its practical application to managing a business has evolved out of strategic planning and strategic management (Fiol & Lyles, 1985; Hosley, Lau, Levy & Tan, 1994), which have recognized that organizational learning is the underlying source of strategic change (DeGeus, 1988; Jashapara, 1993). Much of the quality improvement movement of recent years, with its emphasis on continuous improvement, represented the first widespread, inchoate application of learning organization concepts (Senge, 1990b; Stata, 1989).

Learning organizations tend to have the following characteristics in common (Calvert, Mobley & Marshall, 1994; Watkins & Marsick, 1993):

- They provide continuous learning opportunities.
- They use learning to reach their goals.
- They link individual performance with organizational performance.
- They foster inquiry and dialog, making it safe for people to share openly and take risks.
- They embrace creative tension as a source of energy and renewal.
- They are continuously aware of and interact with their environment.

The label, "learning organization," is commonly used as if it represents a certain type of organization, implying that it is possible to designate certain firms as learning organizations and, at the same time, determine that others are not. In contrast, it seems more useful to think of the learning organization as a model of strategic change. In fact, the learning organization represents the fourth version in a series of strategic change models. The learning organization model is emerging to help firms plan and execute significant organizational change amid rapidly changing business conditions.

## THE FIRST THREE VERSIONS

On an individual basis, each organization learns how to change by taking action, encountering obstacles, and discovering over time how to overcome them. Each version of this cycle (taking action, confronting problems, and adjusting course) is an opportunity for learning. In this process, organizations—at varying speeds and to differing degrees—become more sophisticated in their ability to introduce strategic change.

On a collective basis, organizations have also learned how to change over the past several decades. It is possible to identify three broad versions of this learning process, each of which is dominated by a generally prescribed model of strategic change. This model indicated the preferred methods of how companies can best go about introducing fundamental changes in their business.

## THE FIRST VERSION—FORMAL PLANNING FOCUSED

*If a school or institution uses a formal planning approach, what is the leader's role in ensuring it does not fail?*

The first model focused almost solely on the planning of strategic change by senior management. Strategic planning, as traditionally practiced, reflected this first version approach to change, assuming that if executives came up with excellent plans, the plans would be easily executed, and successful strategic change would result (Gluck, 1986; Morrisey, 1996). This model emphasized the creation of formal, fixed planning documents through a staff-driven, once-a-year event restricted to the most senior executives. Underlying conventional strategic planning was a "predict and plan" premise, which presumed that incipient trends could be detected through the use of sophisticated environmental scanning methods. Based upon such advance warning signals, the organization could get a jump on the competition, formulating and implementing plans that would result in a competitive advantage when the predicted waves of change hit the shore.

This planning-dominated model of change has been seductive for several reasons. The approach is rational and unambiguous, rooted in the quantitative analytical tools of management science. Moreover, it is consistent with traditional command-and-control forms of management, reserving planning to an elite echelon of top management. Perhaps most important, it promises quick action and concrete results as specified by the planning document.

Over the years, even when companies used the most sophisticated scanning and profound planning methods, and even when the plans reflected brilliant and insightful approaches to future competitive positioning, they often failed. In reality, plans frequently stayed on the shelf. When it came down to the details of implementation, the desired changes were often much more complex than originally imagined, requiring more time and resources than previously thought. Speed was also an issue. Many business environments were themselves changing at rates exceeding the capacity or organizations to implement their plans (Henkoff, 1990). Finally, the actions of middle managers, rather than the words of top management, often determined how well plans are implemented. Because middle managers were not usually involved in the planning process, they were often not committed to the plans and, in fact, may not have fully understood them. Moreover, these same middle managers frequently had essential ideas and information that, when not taken into account, weakened the integrity of the plans.

# THE SECOND VERSION— IMPLEMENTATION FOCUSED

A new model emerged in the late 1970s and early 1980s as an attempt to overcome the limitations of the planning-dominated approach. It recognized that coming up with great plans was often not sufficient. Detailed attention needed to be paid to how the plans were to be implemented (Fusch, 1997). For the first time in many companies, middle managers were included in the formulation of strategic plans, and in many cases, detailed execution schemes were developed. Often these implementation plans speculated about potential problems and made contingent plans to overcome them. Increased consideration was also given to the resources (financial, technical, human, and time) needed for plans to happen. A new emphasis was placed upon communicating strategic direction to all affected employees, including detailing any new responsibilities and tasks needed to be performed. Moreover, greater attention was paid to following up on plans, tracking progress, uncovering problems, and resolving impediments at the earliest possible point.

*How prevalent is implementation-focused strategic planning in schools and institutions today?*

Nevertheless, companies still encountered many of the implementation problems identified earlier, such as unexpected delays, inadequate progress, and organizational resistance. Strategic change was clearly more complex than previously imagined. Broad systemic issues (culture, rewards, norms, policies, management styles, etc.) often affected implementation. Moreover, strategic change frequently called for skills and resources that could not be quickly developed in the narrow gap between planning and implementation. Senior executives often let short-term obstacles and internal considerations obscure their ability to provide strategic direction to the firm. Middle managers were occasionally resistant to the radical upheaval of past practices because they were often rewarded for short-term operational results, not long-term strategic successes. Front-line employees who execute the plans often did not understand the need to do things differently. They were ignorant of the competitive forces, technological changes, and marketplace demands that were combining to make their organization's environment so unpredictable and threatening. Nor were they aware of the strategic objectives the firm had established to deal with these uncertainties.

# THE THIRD VERSION—READINESS FOCUSED

Second-version approaches often paid painstaking attention to the details of making strategic change happen. Still there were problems. Short-term considerations frequently diverted attention from long-term strategic goals. In many cases, broad-scale resistance to change persisted, prohibiting the initiatives from taking hold. Implementation often continued to take longer than planned, with new problems arising that no one could have anticipated, given what was known at the time.

Why? Why after involving middle managers in developing a plan for change? Why after fully communicating the new strategic direction to everyone involved? Why after creating detailed action plans for implementation that included contingency measures? Why after assigning sufficient financial, technical, and human resources? Why, after taking all of these steps did so many change efforts based upon the second iteration model still encounter major obstacles?

The reason was a fundamental lack of readiness for strategic change in the company. Rewards often reinforced the status quo. Management styles often clashed with the imperative to involve people in making change happen. People from throughout the company were often unaware of the need to change. And strong norms and culture prohibited change from taking form.

In response to these problems, a new model of strategic change developed. This third version placed as much emphasis upon the creation of readiness for change in the organization as it did upon planning and implementation. This new model of strategic change recognized the importance of three elements—readiness, planning, and implementation.

According to the third version, any successful strategic change was viewed as dependent on a certain degree of readiness for the change within the organization. As a result, it was proposed that any attempts to introduce significant organizational change should be prefaced by a series of steps to enhance readiness. These steps often included the following:

- Building awareness of the need for and communicating a vision of the desired change.
- Creating a climate that is supportive of the desired change by realigning organizational culture, rewards, policies, procedures, systems, and norms to support such change.
- Equipping people throughout the organization with the skills needed to participate meaningfully in planning and implementing strategic change (Barger & Kirby, 1995).

Planning tended to be seen as a more open process, with an emphasis on establishing general goals and direction and using pilot programs to build commitment within the organization. During implementation, there tended to be more concern for engaging frontline employees, as well as suppliers, customers, and other key stakeholders, in working out how plans should be executed.

Most quality improvement efforts of the late 1980s and early 1990s illustrate the third version. Quality improvement programs generally start with

Table 1    Versions of Strategic Planning

| Version | Purpose | Emerged |
|---|---|---|
| First—Formal Planning Focused | Formal, Fixed Planning Documents by Senior Managers | 1940s–'50s |
| Second—Implementation Focused | Complex Implementation of Strategic Change Plans | 1970s–'80s |
| Third—Readiness Focused | Creation of Readiness For Change Along With Planning | late '80s–early '90s |
| Fourth—Integrated Organizational Learning Focused | Integrates Readiness, Continuous Planning, Improvised Implementation, and Action Learning | mid-1990s |

ambitious preliminary preparations designed to create the readiness for change in the organization. A major focus is to build awareness of the critical importance of quality improvement and to convey top management's commitment to a radical new vision of the organization's future, a vision characterized by continuous improvement, employee involvement, and world-class leadership in quality. Another major target of readiness activities is to build a climate conductive to quality improvement by helping managers make a fundamental shift in their management practices, adopting more participative and facilitative styles that support employee involvement in the continuous improvement of quality. Still another target of preliminary readiness activities is the retooling of the workforce through intensive, up-front education and training in quality improvement philosophies and techniques.

*How are some schools and institutions adapting quality improvement programs to be readiness focused?*

## TOWARD THE FOURTH VERSION

Each version of strategic change efforts emerges from the problems encountered in the previous version (see Table 1). So it is that, as a result of the limitations inherent in quality improvement programs and other third-version efforts, a new, fourth version of strategic change is taking shape: the learning organization.

Many quality improvement efforts have been highly successful. Numerous firms have achieved breakthroughs in product and service quality, significantly enhancing customer satisfaction and greatly strengthening their competitive positions (Watkins & Marsick, 1993). But there is also a dark side of quality. Several studies are showing that the quality improvement programs started over recent years, based upon the examples of Baldridge winners or the prescriptions of quality gurus, are experiencing a high mortality rate (Hosley, Lau, Levy & Tan, 1994; The Quality Imperative, 1991; Garvin, 1998). Even Florida Power & Light, the once-heralded example of world class quality improvement, hit the rocks. Its Deming Award-winning quality program was dismantled, and its president, the architect and champion of the effort, left the company under pressure (Main, 1991). In fact, studies indicate that change efforts, when treated as established programs and not unfolding processes, almost always fail (Beer, Eisenstat, & Spector, 1990; Fusch, 1997).

Over the years, even with full management support and substantial investments of time, people, and money, many third-version change programs are being designated failures, even by the people who initiated them (Barger & Kirby, 1995). This seems to be increasingly true for many total quality programs, for several reasons. First, the activities designed to create readiness also established unrealistic expectations that momentous change would happen, and happen fast. In addition, despite eloquent protestations to the contrary, many total quality initiatives were still introduced as fixed programs with short-term objectives. In many cases, organizations also failed to achieve a fully integrated, systemic approach to quality improvement, often neglecting the relationship of quality to business strategy, company structure, and information systems. Maybe most important, many quality programs have been primarily internally focused and past-driven—inducing incremental improvements in past procedures and products rather than the discontinuous disruptions needed to weather tempestuous and turbulent business environments.

Quality improvement efforts are teaching an important lesson. Change cannot be transplanted. It must follow its own natural cycle of planting, growth, and harvest in each organization. To do so, the ground needs to be prepared in advance; old soil must be churned and nourished. These seeds of change need to be sown on the organizational topsoil—the immediate issues facing the organization. These seeds then gradually sprout deep roots that wrap around the firm culture—its management practices, business strategies, structure, and information systems. As it grows, the final fruit takes shape over time. The emerging change is continuously pruned and shaped both by the natural forces of the environment and by the vigilant attention of the gardeners, who water and feed—not on a preplanned schedule, but through personal judgments formed from experience and experimentation. That is the fourth-version model of strategic change, and that is what is meant by the learning organization.

## THE FOURTH MODEL—THE LEARNING ORGANIZATION

Today, a fourth model of strategic change has emerged to compensate for the limitations of the earlier versions—the learning organization. The learning organization can be defined as one in which everyone is engaged identifying and solving problems, enabling the organization to continuously experiment, change, and improve, thus increasing its capacity to grow, learn, and achieve its purpose (Daft & Marcic, 1998). Some authors agree that learning organizations start with the assumption that learning is valuable, continuous, and most effective when shared and that every experience is an opportunity to learn (Calvert, Mobley, & Marshall, 1994; Watkins & Marsick, 1993).

In one sense, becoming a learning organization increases the size of a company's brain. Employees participate in all thinking activities, including strategy, with few boundaries among employees in different departments or between the top and bottom. Everyone communicates and works together, creating enormous intelligence and flexibility to deal with rapidly changing environments.

There are four defining characteristics of the learning organization: constant readiness, continuous planning, improvised implementation, and action learning.

**Constant readiness.** Rather than building readiness for a predetermined change, the organization exists in a constant state of readiness, preparing itself not for any specific change, but for change in general, attuned to its environment and willing to question its fundamental ways of doing business.

Unlike the third version, readiness is no longer a one-time event designed to prepare the organization for a specific change. Instead, readiness consists of a perpetual state of preparedness for change since, amid highly turbulent conditions, the organization needs to be equipped to deal with anything and to reevaluate past assumptions and future directions.

**Continuous planning.** Rather than the creation of fixed plans by a few senior executives, the learning organization develops open, flexible plans that are fully shared and embraced by the entire organization. In learning organizations, the act of planning differs greatly from earlier versions, which often relied on formal, written, detailed programs and procedures. In learning organizations, "revision" may be more important than "vision," with rigid, fixed plans supplanted by flexible, open strategic directions. These plans are not merely top management visions and programs, but are fully embraced and shared by the people involved in making them happen.

**Improvised implementation.** Rather than executing plans by the numbers, the learning organization improvises change, encouraging experimentation, rewarding small wins, and institutionalizing success throughout the organization.

No longer does implementation consist of the note-by-note execution of a prescribed plan. Just as in jazz improvision, where every performer is a composer, in the learning organization, every member—whether on the front line or the executive suite—is a strategic partner. In the fourth version, individuals and teams act in creative and autonomous ways to interpret the strategic direction and make the plans happen. The actual nature of the change gradually reveals itself through the spontaneous and creative actions of people throughout the organization. They coordinate and collaborate with others in the organization who are also experimenting with change. Over time, successes and accomplishments are reinforced and institutionalized, modifying the formal structures, rewards, procedures, and systems of the organization.

**Action learning.** Rather than reevaluating change efforts only at once-a-year planning sessions, or waiting for the slow learning that derives from experience or the traumatic learning that occurs from crisis, the learning organization takes

*What are some of the unwritten implications of moving to the fourth model of decision making for a school or institution?*

action, reflects, and adjusts course as it goes, seeking to enhance the speed and effectiveness by which it learns how to change.

In the fourth version, learning is not something that just happens. It is made to happen. Learning begins when those involved in an activity stop and examine how things are done. In learning organizations, attempts are made to provide frequent, ongoing opportunities for such action-based learning. Learning organizations do not wait for problems to emerge or for crises to arise to compel reevaluation. Reflection becomes part of "the way we do things around here" and is built into the implementation of strategic change. Through this process, they question the original assumptions and search for deep, system ("double-loop") solutions to the problems.

That organizations can learn to change is a captivating idea, with the potential to revolutionize our understandings of competitive positioning, strategic planning, and organizational change. There is a danger, however, that the learning organization will become the newest addition in a long succession of management fads, producing its own generation of quick-fix solutions in a box. That would be both sad and ironic, since what distinguishes this new model of change is the recognition that any fixed program or plan of change is doomed to failure. There is also the hazard that the learning organization will be prescribed as the ultimate cure for afflictions such as stagnancy and surprise. However, even the learning organization model, when perfectly implemented, will not be a panacea for all organizational ills. Companies will still experience problems in making change happen, and time will assuredly expose significant limitations of this fourth model of strategic change. Instead, the learning organization is best understood as part of a broad, fast-moving current of learning that is gaining speed as it heads downstream. The first version led to the second, the second to the third, and the third to the fourth. The fifth version is just around the next bend.

## REFERENCES

Argyris, C., & Schon, D. (1978). *Organizational learning: A theory of action perspective.* Reading, MA: Addison-Wesley.

Barger, N., & Kirby, L. (1995). *The challenge of change in organizations.* Palo Alto, CA: Davies-Black.

Beer, M., Eisenstat, R. A., & Spector, B. (1990). *The critical oath to corporate renewal.* Cambridge, MA: Harvard Business School Press.

Calvert, G., Mobley, S., & Marshall, L. (1994). Grasping the learning organization. *Training,* 48(6), 38–43.

Daft, R., & Marcic, D. (1998). *Understanding management.* Ft. Worth, TX: The Dryden Press.

DeGeus, A. P. (1988). Planning as learning. *Harvard Business Review,* 66(2), 70–74.

Fiol, C. M., & Lyles, M. (1985). Organizational learning. *Academy of Management Review*, 10(4), 803–813.

Fusch, G. (1997). *Organizational change from scientific management to the learning organization: Implications for new work systems*. Washington, D.C.: National Institute of Education (ERIC Document Reproduction Service No. ED 417 329.

Garvin, D. (1998). Does the Baldridge really work? *Harvard Business Review*, 69(6), 80–93.

Gluck, W. F. (1986). Strategic management: An overview. In J. Gardner, R. Rachlin, & H. Sweeny (Eds.). *Handbook of Strategic Planning*, (pp. 1.1–1.36). New York: Wiley and Sons.

Henkoff, R. (1990). How to plan for 1995. *Fortune*, 122 (16), 70–79.

Hosley, S., Lau, A., Levy, F., & Tan, D. (1994). The quest for the competitive learning organization. *Management Decision*, 32(6), 5–15.

Jashapara, A. (1993). The competitive learning organization: A quest for the Holy Grail. *Management Decision*, 31(8), 52–62.

Kieschel, W. (1990, March). The organization that learns. *Fortune*, 122, 133–136.

Main, J. (1991, July). Is the Baldridge overblown? *Fortune*, 123, 62–65.

Morrisey, G. (1996). *Strategic thinking: Building your planning foundation*. San Francisco: Jossey-Bass.

Revans, R. W. (1983). Action learning: Kindling the touch paper. *Management Development*, 21(6), 3–10.

Senge, P. (1990a). *The fifth discipline: The art and practice of the learning organization*. New York: Doubleday/Currency.

Senge, P. (1990b, Fall). The leader's new work: Building learning organizations. *Sloan Management Review*, 7–23.

Stata, R. (1989, Spring). Organizational learning: The key to management innovation. *Sloan Management Review*, 63–74.

The quality imperative. (1991, October). Special issue *Business Week*.

Watkins, K., & Marsick, V. (1993). *Sculpting the learning organization: Lessons in the art and science of systemic change*. San Francisco: Jossey-Bass.

# Futuring: A Complex Adaptive Systems Approach to Strategic Planning

## John Vogelsang

Strategic planning continues to be one of the most frequently requested nonprofit consulting services. Client's constructs of what strategic planning is, however, range from a one-day board and staff retreat to a six-month or longer process involving extensive research of trends, opportunities, and challenges. Most express the hope that the process will help them develop the "right" plan that will provide a map to the future or at least position their organization to survive for the next three to five years. Those who want to conduct extensive research often express the belief that if they can gather the right amount of quality information they can avoid predictable pitfalls and bring about desired outcomes.

To judge from the number of requests and the language people use to describe what they want, we are still in what Richard Pascale (1999) calls the "strategic era:"

> The decade following World War II gave birth to the "strategic era." While the tenets of military strategy had been evolving for centuries, the link to commercial enterprise was tenuous. Before the late 1940s, most companies adhered to the tenet "make a little, sell a little, make a little more." After the war, faculty at the Harvard Business School (soon joined by swelling ranks of consultants) began to take the discipline of strategy seriously. By the late 1970s, the array of strategic concepts (SWOT analysis, the five forces framework, experience curves, strategic portfolios, the concept of competitive advantage) had become standard ordnance in the management arsenal. (83)

However, as Pascale argues in his article about Complex Adaptive Systems, there are new approaches to planning. This article describes the current state of traditional approaches to strategic planning in nonprofits, some emerging approaches, and the potential for further rethinking offered by Complex Adaptive Systems Theory.

## TRADITIONAL APPROACHES

Since its prominence in the 1970s and 1980s, strategic planning has become a method for examining the appropriateness of an organization's mission and for positioning an organization to deal with potential challenges in the future. If one were to include many of the refinements that have occurred over the past twenty some years, the method as they applied in nonprofit settings usually involves:

A set of underlying principles:

- There is a need for a clear, well-understood mission and vision
- The organizational culture must support trust, honesty, and accountability
- The participants need to have strategic/systems thinking and skills
- Well-informed cross-functional, cross group networks are important for gaining the best insights and sharing the process and decisions throughout the organization
- Good communication must be maintained at all times
- The coordinating team needs to define what they consider a successful planning process and articulate that definition clearly to those involved

The process usually includes:

- A Coordinating Committee and/or Planning Committee
- Task Forces to develop sections of the plan
- A planning retreat for internal stakeholders or their representatives and some external stakeholders
- A planning document developed by task forces and the planning committee with assistance from a consultant

The steps in the process, not necessarily in this order, can be:

- Review the organization's purpose, mission, vision and values
- Conduct an external environmental and internal organizational SWOT (What are our Strengths, Weaknesses, Opportunities, and Threats) scan
- Analyze the information from the scan
- Create a discussion document or a way to involve stakeholders in the information that was gathered during the environmental and organizational scan
- Revise the mission statement if necessary
- Revise or create organizational values (if not clarified)
- Create a vision of the future
- Develop strategies to implement the vision
- Identify specific long range goals/objectives
- Design a first year, detailed implementation plan
- Design an evaluation process for the plan

*Which of the steps in the process apply to schools and institutions?*

The strategic planning consultant and the coordinating/planning committee usually share responsibility for accomplishing each of those steps. In earlier approaches to strategic planning, the planning committee or an executive team usually developed the plan with some input from other staff and external stakeholders through surveys, interviews or focus groups. Currently, most agencies attempt to include as many internal and external stakeholders either through the information gathering and/or through a series of large/small group planning meetings to help formulate components of the plan.

# EMERGING APPROACHES TO PLANNING

*What are some benefits of using emerging approaches to planning for schools or institutions?*

A number of approaches to planning have emerged over the past twenty years. They include: Whole-Scale (Dannemiller, 2000), Search/Future Search Conferences (Emery, 1996) (Weisbord and Janoff, 1992), the Conference Model (Axelrod, 2000), and FutureScape (Sanders, 1998). All of these approaches tend to use variations of the traditional process with the following differences:

- They emphasize large and small group ways to involve as many stakeholders in the system (both internal and external) in the planning process,
- They tend to do the environmental and organizational scan in "real time" at a large group meeting (with some scanning done before to shape the questions and process),
- They emphasize looking at the whole system and not parts; that is why they want to have as many representatives of the organization a part of the process,
- They favor visual and metaphoric approaches in addition to rational processes; and
- While developing the usual long-term goals, they tend also to look for short-term immediate changes that can help increase commitment to the overall plan.

Some use Appreciative Inquiry (Cooperrider, 1999) processes and emphasize how to nurture the effectiveness of those aspects of the organization that are valued by the internal stakeholders and produce value for the external stakeholders. Clarifying what the external stakeholders find valuable becomes the focus of the environmental scan. This scan can be done through interviews or focus groups (more traditional approach) or forums and large group meetings.

As practitioners incorporate the emerging approaches and attempt to connect them to clients' requests for more traditional strategic planning, they have developed some interesting hybrid variations. All of the following approaches assume the starting point is revisiting the organization's purpose and mission. In most cases there is a large group environmental scan, or a forum with external representatives, or the more traditional environmental scanning and report writing:

- Develop a three to five year Vision with long term strategies such as we will emphasize collaborative projects with other service providers, we will expand our capacity by emphasizing staff development. Specific goals and objectives are created on a yearly basis in an operational planning process.
- Develop a three to five year vision, affirm that the major strategy will be entrepreneurial development of opportunities, and identify criteria for how to decide among the many opportunities.
- Examine how people currently spend their time and energy and identify the emerging strategies and practices that are and could continue to move the organization forward. Choose how to support or further develop those

strategies and design goals and objectives to accomplish that. The emerging strategies may lead to a re-examination of the mission.

- Instead of developing a plan, identify key strategic questions that become the topic of regular board and staff meetings. Such questions include: Who are our customers and how are they changing? How do we deal with an economic downturn? What are emerging service needs? As a product of the discussions the board and staff formulate long range strategies that inform operational decisions.

# COMPLEX ADAPTIVE SYSTEMS THEORY'S INFLUENCE ON STRATEGIC PLANNING

Most of the practitioners of the new approaches to planning say they draw upon Theoretical Biology, Quantum Physics, and Chaos Theory, particularly theories of self-organization, nonequilibrium, complementarity, and the "butterfly effect"—minute fluctuations can produce large scale changes. Another influence on management theory and strategic planning is Complex Adaptive Systems Theory that attempts to understand how physical, biological and social systems operate. When people describe Complex Adaptive Systems they commonly include many of the following characteristics:

- **Agents with schemata.** The agents interact with each other constructing and reconstructing schemata (assumptions, expectations, values, habits) that organize their relations at the local level. They are continually coming together to understand the world and each other, form judgments, fashion the future, and to sustain their relations. Their act of responding to and interpret what they experience involves constructing, reconstructing, and modifying their schemata.
- **Global patterns of relationship emerge.** As the agents interact locally, adapt to each other, and generate variety and complexity in their schemata they construct coherent and global patterns of interacting: rituals, structured relationships, communication systems, commonly held criteria for making decisions (operating values), a shared purpose, and organizations. This emergence of self-organization comes from a range of valuable innovations to unfortunate accidents. Misunderstandings and miscues offer variable ways of interacting and opportunities to reshape the assumptions and expectations that have become global patterns. Each contributes to the continual change going on in the organization. Each time the members solve problems individually and together they self-organize and release variety into the system. The system will wind down unless replenished with energy generated by internal and external relations and the subsequent innovations and mistakes.
- **Coevolution at the edge of chaos.** Complex Adaptive Systems exist at the boundary regions near the edge of chaos where the frozen components

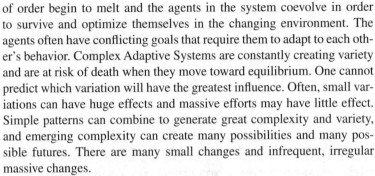

of order begin to melt and the agents in the system coevolve in order to survive and optimize themselves in the changing environment. The agents often have conflicting goals that require them to adapt to each other's behavior. Complex Adaptive Systems are constantly creating variety and are at risk of death when they move toward equilibrium. One cannot predict which variation will have the greatest influence. Often, small variations can have huge effects and massive efforts may have little effect. Simple patterns can combine to generate great complexity and variety, and emerging complexity can create many possibilities and many possible futures. There are many small changes and infrequent, irregular massive changes.

- **System evolution based upon recombination.** In every interaction the agents enact historic patterns—the previously formed schemata—with slight or major variations. The agents are able to recognize the patterns, experience the difference, and choose to reconstruct them or construct new patterns. Thus there is consistency yet difference. The system generates novelty without abandoning the best elements of its past. The system is also resilient: flexible and open to learning in order to evolve while being durable and consistent with its schemata—purpose, values, rituals, and relations.

- **No one point of control.** For a Complex Adaptive System to survive it must cultivate variety, but it is an illusion to think that one can direct the variations. One can only disturb the system and be mindful of what is happening. At the same time one cannot be separate from the system—stand outside and influence its direction. One can only influence the rules, the relationships, the choices made as a participant in interactions while being influenced by others. (Anderson, 1999; Kauffman, 1995; Pascale, 1999; Rouse, 2000; Stacey, 2001)

*What is an example of a small variation having a huge effect or a massive effort having little effect on a school or institution?*

Attempts to apply earlier versions of Complex Adaptive Systems theory to organizations often rejected or de-emphasized strategic planning in favor of organizational learning processes for challenging existing mental models of behavior in organizations in order to learn how to rapidly adapt to a changing environment (Phelan, 1995). If small variations can have huge effects and massive efforts may have little effect it is difficult to identify historic and emerging patterns that can be projected into the future in a planning process. Thereby, it is argued that the organization needs to develop learning processes that will enable it to adapt to the many unexpected changes. The emphasis on learning organizations has contributed to efforts to foster self-organization and co-evolution in organizations through such techniques as learning circles, peer learning groups, communities of practice, and systems thinking. There may not be a predictable future but there is still a need to engage in futuring—continually constructing a future. We need ways to answer are we engaged in the most appropriate activities and relating in the most appropriate way to our stakeholders that contribute to our resilience and optimization in this particular patchwork of current and emerging relationships.

When we combine the emphasis on learning organizations and with the need to construct a future we have such planning concerns as:

- How can we be clear about our purpose and values and use them to structure modes of communication that support interconnectedness among the various stakeholders?
- How can we optimize and construct relationships in the organizations so to foster complexity, self-organization, and futuring?
- How can we encourage resiliency in the organization—the flexibility, durability, openness to learning, and decision making and problem solving skills to make complex, reliable decisions in the presence of massive and often conflicting input as we coevolve between order and chaos?
- How can we find the unique, alternative outcomes already contained in the current situation and its history, as different from creating an unknown future?
- How can we disturb/get the attention of the organizational system?

# TECHNIQUES

If strategic planning is a way of asking are we engaged in the most appropriate activities and relating in the most appropriate way to our stakeholders that contributes to our fit and optimization in this particular patchwork of current and emerging relationships, there are some aspects of the traditional methods that are helpful and many that need to be modified. Instead of a rational, step by step planning process that produces the "right" goals that will allows us to exercise some control over the future, we need to develop mindfulness as we move between chaos and order. Some of the possible ways this can be done are:

## Shaping the Context for Planning

As with traditional strategic planning the process can benefit from a well-informed, cross-functional, and representative coordinating group and an organizational system that supports trust, honesty, and accountability. The group needs to decide:

- How ready is the organization for developing a strategic plan? Are there far too many changes/crises happening or is the staff highly resistant to changing their patterns of work? If there are too many changes, the group may consider ways to foster relationships in the organization that encourage mutual learning and construction of adaptive techniques to the rapid changes (organizational learning approaches). Or they could use this time as an opportunity to revisit the mission and values and develop strategies that will help the immediate situation and provide some guidance for at least the next 2 years. If there is a high level of resistance, the group may want to look at ways to modify the relationships among the staff in order to develop possibilities that have been ignored. Are there some groups that could be cross-functional or work on joint projects?

- Is there sufficient trust and a sufficient functioning level in the relationships that would support honest feedback and discussion, and is there a willingness to learn and create together? If there is not, how can the process itself contribute to creating this atmosphere of trust and learning?
- Will the organization commit the needed time and money to the process?
- How can the coordinating group members be aware of the dynamics in their group in order to be more mindful of what is contributing to or hindering communication among the staff?
- What will be their criteria for deeming the planning process a success?
- Who will be involved and how?
- What will be the steps in the process?

Clarify, review, and affirm the core purpose, mission, values, desired outcomes, and criteria for making decisions that influence the stakeholders.

In Complex Adaptive Systems the agents are interconnected through commonly held criteria for making decisions (operating values) and a shared purpose that also informs the way they relate to each other and the stakeholders. As with the traditional and emerging processes described above, the coordinating group needs to involve the whole system in clarifying and reaffirming what difference (outcome) the agency is trying to achieve with its stakeholders, how they will know if they have achieved that difference, and what are the values/criteria that will influence what practices, methods, and resources they will use to achieve those outcomes.

## Fostering Relationships and Systems and Modes of Communication

*How does a Complex Adaptive System approach to planning differ from the learning organization approach as outlined by Rowden in reading 3?*

A Complex Adaptive System approach to Strategic planning is an opportunity to reconstruct relationships and construct possibilities through dialogue and networking among both internal and external groups. This means a shift in emphasis. As in traditional and emerging strategic planning approaches, meetings among stakeholders still have a role in generating information for decision-making, but they have a larger role in nurturing the relationships that contribute to constructing possibilities and encouraging self-organization. Instead of a traditional organizational and environmental SWOT analysis, the agency may use Appreciative Inquiry and other ways to look for the changes already happening or about to happen. There may be a series of large (whole system) and small group meetings of both internal staff and external stakeholders in order to create the opportunity for new relationships and better communication. The agency may try to understand the various relationships it has with its stakeholders and other community entities and how they and the stakeholders influence those relationships. The staff may want to explore their assumptions about the past, present and future and how those assumptions are affecting how the staff relates to each other and to the stakeholders. . . .

## Choosing Strategies that Increase Resiliency and the Ability to Perform Complex and Reliable Decision Making

Beinhocker (1999) recommends that instead of choosing singularly focused strategies, organizations need to cultivate multiple strategies, many of which will operate in parallel in order to encourage co-evolution. The multiple strategies that can increase the resiliency of an organization are 1) those that deepen and extend current practices, 2) those that create new practices, and 3) those that plant the seeds for future developments. While emphasizing the first, organizations that continue to optimize in their particular fitness environment commit varying degrees of resources to the other two.

In forming strategies, the coordinating group (and the whole system through group meetings) can be mindful of the continual changes happening in the organization and decide how to foster those that fit the mission, values, and criteria. They can discuss what are the changes they want:

- To acknowledge—because they are already happening and they deepen and extend current practices
- To influence—because they need some support and direction to occur and they have the potential to further improve current practices and/or create new practices
- To make happen—because they are new possibilities: new practices or the seeds for future development

In order to contribute to continuing resiliency, planning strategies could include ways to foster the organizational learning processes mentioned earlier. These could include instituting and supporting opportunities for cross-functional and staff in the same program to come together for peer learning groups, case conferences, and mutual problem solving sessions.

A Complex Adaptive System approach to strategic planning builds upon organizational learning methods while it emphasizes mindfulness, mission and values based decisions, fosterng relationships and systems of communication, and continuing to construct possibilities that contribute to an organization's self-organizing and resiliency in its immediate and distant environment. A vision of a near or distant future and the strategic plan itself are not blueprints for a future state but ways to prepare an organization to be more mindful of the constant changes and possibilities happening in the present.

# REFERENCES

Anderson, P. 1999. "Complexity Theory and Organization Science." *A Journal of the Institute of Management Sciences*, v. 10, 3, May/June.

Axelrod, R. 2000. *Terms of Engagement.* San Francisco: Berrett-Koehler Publishers, Inc.

Beinhocker, E. D. 1999. "Robust Adaptive Strategies." *Sloan Management Review*, Spring.

Cooperrider, D., P. F. Sorensen, and D. Whitney. 1999. *Appreciative Inquiry: Rethinking Human Organization Toward a Positive Theory of Change.* Champaign, IL: Stipes Publishing.

Dannemiller, K. and Associates. 2000. *Whole-Scale Change.* San Francisco: Berrett-Koehler Publishers, Inc.

Emery, M. 1996. *The Search Conference.* San Francisco: Jossey-Bass, Inc.

Kauffman, S. 1995. *At Home in the Universe.* New York: Oxford University Press.

Pascale, R. 1999. "Surfing the Edge of Chaos." *Sloan Management Review*, Spring, 83–94.

Phelan, S. 1995. "From Chaos to Complexity in Strategic Planning." Paper presented at the 55th Annual Meeting of the Academy of Management, Vancouver, BC.

Regine, B. and R. Lewin. 2000. "Leading at the Edge: How Leaders Influence Complex Systems." *Emergence*, v. 2, 2.

Rouse, B. 2000. "Managing Complexity: Disease Control as a Complex Adaptive System." *Information Knowledge Systems Management*, v. 2, 2.

Sanders, I. 1998. *Strategic Thinking and the New Science.* New York: The Free Press.

Stacey, R. 2001. *Complex Responsive Processes in Organizatons: Learning and Knowledge Creation.* New York: Routledge.

Weisbord, M. and S. Janoff, 1992. *Future Search.* San Francisco: Berrett-Koehler Publishers, Inc.

# ISSUE SUMMARY

———————————————————————●

All schools and institutions need to plan and look ahead. For decades, this process has been carried out in a formal manner, using analytical quantitative methods to predict actions that must be taken. Too frequently, the final plan was a carefully detailed document that did not have impact on daily organizational life.

Today, formal planning of the "review and act" type is being set aside for approaches that reflect new concepts and theories about educational organizations and their larger environment. *Whole-scale, conference model, futuring, appreciative inquiry:* these approaches can be clustered under the term *emergent.* Many emergent approaches incorporate some aspects of traditional strategic planning but move further in scope and depth. Taken together, emergent strategies typically pay attention to the whole system and use images of change (visual or metaphoric) in addition to narration and statistics.

Key to the success of emergent approaches is broad involvement of participants at all levels of the institution. Planning becomes the work of everyone, not chief administrators or a select few. Kanter uses the metaphor of improvisational theater to describe the strategizing work of the educational organization: "It shifts attention from the dynamics among members of a project team to the way in which an organization as a whole can become an arena for staging experiments that can transform the overall strategy" (2002, p. 76).

For many organizational leaders, the process of looking ahead is more important than the resulting strategy plan document. By discussing the mission, creating action plans, reviewing data, and clarifying values, constituents think strategically about their school or institution. The document itself contains the plan, but the process of deliberation is what builds understanding and consensus about the future.

Deliberation and discernment are at the heart of a learning organization. If an organization develops its own learning processes, it is better able to adapt and become resilient in ever-changing conditions. With an emphasis on learning and adapting rather than reviewing and perfecting, it is no wonder that strategic planning is evolving.

Appreciative inquiry is an additional approach to strategic planning that has much to recommend it. This model has three unique characteristics: assessment of current strengths and assets, involvement of all constituents, and extensive use of narrative and dialogue. As the term *appreciative* indicates, the process involves discovering what is going well and building on those strengths. More than asset mapping, this form of inquiry is strategic because it includes envisioning what the learning organization desires to be in the future.

# ISSUE HIGHLIGHTS

- Calendar-driven, task-focused planning processes are becoming irrelevant for many organizations.
- Changing the timing and focus of planning also changes the nature of strategizing from "review and approve" to "discuss and decide."
- Planning that is continuous and decision-oriented must be staffwide work rather than committee work.
- Collaborative, strategic problem solving is a deeper level of planning that leads to sustained improvement of student outcomes.
- Earlier versions of strategic planning focused on detailed implementation schemes or on readiness for change.
- Quality and improvement initiatives often fail because they are not well integrated, are based on short-term expectations, and are limited to existing procedures.
- The strategic era is being replaced by the knowledge management era, which is leading to emergent strategic planning approaches.
- Organizations are realizing the need to continually construct a future and are using futuring strategies for their planning work.
- Complex adaptive system theory contributes a more holistic perspective to strategic planning, enabling an organization to do more "out of the box" thinking.

# CRITICAL THINKING

In "Beyond Data: The World of Scenario Planning," George Goens contends that old approaches to strategic planning aren't working:

> Strategic planning has taken school districts . . . by storm in the past decade. Consultants have made bundles helping districts and state departments of education put their strategic goals into data-driven terms, defining benchmarks, establishing metrics and determining measurable performance standards.
>
> But even the best-laid plans, as the old saw says, can be circumvented by people or unanticipated events. The world and life intervene, shattering the cause-and-effect basis for those plans. Hence the problem, because leadership involves more than analyzing data and making decisions. You cannot change schools by painting by the numbers.

Essentially Goens is advocating for planning that moves beyond tangible and quantifiable elements. Intangible factors are often ignored, simply because they cannot be placed on data tables for analysis. Demographics, economics, and politics are all the source of great risk for organizations and should not be ignored.

Scenario thinking is an appropriate approach for incorporating these intangible factors. By creating scenarios—different versions of the future—constituents bring multiple perspectives to planning. The result is a more comprehensive approach to long-term improvement and achievement.

# ADDITIONAL READING RESOURCES

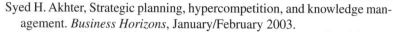

Syed H. Akhter, Strategic planning, hypercompetition, and knowledge management. *Business Horizons*, January/February 2003.

Eric D. Beinhocker and Sarah Kaplan, Tired of strategic planning? *McKinsey Quarterly*, Special Edition, 2002.

George A. Goens, Beyond data: The world of scenario planning. *The School Administrator*, April 2001.

Rosabeth Moss Kanter, Strategy as improvisational theater. *MIT Sloan Management Review*, Winter 2002.

Sherry Rockey and Laverne Webb, Organizational change inside and out: The impact of an appreciative inquiry. *Journal for Nonprofit Management*, 2005.

Southwest Educational Development Laboratory, *Working Systemically to Increase Student Achievement*. At www.sedl.org/ws/stages.html

For more information on planning strategies, check these sites:

Appreciative Inquiry Commons http://appreciativeinquiry.case.edu/

Association for Strategic Planning www.strategyplus.org/

Data Use http://edadmin.edb.utexas.edu/datause/index.htm

Strategic Planning: Is It Worth the Effort? www.weleadinlearning.org/feb06rjj.htm

# ISSUE 3

# What Is the Right Balance of Central Authority and Site-Based Autonomy?

For leaders of educational systems, the debate over balance of authority and autonomy is not new, but it *is* escalating. This controversy is due mainly to a growing reform agenda for institutions that have failed to meet even basic goals. One result is the emergence of new models of schools and institutions that bring with them differing expectations for leadership. New ways of operating schools make the CEO model a mandate for some systems, which causes a shift in central authority. In other systems, another model calls for less local autonomy, in order to achieve high performance across every school.

Today, what we have across the United States is a conflict of structure. Some educational system structures are what Mintzberg calls "machine bureaucracy." The goal of machine structures is performance-to-regulation, not problem solving. Other structures are "professional bureaucracy," where local problem solving and decision making are the drivers of performance. What has led to this wide range of structures is a powerful mix of federal regulations, public opinion, and political ideologies. (For more information on the impact of these and other dynamics on school structure, check Hoy & Miskel, 2004, Chapter 3.)

Within the current milieu, can there be a right answer to the right balance of central authority and local autonomy? The leadership role depends on many factors. According to some experts, an emphasis on instructional leadership places the local administrator in charge of ensuring that students reach higher levels of achievement and no one can argue with that. For others, improvement goals are unified and mandated, placing the central office in charge of performance and effectiveness. Some view site-based autonomy as the counterbalance to remote, uninvolved leadership, while others see central executive leadership as the means to more efficient and responsible decision making.

A couple of years ago I had the unique opportunity to be part of a working group charged with finding out the best balance of authority and autonomy. I contributed to the research design, data gathering, and drafting of a report entitled "Beyond Islands of Excellence." This important research was sponsored by the Learning First Alliance, a coalition of education associations in Washington, DC. During the course of our research on selected school systems around the United States, it became clear that while individual leaders can successfully lead individual schools through reform, it takes a much broader ensemble of leaders to lead an entire system to success:

> . . . during the course of the reforms, the districts extended the leadership from a few traditional positions—the superintendent and principal—to include other actors: assistant principals, teacher leaders, central office staff, union leaders, and school board members. In addition, in most districts, external actors— representatives from state offices, universities, and communities—worked in a coordinated manner with district staff. In these districts leadership was not simply shared; most stakeholder groups took on the elements of reform they were best positioned to lead. (Togneri & Anderson, 2003, p. 31)

These systems found a model that worked well for them, one of broad collaboration, high trust, and willingness to redefine leadership. Leaders of these systems were not intimidated by sharing their leadership, rather they acknowledged that others had "comparative advantage" in particular areas (Elmore).

The readings selected for this issue provide still other models for balancing authority and autonomy. The first reading is from a survey of top school officials across the United States. "Theory of Action" reports the results of a study on instructional leadership commissioned by the Education Week Research Center. This poll of school superintendents is an eye-opener. It is clear that superintendents believe they must take a more assertive role in making instructional decisions for the local level. The report verifies that instructional leadership is shifting from localized to centralized. What is also clear is that curriculum is no longer a matter for school leaders to decide. Bottom line: If schools are going to improve radically, it will be due to the strength of central leadership.

"Schools Take a Lesson from Big Business" is an insightful comparison of decentralization in business and schools. Author Del Jones uses the term *autonomy zone* to describe the tendency of large-city school systems to increase the number of schools that are making major decisions *in loco*. Just how many school districts are we talking about? Not many. Jones claims that decentralization is making inroads mainly in the "giant" or mega-city districts. For principals of autonomous schools, the benefit is space to be entrepreneurial, to negotiate inflexible regulations, and to redirect resources. Unlike the findings of the Education Week poll in the previous reading, these giant districts see decentralization as the only valid means of high performance.

In "Educational Leaders as Caring Teachers," Nel Noddings takes a philosophical stance by starting her argument with the nature of the educational enterprise. She reopens the question of the means schools and districts use for achieving aims and establishing levels of proficiency—which are givens for many institutions. Noddings makes the case against pre-given educational aims, goals, and objectives by contrasting two theories of motivation—extrinsic and intrinsic. If the driving force behind a school is intrinsic motivation, it only makes sense that the leaders and teachers will want more choice about curriculum and goals and ultimate ends of education. Noddings argues that caring leaders need to be teachers—holding the demands of central authority in check in order to use locally determined means for reaching the highest educational aims.

Peter Eisinger and Richard Hula pull no punches in "Gunslinger School Administrators." Within the world of school reform, one cluster of reforms is all about centralizing authority in educational organizations. Out of this context, Eisinger and Hula paint a picture of the nontraditional outsider (individual without public education experience or credentials), unencumbered by bureaucracy and outdated regulation (in both central office and individual schools), who is recruited to clean up the place (the entire district). These superintendents are using their management experience to make super-sized changes. In some cases, the "gunslinger" superintendent turns the district over to private management firms. Others are delegating instructional/organizational responsibility to a second-in-command. Keep in mind that communities hiring this type of superintendent tend to be large urban cities with district operations, internal working relationships, and accreditations procedures that are very complex. The authors' study yields some startling facts about the success of the gunslinger leader.

With so much attention given to the authority/autonomy controversy, the fundamental question is: who should lead in matters of teaching and learning?

## SOURCES

Jeff Archer, Theory of action. *Education Week*, September 14, 2005.

Del Jones, Schools take a lesson from big business. *USA Today*, March 9, 2006.

Nel Noddings, Educational leaders as caring teachers. *School Leadership and Management*, September 2006.

Peter K. Eisinger and Richard C. Hula, Gunslinger school administrators. *Urban Education*, November 2004.

# Theory of Action

Jeff Archer

Not long ago, a popular theory about school improvement went something like this: Put in strong principals and dedicated staff members, and then get out of their way. When it came to improving teaching and learning, the thinking went, the central office had little to add.

The upshot was an era of policies that limited the role of district-level leadership in matters of instruction. Site-based management and "whole-school reform" models flourished in the 1990s on the premise that individual schools alone could raise achievement.

And the idea worked. Or rather, it worked for some schools, while others languished. As a result, a new consensus is emerging in the field that strong district leadership is needed to bring about large-scale improvement—now a mandate under the federal No Child Left Behind Act.

"Either you believe in district reform, or you're going to have to be extremely patient in waiting for a school-by-school turnaround," says Jane Hammond of the Stupski Foundation, a Mill Valley, Calif.-based group that helps districts with strategic planning.

*Education Week* is focusing on leadership at the district level for its second annual "Leading for Learning" special report. The key question is: What strategies should district leaders pursue to influence the quality of teaching and learning?

To answer that, we tell the stories of two school systems that re-established the role of the central office in guiding instructional improvement: the 10,000-student Gilroy Unified schools in California and the 26,000-student Clarksville-Montgomery County system in Tennessee.

The two districts—both of which work with the Stupski Foundation—have sought greater consistency across schools in content and teaching methods. They've created new ways for teachers to learn together and use student data. And, they've each seen more students succeed academically.

To get a sense of how widespread such approaches are, the Education Week Research Center also commissioned a poll of superintendents that asked what practices they use to improve instruction. The results show district leaders across the country embracing many of the strategies employed in Gilroy and Clarksville-Montgomery County.

True, districts still reflect a range of approaches. Some are more explicit in telling schools what instruction should look like—a method that some are

*What are implications of increasing the role of district-level leadership for school-level leaders?*

now calling "managed instruction." Others prefer to set broader boundaries and then step in where they see problems.

Many experts see the growing assertiveness of district leaders as a natural consequence of the movement for higher academic standards that has dominated education policymaking for more than a decade. It's too much, they say, to presume that every school has within it the capacity to bring its students to the levels of achievement now demanded of them.

"When you have a policy environment now that expects change to occur at scale, that means that districts have to improve all schools, essentially simultaneously," says Warren Simmons, the executive director of the Annenberg Institute for School Reform, located in Providence, R.I.

Tellingly, the Bill & Melinda Gates Foundation—one of the strongest promoters of designs for small schools—has drafted a new white paper arguing that schools are most likely to succeed if they're part of a supportive district, or, in the case of charter schools, part of a larger network of schools.

"We've spent over a billion dollars on almost 2,000 schools, and what we found is that most people don't know what to do, and how to do it," says Tom Vander Ark, the executive director for education at the Seattle-based foundation.

Mounting evidence suggests that effective schools are most often found in districts with strong systemwide guidance. In 2002, the Council of the Great City Schools identified some parallels among improving districts in an influential report, "Foundations for Success."

The council described strategies employed in Charlotte-Mecklenburg, N.C.; Houston; Sacramento, Calif.; and the subset of schools in New York City then known as the Chancellor's District.

Each district had a common curriculum, and had set up training and monitoring systems to ensure consistent approaches toward instruction across schools. The districts also made frequent use of student-performance data to inform educators' decisions.

"You have to take responsibility for the overall instructional program," says Michael D. Casserly, the executive director of the Washington-based council, "rather than just abandon that to the individual schools without providing direction, technical assistance, or professional development, and just hoping for the best."

Chrys Dougherty, the director of research at the National Center for Educational Accountability, says much the same is true in most of the districts named as finalists and winners for the annual Broad Prize for Urban Education, which recognizes improved student performance.

"When you go to effective schools that are in a district that has certain things in place, they will say their job was made infinitely easier by the fact that the district did these things," says Dougherty, whose Austin, Texas-based center collects the data used to make the Broad Prize selections.

On the surface, this larger role for the central office might seem at odds with the concurrent push to give families more options. Some of the biggest urban districts, for example, are creating large numbers of new schools with different designs—what's come to be called a "portfolio" model.

Likewise, decentralized decisionmaking still has plenty of proponents, as seen in the number of districts giving school sites more power to hire whom they want and to spend their budgets as they see fit.

*What is driving the need for district leaders to be more active in guiding instruction?*

But strong district leadership is needed for empowerment of school sites to succeed, says Joseph Olchefske, a former superintendent of the Seattle public schools. As a district chief, he gave schools considerable leeway to design their own programs, but that didn't mean anything goes.

"You've got to set standards, you've got to create and implement assessments that are for all kids, regardless of the school, and have very clear accountability, which means consequences," says Olchefske, who is now the managing director of a new consulting group at the American Institutes for Research, located in Washington.

Michael Fullan, an expert on school system management at the University of Toronto, says one of a superintendent's biggest challenges is finding the right balance between central authority and site-based autonomy. Ideally, he argues, schools should feel ownership of a common vision of instruction.

"If you're too loose, you don't get the focus, but if you're too focused, you get prescription, and narrowness, and rebellion," he says. "The holy grail of school reform on a large scale is large-scale ownership."

Whether most districts in the United States can achieve that balance remains to be seen. But as the survey results and the stories of the two districts in this report suggest, few district leaders are leaving things to chance.

# ARTICLE 3.2

# Schools Take a Lesson from Big Business

Del Jones

## DECENTRALIZING HELPS WHEN ORGANIZATIONS GET UNWIDELY

Of ideas for improving the public schools, none sounds more dull and dreary than decentralization.

Yet since DuPont introduced decentralization to business nearly 90 years ago, large companies have stumbled across few ideas that have better withstood the test of time. Now, momentum is building from New York City to San Francisco to Miami to decentralize public schools and drag them into the 1920s.

There are 12 school districts in the USA that have more than 10,000 teachers, and that's not counting non-teaching employees. Companies that grow past 1,500 employees start to bulk up at the center and become bureaucratic, says UCLA management professor William Ouchi.

Just as General Electric's Jack Welch spent much of his 20-year career as CEO fighting bureaucracy to create an environment of small companies at the behemoth corporation, some school systems are recognizing that *principals* know their neighborhoods. Decentralization, often called autonomy, takes billions of dollars away from superintendents and the legions of central office minions and turns it over to those schools and principals.

The movement goes back 30 years to Edmonton, Alberta, where principals today control 92% of the money, and local voters have consistently indicated in school board elections that they will have it no other way.

But elsewhere the movement has been slow. Public schools have the luxury of resistance because they can't go out of business. "Unlike the woolly mammoth," schools can persist in a state of failure, says Ouchi, a longtime proponent of the push. Also, not every neighborhood school, principal and teacher welcomes the accountability that decentralization brings. It may sound nice to be in charge of a $10 million high school budget until you find out that you, not school boards and superintendents, take the heat for tough choices, such as cutting funding for the school band.

Decentralization is, however, starting to make inroads into giant school districts. In January, New York City decided to increase the number of schools in its autonomy zone from 58 to more than 200, turning the nation's largest school system into a serious player in the decentralization movement. Today, Miami-Dade County Public Schools (No. 5) will hold committee meetings with the

**100**

goal of giving 18 schools freedom from district control to tailor their staffing and purchasing. That decision is to be made by the school board next week.

Seattle and Houston (No. 8) decentralized 10 years ago, followed six years ago by San Francisco and St. Paul. Boston and Chicago (No. 4) have small experiments. Oakland jumped in with a district-wide program last year, and Hawaii (No. 10) started it statewide this year.

School boards have it under consideration in Charlotte (No. 24) and Las Vegas (No. 7), says Ouchi, who gained respect in 1981 when many were predicting that the runaway world economic power of the future would be Japan. Ouchi refuted the defeatism in his business best seller Theory Z: How American Business Can Meet the Japanese Challenge. His refocus today on education is attracting other top management experts into the field, and—for the first time in 50 years—the *Academy of Management Journal* (www.aomonline.org) concentrated on public education in its January issue.

"When I was principal of a big high school in Los Angeles, I never saw the damn phone bill," unless asked to reprimand someone for making "bizarre calls to Afghanistan," says Michael O'Sullivan, president of the Associated Administrators of Los Angeles, a union for principals.

Many principals prefer it that way, and the annual turnover rate for principals edges up from 12% to 15% when decentralization is introduced, Ouchi says.

*Why is decentralization difficult for some school principals?*

## A New Breed of Principals

But those who leave are often replaced by principals like Clover Codd, 31, who sees decentralization as entrepreneurial.

Codd is in charge of a $1.6 million annual budget at Loyal Heights Elementary in Seattle, where schools are autonomous, dollars follow students, and parents can choose within geographic clusters of six to eight schools. "I like to think my job is on the line," if test scores were to plummet at Loyal Heights for consecutive years, says Codd, who saved the school enough money to hire a part-time counselor to work with students on mental health.

That's the way it's designed to work, Ouchi says. Under decentralization, the heat might get turned down at night or the gym floor might go another year without refinishing. In the past, if a school made such efforts to save money, the funds would only be sent back to the central office to be spent by someone else. Now it stays where it may mean a part-time reading instructor. When substitute teachers are paid by headquarters, teachers call in sick more often. When money saved on substitutes comes back to the school, absenteeism falls 40%, Ouchi says.

Principals at high schools in New York City's autonomy zone have given up assistant principals, guidance counselors and attendance clerks. But they have been able to add so many teachers with the same budget that the number of students a teacher sees each day has been driven down from 160 to 60, Ouchi says.

This flexibility to redirect resources is a lesson DuPont learned after it took its World War I gunpowder profits, expanded into an unwieldy conglomerate and nearly went broke, says John Smith, a Lehigh University professor who specializes in the history of industry. As a last resort, division heads were given control of their budgets and promoted or fired based on division profits and losses. Today, companies such as Texas Instruments give semi-autonomy to just about everyone with managerial authority. Decentralization spurs innovation and creativity by making supervisors "the master or mistress of their own destiny," says Texas Instruments Vice President Marcia Page.

But even in business, decentralization is a work in progress. Sara Lee struggled when it became the ultimate in decentralization, a holding company for independent divisions that made everything from Wonderbras to Jimmy Dean Sausage. New CEO Brenda Barnes says the company was so decentralized that there was no knowledge-sharing or camaraderie from one division to another. She is trying to balance the efficiencies of decentralization while getting Sara Lee's 137,000 employees to feel part of the whole rather than islands. Barnes says decentralization makes sense for public schools, but it can't be used for everything. For example, information technology "has to be centralized, or you wind up with a hodgepodge that doesn't talk to each other," she says.

Ouchi says schools have no choice but to decentralize if they want to succeed. Since 1932, the number of public school students has doubled to 50 million, yet the number of school districts has declined from about 127,000 to 16,000. New York City and Los Angeles now have budgets as large as Dell Computer or Johnson & Johnson.

*What factors of decentralized schools contribute to increased performance?*

Ouchi's reputation from Theory Z gave him the clout to raise $1 million for ongoing research on decentralized schools. He concludes that they consistently outperform traditional public schools. For example, math and reading scores have improved more in decentralized Houston than in Los Angeles, both large school districts with similar demographics. But accurate comparisons are never easy in education and have proven subject to manipulation. In this case, Houston was found to be undercounting its dropouts.

## Criticism Clashes with Praise

"Decentralization is a terrible idea that would be a disaster," says A.J. Duffy, president of United Teachers Los Angeles. Too many principals and assistant principals are "demigods who take credit for what teachers do and blame teachers for what goes wrong," and they would become more "mean spirited" if given the power of the purse, he says.

Decentralization works in industry, Duffy says, because employees can find a similar job elsewhere if they have an abusive boss. "You can't do that in schools," he says. "You either work there, or you become a welder."

But decentralization probably serves to weed out bad principals, says former astronaut Sally Ride, who straddles the worlds of education and business as the owner of Sally Ride Science, which encourages girls to pursue science and math careers. Ride concurs that there are bad principals, which is why there "is value in having their feet held to the fire."

Ouchi points to large private school systems, which decentralized long ago. The Catholic schools in New York City have a central office staff of 22. The public schools have 10 times as many students, which should translate into a central office staff of 220, Ouchi says, but the actual number is 25,500.

Educators such as Duffy find decentralization one more business intrusion on schools when "the Delphis, the Enrons, the WorldComs" prove that business is far from the perfect role model.

Critics worry that principals could skim money from schools, but that has proved unfounded, probably because $500 to an individual school is a lot of money and would be noticed, whereas it's a rounding error in the $13 billion Los Angeles Unified School District, Ouchi says. Even those like former Los Angeles principal O'Sullivan, who agrees that decentralization is a good idea, say it's just another flavor of the month that will be implemented and abandoned with each new mayor and superintendent.

*What are some pros and cons of decentralization?*

Ouchi sympathizes and agrees that schools have long been whiplashed by one idea replacing the next. But he says decentralization will stick, as it has for 30 years in Edmonton, because schools and parents resist new regimes if they attempt to take back the money.

# ARTICLE 3.3

# Educational Leaders as Caring Teachers

## Nel Noddings

*Good leadership varies with the sort of enterprise to be led. We would not put the CEO of a large clothing manufacturer, inexperienced in warfare, in charge of a military expedition. Now and then highly successful people from one field are recruited to lead an entirely different enterprise, but their duties are usually limited, and often they are mere figureheads. At the level where field-related decisions must be made we need leaders who know the field. Leadership in education requires both breadth and depth of knowledge about education. At the very least, an educational leader should have a defensible position on the aims of education, on a theory of motivation and on what constitutes ethical practice.*

## WHAT SORT OF ENTERPRISE IS EDUCATION?

Despite much talk in the last few decades about products and outcomes, education differs radically from manufacturing in its aims. At its best, education does not try to produce a uniform product. Designed to develop the various talents and interests of all students, it satisfies its mission when its graduates show that these varied talents have in fact been developed. From this perspective, the best education increases some important differences; it does not aim at uniformity. The best schools, both pre-college and undergraduate, turn out people who will one day be mathematicians, artists, business leaders, engineers, diplomats, nurses and members of a host of other professions and occupations.

Education seeks multiple aims. Not only does it reject the idea of a uniform product, it also rejects the notion that its only aim is either academic or vocational, i.e. to prepare precisely the mathematician, artist or diplomat. An education worthy of its name will help its students to develop as persons, to be thoughtful citizens, competent parents, faithful friends, capable workers, generous neighbors and lifelong learners. It will try, too, to develop aesthetic, ethical and spiritual sensitivity. It offers programs and activities designed to enhance these ends and it tries to choose means compatible with them. Where possible, it avoids coercion. It prefers the language of invitation, offering, encouragement, guidance, sharing, advice and trying-out to that of requirement, compulsion, prescription, testing and assignment.

Moreover, education in liberal democracies serves two great interests that are always in some tension. State sponsored schools must serve the interests of the state; they must produce competent workers and citizens. However, they must also develop the individual talents and interests of their students. In theory there should be no conflict here because liberal democracies thrive when their citizens' individual talents are highly developed. In practice, of course, many conflicts, both potential and actual, arise and the tension, while shifting in focus, is always there.

Some years ago the president of Stanford University explained informally why he resisted a new direction planned by a regional accrediting agency. The agency had asked colleges and universities to list the outcomes they sought and describe their ideal graduate in some detail. The president protested that people come to Stanford with a great variety of respectable expectations, both professional and personal. The university tries to provide opportunities for students to analyze, refine and meet these expectations. And there is no honest and useful way to describe the Stanford graduate.

*Who should set levels of proficiency for K–12 students?*

However, one may ask, are there not some identifiable skills, some knowledge and attitudes that an educational institution should expect of all its students? The answer to this is a cautious yes. Certainly, we expect elementary schools to turn out students who can read, write an intelligible message and perform basic arithmetical operations. But to what level of proficiency? This is not an easy question to answer, and responding reasonably to it requires some knowledge of each student whose proficiency will be assessed. It cannot be adequately answered by looking only at the task or by establishing a median on some test and then insisting that it should be the mark of proficiency for everyone.

At the undergraduate level of education we can name some ideal aims for our graduates—critical thinking, tolerance of ambiguity, concern for the common good, heightened aesthetic sensibility and self-actualization—but we cannot measure these hoped-for outcomes precisely and we surely cannot establish them as requirements for graduation. But despite the fact that universities cannot guarantee their attainment nor even agree on exactly what constitutes each ideal, universities would be poor places—morally bankrupt places—if they did not seriously pursue such aims.

Questions involving the aims of education and the means chosen to achieve them are profound questions. They require continual examination, critical thought and reflection. Sometimes, at the level of classroom instruction on a specific skill, we can answer the question of expectations quite precisely. We might say, for example, that after specific instruction on a mathematical skill X most of our students should get at least 80% on a quiz testing their competence on X. But what do we mean by 'most'? And if a few do not reach 80%, what should we do for them? And why 80% instead of 70 or 90%? And why did we choose to teach X in the first place? I am not suggesting that there are no adequate answers to these questions. I merely point out that we rarely bother to ask them. Good teachers should never stop asking them.

## CARING TEACHERS

Caring teachers listen and are responsive (Noddings, 2003). Like all responsible adults, teachers infer certain needs for their students. Indeed, most of the material taught in schools represents inferred needs. I am making a distinction here between expressed needs—those that arise within the person having them—and inferred needs—needs identified by outside decision-makers and imposed on those said to have them (Noddings, 2002). Students rarely express a need to learn the things we require of them. But caring teachers hear their students' expressed needs, whether those needs are expressed verbally or in some other way. What should be done with expressed needs? Sometimes, in the progressive tradition we acknowledge and direct expressed needs towards the inferred needs already identified. Sometimes, the task is more one of balancing expressed needs and inferred needs. At a simple level the idea is that by meeting some of their expressed needs (provided they are not harmful) we win students over and they become more willing to work on the needs we have identified. But we may also use the balancing strategy because we need time to observe what happens and to see how the chosen activity might best be developed educationally. Finally, there are times when students' expressed needs seriously challenge one or more of our inferred needs. Then we might ask that profound question: why am I teaching X; why do I infer that my students need to learn X? The outcome of our reflection may be a more solid justification for teaching X, and then we turn to the balancing or negotiating strategy. Or it may be an astonishing revelation: they don't need X! Or this child does not need X. Maybe I'll have some students work on X and provide something different for others.

What motivates students to learn? Clearly, needs, wants and desires are instrumental. Caring teachers listen to their students and plan to work with their expressed needs, but they are careful to distinguish between passing or capricious wants and the fairly stable ones I have been calling expressed needs. Most of the time good teachers can easily substitute genuine and valuable interests for some passing desire their students evince. However, sometimes, as John Dewey reminded us, capricious activity is actually induced by faulty teaching—usually by insisting that students engage in an activity for which they are unmotivated (Dewey, 1916). Then the great desire is to disrupt things, to get rid of this hated activity or expectation.

Today teachers are urged to motivate students. Aims, goals and objectives, all posited somehow as needs students should satisfy, are established a priori, before any interaction with students. Then it becomes the job of teachers to motivate students to learn material they have not chosen and, perhaps, would prefer to avoid (Noddings, 1997). Can this be done without inviting the capricious desire to disrupt things? If so, what other risks are incurred in the doing?

In the period roughly from the mid 1950s through most of the 1970s management experts in both industry and education seemed to be vitally interested in theories of motivation. A book on managerial psychology from which I studied in 1970 (Leavitt & Pondy, 1964) opens with an article by Abraham Maslow, and Maslow's (1970) theory of intrinsic motivation was widely discussed by educators. The important idea, reminiscent of what Dewey had already promoted in education, was to challenge the prevailing theory of external motivation.

That theory is sometimes called the 'carrot and stick' theory. The basic idea is that managers (and teachers) must offer clear rewards and punishments to get people to do what managers want them to do. Teachers have typically used both rewards and punishments to entice or force children to learn things in which they are not interested. Enlightened advocates of this theory have concentrated more on rewards, or positive reinforcement (Skinner, 1953, 1964), than on punishment. Today, however, a whole system has been established in the USA based on sanctions and punishments. Students, teachers, administrators and whole schools are to suffer punishment if they do not meet the expectations laid down by government (Kohn, 2000; Linn, 2003). Students, even young children, are retained in grade if they do not pass standardized tests, teachers are denied bonuses if their students' test scores are not satisfactory, administrators are fired or transferred and whole schools may be structured.

We should consider the effects this motivational approach has on moral life as well. People who are coerced and punished in the interests of accomplishing specific aims or objectives are likely to use questionable methods of compliance if they find themselves unable to meet the objectives. School children may cheat. Teachers may eliminate much valuable material from the curriculum and concentrate on test items. Administrators may move students from school to school to manipulate their statistics and engage in various forms of triage to bring classes and groups to the required median score. Policy-makers at the state level may engage in questionable practices to establish proficiency levels and expectations for adequate yearly progress.

A second theory, well described by Dewey and Maslow, concentrates on intrinsic motivation. This theory, introduced above, takes a more generous view of human beings and their motivation. When people are interested, they want to learn or to further the success of a company for which they work. The right move for teachers and managers, then, is to maintain that intrinsic interest. When that cannot be done, caring teachers and managers employ the balancing/negotiating strategy mentioned earlier and work toward a revival of intrinsic interest. Advocates of this theory testify to improved relationships, a higher level of trust and greater job satisfaction. Do we also get better results? To answer this question, we have to return to our profound questions, and the initial answer has to be that it depends on how we define 'results'. As George Orwell (1981) pointed out, teachers can get 'better results' in terms of test scores, obedience and immediate responses by beating and humiliating students. But that is hardly the road to lasting learning or caring attitudes.

*Does theory two (intrinsic motivation) fit the aims of public education today?*

I should say a little more on these two competing theories of motivation. Many idealistic young teachers are attracted to theory 2 (intrinsic motivation), and I confess that I am still a strong advocate of it. But that does not mean that we should never use strategies drawn from theory 1. Indeed, the balancing/negotiating strategy that I mentioned with approval contains the seeds of something like a reward: we'll do what you'd like for a while, but then perhaps you will do what I'd like. If the strategy is undertaken simply to sugar coat the lesson intended by the teacher, it is likely to backfire (see Dewey, 1916). But if it is done out of respect for the students' interests and the possibility remains open that a whole new project or approach may emerge, the strategy is transformed into cooperative living.

Pressing the matter a little further, we may see that it is impossible and perhaps even undesirable to maintain a pure approach to motivation. Even intrinsic motivation can be badly warped by schooling and parenting practices. The desire for approval, for example, is an admirable human desire, but it can be corrupted into a single-minded campaign for high grades. Failing to recognize the pernicious quality of this 'achievement motivation', teachers often express high praise for students who have actually lost all intrinsic interest in learning (Pope, 2001). To get things back on track teachers might have to use a reinforcement schedule of some sort to help students believe that approval of them as persons does not depend on their getting high grades. Exclusive use of one method, stubborn adherence to a single theory or perspective, can verge on idolatry and it may not serve the best interest of students. For caring teachers the child is more important than the theory.

## CARING LEADERS

Educational leaders, like teachers in general, should probably find motivation theory 2 more attractive than theory 1. Teachers are already motivated—they do not need external rewards and punishments, although of course they might appreciate higher pay and positive public recognition. Most people enter teaching because they want to make a difference in the lives of young people. In the Stanford Teacher Education Program this reason has topped all others for years. A second reason, also consistently in the top three, is to use, enjoy and learn more about a beloved subject. It isn't easy to find an occupation other than teaching that will pay one to study English literature, European history or poetry, or even art, music or drama.

Caring leaders recognize these intrinsic interests and try to protect them. A good reason for promoting smaller classes is that teachers and students are more likely to form the kinds of relationship conducive to 'making a difference'. Leaders who recognize this do not require proof that smaller classes will produce higher test scores. Smaller classes may actually do so, but higher test scores are not the main point. Similarly, a reasonable degree of teacher choice with respect to curriculum must be protected. No vital teacher-intellectual wants to teach a tightly prescribed curriculum and she or he may not want to teach the exact same topics year after year. Indeed, such a system encourages intellectual laziness. The intellectual excitement that comes with choice should be cherished and actively promoted.

But surely an institution and its leaders have a responsibility to ensure that students acquire certain skills, gain some specific knowledge and come to understand fundamental concepts. Of course. And we can add to these three great aims many mentioned earlier. This is why caring leaders must keep aims talk alive. What are the main academic goals we seek? Why? What other aims should guide our work? Are the means suggested compatible with these aims? Are they compatible with a defensible moral view? If we change topics from year to year will the change contribute to or detract from our major aims and goals? Such continuing discussion is essential if we are to avoid the pervasive mindlessness deplored decades earlier in education (Silberman, 1970). If anything, however, that mindlessness has increased in the last few years. The major justification now for teaching a topic is that it appears on the required standardized test, and it is by no means clear that there is any real justification for its appearance there.

Caring leaders should be teachers. They need not, indeed cannot possibly, be experts in every subject. But they can listen, ask probing questions and lead discussions. They can make it both comfortable and rewarding for teachers to seek help instead of trying to hide their weaknesses, doubts and failures. They can serve as models of critical thinking by showing that they continually question even the methods and procedures that they themselves have officially advocated.

Leaders, like classroom teachers, have to balance the objectives of higher authority with those of their staff. Can we meet the demands of the state and central office and still pursue those ideals for which we entered the profession? In the USA today my sense is that this is becoming more and more difficult. It will take intelligence, faith and courage to stand by our convictions on how people learn, what motivates them and what is worth learning.

Finally, caring leaders invite participation and responsible experimentation. They avoid coercion whenever possible. When a promising idea arises a caring leader may offer to support those who would like to try it. I have been campaigning for years to implement a system in which teachers and students can stay together for several years (by mutual consent) rather than the typical one year. This practice has many attractive features (Flinders & Noddings, 2001) and it may yield desirable cognitive, social and affective results. However, I would never mandate it. Rather, I would offer support to those who want to try it. When we force people to employ specific means we risk losing the very ends for which the means were chosen. Of course, if we never question what these ends are and why they have been chosen, we have no cogent reason for examining the means. We just go with 'what works', never mind why we are interested in the things toward which we are working or what may be lost in our choices. We can do better than this, and caring leaders must show the way.

*What training is essential for leaders who want to become caring teachers?*

# REFERENCES

Dewey, J. (1916) *Democracy and education* (New York, Macmillan).

Flinders, D. & Noddings, N. (2001) *Multiyear teaching: the case for continuity* (Bloomington, IN, Phi Delta Kappa).

Kohn, A. (2000) *The case against standardized testing* (Portsmouth, NH, Heinemann).

Leavitt, H. J. & Pondy, L. (Eds) (1964) *Readings in managerial psychology* (Chicago, IL, University of Chicago Press).

Linn, R. (2003) Accountability: responsibility and reasonable expectations, *Educational Researcher,* 32(7), 3–13.

Maslow, A. (1970) *Motivation and personality* (New York, Harper & Row) (Original work published 1954).

Noddings, N. (1997) Must we motivate?, in: N. Burbules & D. Hansen (Eds) *Teaching and its discontents* (Boulder, CO, Westview Press), 29–44.

Noddings, N. (2002) *Starting at home: caring and social policy* (Berkeley, CA, University of California Press).

Noddings, N. (2003) *Caring: a feminine approach to ethics and moral education* (2nd edn) (Berkeley, CA, University of California Press).

Orwell, G. (1981) *A collection of essays* (San Diego, CA, Harcourt Brace).

Pope, D. C. (2001) *"Doing school": how we are creating a generation of stressed out, materialistic, and miseducated students* (New Haven, CT, Yale University Press).

Silberman, C. E. (1970) *Crisis in the classroom: the remaking of American education* (New York, Random House).

Skinner, B. F. (1953) *Science and human behavior* (New York, Free Press).

Skinner, B. F. (1964) The science of learning and the art of teaching, in: H. J. Leavitt & L. Pondy (Eds) *Readings in managerial psychology* (Chicago, IL, University of Chicago Press), 79–89.

# Gunslinger School Administrators: Nontraditional Leadership in Urban School Systems in the United States

## Peter K. Eisinger and Richard C. Hula

Educators, political leaders, and the public in the United States share a broad consensus that school systems in the larger urban areas are not meeting the educational needs of the children they are charged to serve. High dropout rates, disciplinary problems, chronic truancy, and most important, low test and achievement scores are seen as evidence of the incapacity of public educational institutions to achieve their most basic goals (Hill & Celio, 1998). These concerns underlie what Richard Elmore (1997) has called a cottage industry of school reforms, so varied and numerous that the schools are virtually awash in innovation (see also Payne, 2001).

Perhaps the most visible broad class of reforms focuses on various ways of decentralizing authority and responsibility in the school system. Here, the assumption is that parents and teachers—those closest to the children—know best how to educate them. Some of these reforms involve market-based experiments that devolve influence to parents by seeking to provide greater choices through vouchers or charter schools (Finn, Manno, & Vanourek, 2000; Witte, 2000). Others are school-based, including curricular modifications, pedagogical experiments, and teaching corps enhancements. Still another set of decentralizing reforms addresses governance and administrative issues by devolving these functions to the school or subdistrict-level through various forms of site-based management (David, 1995; Malen, Ogawa, & Kranz, 1990; Wohlstetter & Mohrman, 1994). Each of the reforms takes aim at traditional school systems that are seen as major impediments to fundamental change.

A second category of recent reforms focuses on the power of leadership. Like those focused on decentralization, leadership reform efforts typically assume that poor education outcomes are the result of structural faults with the education system itself. In contrast to the efforts to decentralize influence to schools or parents through various sorts of site-based management and school choice arrangements, leadership reforms often seek to move in precisely the opposite direction. They seek to centralize authority in the effort to enhance accountability and overcome the impediments of school board politics and bureaucratic inefficiencies (Hunter & Swann, 1999). Examples of centralizing initiatives include mayoral and state takeovers of school systems (for example,

*What factors lead to the assumption that poor education outcomes are the result of structural faults with the education system itself?*

Detroit, Philadelphia, Chicago), efforts to curtail or even abolish school boards (New York, Boston), and the appointment of CEOs rather than school superintendents as a way of emphasizing the need for tough-minded management (New Orleans, Oklahoma City, Baltimore, among others).

One variant of these centralizing reforms presents an intriguing departure from past practice: In the search for strong, centralized leadership, some cities have consciously decided to recruit a school CEO or superintendent whose professional backgrounds lie entirely outside of the sphere of public education. In a field in which advancement has typically required an advanced degree from a school of education, as well as a combination of teaching and administrative experience in the schools, these retired military officers, stockbrokers, business executives, and attorneys stand out. These nontraditional school superintendents come to their new jobs often unable to distinguish, as one observer put it, between a Carnegie unit and a cantaloupe (Mathews, 1999). Nevertheless, cities are seeking out such leaders for their assumed independence, management expertise, and decision-making abilities, judging these attributes more important than professional training and experience in public education.

We liken these education outsiders, these nontraditional school system leaders, to the "gunslinger" of American frontier mythology, the stranger, like Shane, who rides into town and solves a menacing problem that the townsfolk cannot manage themselves.[1] This article explores the gunslinger phenomenon in public education leadership by describing it, specifying the conditions under which cities resort to this sort of reform, and exploring its implications for public education.

## THE GUNSLINGER MODEL

The main diagnosis that leads a city to turn its schools over to a gunslinger from outside the education profession is the conviction that the crisis in the public schools can be traced in large measure to its character as a closed system, wedded to traditional and inefficient ways of operating, resistant to truly new ideas, and unresponsive to community desires. Elected school boards are seen as mired in the petty rivalries of turf wars and identity politics. Teachers unions are portrayed as determined to protect work rule prerogatives and enhance pay and benefits rather than focusing on the educational interests of children. The huge urban school bureaucracy is seen as a self-protective hotbed of competing fiefdoms—inefficient, antiquated, inflexible, and sometimes even corrupt. The product of such school systems, according to this perspective, is the manifest failure of their children to graduate with the basic literacy and numeracy skills that will make them employable or educable at the college level. The function of the gunslinger, therefore, is to ride into town and tame or even replace the school board, challenge the unions, master the bureaucracy, and for good measure, galvanize students and their parents to commit to higher achievement.

How communities decide to seek a gunslinger varies from place to place. In several cases, the infrastructure of the traditional school leadership hierarchy was cleared away by state action. In Chicago and Detroit, for example, the state legislature abolished the elected school boards in the two cities and concentrated power in the hands of the mayors. In the former, the mayor chose a trusted lieutenant in Paul Vallas; in the latter instance, the mayor's role was to appoint a new school board, which in turn sought out an interim school CEO in the gunslinger mode. Changes in the leadership of Philadelphia schools occurred against the backdrop of state threats to take over the school system and turn it over to private management. In most of the other cities—for example, in New York under both Mayor Giuliani and Mayor Bloomberg—the choice of a gunslinger was purely a local decision, not prompted by state power.

*How might skeptics view the decision of a state legislature to abolish an elected school board and concentrate power in the hands of the mayor?*

Perhaps the earliest example of this new breed of school administrators was Howard Fuller, who managed the Milwaukee school system from 1991 to 1995. Fuller, who had no background in public education, came to the job from his position as the director of the Milwaukee County Department of Health and Human Services. Since Fuller was appointed superintendent of the Milwaukee schools, at least 22 other school systems (some more than once) among the nation's 100 largest have drawn their leadership from the ranks of retired military officers (Seattle, Washington, D.C., New Orleans, Duval County), business and finance (New York, Philadelphia, Minneapolis, Seattle), law (San Diego, Philadelphia), government (Los Angeles, Baltimore, Chicago), or academia (Detroit). Of these, 15 are still in charge of their respective school systems (see Table 1).

Gunslingers seem to be attractive to reformers for at least four related reasons:

**Intellectual openness** • To frustrated parents and politicians, urban public education seems encumbered by reform-of-the-month fads, mysterious professional jargon, and an unbending commitment to formal accreditation procedures for teacher certification. Furthermore, school systems often appear to be hostage to teachers unions that operate according to well-worn models of industrial unionism. Gunslinger superintendents are attractive in this context because they appear to be free (or even unaware) of the dogmas of the education profession and organized school labor. Certainly, this new category of education administrators has no exposure to the standard education school curriculum. They have not shaped their professional identity by championing particular education approaches or practices. The hope in bringing in a gunslinger is that he or she will be open to new ideas and perhaps even radical approaches to teaching, teachers, and curriculum matters.

Gunslingers do not always disappoint. When David Adamany became interim CEO of the Detroit school system, he immediately proposed hiring "nontraditional teachers," by which he meant college graduates in fields other than education. The Detroit teachers union vehemently opposed the idea. In Seattle, John Stanford eliminated teacher seniority as the basis for school

Table 1 Large Urban District Gunslingers

| | Leadership Role | School System | Year | Professional Background |
|---|---|---|---|---|
| **Current nontraditional school leaders** | | | | |
| Stephen Adamowski | Superintendent | Cincinnati | 1998 | Assistant commissioner of education |
| Alan Bersin | Superintendent | San Diego | 1998 | U.S. attorney |
| A. G. Davis | CEO | New Orleans | 1999 | U.S. Marines colonel |
| Richard DiPatri | Superintendent | Broward County | 2000 | State education commission |
| Pasquil Forgine | Superintendent | Austin, TX | 1999 | Government administrator |
| John Fryer | Superintendent | Duval Co. | 1998 | USAF major general |
| William Harner | Superintendent | Greenville County | 1998 | Military |
| Jules Klein | Chancellor | New York City | 2002 | Lawyer and business executive |
| Mike Moses | Superintendent | Dallas | 2000 | Commissioner of education/ university assistant provost |
| Joseph Olchesfske | Superintendent | Seattle | 1999 | Banker |
| Joseph Redden | Superintendent | Cobb County | 2000 | Military |
| Roy Romer | Superintendent | Los Angeles | 2000 | Governor of Colorado |
| Jim Scherzing | Superintendent | Portland | 2001 | District CFO, legislative staff |
| Roscoe Thornhill | Superintendent | Polk County | 2000 | Government administrator |
| Jerry Wartgov | Superintendent | Denver | 1998 | University president |
| **Former nontraditional school leaders** | | | | |
| David Adamany | CEO | Detroit | 1998–1999 | University president |
| Julius Becton | Superintendent | Washington, DC | 1996–1998 | Army lieutenant general |
| Robert Booker | CEO | Baltimore | 1998–2000 | Government CFO |
| Howard Fuller | Superintendent | Milwaukee | 1991–1995 | Government administrator |
| Philip Goldsmith | Int. CEO | Philadelphia | 2000–2001 | Banker |
| David Hornbeck | Superintendent | Philadelphia | 1994–2000 | Attorney |
| Peter Hutchinson | Superintendent | Minneapolis | 1993–1997 | Business executive |
| Harold Levy | Chancellor | New York City | 2000–2002 | Finance |
| John Stanford | Superintendent | Seattle | 1995–1997 | Army major general |
| Paul Vallas | CEO | Chicago | 1995–2001 | City budget director |

selection and instituted a process that allowed teacher "leadership teams" in the schools to select their own staff.

More common, what the community hopes will be openness to new approaches turns out to be the embrace of a shotgun strategy: In the absence of a commitment to a particular method or curriculum or standard, gunslingers try a little bit of everything all at once. For example, Harold Levy, the Wall Street lawyer and financial manager who headed the New York City school system under Mayor Rudolph Giuliani, introduced what one writer described as "a blizzard of reforms." His approach was characterized as "pragmatic, see-what-works" (Packer, 2001). Adamany, too, finally resorted to proposing a multitude of different ideas: an end to social promotion, mandatory summer school, arresting parents of chronic truants, smaller classrooms, nontraditional teachers, linking teacher pay to performance, longer school days, and more.

Recognizing that in fact they know little about teaching children in public schools, the gunslinger superintendents tend to hire second-in-command instructional administrators whose training and experience conform to the professional norms (Hurwitz, 2001; Mathews, 1999). Alan Bersin, superintendent of the San Diego schools, brought in Anthony Alvarado to be his chancellor of instruction. Alvarado had made his reputation as a superintendent of the East Harlem school district and then as chancellor of the New York City school system. Roy Romer, the former governor who heads the Los Angeles schools, has relied on Maria Gutierez Ott, a former school district administrator from a community in Los Angeles County, to serve in a similar capacity. Levy of New York City also delegated much of the instructional leadership to a chief education officer who reported to him, as did Paul Vallas of Chicago. In the end, then, the vaunted intellectual openness of the gunslinger superintendents often finds its counterweight in the very traditionally trained deputies who actually assume responsibility for devising and administering the instructional and curricular programs.

**Organizational independence** • Gunslinger superintendents or CEOs were never functionaries in a local school bureaucracy nor are they products of its culture.[2] In fact, one of their chief functions is to challenge that culture, which is seen by many members of the public as obstructionist, hide-bound, and self-seeking. Gunslingers are not insiders. As Howard Fuller, the Milwaukee superintendent in the early 1990s, remarked, "Because I came from the outside, I was not married to the system" (Mathews, 2001, p. 11). Paul Vallas emphasized his independence by proclaiming, "I'm in a great position. I don't want to be a lifetime school superintendent. I don't want to be an education consultant when I'm done here" (Mathews, 2001, p. 11).

This organizational independence is presumed to free gunslingers to focus on restructuring initiatives that traditional superintendents might feel constrained to undertake. Gunslingers have no career at stake, no reputation to protect and enhance for the next superintendency, freeing them, as Harold Levy once said, to undertake "ruthless leadership that is prepared to tackle really ancient problems of management" ("The Outsiders Take Over," 2000). Often, the first impulse is to cut out layers of administration. Thus, on coming into office, Levy reduced the number of people in the central office, Fuller eliminated area superintendents and flattened the bureaucracy, and Vallas replaced nearly every department head. In Seattle, John Stanford consolidated services such as transportation, maintenance, landscaping, warehousing, and purchasing, each of which had been so many independent fiefdoms in district offices. Adamany in Detroit actually stripped the bureaucracy of certain of these same functions and contracted them out to private vendors. Little of this reorganization has a direct bearing on classroom processes or performance, but it represents a powerful signal to the school district employees that an assertive leader is in charge and to the community that the leader is no captive of the bureaucracy.

**Results orientation** • Mathews (1999) has argued that many traditional school superintendents are at best ambivalent about standardized testing. Gunslingers, however, are thought to be more comfortable with achievement measures, because in the corporate and military worlds from which gunslingers are often drawn, success is continually assessed by the use of quantifiable indicators. "Wherever a nontraditional superintendent has been hired," Mathews (2001) writes, "the first administrative changes have almost always pushed the school staff toward making more frequent and more accurate measurements of what is going on" (p. 6).

It is not, in fact, clear empirically that these education outsiders are more prone to adopt benchmarks or standards than their counterparts who come to school superintendencies through the traditional ranks. But there is certainly a perception that standards and testing are no-nonsense gauges and that people from less sentimental worlds than public education are more suitable administrators in these circumstances. Certainly, standards-based assessment—not simply of students but of teachers and administrators as well—is consistent with the calls for accountability that have led to the use of gunslingers as a way of centralizing authority over the competing bureaucratic fiefdoms and union domains.

**Modern management skills** • The gunslinger superintendents are first and foremost administrators out of the new public management mold. They speak of pleasing their "customers," and they promise to bring "business practices" to bear on everything from personnel assessment to purchasing (Hurwitz, 2001; Mathews, 2001). They institute quality control procedures and internal audits. Gunslinger CEOs in Chicago, Seattle, and Detroit privatized certain functions that had long been performed in-house, and they consolidated others. In New York, Harold Levy was surprised to find that the youngest teachers and the least experienced administrators were working in the weakest schools. In the business world, Levy noted, "If you've got branches or distant offices that don't work well, you put your strongest managers there" ("The Outsiders Take Over," 2000).

Gunslingers almost invariably focus first on management reforms when they come into office. Management reform is a manageable challenge in a way that boosting student achievement among grade-school children from overwhelmingly impoverished families is not. One issue for the gunslinger superintendents and CEOs is whether they can move from a management reform agenda to the more difficult and often controversial education reform agenda without seeming to cede the latter function to their education deputies. Gunslingers recognize that they are not educators, but they want to be leaders of the education system. Another issue is whether the public will recognize their management skills and reward them for their success in this domain. It is not clear that a public worried about its children's ability to learn and graduate is at all concerned with the rationalization of the school district purchasing procedures or the challenge to teachers-union working conditions prerogatives.

## SCHOOL SYSTEM CHARACTERISTICS AND NONTRADITIONAL LEADERS

What are the characteristics of school systems that have hired gunslinger school leaders? To determine whether the resort to non-traditional administrators is random or not, we surveyed the nation's 100 largest school systems, covering the period 1995–2002. In the analysis that follows, any school district that had a gunslinger school superintendent or CEO at any time in this period is classified as having "nontraditional" leadership, even if in 2002 the district had returned to a superintendent with traditional education credentials.[3]

The initial sample was the 100 largest districts as reported in the National Center for Educational Statistics' Common Core Data (CCD).[4] The CCD includes three categories of information: descriptions of school and school districts, data on students and staff, and fiscal data on agency revenues and expenses. The Department of Education collects annual data from all of the approximately 16,000 school districts in the country. Because the data are collected on an annual basis, specific districts can enter and drop out of the list of the largest 100. Using annual CCD from academic year 1993–1994 to 1997–1998 results in a total of 111 districts that appeared in the largest 100 list for at least 1 year.

Data on leadership transition in the districts were obtained from two primary sources. First, district Web pages were identified and reviewed. These pages were searched for information on system-wide efforts of educational reform and leadership change. Particular attention was given to the background of current administrative leaders in the district and the process by which those leaders were chosen. Those districts that did not provide information on recent leadership transitions were contacted directly and were asked to provide basic information on current district administrators and how those administrators were selected.[5]

It is clear that gunslingers have been more common in larger rather than smaller school systems. The three largest systems in the nation—New York,

Los Angeles, and Chicago—have all been run by nontraditional school administrators. Detroit, Philadelphia, and San Diego are also among the 15 largest in the country. Table 2 shows that even among the 94 largest school districts for which we were able to find data, gunslingers (in all the tables, gunslingers are called nontraditional leaders) are more prevalent in central city school districts than in large suburban, consolidated or county-based school systems. The average size of the student population in systems run by traditional superintendents is 83,137, but in gunslinger school districts it is 182,488. The choice of gunslingers is not unknown in smaller places: For example, Oklahoma City and Kansas City, neither of which falls in the largest 100 systems, hired former military officers to run their systems. In general, however, gunslinger leadership is a big-city, big school district phenomenon.

Table 3 shows that the student demographic composition of school systems led by gunslingers tends to be Blacker and poorer than those run by traditional school superintendents. Almost half (44%) of the students in systems run by nontraditional leaders are Black, compared with 27% in schools with superintendents from the education profession. Gunslinger leadership is particularly associated with percentage Black in the student population but not percentage Hispanic. It is also related to the prevalence of poverty among the students. Using the percentage of students who qualify for free lunch as a proxy for poverty among the student body, we can see that on average, gunslingers administer systems where half (53%) of the students come from poor families, compared with 37% of the students in large systems with traditional leadership.[6] Student socioeconomic differences are, of course, a reflection of community characteristics. Median income among families with children is lower in gunslinger systems than in communities that hire traditional superintendents.

## GUNSLINGER LEADERSHIP AND SCHOOL SYSTEM DISTRESS

Big, predominantly poor and minority school systems are those most likely to be perceived as operating in a state of acute crisis and thus suitable targets for

Table 2   Geographic Distribution of School Districts by Leadership Type

|  | Leadership Type | |
| --- | --- | --- |
|  | **Education-Based** | **Nontraditional** |
| Central city | 44 | 21 |
| Suburban | 33 | 1 |
| Number of students | 83,133 | 182,488* |

*Difference of means test significant at .005 level.

Table 3    Composition of School Population by Type of Leadership

| | Leadership Type | | # School Districts Surveyed | Significance[a] |
|---|---|---|---|---|
| | Education-Based | Nontraditional | | |
| % minority | 51 | 67 | 98 | .008 |
| % Black | 27 | 44 | | 98.003 |
| % Hispanic | 17 | 18 | | 98.819 |
| % qualifying for free lunch | 37 | 53 | 81 | .005 |
| Median income of families with children | $35,767 | $30,384 | | 98.06 |

[a] Significance of $F$ ANOVA.

radical reform solutions. These perceptions are rooted in reality to a certain degree. Generally, students in big urban school systems perform more poorly on standardized tests than their suburban and out-state counterparts do. Graduation rates are lower and college matriculation is less common. Thus, these troubled big school systems loom large in the perceptual map of their respective states, even though there may in fact be far smaller, Whiter school districts that perform even more poorly (as in Michigan, for example, where the worst performing districts in terms of standardized test scores are several small, rural, largely White school districts). So, too, in the national public eye, the very largest districts in the country—New York, Los Angeles, Chicago—serve to establish a national standard of dysfunction.

Our data suggest, however, that school systems run by gunslinger leaders are not significantly more troubled by any measure than big city systems run by traditional leaders. For example, consider comparative dropout rates. We were able to obtain information on dropout rates for only 52 of the largest school systems, but Table 4 reports that similar proportions of students drop out in gunslinger and traditional systems. It would be difficult to conclude that high dropout rates make a school district more likely to consider gunslinger administrators.

Similarly, student performance on standardized tests does not seem consistently worse in school systems that have gunslingers at the helm. We compared students in the two types of school systems on how far below state norms they scored.[7] Although the average reading and math scores of students in systems led by gunslinger administrators tended to be farther below the state averages on standardized reading and math tests than the scores of their counterparts in traditionally led schools, the differences again did not reach statistical significance, using a simple analysis of variance $F$ test.

Table 4    Education Outcomes by Type of Leadership

|  | Leadership Type | | |
|---|---|---|---|
|  | Education-Based | Nontraditional | Significance[a] |
| % dropout, 1996 | 5.8 | 5.4 | 52.51 |
| % dropout, 1999 | 5.4 | 7.8 | 52.07 |
| % difference between district and state reading score | −23 | −32 | 40.59 |
| % difference between district and state math score | −26 | −53 | 36.30 |

[a] Significance of $F$ ANOVA.

What these data suggest is that, first of all, there is no evidence to indicate that systems that seek out a gunslinger are necessarily the worst performing. At best, we can say that the resort to gunslinger leadership is a response to extremely poor educational outcomes, but these sorts of outcomes are common in most large urban school districts and relatively less common in middle-class school systems. Thus, once some threshold of educational distress has been passed, the particular conditions that lead to the choice of a gunslinger likely have less to do with comparative degrees of dysfunction than of idiosyncratic community dynamics. That is an issue yet to be explored.

## GUNSLINGER LEADERSHIP AND SCHOOL REFORM

It is too early to tell whether gunslinger leadership will raise educational achievement in the nation's troubled big city school systems. In Chicago, test scores did seem to rise slightly during Paul Vallas's early tenure, but then they evened out and even declined in some cases as his time in office came to a close. Standardized test scores rose over the first 3 years of John Fryer's superintendency in Duval County, Florida. In Detroit, however, standardized test scores were lower in 2001 than they had been in 1999 after David Adamany's 1-year gunslinger term (New Detroit, 2002). But we generally lack systematic and comparable data for other cities. The turn toward nontraditional leadership in public school systems is interesting on several counts, however, whatever the educational outcomes.

First, the appointment of a nontraditional school administrator is distinguished by the fact that it is an unusual response to the urban educational crisis. It does not fall within the orbit of educational innovations and options. It represents an effort to think outside the boundaries of the normal, to shock the system. It suggests a determination to wipe the slate clean, an effort to challenge all assumptions about the sources of wisdom and competence in public education that might have been taken for granted.

Second, a related point is that hiring gunslingers poses the question of whether the skills required to run a big city school system are in fact those learned in the professional schools of education. To bring in a gunslinger to run the school system suggests that the community believes other skills are more important in a time of educational crisis than those learned through teaching or through advanced training in educational administration.

What the choice of a nontraditional school leader seems to suggest is that many people in positions of responsibility appear to have lost faith in the education profession as a profession. The resort to gunslinger leadership is nothing short of a challenge to the competence of education professionals. A profession claims special, sometimes unique, abilities in the management or pursuit of some activity, such as the law or medicine or education. But those claims by education professionals are no longer uncontested by state legislators in states that have taken over school systems or passed enabling legislation, by mayors who seek control of the schools themselves, and by business leaders tired of stories of administrative incompetence and inefficiency in the school bureaucracy. Just as war is too important to leave to the military, so in this view is the administration of public education too important to leave to graduates of professional schools of education.

Third, by appointing a gunslinger school leader, a community signals that the primary skills it values and wishes to bring to bear involve not the ability to teach or to understand teaching or learning but rather the ability to impose order on a disordered system. The assumption here is that order is a prerequisite to education and learning, that order is the first order of business. It is noteworthy to recall that the gunslingers make no pretense about understanding the process of public education. Most of them delegate this function to their second-in-command.

Thus, the first things that nontraditional school administrators tend to do is to impose order on the chaotic bureaucratic operations of the school district. They are not educational innovators. The management of bureaucratic organizations is something that these former military and business and government executives understand. They seek to bring order by streamlining, consolidating, and rationalizing, all in the effort to reduce inefficiencies and duplication and to increase accountability.

Some of the gunslinger leaders see the fragmented union landscape (Detroit school officials had to bargain with 18 different unions; Chicago with 29) as a picture of disorder. Thus, some have challenged the teachers unions, portraying them as a divisive force and obstacle to innovation. Adamany in Detroit and Vallas in Chicago also took on the various in-house staff and maintenance unions, contracting out their jobs to private companies.

Fourth, the appointment of a school leader whose central mission is to bring order to a disordered system as a way of addressing its failures suggests a different learning paradigm. It suggests that the effects of the imposition of order

*Why do districts that are **not** the worst performing prefer non-traditional administrators?*

from the top will work their way down through the system to the classroom and perhaps into the community. Order at the top is supposed to bring order to the classroom and perhaps even galvanize disorganized families and communities to take education seriously. Administrative change at the top, it is hoped, will create the conditions, presently lacking, for learning in the classroom.

The notion that order, unity, discipline, and accountability are preconditions for learning may be valid. The problem with this idea, however, is that we have no evidence yet that educational outcomes—that is, test scores and dropout and graduation rates—can be affected by administrative leadership changes at the top. There is no theory of educational achievement that attributes variations in education outcomes to administrative styles at the top of the system. Thus, the resort to gunslingers in urban school systems risks creating expectations for which there is no intuitively persuasive support. In the movies, we expect the good guy gunslinger like Shane to ride off triumphantly into the sunset. In real life, however, gunslinging is a high-risk proposition that is just as likely to lead to ignominious defeat and community disappointment because expectations were based on the wrong paradigm.

## ENDNOTES

1.  The term is used in Henig, Hula, Orr, and Pedescleaux (1999) as a description of an entrepreneurial superintendent brought into town to face down recalcitrant bureaucrats (p. 8). We have built on and broadened this idea of the outsider.
2.  Joel Klein, chancellor of the New York City schools under Mayor Bloomberg, took a brief leave from law school to teach sixth graders in the city's schools until he was called up into military service.
3.  It is hardly surprising that the operational definition of nontraditional administrator was subject to some ambiguity. For example, some superintendents/CEOs had administrative positions in education-related areas but not as administrators in a local school system. Examples include individuals who served in various roles in the federal department of education and various state education commissions. For the purposes of this article, such individuals were considered gunslingers because they clearly are out of the traditional advancement pattern for local superintendents.
4.  For a review of the CCD dataset, see http://nces.ed.gov/ccd/aboutccd. html#top.
5.  Information on past superintendents/CEOs was collected in a less systematic fashion and was obtained from a number of sources including school system Web pages, media reports, and citations in the education reform literature.
6.  Under the federal school lunch program, meals are free to children from families with a gross income at or below 125% of the federal poverty line.

7.  It is impossible to compare school districts directly because the scores were not equivalent across districts.

# REFERENCES

David, J. (1995). The who, what and why of site-based management. *Educational Leadership*, 53(4), 4–9.

Elmore, R. (1997). The paradox of innovation in education: Cycles of reform and the resilience of teaching. In A. Altshuler & R. Behn (Eds.), *Innovation in American government* (pp. 246–273). Washington, DC: Brookings.

Finn, C., Manno, B., & Vanourek, G. (2000). *Charter schools in action*. Princeton, NJ: Princeton University Press.

Henig, J., Hula, R., Orr, M., & Pedescleaux, D. (1999). *The color of school reform*. Princeton, NJ: Princeton University Press.

Hill, P., & Celio, M. B. (1998). *Fixing urban schools*. Washington, DC: Brookings Institution.

Hunter, R., & Swann, J. (1999). School takeovers and enhanced answerability. *Education and Urban Society*, 31, 238–251.

Hurwitz, S. (2001). The outsiders. *American School Board Journal*, 188(4), 10–15.

Malen, B., Ogawa, R., & Kranz, J. (1990). What do we know about school-based management? A case study of the literature—a call for research. In W. Clune & J. Witte (Eds.), *Choice and control in American education* (Vol. 2, pp. 289–342). New York: Falmer Press.

Mathews, J. (1999). On-the-job learning of nontraditional superintendents. *The School Administrator*, 56(2), 28–33.

Mathews, J. (2001). Nontraditional thinking in the central office. *The School Administrator*, 58(6), 6–11.

New Detroit, Inc. (2002). *A progress report: School improvement in the Detroit public schools*, Phase I. Detroit: Author.

Packer, G. (2001, March 11). The suit. *New York Times Magazine*, pp. 52–57.

Payne, C. M. (2001). So much reform, so little change: Building-level obstacles to urban school reform. In L. Joseph (Ed.), *Education policy for the 21st century* (pp. 239–278). Chicago: Center for Urban Research and Policy Studies.

The outsiders take over. (2000, June 19). *Time*, pp. 36–37.

Witte, J. (2000). *The market approach to education*. Princeton, NJ: Princeton University Press.

Wohlstetter, P., & Mohrman, S. (1994). *School-based management: Promise and process*. New Brunswick, NJ: Consortium for Policy Research in Education, Rutgers University.

# ISSUE SUMMARY

C learly there is divided opinion on the right balance of authority and autonomy in an educational system. To a certain extent, the right balance depends on the scope of change demanded by the public and legislators. The pressure is definitely heaviest on educational leaders in underperforming schools and institutions. But what is different about the scope of change that impacts leaders more directly?

It is interesting to compare the scale of school reform efforts two to three decades ago with current reforms. Today's efforts are all-encompassing, affecting every level of operation, whereas earlier reforms were smaller-scale, limited to instructional design or curriculum or classroom arrangement. Essentially, educational leadership was not the direct focus of past reforms, whereas now it is front and center. The issue of authority/autonomy is a vital one for leaders to consider. With so many reforms being attempted at once, the leader's role as change-agent becomes pivotal.

Unfortunately, state-level reform efforts are proving to be risky to the success of educational leaders. The reason is that such efforts "often ignore the important contributions of more school-focused policies" (Epstein, 2006, p. 5). In a summary of data from an extensive study of reform "fallout" Epstein concludes:

> The desire to reform the educational system in response to high levels of public concern is not surprising. However, research on the implementation of large-scale educational reforms suggests that they rarely achieve the many subgoals that they aspire to and seldom serve as a stimulus for measurable changes at the societal level...virtually all case studies of school improvement efforts show that unpredictable "normal crises," such as strikes, superintendent or principal turnover, or the introduction of new and competing change programs from outside of the school can both sidetrack successful programs and bolster lagging efforts. (p. 6)

At the heart of the myriad issues involved in this era of radical reform is a deceptively simple question for educational leaders: who leads what?

## ISSUE HIGHLIGHTS

- Some experts believe strong system leadership is needed for large-scale improvement, while other experts believe decentralization is key to improvement.
- Central authority can result in more consistency in curriculum and teaching methods, which lead to higher academic success.
- Decentralization allows leaders more autonomy and flexibility.
- Redirecting resources and staff, ridding the organization of excess bureaucracy can be positive effects of decentralization.

- Negative effects of decentralization include inappropriate power-wielding and the tendency to make short-term decisions with long-term consequences.
- Caring leaders understand intrinsic interests and act to protect them, not yielding total control to state and central authority.
- Forcing leaders to employ specific means results in losing the right to question and to make local choices.
- The number of nontraditional leaders in urban systems is on the rise.
- Nontraditional leaders are viewed as being able to entertain new and radical approaches to teaching and learning and maintain organizational independence.

# CRITICAL THINKING

William Ouchi is a business educator, author, and theorist who has turned his attention to educational systems. He and fellow authors posit that decentralization is a must for large public education systems, although he acknowledges most educators view this with skepticism:

> Local solutions and autonomy, along with it accountability—these are the kinds of things we in management research focus on. Unfortunately, you won't find many people in education who have an interest in studying this topic. . . . Few business organizations that live in a competitive world could survive that much growth without fundamentally altering their organizational form through decentralization. But school districts, not living in a competitive world, have not changed their form. They remain every bit as centralized today as when they were one-fifteenth their present size. But the fact that they don't go out of business doesn't mean they aren't failing. The evidence is very clear that satisfaction with public schools has been eroding steadily for the past 30 or 40 years. (Ouchi et al., 2005, p. 933)

Contrast Ouchi's viewpoint with Eisinger and Hula's research findings of the 100 largest school systems in the United States.

- Systems run by gunslinger leaders are not significantly more troubled than systems run by traditional leaders
- Student performance on standardized tests does not seem consistently worse in systems that have gunslingers at the helm
- The conditions that lead to the choice of a gunslinger likely have less to do with comparative degrees of dysfunction than of idiosyncratic community dynamics (Eisinger & Hula, 2004, pp. 632–633).

The question for critical thought is why state legislators or mayors or business leaders prefer to choose a nontraditional school leader.

## ADDITIONAL READING RESOURCES

Richard F. Elmore, *Building a New Structure for School Leadership*. The Albert Shanker Institute, 2000.

Kitty Kelly Epstein, *A Different View of Urban Schools: Civil Rights, Critical Race Theory, and Unexplored Realities*. Peter Lang, 2006.

Wayne K. Hoy and Cecil G. Miskel, *Educational Administration: Theory, Research, and Practice* (7 ed.). McGraw-Hill, 2004.

Henry Mintzberg, *The Structuring of Organizations*. Prentice Hall, 1979.

William Ouchi, Richard Riordan, Linda Lingle, and Lyman Porter, Making public schools work: Management reform as the key. *Academy of Management Journal*, December 2005.

Wendy Togneri and Stephen E. Anderson, *Beyond Islands of Excellence: What Districts Can Do to Improve Instruction and Achievement in All Schools—A Leadership Brief*. Learning First Alliance, 2003.

For more information on central authority vs. site-based autonomy, check these sites:

Learning First America's *Beyond Islands of Excellence* www.learningfirst. org/publications/districts/

Education Week's *Learning to Lead* www.edweek.org/ew/articles/2005/09/ 14/03leader-about.h25.html

# U N I T 2

# Context of Educational Leadership

In times of change, learners inherit the Earth, while the learned find themselves beautifully equipped to deal with a world that no longer exists.

—Eric Hoffer

School matters like performance, culture, and improvement are at the heart of daily operations and leaders may think they have learned all they need to know about them. Some school matters can easily be thought of as fundamental givens or as resistant to change, but that would be a mistake. Issues related to the context or milieu of the organization are often the most complex to tease apart and analyze. Yet they cannot be ignored because they make a profound contribution to effectiveness and improvement.

*Performance assessment* is an essential process, not likely to disappear from sight. What makes this process problematic and issue-laden for many educational leaders is tying student achievement to teacher performance. This direct linkage changes the nature of teacher work dramatically, as is obvious in the range of viewpoints presented in the readings. One author contends that when principals rate teachers, a lot of negative things can happen, despite good intentions. Another author proposes that traditional performance measures are no longer worthwhile. Another examines problems in evaluating the performance of teams.

The final viewpoint on the issue of performance assessment proposes a new way of evaluating teachers.

The readings on *systems thinking* provide different viewpoints on how leaders become systems thinkers. At heart, a systems thinker knows the importance of asking questions instead of giving answers. Asking how can I help you deal with today's reality and manage change is very different from declaring I know what you need to do. Beyond the clichés and short lists that often mark change literature, the systems approach places decision making and strategic planning in their rightful context. Taken together, the readings establish a framework of theoretical knowledge and practical experience that enables leaders to become more adept at viewing patterns from the balcony, instead of getting tangled up on the floor.

One of the least analyzed factors of student achievement is *organizational culture*. Some view this factor as too nebulous to shape, much less to control. Yet educators recognize that a strong positive culture is a fundamental component of student success. This stance is reflected in a reading that describes culture as the hidden curriculum of schools. A counter viewpoint is offered in a reading that posits the question: can school culture change? Daily interactions in a school can sometimes be dysfunctional but no one has the skills to correct them. The final reading is a close look at the passive-aggressive behaviors of people in organizations and what leaders can do to lessen dysfunctional behaviors.

*Reform* is in the bloodstream of educational institutions. Until recently reform was localized, even optional—like a vitamin for better health. Now reform is comprehensive, even pervasive—like a transfusion of the entire system. Because current educational reforms are so widespread, the first viewpoint deals with the capacity to adopt reforms and innovations. But are current reforms—pervasive as they are—sufficient in this age of knowledge-creation, competitiveness, and innovation? No, according to a report commissioned by the National Center on Education and the Economy. Another viewpoint questions whether education reforms per se are adequate when economic, political, and social reforms are ignored. A companion viewpoint makes the case that schools with showcase reforms often overshadow other schools in the system, which is a social justice issue leaders should consider.

**Issue 4:** What Performance Assessment Practices Should Educational Leaders Consider Today?

**Issue 5:** How Can a Systems Approach Help Educational Leaders Manage Change?

**Issue 6:** How Do Educational Leaders Shape Organizational Culture?

**Issue 7:** What Do Educational Leaders Need to Understand about Organizational Improvement and School Reform?

Quote: Eric Hoffer, *Reflections on the Human Condition*, HarperCollins, 1973.

# ISSUE 4

# What Performance Assessment Practices Should Educational Leaders Consider Today?

Performance assessment is standard operating procedure for schools and institutions, so why should leaders bother to think about which practices make sense for today's educational systems? For decades the formula has been simple: The administrator observed the faculty member and completed a simple form. After all, annual review was really pro forma because compensation has been based on education and experience. But times have changed and demand for high performance is a very public and very controversial issue. Whether the educational organization is a school, a college, a professional association, or an agency of government, people want to know if its faculty and staff are actually improving teaching and learning. The public may not be interested in the organization's internal processes, but they are definitely interested in its outcomes.

Increasingly, educational leaders are called on to influence an organization's performance. This may seem an obvious role for leaders; however, organizational practices in supervision and assessment are still underdeveloped:

> A change in mindset and culture is required to develop and use performance measures to improve performance. Agencies can lay the foundation for these changes by encouraging and fostering the use of performance measures. This will happen only if senior managers support and participate in the process itself. (Patrick T. Plunkett, *Eight Steps to Develop and Use Information Technology Performance Measures Effectively*. Washington, DC: General Services Administration, ND)

The "change in mindset" started with the federal government's first performance measurement legislation in 1993—the Government Performance Results Act. Since then, performance measurement has become a significant part of administrative practice, not only for government agencies but for corporations and nonprofits. The move by schools and institutions to adopt performance-based budgeting, merit pay, and balanced score cards are obvious signals that performance measures deserve more attention.

Of all the review processes an organization undertakes, employee performance may be the most neglected. The tools have been around for so long and are so standardized that leaders often take them for granted. But which review processes make sense today? Isn't one process as good as another? Obviously this is not the case. As the systems approach penetrates educational organizations, leaders are beginning to question conventional performance measurement that stands separate from other aspects of the organization. From a systems approach, the alignment process starts with reviewing institution-wide goals and objectives, then outlining strategies, then identifying resources, and *then* choosing appropriate performance measures. Leaders need to be clear about what employees will be responsible for in order to generate specific performance criteria. It's a matter of linking everything together, from mission to goals to actions to results to assessment.

The first roundtable viewpoint deals with leaders' ability to predict performance. "When Principals Rate Teachers" describes the results of a study of school leaders who rated teachers on a variety of performance criteria. In addition to specific characteristics, leaders assessed teachers' ability to improve math and reading achievement. Keep in mind that these leaders did not use achievement test data to assess performance, yet they were able to do a good job of accurately assessing teachers' effectiveness. So is a leader-led assessment of performance as good as a performance review process based on student standardized scores? This reading tells the best and the worst that can happen when leaders rate teachers.

A newer way of reviewing professional performance is the 360-degree assessment, a multi-source feedback system. Essentially, a teacher or staff member is provided with confidential feedback from several people, including peers, administrators, perhaps parents or students. Rather than one administrator measuring the individual against standards, the input comes from numerous sources. Ideally, the results of feedback are used to verify strengths and determine areas of development. In the second reading, "Assessment Alternatives: Appraising Organizational Performance," Ralph Jacobson explores some of the issues related to 360-degree feedback. Jacobson is not completely convinced about the effectiveness of this assessment process; he contends there are simpler, more effective ways to provide feedback that will improve individual and organizational performance.

Another question leaders are asking is what to do about team evaluation. Is traditional individual performance assessment appropriate or should more wholistic measures be used for teams? The authors of the third reading respond to this question on the basis of a national survey of organizations that utilize teamwork. The findings discussed in "Project Teams: How Good Are They?" indicate that performance review of teams is woefully lacking. The practices of teams and the assessment of team members are not yet aligned, which leaves leaders wondering how to manage an initiative if teamwork cannot be assessed effectively.

"It's Time to Rethink Teacher Supervision and Evaluation" paints a depressing scenario of current performance review practices. In a surprising twist, the author proposes that the theory behind current practice may be wrong, thus placing blame on our assumptions, not on supervisors and leaders. Marshall's premise is that leaders conduct "microevaluations," which are an incomplete picture of instruction. The trouble is microevaluations are a conventional practice that does not fit with the high-stakes environment of teachers and their students. For Marshall, this is incongruous and needs to be rethought.

Performance review, once regarded as a routine practice, is increasingly seen as a thorny issue for leaders. The conventional practices of earlier times are no longer viable, leaving organizations to search for better matches between contemporary mandates for student achievement and performance assessment of teachers.

## SOURCES

Brian Jacob and Lars Lefgren, When principals rate teachers. *Education Next*, Spring 2006.

Ralph Jacobson, Assessment alternatives: Appraising organizational performance. *Chief Learning Officer*, November 2005.

Howard M. Guttman and Andrew Longman, Project teams: How good are they? *Quality Progress*, February 2006.

Kim Marshall, It's time to rethink teacher supervision and evaluation. *Phi Delta Kappan*, June 2005.

# When Principals Rate Teachers

## Brian Jacob and Lars Lefgren

Elementary- and secondary-school teachers in the United States traditionally have been compensated according to salary schedules based solely on experience and education. Concerned that this system makes it difficult to retain talented teachers and provides few incentives for them to work to raise student achievement while in the classroom, many policymakers have proposed merit-pay programs that link teachers' salaries directly to their apparent impact on student achievement.

Until recently, only a handful of isolated districts had attempted such programs. Now entire state systems are moving toward merit pay, with new policies established recently in Florida and Texas requiring districts to set teachers' salaries based in part on the gains their students are making on the state's accountability exam.

Implementing a merit-pay system, however, comes with challenges. Students often have more than one teacher but take only one high-stakes test. How do we know which teacher to reward? If students are not tested annually in each subject, how do we determine the merit of a teacher in a year without testing? How do we fairly assess the impact of a teacher during a testing year if we do not know how students performed during the previous school year? Can a merit-pay system overcome these obstacles?

One option is to turn to principals and ask them to help determine the size of pay raises. Such subjective performance assessments are already used to evaluate untenured teachers, and they play a large role in promotion and compensation decisions in other occupations. While principals can and do judge teachers' performance, however, there is little good evidence on the accuracy of their judgments.

The research reported in this paper fills this gap. We found that principals in a western school district did a good job of assessing teachers' effectiveness. In fact, principals are quite good at identifying those teachers who produce the largest and smallest standardized achievement gains in their schools (the top and bottom 10–20 percent). They are less able to distinguish among teachers in the middle of this distribution (the middle 60–80 percent), suggesting that merit-pay programs that reward or sanction teachers should be based on evaluations by principals and should be focused on the highest- and lowest-performing teachers.

## A REPRESENTATIVE SAMPLE

We surveyed all 13 elementary-school principals in a midsized school district, that asked to remain anonymous, in the western United States. We asked them to rate the teachers in their schools on a variety of performance dimensions. The survey, conducted in February 2003, provides evaluations by their principals of 202 elementary-school teachers in grades 2 through 6.

The teachers included in the study are fairly representative of elementary-school teachers nationwide. Sixteen percent of them are men, the average age is 42, and average teaching experience is 12 years. Most of these teachers attended a local university; 10 percent attended another in-state college; and 6 percent attended a school out of state. Seventeen percent of them have a master's degree or higher, and most are licensed in either early childhood education or elementary education. Finally, 8 percent of the teachers in our sample taught in a mixed-grade classroom in 2002–03, and 5 percent were in a "split" classroom, sharing a single contract and dividing the school day with another teacher. The students in grades 2 through 6 in the district are predominantly white (73 percent), with a sizable ethnic minority (Latino students compose 21 percent of the elementary population); 48 percent of them receive a free or reduced-price lunch. Achievement levels in the district are almost exactly at the average of the nation (49th percentile on the Stanford Achievement Test).

All elementary-school students in the district take a set of exams each year, in reading and math. These multiple-choice, criterion-referenced tests cover topics that are closely linked to the district's learning objectives. While student achievement results have not been linked to rewards or sanctions for schools until recently, the results of the exams have been distributed to parents annually for at least the past decade, years before implementation of the No Child Left Behind law. This latter fact is important because our study relies on a consistent data set covering the years 1998 through 2003. The district has not had a merit-pay program for teachers at any time during this period.

*Why is it important to avoid a "value-added" measure of student learning in linking student achievement data to teacher performance?*

To ensure that we could link student achievement data to the appropriate teacher, we limited our sample to classroom teachers, omitting music and gym teachers as well as librarians. We excluded kindergarten and first-grade teachers because earlier achievement exams were not available for their students; this prevented us from developing a "value-added" measure of student learning. We retain in our analysis the small number of teachers who share a contract, each teaching only half of the school day. For our analysis, the gains made by students in these classes count toward the estimated value added of each of the two teachers.

## CAN PRINCIPALS IDENTIFY EFFECTIVE TEACHERS?

Principals were asked not only to provide a rating of overall teacher effectiveness, but also to assess, on a scale from one (inadequate) to ten (exceptional), specific teacher characteristics (ten altogether), including dedication and work ethic, classroom management, parent satisfaction, positive relationship with administrators, and ability to improve math and reading achievement. Principals were assured that their responses would be completely confidential and would not be revealed to the teachers or to any other employee of the school district.

While there was some variation among principals, the overall assessments they gave teachers were generally quite high, with an average of 8.1. Only 10 percent of the assessments fell below a 6, and the average rating for the least-generous principal was still a 6.7. At the same time, principals did not simply assign similar scores to each of their teachers. In fact, the principals generally used 5 to 6 different ratings for the teachers in their school.

Because principals differ in the generosity and degree of variation in the ratings they give, we placed all the ratings on the same scale by subtracting from each teacher's rating the average rating given by that teacher's principal and then dividing by the principal's standard deviation. We did this separately for each specific aspect of teacher performance about which principals were asked.

We compared a principal's assessment of how effective a teacher is at raising student reading or math achievement, one of the specific items principals were asked about, with that teacher's actual ability to do so as measured by their value added, the difference in student achievement that we can attribute to the teacher. To estimate the value added by a teacher, we examine the performance of her students after accounting for a wide variety of student and classroom characteristics that could affect achievement independent of the teacher's ability. These characteristics include race, gender, eligibility for the federal lunch program, limited English proficiency, and, most important, previous student achievement. We also take advantage of the availability of data on the same teachers from as far back as the 1996–97 school year; this enables us to distinguish long-term teacher quality from the possibly idiosyncratic performance of a class in any one year.

We find a positive correlation between a principal's assessment of how effective a teacher is at raising student achievement and that teacher's success in doing so as measured by the value-added approach: 0.32 for reading and 0.36 for math. These correlations are based not on a principal's overall rating of the teacher, but rather on the principal's personal assessment of how effective the teacher is at "raising student math (or reading) achievement." Previous studies of evaluations by principals have used only the overall rating of the teacher, a less direct assessment of a teacher's ability to raise student performance. Using the overall rating in that way could compromise the accuracy of subjective performance evaluations, especially if principals value characteristics of teachers that are unrelated to their effect on student performance. Our findings lead us to conclude that principals are able to identify accurately this dimension of teacher effectiveness.

Why aren't these correlations even higher? One possible explanation is that principals focus on the average test scores in a teacher's classroom rather than on student *improvement*. There is some evidence for this conjecture. The correlation between ratings by principals and the average test scores of a teacher's students is significantly higher than the correlation between ratings by principals and the teacher's value-added rating in reading (0.56 versus 0.32), though not in math.

Another reason could be that principals focus on their most recent observations of teachers. We do find, for example, that the average achievement gains in a teacher's classroom in 2002–03 is a modestly stronger predictor of the principal's rating than the gains in any previous year. In theory, it is possible that principals are correct in assuming that a teacher's effectiveness changes over time so that teachers' most recent experience is the best indicator of their actual effectiveness. If that were the case, however, we would expect to find that principals' ratings are more highly correlated with value-added measures that have been adjusted to account for the fact that teachers tend to be less effective in their first one or two years in the classroom. In fact, the correlation between principals' ratings and experience-adjusted value-added measures is no higher than the correlation with our baseline value-added measures. The bigger mistake principals make, it seems, is not adequately accounting for students' incoming ability.

While informative about principals' overall abilities, a simple correlation does not tell us whether principals are more or less effective at identifying teachers at certain points on the ability distribution. We therefore estimated the percentage of teachers that a principal can correctly identify in the top group within his or her school. We found that the teachers identified by principals as being in the top category were, in fact, in the top category according to the value-added measures about 52 percent of the time in reading and 69 percent of the time in mathematics. If principals randomly assigned ratings to teachers, we would expect the corresponding probabilities to be 14 and 26 percent, respectively. This suggests that principals have considerable ability to identify teachers in the top of the distribution. The results are similar if one examines principals' ability to identify teachers in the bottom of the ability distribution.

*What are some factors that make it difficult for principals to distinguish among teachers in the middle of the ability distribution?*

Despite their success with the top and bottom of the distribution, principals are significantly less successful at distinguishing among teachers in the middle of the ability distribution. Principals correctly identify only 49 percent of teachers as being better than the median teacher in their school in boosting students' reading scores, relative to the 33 percent that one would expect if principals' ratings were randomly assigned. Principals appear somewhat better at distinguishing between teachers in the middle of the distribution in math (they correctly placed 54 percent of teachers above the median, compared with the 26 percent expected if ratings were random), but they again appear to be better at identifying the best and worst teachers.

One reason that principals might have difficulty distinguishing between teachers in the middle is that the distribution of teachers' value-added ratings is highly compressed. However, our analysis of the data suggests that this is not the case. Teachers who receive ratings at or close to the median in the school have estimated value-added measures that are quite widely dispersed.

# WHAT CHARACTERISTICS OF TEACHERS DO PRINCIPALS VALUE?

Of course, the effects of moving to a system of compensation based on assessment by principals depend on the relative importance they place on a teacher's ability to raise standardized test scores when making overall assessments of teachers' effectiveness. While such preferences could theoretically be set by district administrators or other policymakers, it is likely that principals would retain some autonomy over personnel decisions, so their preferences are important to investigate. We therefore compared principals' overall rating of each teacher with their assessment of various teacher attributes to examine how principals value different dimensions of quality in teachers.

Perhaps not surprisingly, teachers' ratings on many (though not all) of the individual survey items are highly correlated. Based on the relationships between the questions, we created three groups of teachers' quality characteristics and reanalyzed the results. The first group captures what might be described as traditional teaching ability and includes the ratings of classroom management, organization, and ability to improve students' test scores. The second, including the principal's assessments of a teacher's relationship with colleagues and administrators, measures a teacher's collegiality. The third measures student satisfaction and includes the principal's ratings of student satisfaction and the teacher as a role model.

Ability, collegiality, and student satisfaction all contribute independently to a principal's overall evaluation of a teacher, but principals weigh the set of questions measuring teachers' ability to improve student achievement and to manage a classroom most heavily. An increase of one standard deviation in a principal's evaluation of a teacher's management and teaching ability, for example, is associated with an increase of 0.56 standard deviations in the principal's overall rating. In comparison, an increase of one standard deviation in teacher collegiality is associated with an increase in overall ratings of roughly one-third of a standard deviation in overall rating. Meanwhile, teachers scoring one standard deviation higher in student satisfaction score just 0.15 standard deviations in their overall rating, all else being equal.

# PREDICTING PERFORMANCE

We should care about the quality of principals' assessments of teacher quality not just for their reliability in a merit-pay system, but also for their ability to identify teachers who will continue to improve student achievement. In order to get a sense of how well principals' assessments forecast teachers' performance, we examined how well these assessments predict future student achievement gains. For our February 2003 survey of principals, that meant evaluating scores on the spring 2003 tests. We compared the predictive accuracy of a principal's assessment of teacher effectiveness with the predictive accuracy of a teacher's value-added rating. We also measured the accuracy of the traditional determinants of teachers' salaries, experience and education, in predicting those scores. Throughout, we accounted for differences in previous student achievement, student demographics, and classroom characteristics.

Our findings suggest that ratings by principals, both overall ratings and ratings of a teacher's ability to improve achievement, effectively predict a student's future achievement gains (see Figure 1). Students whose teachers receive an overall rating one standard deviation above the mean are predicted to score roughly 0.06 standard deviations higher in reading than students whose teacher received an average rating. By way of comparison, students receiving free or reduced-price lunch in the same district experience achievement gains approximately 0.16 standard deviations lower than similar students who are not eligible for such programs. Assignment to a teacher with a favorable evaluation by her principal appears to be more important for math performance. An increase of one standard deviation in the principal's evaluation predicts an

### Figure 1   Principal Distinctions

*Principals do a reasonably good job of identifying those teachers who are better (and worse) at raising student test scores. Not surprisingly, the best way to predict how effective a teacher will be is to find out how effective the teacher has been in the past. Differences in teacher's salaries within a school system are entirely unrelated to teachers' effectiveness.*

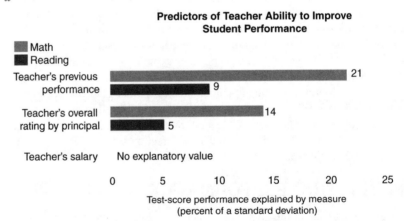

*Note:* The figure shows the degree to which an increase of one standard deviation in each variable is related to student achievement in 2003. Previous performance is measured by the teacher's estimated success in raising test scores between 1998 and 2002. The analysis controls for student demographic characteristics, classroom characteristics, fixed effects for grade and school, and lagged math and reading scores. All reported effects are significant at the 0.05 level.

*Source:* Author's calculations from district's data.

increase of 0.14 standard deviations in math performance, roughly on par with the disadvantage associated with coming from a low-income family.

Measures of teachers' value added in previous years are an even better predictor of future gains in students' achievement than are principal ratings. These results, which are similar for math and reading, suggest that teachers' impact on student achievement, as measured by simple value-added measures of teacher effectiveness, remain fairly stable over time and that principals' ratings effectively capture a substantial fraction of these stable differences in teachers' effectiveness.

We do not find any statistically significant relationship between the number of years a teacher has taught and students' achievement, though this is probably due to the necessary omission of first-year teachers (because we cannot measure their value added for a previous school year). Other studies have found that first-year teachers tend to perform worse on average than experienced teachers. Education does have some predictive power. Teachers with advanced degrees have students who score roughly 0.10 standard deviations higher. We hesitate to say that education itself is producing these gains, because a teacher's level of education is likely to be associated with personal characteristics not accounted for in our analysis, and these may be the very factors responsible for the improvements in student achievement.

Perhaps our most interesting finding is that the salaries teachers in this district received in 2002–03 bore no relation at all to their impact on student achievement. Students with highly paid teachers made no more progress than those with teachers who had low salaries.

## CONCLUSIONS

In sum, our results suggest that student achievement (as measured by standardized test scores) would probably improve more under a system based on principals' assessments than in systems where compensation is based solely on education and experience. This is because principals would be able to identify and reward the very best teachers while, at the same time, identifying the least competent teachers for remediation or dismissal.

To the extent that the most important staffing decisions involve sanctioning incompetent teachers and rewarding the very best teachers, a principal-based assessment system may affect achievement as positively as a merit-pay system based solely on student test results. Moreover, evaluation by the principal has the potential to offset some of the potential negative consequences of test-based accountability systems. If principals can observe inputs as well as outputs, they may be able to ensure that teachers increase student achievement through improvements in pedagogy, classroom management, or curriculum rather than teaching to the test. Principals can also evaluate teachers on the basis of a broader spectrum of educational outputs in addition to test scores that parents may value. At the same time, the inability of principals to distinguish between a broad middle range of teacher quality suggests caution in

*How much responsibility should principals have for monitoring teachers' effectiveness?*

relying on principals for fine-grained performance determinations, as might be required under certain merit-pay policies.

Two important caveats to consider when interpreting our results. First, we conducted our analysis in a context where principals were not being evaluated on the basis of their ability to identify effective teachers. It is possible that principals' ability to identify the best-performing teachers would be enhanced by a school system where the principals had more responsibility for monitoring teachers' effectiveness. At the same time, social or political pressures might make principals less willing to assess teachers honestly if their judgments directly influenced teachers' compensation. Second, our analysis focuses on the *source* of the teacher assessment; we do not address the type of rewards or sanctions associated with teacher performance. This is clearly an important dimension of any performance management system, and one would not expect either a principal-based or a test-based assessment system to have a substantial impact on student outcomes unless it were accompanied by meaningful consequences.

# Assessment Alternatives: Appraising Organizational Performance

## Ralph Jacobson

Considerable corporate time and resources are devoted to providing feedback to employees. In general, the vast majority of human resources professionals use the 360-degree competency assessment process as a primary means to provide feedback to employees regarding their performance. Employees, with the support of their managers, are expected to analyze this feedback to determine their strengths and weaknesses and to develop a plan to enhance their personal productivity and effectiveness. The process has become so widespread that its power to shape positive behaviors is accepted as fact. Legions of consulting organizations are willing to assist in devising competencies and generating feedback reports. But does the considerable time and investment devoted to this feedback process actually deliver a significant return? Do the reports and discussions with managers actually improve performance?

The issues involved with the 360-degree assessment include the determination of competencies, interpretation of results and subsequent efforts to use the data to create development plans. There are simpler, more cost-effective and more powerful methods for providing feedback that are more likely to improve individual and organization performance.

## VALIDITY: DETERMINING THE RIGHT COMPETENCIES

To achieve statistical validity and ensure that the targeted competencies positively impact performance, managers must first identify the most competent employees. Then, they can pinpoint the specific knowledge, skills and abilities of these individuals that account for their higher performance. Establishing the validity of this data requires rigorous collection of job-specific behaviors and comparisons between highly and less productive employees. Further, focus groups, expert panels, behavioral interviews and psychological tests are often used to confirm that the right competencies have indeed been identified.

Because validating competencies is expensive and time-consuming, most human resources professionals avoid this expense by selecting a number of competencies from pre-established lists. Alternatively, they may decide to develop a competency list through the use of focus groups of senior organizational leaders. Such lists may or may not identify the competencies that lead to outstanding performance.

*What is the value of using a pre-established list of competencies for assessing teacher performance?*

# SoftBrands: The Toolbox Approach to Organizational Success
## Ralph Jacobson

SoftBrands is a provider of enterprise-wide software solutions focused on the hospitality and manufacturing industries. For David Gahn, vice president of the Americas for Softbrands, building the success of the organization was a new assignment. But for Randy Tofteland, SoftBrands' president, it was an unresolved challenge that had been delegated to two previous vice presidents. The U.K. division, which the organization had acquired through a merger many years ago, continued to be a drain on the corporation. Tofteland charged Gahn with the task of either quickly fixing the ailing division or divesting it.

Previously, Renee Conklin, vice president of human resources, had invested heavily in traditional types of leadership training that emphasized 360-degree competency feedback and learning about personality types. Though a few individual leaders may have found some of this knowledge personally useful, the training clearly had not impacted business results. Although the company's leaders were highly seasoned, none of them had faced such a difficult and competitive market. Developing leaders who could face challenging assignments was central to the organization's long-term success.

Leaders at SoftBrands required an alternative development process that would help them quickly improve business performance. Conklin shifted her leadership development approach to provide the top and middle management teams with toolbox training, which was specifically designed not to improve their individual leadership capabilities, but to teach the leadership groups how to address current organizational leadership challenges. The toolbox training provided specific leadership language, the leader's map and the leadership tools to address the organization's challenges.

Gahn gathered together the employees of the U.K. division. With them, he used the leadership change map and the tools to analyze the market, develop scenarios, determine the organization's critical core competencies, and identify and balance the paradoxes that stood in their way. Through this process, he was able to gain employee commitment to a new strategic scenario. Tofteland was delighted with the newly crafted strategic plan and gave the U.K. division the permission, time and the resources needed to reframe its future.

In early 2002 Terry Peterson, who was responsible for the company's service contract business, watched first-quarter revenues fall quickly.

Prior to the leadership toolbox training, Peterson would have felt compelled to cut expenses and lay off employees. This time, however, he took a different route. He pulled out the leader's map and applied the leadership tools to the task at hand. Rather than follow his usual practice of tightening up, Peterson openly shared the current business reality with the employees and invited them to participate in the process of reinventing their future.

The organizational results achieved by the use of the newly learned leadership tools were astounding. At the end of the first year, revenues of the U.K. division grew 30 percent, almost all of which fell to the bottom line. While the annual industry market growth rate for manufacturing software in the year following the training was 3 percent, the U.K. division delivered a whopping 23 percent increase in revenues. By the end of the second quarter of 2002, Peterson's contract services group had erased the shortfall of the first quarter and exceeded the yearly budget revenue forecast as a result of the five new products that had been produced with the help of the leadership tools.

These two leaders learned that powerful results can be achieved by using the right leadership tools. They learned how to effectively involve employees in the process of analyzing the competitive environment and how to put in place an infrastructure for realizing financial success. Overwhelming market challenges could have led to the worst experiences of their long careers. Instead, Peterson and Gahn successfully navigated changes that led to both organizational success and high levels of personal satisfaction.

Though it has been three years since their first and only formal leadership toolbox training, the leadership map and the tools remain central aspects of SoftBrands' leadership strategies.

## ORGANIZATION-WIDE COMPETENCIES

Applying a short list of competencies to all employees or to broad job categories could simplify the feedback process, reduce the upfront expenses and support a common set of values and norms. Also, learning efforts may be more efficient when focused around a narrow set of topics. Though a short list of competencies for an entire organization can support working together more effectively, the compromised list is less likely to identify the feedback that is needed to improve specific job performance of each individual. The effectiveness of this approach is therefore significantly diminished.

*Why are predetermined competencies for a 360-degree assessment **not** a good idea?*

## FOCUS ON THE JOB

Most jobs require an array of competencies, which are usually defined from the perspective of individual managers. But flatter organizational structures and greater use of cross-functional teams require groups of people to perform in ambiguous and free-flowing situations. Knowing how employees should and do perform in specific group or project situations may be more important than knowing how they perform as individual contributors. The utilization of a unique combination of skills and personalities within a larger, constantly shifting structure determines organizational performance. A competency that is viewed as effective within the context of an individual job may be ineffective in a team environment. The general competency approach may not distinguish between these two work requirements.

## THE ASSESSMENT PART OF THE PROCESS

In the usual 360-degree competency assessment, co-workers and managers are given a list of competencies and a set of behavioral anchors for each to use in evaluating individual employee performance. They are then asked to check their level of agreement or the frequency with which the employee must use each competency to perform in an excellent manner. Two clear issues emerge with this method of assessment. Generally, five to eight people are asked to make the assessment. As a result of the small sample size, one or two answers will have a significant impact on the averaged score for that item. Further, because relatively few people write in the comment sections on the form to clarify and further describe the behaviors they have observed and the rationale for their ratings, it is difficult to specify the context in which they expect a particular competency to be exhibited. Thus, the numerical score is likely an insufficient indicator of the behaviors that are expected to lead to desired employee performance.

## INTERPRETATION OF RESULTS

*What is the theory behind the argument that the purpose of competency assessment is developing the strongest or most critical competencies?*

Most people are content with their performance of competencies where feedback suggests they are performing in the average to above-average ranges with respect to their peer group. However, feeling content with an average score on a critical competency may be an ineffective strategy for driving sought-after performance.

In their book "The Extraordinary Leader," authors John Zenger and Joe Folkman, Ph.D., demonstrate empirically that the best leaders possess a few truly outstanding competencies. Leaders whose competency scores fall completely in the average range are perceived to be only 34 percent effective. Those with one strength above average are perceived to be 64 percent effective. Those with three strengths above average are perceived to be 80 percent effective.

The purpose of competency assessment should be to pinpoint and develop those few critical competencies that yield extraordinary and disproportionate performance. This is a more effective development strategy than shoring up less important competencies so that they are all perceived to be in at least the average range.

# DEVELOPMENT PROGRAMS

Managers are expected to work with employees to develop approaches to improve targeted competencies, but few managers have the expertise to actually develop such a plan. For example, managers have difficulty effectively differentiating those skills that can be taught from innate abilities that are less likely to be improved with development activities. Trying to improve what are viewed as innate abilities is likely to frustrate employees.

Employees are more likely to improve their performance by practicing new behaviors in a work environment that allows room for experimentation and offers specific, timely and helpful feedback. Unfortunately few managers today believe they can allow employees to focus on anything other than immediate work issues. Without management support, employees are likely to revert to old behaviors. In such situations, performance feedback will have only a momentary impact on employee performance.

# FEEDBACK ALTERNATIVES

On its face, the competency assessment process appears logical and relatively easy to administer. In reality, the process falls short of the goal of improving individual and organization performance. Two alternate approaches are far more effective: providing direct feedback and using leadership tools that are simple to learn and proven to have bottom-line impact. The direct-feedback approach actively involves the employee and all critical stakeholders in the improvement process. The leader's toolbox approach skips the diagnostic assessment completely and instead provides a common language for leadership at all levels, as well as many management and leadership tools to more directly achieve bottom-line improvement.

In the traditional 360-degree competency approach, employee feedback remains confidential, presumably to encourage honest responses. Major stakeholders, such as peers and associates, have little involvement in the individual's performance improvement beyond providing the initial assessment. This limited responsibility causes several problems. First, most organizational performance requires people to work together to make things happen. Even when one person improves his or her performance, the group may not perform better. More importantly, significant behavior change takes time and encouragement. Colleagues who are accustomed to an individual's on-the-job behaviors may not notice an improvement in performance or provide the necessary encouragement to sustain the improved on-the-job behaviors.

Marshall Goldsmith and Howard Morgan studied more than 86,000 people for their article, "Leadership is a Contact Sport: The 'Follow-up Factor' in Management Development," in Strategy+Business (September 2004). They state that the most critical factor in achieving positive long-term improvement is consistent, ongoing interaction and follow-up with colleagues. Dramatic performance improvement did not result from the assessment itself, but from the mutual discussion about development priorities with co-workers over time. Individuals who did not have the benefit of ongoing dialogue "showed improvement that barely exceeded random chance." Creating direct and frequent dialogue about performance has far greater impact than simply assessing behavior.

Within the direct feedback approach, the role of human resources professionals shifts from providing assessments to teaching people how to ask for and receive feedback. They train managers and internal coaches to help employees process feedback information and to create effective development plans. In this approach, responsibility for performance improvement shifts from the human resources professionals to managers and employees. Direct feedback creates opportunities for honest dialogue between people and provides the impetus for them to work closely and effectively with one another.

Many excellent leadership tools are described in great detail in business books and articles, but few of these tools are actually adopted in practice. It is more effective to encourage leaders at all organization levels to use a common leadership language and to employ processes and tools that can be applied to a broad range of organization challenges. Teaching leaders how to develop organization and functional strategies, engage critical stakeholders and coach employees in their improvement processes will more likely lead to successful implementation of large-scale organizational change. When leaders at all levels realize they face common obstacles to success, they are then more likely to open themselves to learning and personal growth. Learning and sound leadership practices address an organization's performance needs for the long run.

When using the toolbox methodology, the role of the human resources professional shifts from delivering individual assessments to determining the leadership language and processes that will have greatest impact on the organization's success. The human resources professional works closely with senior management to create practice fields in which to apply new learning to real, ongoing business issues. Creating a direct relationship between learning and organizational performance shifts responsibility for learning, thinking and development to senior leaders, where it rightly belongs.

*What are some of the strengths and weaknesses of the direct feedback approach?*

## SUGGESTIONS FOR THE 360-DEGREE APPROACH

If you do decide to use the competency approach, consider the following suggestions:

- Undertake the rigorous process of defining those few behaviors that truly make a difference to organization's success. Avoid selecting competencies from a pre-established list.
- Identify your organization's core organization competencies, which Gary Hamel and C.K. Prahalad define as the integration of skills, technologies and knowledge across the organization that provides disproportionate

competitive advantage. Critical core competencies are difficult for competitors to emulate and are perceived by customers as delivering significant value. The contributions of employees toward shaping the organization's core competence can then become a significant determinant of critical individual competencies.

- Rather than expecting employees to fill out a standard competency questionnaire, teach employees how to actively participate in the process of defining critical competencies. Ask them to be precise, to describe in detail the specific behaviors that support their conclusions. Tell them how to avoid such common evaluation problems as the halo and devil effects.

- Provide development opportunities that will support employees' strengths. Focus only on those areas of weakness that will make a significant difference to effective performance on the job.

# ARTICLE 4.3

# Project Teams: How Good Are They?

## Howard M. Guttman and Andrew Longman

*How do project teams function in K–12 schools?*

**P**roject teams have become the basic work units of the modern enterprise. The ability to complete projects on goal, on time and on budget will likely set apart winners from wannabes in the years ahead. But attaining project success is a tough challenge. In 2004, the Standish Group found 51% of the IT projects it surveyed were seriously late, over budget and off goal.[1]

The IT function is not alone in its project failures, as we all know from the "big bombs" featured in the media over the past several years. Consider these:

- **DaimlerChrysler's troubled Smart car division.** The company's missteps hobbled what should have been a car that was a perfect fit for its time.[2]
- **Huge weapons systems being developed for the Pentagon.** A Government Accountability Office review of 26 weapons systems found the total cost of these programs had increased nearly 15% over the first full-cost estimates.[3]
- **The FBI's Virtual Case File system.** The agency declared an official end to its floundering $170 million effort to overhaul its computer software and said it would take at least three and a half years to develop a new system.[4]
- **The Big Dig, a Boston public works project.** Twenty years and billions of dollars later, there are continued budget overruns, investigations of fraud and a newly opened tunnel with blocked fire exits, falling debris and leaks.[5]
- **Hurricane Katrina response.** Poor project planning and execution, from the White House to the New Orleans mayor's office, turned a natural disaster into a political, economic and human catastrophe.

These examples and countless others raise a number of key questions:

- In general, how are projects currently being managed in organizations?
- How well are individual projects led, planned and executed?
- What causes projects to veer off track?
- What is life like on the typical project team?

To answer these questions, *Quality Progress* teamed up with the consulting firms of Guttman Development Strategies and Kepner-Tregoe. In September 2005, *QP* e-mailed our survey on project team performance to about half its readership. Of the 46,828 people who received the survey, 1,905 responded, for a 4% response rate. Twenty-nine percent of respondents were individual contributors, 42% were first-line and middle managers, and 15% were senior managers. Respondents represented a cross section of industries. Approximately half worked for companies with more than $200 million in revenue and 1,000 employees.

We asked both quantitative and qualitative questions. The qualitative ones asked respondents to identify the most important reasons for project success and failure in their organizations. A representative sampling of answers, called "Voices From the Workplace," is sprinkled throughout the text that follows.

## PROJECT TEAMS: THE BIG PICTURE

From the quantitative responses, a somewhat conflicting picture of projects emerges. On one hand, many respondents were positive about the quality and effectiveness of their organizations' project teams. But few rated their overall project performance as excellent, and, more disturbingly, a significant number reported performance was mediocre at best. When you cut to the heart of the findings, two essential facts stand out:

1. Fewer than half (46.9%) of the projects under way in respondents' organizations always or often meet their goals.
2. Fewer than one-third (32.6%) are always or often completed on time and on budget.

Given these numbers, it's not surprising fewer than half our respondents said their organizations' financial performance was in the top third of their respective industries.

To learn more about what is working and what isn't on project teams, we drilled down, asking respondents a series of specific questions about the way projects are generally managed in their organizations. We began by probing five areas vital to an organization's project success:

1. **Project alignment and goals.** Whether the analogy is with the human anatomy, automobiles or organizations, alignment implies things are effectively lined up to achieve maximum performance. When it comes to projects, how aligned are they, across the board, with overall organization strategy? The good news is 70% of respondents reported their projects were aligned. Yet, nearly one-third reported their projects were off strategy.

    Fuzzy or unrealistic goals kill project effectiveness. While slightly more than half (54%) said their organizations' project goals were often or always clear and attainable, the remaining 46% reported this is only the case sometimes, rarely or never. This points to a significant potential problem related to goal clarity and realism.

2. **Resources and staffing.** This area has frequently been a lightning rod for organizational conflict, and survey responses affirmed it still is.

More than two-thirds of respondents said their organizations' project teams are only sometimes, rarely or never given sufficient resources to accomplish their goals. Insufficient resources was also the most common answer to the open-ended question "What is the most common reason for the failure of projects in your organization?"

More than half our respondents did not think the right people were always or often selected to lead or serve on project teams. In answer to a related question, 84% said employees rarely, if ever, were relieved of their routine job responsibilities while serving on a project team.

3.  **Training and development.** Eighty percent of respondents said only sometimes, rarely or never do employees receive training in project management methodology before serving on a project team. It's probably no coincidence that 62% reported project teams throughout the organization don't often follow a standard methodology to define, plan and implement projects.

4.  **Rewards and recognition.** While the drive to excel may spring from deep within, sustaining that drive over the long term requires ongoing rewards and recognition. So, are project teams receiving sufficient rewards? It seems not—58% of respondents said only sometimes, rarely or never is the successful completion of projects recognized publicly by top management.

    Not many teams receive financial rewards/bonuses for the successful completion of projects, with more than 87% of respondents reporting these are given only sometimes, rarely or never. In nearly 61% of the cases, there is no link between employees' annual reviews and their performance on project teams.

5.  **Senior executive team.** Because top teams exercise an almost gravitational pull on the collective psyche of an organization, we asked for an assessment of the following statement: "Our senior management team serves as a positive role model for project management." Seventy percent of respondents said this occurs sometimes, rarely or never.

    Of all the survey findings, we find this to be the most troublesome. You can have clear, specific and attainable project goals. You can embed the right project management processes and methodologies and train project teams to use them. You can tweak rewards and recognition. But unless the senior team demonstrates high performance, teams elsewhere in the organization will follow the wrong example.

*What prevents leaders from serving as positive role models for project teams?*

Overall, the responses to this section of our survey should raise serious red flags about how organizations view and manage projects. The bottom line: While responses reveal a large number of projects are sufficiently well managed, many others are not. Though these may never show up on a future list of big bombs, continued poor performance will likely compromise the organization's competitive vitality.

# PROJECT TEAMS: UP CLOSE AND PERSONAL

The survey results painted a picture not only of how organizations manage projects in general but also of the personal experiences of respondents when serving on typical project teams—as team leaders, members or facilitators. Not surprisingly, a comparison of the responses of these three groups shows a slightly more optimistic view from the team leaders. Otherwise, among all three groups, the picture that emerged was one of sharp contrasts, with many respondents reporting very good to excellent experiences and many others describing teams that needed substantial improvement.

We began by asking for an assessment of the typical team's goals and roles:

- Two-thirds answered their teams' overall goals were very clear, which is good news—except for the remaining third, who said their goals were only somewhat clear or not at all clear.
- While it's one thing to be clear about your team's overall project goals, it's quite another to be clear about the individual roles of you and the person sitting next to you on a project team. Here again, while the majority (57%) said they were clear about these roles, a significant number (42%) said they were not.

Think of project management processes as organizing principles for team performance. How many typical teams followed standardized processes during their project? Once again, there was good news and bad. Sixty-two percent of respondents said their teams had followed a visible, common project management process—but the remaining 38% said a process wasn't used or they weren't sure. Similarly, 56% said their teams had used a common process for problem solving and decision making, but 43% weren't sure or said the teams hadn't used such a methodology.

We next probed the interactions and behavior of the team members. A house divided does not allow for a high performance team. Energy gets diverted from meeting project goals to dealing with dysfunctional behavior and subterfuge, which is why we asked how well typical project teams handled this critical issue.

The good news: On a scale of one to five—with one equivalent to no tolerance for confrontation/conflicts suppressed and five meaning tensions surfaced and were confronted and resolved—about half (51.3%) gave their teams a four or five. Those teams dealt with conflict in an open manner. But that leaves nearly as many respondents (48.2%) who rated their teams' performance in this area three or lower. And, while only 8.3% reported the team spent more than half its time dealing with unresolved conflict, more than 90% said the team had spent up to half its time in this unproductive activity (62.2% up to a quarter of their time, 28% between one-quarter and one-half of their time).

One of the hallmarks of a high performing team is the degree to which its members see themselves as responsible for the success of the team as a whole, rather than being narrowly "me" focused. Here again, responses were split, with nearly 60% feeling very to highly responsible for the success of their fellow team members and the other 40% feeling no or little responsibility for others.

In terms of intrateam communication, the picture was not much better: On a scale of one to five, with one equivalent to not at all effective and five very effective, nearly 44% of respondents answered one, two or three.

The final questions in the set dealing with experience on a typical project team related to project outcomes. On the positive side, 82% of those who responded said their projects were completed, and 89% said the projects met their goals. However, 36% reported the projects were late, and 26% said they came in over budget, indicating that meeting project goals is often a costly and time consuming enterprise.

## PROJECT LEADERSHIP

In today's project environment, the leader-follower paradigm seems like an antiquated relic from the past. Teams reach the highest levels of performance when members step up to assume greater responsibility for thought leadership and results. Today's project leaders are less directors and more facilitators of team performance. One of their major roles is to keep resources focused and help the team set guidelines for decision making and behavior.

How well does the typical team leader carry out this role? When we asked respondents to tell us how effective their teams' leaders were at helping teams meet their goals—on a scale of one to five, with one being not at all effective and five being very effective—42.5% gave the leader three or less. And, when asked to rate the team leader's overall project management skills on a scale of one to five, with one being poor and five excellent, nearly half gave the team leader a grade of three or less.

Our last two questions about project leadership focused on interpersonal relations. First, we asked how effective the team leader was in managing conflict among team members. With one being poor and five excellent, more than half rated their leaders' conflict management skills three or less. When asked to describe their leader's behavioral style, fewer than half of team leaders were characterized as having a healthy, assertive way of interacting. The remaining half was split nearly equally between the less effective nonassertive and aggressive styles.

Overall, responses indicate there is an across-the-board deficiency of leadership capabilities. In a significant number of cases, project leaders are lacking many of the process and behavioral skills necessary for project success.

## PATHWAYS TO CHANGE

In general, survey respondents reported that, on a significant number of projects, processes are loose, informal and left to chance. In many cases, team behavior is poorly managed and less than productive.

Stepping back from the survey data, how can all projects—those that are performing badly and those that are just average—be improved? One answer: Provide more resources. After all, nearly three-quarters of respondents reported projects were under resourced sometimes, often or always. But this solution may not be realistic, given the resource constraints in most organizations. And it is certainly simplistic, in light of the array of other factors that respondents say lead to project failure. Sadly, there is no one silver bullet.

Based on the survey data and our consulting experiences, moving project teams to higher levels of performance requires an integrated approach that addresses four major areas:

*What is the leader's role in dealing with the issue of scarce resources for project teams?*

1. **Leadership.** Top management teams must learn to serve as role models of high performance. They must become aligned strategically, reach agreement on business goals, be clear on roles and responsibilities, determine ground rules for decision making and strive for transparency in business relationships. In addition, the organization's leaders must provide visible and meaningful support for projects throughout their organization. This includes prioritizing the organization's portfolio of projects to avoid the stop-start syndrome and project overload, providing rewards for superior performance on projects and providing team leaders and members with the requisite technical, process and interpersonal skills needed to succeed.

2. **Process discipline.** As organizations become more matrixed and project teams more cross functional in nature, there is a need to move beyond a helter-skelter project management approach. Project management has evolved into a discipline, and organizations would do well to absorb project management processes, transfer them throughout the ranks and build a knowledge management legacy system that captures lessons learned. Seat-of-the-pants problem solving and decision making on projects is not working. It is crucial for project teams to employ a common, systematic process for resolving the problem solving, decision making and planning issues that come before them.

3. **The performance system.** Think about project teams as mini performance environments that must be carefully managed. Team members must be clear on project goals and the end game, possess the right skills, receive accurate and timely feedback and be aware of the positive and negative consequences for various behaviors.

4. **Interpersonal dynamics.** Given all the performance pressure on project teams and the mounting complexity of the environments in which they operate, it is not surprising that such teams have become holding pens for unproductive behavior. Such behavior takes many forms: putting functional self interest over team accomplishments, engaging in conflict (both overt and hidden), adopting a nonassertive or aggressive style, passing the buck, playing follow the leader and hesitating to confront

one another's poor performance and unacceptable behavior. To eliminate these negative behaviors, all project teams should go through the same alignment process as the senior team and receive training in conflict management and related skills.

While many respondents report experiencing project success, almost all point to an urgent need for improvement. To begin your improvement efforts, ask yourself how your organization's responses would compare to those we received. Then, look to leadership, process discipline, the performance system and interpersonal dynamics as prime targets in which to make the changes that will propel project teams to the next level of performance.

## REFERENCES

1. Frank Hayes, "Chaos Is Back," *Computer World*, Nov. 8, 2004, p. 70.
2. Mark Landler, "DaimlerChrysler To Scale Back MiniCar Unit," *The New York Times*, April 2, 2005, p. C1.
3. Tim McLaughlin, "Report Says Weapons Are Costing More Than Promised," *St. Louis Post-Dispatch*, April 1, 2005, p. A16.
4. Eric Lichtblau, "FBI Ends a Faltering Effort To Overhaul Computer Software," *The New York Times*, March 9, 2005, p. B16.
5. Eileen McNamara, "The Big Dig and Blame Games," *Boston Globe*, Dec. 17, 2003, p. B1.

# It's Time to Rethink Teacher Supervision and Evaluation

## Kim Marshall

A principal boasts that he spends two hours a day in classrooms. And it's true—he really does visit his school's 17 teachers daily, chatting with students and occasionally chiming in on a lesson. But when teachers are asked what kind of feedback they get, they say the principal rarely talks to them about what he sees when he strolls through their classes.

A principal gets complaints from several parents about a history teacher's problems with discipline but is so overwhelmed that she rarely visits his classroom. When she does her required observation of his class, she sees a carefully planned lesson featuring an elaborate PowerPoint presentation and well-behaved students. The principal feels she has no choice but to do a positive write-up of this lesson and give the teacher a satisfactory rating.

A principal spends four entire weekends in April and May completing teacher evaluations just before the deadline. He puts the evaluations into teachers' mailboxes with a cover note attached that reads, "Please let me know if you have any concerns and would like to talk. Otherwise, sign and return by tomorrow." All the teachers sign, nobody requests a meeting, and there is no further discussion.

A well-regarded veteran teacher hasn't been evaluated in five years and rarely sees the principal in her classroom. She takes this as a compliment—her teaching must be "okay." And yet she feels lonely and isolated with her students and wishes the principal would pay an occasional visit and tell her what he thinks.

A sixth-grade teacher has good classroom management and is well liked by students and parents, but his students do poorly on standardized tests. A new principal mentions the disappointing scores, and the teacher launches into a litany of complaints: he always gets the "bad class," most of his students come from dysfunctional families, and he's tired of being asked to "teach to the test." Later that day, the union representative officiously tells the principal that she can't mention test results in a teacher's evaluation.

A principal observes an elaborate hands-on math lesson in a veteran teacher's classroom and notices that the teacher is confusing the terms *mean, median,* and *mode.* The principal notes this error in his mostly positive evaluation, and, in the post-observation conference, the teacher suddenly begins to cry. Ten years later, at his retirement party, the principal asks the teacher what lesson she took away from this incident. "Never to take a risk," she replies.

*How could supervision and evaluation worsen a teacher's effectiveness and therefore decrease student achievement?*

The theory of action behind supervision and evaluation is that they will improve teachers' effectiveness and therefore boost student achievement.[1] This assumption seems logical. But the vignettes above raise a troubling question: what if the theory is wrong? This article takes a close look at this possibility and explores an alternative theory of action.

# WHY DO SUPERVISION AND EVALUATION OFTEN MISS THE MARK?

I believe there are 10 reasons why the conventional supervision and evaluation process is not an effective strategy for improving teaching and learning.

1. *Principals evaluate only a tiny amount of teaching.* If a teacher has five classes a day, that's 900 periods each school year. A principal who formally evaluates a teacher for one full class period a year (a fairly typical scenario). . . .

In this case, the principal evaluated 0.1% of the teacher's instruction. The other 99.9% of the time, the teacher was working with students unobserved. Even if the principal made three full-class evaluation visits a year, as required by some districts, that would still leave the teacher alone with students 99.7% of the time. No matter how observant and well trained the principal is, no matter how comprehensive the evaluation criteria are, and no matter how detailed the feedback is afterwards, this is ridiculously thin supervision of the school's most important employees. Principals who spend this little evaluative time in classrooms are basically bluffing, hoping that teachers will think they know more than they really do. Without expensive increases in administrative staffing—politically impossible in most districts—the amount of time principals spend formally observing each teacher is not going to change. Let's face it: teachers are on their own most of the time, and our schools depend heavily on their competence and professionalism.

2. *Microevaluations of individual lessons don't carry much weight.* Many school districts try to compensate for how little time principals spend in individual classrooms by requiring extremely thorough evaluations of lessons that are formally observed. Administrators are asked to script everything the teacher says and write a detailed account of exactly what happened in the class. A perceptive and well-trained principal can see a lot in a single lesson and give the teacher copious feedback on classroom management, student engagement, "accountable talk," clarity, momentum, wait time, bulletin boards, and so forth. But these elaborate write-ups don't mean a lot to most teachers; they know how little the principal sees of their day-to-day struggles, curriculum planning, grading, work with colleagues, parent outreach, professional growth, and routine duties. Even if the evaluation is complimentary, it usually gets filed in a nanosecond. Except in extreme (and quite rare) cases when a principal gives an unsatisfactory rating, evaluation is a pro forma process that has very little influence on what teachers do on a daily basis.

3. *The lessons that principals evaluate are often atypical.* The only way that microevaluating lessons can give an accurate picture of a teacher's overall classroom performance is if the observed lessons are truly representative. But this is often not the case. When teachers have advance notice of an evaluation, they can present a glamorized lesson for the principal's benefit. Even if they don't, the presence of a top-level authority figure in the classroom usually reduces discipline problems and results in a more orderly lesson than students generally experience. These two factors can work in teachers' favor, giving the principal an unrealistically positive view of their teaching. You'd think that principals would be wise to these dynamics, but they are often so stressed and overwhelmed that they play along, treating clearly atypical teaching as typical. When this happens, teachers get an unfortunate message: it's okay to do "special" teaching when the principal visits and "ordinary" teaching for students the rest of the time.

Evaluation visits can also distort reality in a negative way: some teachers get so nervous when the principal arrives that they go to pieces. This is every teacher's nightmare—one screwed-up lesson and the other 99.9% of the year will be painted with the same evaluative brush.

Surely the principal has other sources of information to correct egregiously off-target observations, including informal visits, quick impressions of teachers interacting with students, parent comments, colleagues' impressions, and gossip. But these time-honored sources of information, even when accurate, aren't "admissible" in official evaluations. Principals have little choice but to go by the book and use the information from formal evaluation visits, even when it's bogus.

4. *Isolated lessons give an incomplete picture of instruction.* Although the lesson is the fundamental building block of teaching, it's only a small part of a teacher's effort to inspire students and convey knowledge and skills. To grasp the bigger picture, a principal needs to know more: What curriculum unit is this lesson part of? What are the unit's "big ideas" and "essential questions"? How does this unit align with state standards? How will students be assessed? Principals may try to ferret out these missing pieces by asking for lesson plans and conducting pre- and post-evaluation conferences with the teacher, but evaluations are still tied to the lesson that was observed.

This is a shame, because it's impossible to teach most state standards in a single lesson; it's a huge leap from big-picture goals like "understanding number sense" to planning a single lesson. *Unit* plans, which describe a teacher's game plan for teaching skills and concepts over a three- to five-week period, tell far more about whether instruction is coherent and aligned. But principals rarely see unit plans or the assessments that teachers give at the end of their units.

5. *Evaluation almost never focuses on student learning.* In virtually all school districts, teacher unions have been successful in preventing their members from being evaluated on whether students actually learn what's being taught. Unions are right to object to accountability on norm-referenced tests,

since these assessments are not designed to be "instructionally sensitive."[2] Before-and-after, "value-added" assessments are better, but even their most fervent advocates don't think it's fair to use them to evaluate a teacher after only a year of instruction.

Does this mean that principals have no way of evaluating teachers on whether students are learning? Surely a principal can get a sense of how much students are picking up by walking around classrooms, looking over their shoulders, and asking them probing questions. But this approach has three problems. First, many principals are required to produce detailed narratives after each evaluation visit and can't walk around and write furiously at the same time. Second, even if principals manage to check in with a few students during classroom visits, it's hard to tell whether the whole class understands the lesson that day—let alone a few weeks later. To really know if teachers have been successful, principals need to see students' scores on good unit assessments—which they almost never do. Third, even if principals can get their hands on interim assessment results, such evidence is not admissible in evaluations.

So principals have little choice but to focus on teaching performances versus learning results, on chalkboard razzle-dazzle versus deep understanding, on beautiful bulletin boards versus demonstrated proficiency. Constrained by the supervision/evaluation process, principals overmanage the occasional lesson and undermanage the bigger picture of whether teachers are truly making a difference in student learning.

6. *High-stakes evaluation tends to shut down adult learning.* Even though many teachers don't respect the evaluation process, it still makes them nervous. Their collective bargaining agreements may provide good protection, but teachers harbor irrational fears that every time the principal walks into their classrooms, clipboard in hand, their jobs are on the line. Formal evaluations raise the level of tension and anxiety and make it more difficult to admit errors, listen, and talk openly about areas that need improvement. Any time evaluative comments are put in writing, the parties involved tighten up: the principal is less likely to tell the whole story for fear of facing a grievance, and the teacher is less likely to talk about how things are really going. In all too many evaluative interactions, teachers put on their game face and get through the process with as little authentic interaction as possible. The principal owns the feedback, not them.

This kind of process destroys a golden opportunity for professional growth. The real challenge of supervision and evaluation is to activate (or amplify) a supervisory voice inside teachers' heads that will guide them in their work with students. Conventional supervision and evaluation seldom accomplish this goal. In fact, the exact opposite may occur, with teachers waiting nervously for their principal to judge them and putting up a wall of resistance to any criticism. Where do teachers go for helpful feedback on their teaching? Usually they turn to a colleague, a spouse, a family member, students, parents—or nobody.

An unintended consequence of this whole dynamic is the growth of a certain emptiness in the professional relationship between teachers and school

*How can the formal evaluation process result in adult learning?*

leaders. If principals are rarely in classrooms, it's hard to have meaningful professional conversations with teachers. And if principals aren't setting the tone, it's less likely that assistant principals, team leaders, department heads, and colleagues will have serious conversations about teaching and learning. This kind of instructional vacuum can result in faculty lounge conversation dominated by topics outside of the school, gossip, and funny—and not-so-funny—stories about kids.[3]

7. *Supervision and evaluation reinforce teacher isolation.* One of the American principal's toughest challenges is counteracting two tendencies prevalent in our schools: teachers not working with their colleagues and the "educator's egocentric fallacy"—I taught it, therefore they learned it.[4] In far too many schools, teachers who teach the same subjects at the same grade level don't work together, missing out on the synergy of collaboration and wasting precious time reinventing the wheel. Because principals evaluate teachers in private meetings and confidential documents, evaluation reinforces this isolation and is rarely a vehicle for getting teachers to talk to one another, which detracts from teachers' sense of responsibility to their grade-level or department team.

Evaluation is also an ineffective tool for countering our natural tendency to assume that if something is taught (i.e., explained or demonstrated), it is automatically learned.[5] Because the supervision and evaluation process doesn't focus on team curriculum planning, assessment, and student learning, it doesn't prod teachers to emerge from their isolation and reflect with their colleagues on what they need to change in order for more students to succeed. Without this impetus, teachers gravitate toward the default setting: self-contained, activity-centered lessons or marching through the textbook.

8. *Evaluation instruments often get in the way.* Good teaching is extremely complex and challenging, and research tells us there is more than one way to get students to learn. It takes experience and savvy for a principal to grasp the subtleties of a classroom; it's even more demanding for a principal to capture them in writing; and it's *really* challenging to criticize a teacher's performance in a way that is heard. Some principals are good at all three—observation, write-ups, and "difficult conversations." Unfortunately, many principals are not, and the training needed to bring them up to speed is woefully lacking. The legendary klutziness of school administrators has motivated unions to work overtime to negotiate "principal-proof" evaluation formats and procedures to protect their members from unfair evaluations. Districts, on the other hand, push for evaluation tools that make it possible to build a case to dismiss incompetent teachers. The resultant evaluation tools are rarely conducive to fostering an honest, open, and pedagogically sophisticated dialogue between principals and teachers.

9. *Evaluations often fail to give teachers "judgmental" feedback.* This seems like an odd statement, since all evaluations judge teachers. But many evaluation instruments allow principals to fudge teachers' general status with an overall "satisfactory" rating and a lot of verbiage. These evaluations don't tell teachers where they stand on clearly articulated performance standards,

don't give clear direction on the ways in which teachers can improve their performance, and don't answer the question teachers really care about (and often dread): *How am I doing?* This kind of evaluation is unlikely to motivate a mediocre teacher to improve—or spur a good teacher on to excellence.

10. *Most principals are too busy to do a good job on supervision and evaluation.* Discipline and operational duties are so insistently demanding that teacher evaluation often disappears from principals' calendars until contractual deadlines force them to get serious.[6] When evaluation crunch time arrives, principals fall into three types—saints, cynics, and sinners. The saints go by the book, and evaluation consumes their lives for weeks at a time. I know a principal who routinely spends eight to 10 hours on each teacher evaluation: pre-observation conference, lesson observation, write-up (like a little term paper every Saturday, she says), and post-observation conference. Principals who choose to commit this amount of time (or are required to do so by their superiors) have no alternative but to shut themselves in their offices for days at a time—or spend evenings, weekends, and vacations at their desks at home. Ironically, this reduces the amount of time the saints spend in classrooms doing low-key supervision—coaching, encouraging, and gentle correction.

The second type of principal heaves a sigh, sits down at the computer, and bangs out the required evaluations as quickly as possible. Administrators in this category have grown cynical about the evaluation process and don't believe their write-ups will produce better teaching and learning, but they feel they have no choice but to do them.

The third, more daring, group of principals *simply don't do evaluations* (or evaluate only the occasional egregiously ineffective teacher). These sinners ignore contractual requirements and dare the system to catch them. Since evaluation is in the same category as a trip to the dentist for many teachers, they tend not to complain if their principal "forgets" year after year. And principals' superiors are often none the wiser—or choose to wink at these omissions.

So here's the question: are the saints, who spend hours on each evaluation, more effective at improving teaching and learning in their schools than the cynics and the sinners? Shocking as it may seem, the answer in many cases is no. This is because the conventional supervision and evaluation process is not the best way to truly change what happens in classrooms. Principals need a better way to observe, support, and judge teachers—a way that is more accurate and time efficient and more closely linked to an effective strategy for improving teaching and learning.

## LINKING SUPERVISION AND EVALUATION TO HIGH STUDENT ACHIEVEMENT

I've argued that the theory of action behind supervision and evaluation is flawed and that the conventional process rarely changes what teachers do in their classrooms. Here is an alternative theory: *The engine that drives high student achievement is teacher teams working collaboratively toward common curriculum expectations and using interim assessments to continuously improve teaching and attend to students who are not successful.* Richard DuFour, Mike Schmoker, Robert Marzano, Douglas Reeves, Jeffrey Howard, Grant Wiggins, Jay McTighe, and others believe that this approach is a critical element in high achievement. I agree, but with a proviso: if a school adopts this theory, it must change the way teachers are supervised and evaluated. If it doesn't, the principal won't have the time, energy, and insight to get the engine started and monitor it during each school year.

Why are the principal's time and focus so crucial? Because teacher collaboration is countercultural in most American schools and rarely happens without impetus and support from outside the classroom. Principals are in the best position to provide the support, and rigorous state standards and high-stakes tests can provide the impetus. Standards and tests present a common challenge (a common enemy, some would say) that makes it easier for principals to get teacher teams to buy into working toward ambitious, measurable learning for students.

Of course principals still need to evaluate teachers every year or two, as required by most states, and they also need to give honest and timely feedback to ineffective teachers and have the guts to fire them if they don't improve. But the essence of what I'm recommending is a shift away from a process owned by the principal, in which most of the energy goes into evaluating individual lessons, to a more dynamic, informal process owned by teacher teams. To make this happen, we need to shift:

- from periodically evaluating teaching to continuously analyzing learning;
- from inspecting teachers one by one to energizing the work of teacher teams;
- from evaluating individual lessons to supervising curriculum units;
- from occasional announced classroom visits to frequent unannounced visits;
- from detailed scripting of single lessons to quick sampling of multiple lessons;
- from faking it with distorted data to conducting authentic conversations based on real data;
- from year-end judgments to continuous suggestions and redirection;
- from comprehensive, written evaluations to focused, face-to-face feedback;
- from guarded, inauthentic conversations to candid give-and-take;
- from teachers saying, "Let me do it my way" to everyone asking, "Is it working?";
- from employing rigid evaluation criteria to continuously looking at new ideas and practices;
- from focusing mainly on bad teachers to improving teaching in every classroom;
- from cumbersome, time-consuming evaluations to stream-lined rubrics; and
- from being mired in paperwork to orchestrating school-wide improvement.

# TWELVE STEPS TO LINKING SUPERVISION AND EVALUATION TO HIGH SCHOOL ACHIEVEMENT

These shifts will not happen by themselves. To recover from ineffective practices and to address widening achievement gaps, principals might try the following 12-step program.

1. *Make sure the basics are in place.* These include time scheduled for teacher teams (grade-level teams in elementary schools and subject-area teams in secondary schools) to meet on a weekly basis, preferably in uninterrupted 90-minute blocks; crystal-clear, end-of-year expectations for learning that are aligned with state standards; common assessments, which can be written by teacher teams or purchased, to measure learning and diagnose needs at the end of each year and at intervals during the year; common rubrics for consistently scoring student writing and open-ended responses; and exemplars of student work at the advanced, proficient, basic, and below-basic levels.

2. *Decide on the irreducible elements of good teaching.* For principals and teachers to communicate well about what's happening in classrooms, there must be a common language regarding the basics of effective teaching. Most evaluation checklists are way too long to remember. A handy acronym for the five elements that every classroom should have is SOTEL: *safety*—students feel physically and psychologically protected; *objectives*—the goals of the curriculum unit are evident; *teaching*—learning experiences are skillfully orchestrated; *engagement*—students are leaning forward, involved in the learning process; and *learning*—there is evidence, either during the lesson or on follow-up assessments, that students have learned what was taught.

3. *Systematically visit all classrooms on a regular basis.* Principals need to be in classrooms frequently for a reality check on how things are going. But how frequent is "frequently," and how much time does a principal need to be in a classroom to see how things are going? The answers to these two questions are crucial because there's a direct relationship between the length of each visit, the number of classrooms a principal can see each day, and the quality of information that is gathered. Shorter visits mean the principal can cover more classrooms, but visits that are too short yield superficial data.

Most principals make four types of classroom visits: 1) very brief, "showing the flag" appearances; 2) "walkthroughs" lasting a few minutes, with particular attention to student work on bulletin boards; 3) five- to 15-minute mini-observations focused intently on teaching and learning; and 4) full-period, formal observations with detailed note taking. All four types of visits are useful, but as I have argued previously,[7] the third type is optimal for teachers whose basic competence is not in question. Mini-observations allow the principal to fit as many as five substantive visits into a busy day, and, if the visits are unannounced and the principal is focused and perceptive, they yield the most accurate data on how well teachers are performing.

A principal who is self-disciplined about making three to five mini-observations a day can get into all the classrooms in a medium-sized school every two weeks, systematically sampling the quality of teaching in chunks of time that can be fitted into a busy day. Using this approach, a principal can take 12 to 15 "snapshots" of every teacher's performance in the course of the year and compile a "photo album" of each one's overall performance. The total time the principal spends in each teacher's classroom is not much longer than that spent in the conventional evaluation model described earlier, but the accuracy of the information gained is far superior.

*What are the pros and cons of taking "snapshots" of teachers' performance?*

There's an additional bonus for peripatetic principals: they get to know students better and pick up information that can be useful in understanding learning problems, resolving discipline situations, and talking with parents.[8] Frequent classroom visits also convey an unmistakable message to teachers: "You never know when I'll drop in, and I expect good teaching to be going on whenever I do." If the principal sees something of concern (for example, a student being publicly humiliated), it's time to shift gears to a formal reprimand or a traditional full-lesson evaluation.

4. *Give teachers prompt, face-to-face feedback after every classroom visit.* Teachers should not be left in the dark about what the principal thinks, and personal feedback is far preferable to sending e-mails or leaving notes in teachers' mailboxes. In an informal, low-threat, private conversation, teachers are more likely to relax and engage in honest give-and-take about how things are going. These conversations go best when the principal's feedback focuses on one or two specific points—e.g., an appreciative comment about the way the teacher drew a shy student into the discussion, or a critical comment about the fact that the hands-on activities weren't focused on the unit objectives. Follow-up talks are most effective when they happen within 24 hours: "Better 120 seconds of feedback the same day than a five-page essay delivered a month later," says Douglas Reeves.[9]

In each of these follow-up conversations, principals should make a point of asking about student learning: "How is the Egypt unit coming?" "What Fountas-Pinnell levels have your lowest reading groups reached?" "How did the algebra test go?" If a principal has established a trusting climate, a teacher should be able to say, "My team just spent two weeks teaching the concept of borrowing, and the kids bombed on our quiz. Can you help us figure out what happened?" Teachers should know that their boss is keenly interested in results and should be comfortable reaching out for support.

5. *Require teacher teams to develop common unit plans and assessments.* The best way to ensure that teaching is done right the first time (versus having to provide corrective instruction for substantial numbers of students after the fact) is to have teachers work in teams to plan each curriculum unit with the end in sight.[10] Before they dive into teaching, teacher teams should work backwards from the state standards to identify clear learning objectives, decide on the big ideas and essential questions of the unit, draft assessments they will use to determine whether students have learned what was taught, create

a game plan and calendar for instruction, and run the plan by the principal for feedback.

The three- to six-week curriculum unit is an ideal chunk of instruction for principals to supervise—far better than an individual lesson. A principal who has reviewed a unit plan can check out alignment in classrooms, look at how kids are responding, suggest midcourse corrections, and ask about student learning. Are examining unit plans and following up with teachers time-consuming? Yes. Are these activities a better use of a principal's time than lesson write-ups that are ignored by teachers? Absolutely!

By far the hardest part of implementing this approach is getting teachers to plan together in the first place. Teachers in the U.S. are accustomed to autonomy, and it takes a tenacious principal to foster this kind of collaboration. It's essential, though, because teams plan better than teachers working solo, and teams generate stronger ideas, provide better support, and increase the likelihood that the supervisory voice will be in each teacher's head as the unit unfolds.

6. *Require teams to give common interim assessments.* If formative assessments are of high quality—not just clones of multiple-choice end-of-the-year tests—they can give teachers valuable insights into what students are learning and not learning.[11] It's vital for teams to meet after each unit or quarterly assessment to look at the results and collectively answer these three questions: What percentage of students scored at the advanced, proficient, basic, or below-basic levels? In which areas did students do best, and where were they confused and unsuccessful? What is our strategy for addressing the weakest areas and helping students who are struggling?[12] A powerful enhancement to interim assessments is for teams to set SMART goals—Specific, Measurable, Achievable, Results-oriented, and Time-bound (for example, 85% of our first-graders will be reading at Level I on the Fountas-Pinnell scale by June)—at the beginning of the year and to track progress each quarter.

Teacher ownership of this process is vital; it's better for a teacher to chair team meetings, ideally on a rotating basis, even if the principal has the time. Teachers need to have a clear mission for their meetings (experimentation, continuous improvement, and results), contractual time to score assessments, common planning time during or after the school day to analyze and discuss data, an outside facilitator (unless there is unusually strong leadership within the team), and occasional drop-in visits by the principal to give support and contribute ideas.

7. *Have teams report on student learning after each unit or quarter.* Lots of schools suffer from data overload and insufficient analysis and follow-through. The principal can help teams crystallize their thinking by asking for a *brief,* informal report on the three questions above and on one additional question: How can I help? It's crucial that these reports, which can be submitted either in person or in writing, are low-stakes, nonthreatening, and nonbureaucratic. Teams shouldn't be bogged down in paperwork and must feel they can be creative, try new things,

admit mistakes, and engage in an informal give-and-take about what's working and what needs to be improved.

To summarize, let's contrast how a principal evaluates a teacher using the conventional model with the process that would be followed under the proposed model:

| Conventional Model | Proposed Model |
|---|---|
| Pre-observation conference | Teacher team develops unit plan |
| Lesson plan | Team writes common assessments |
| Lesson observation | Principal gives feedback on these to |
| Evaluation write-up | team |
| Post-observation conference with teacher | Team meets during unit to share ideas |
| Occasional walkthroughs | Brief principal visits to classrooms |
|  | Face-to-face feedback to teachers |
|  | Team gives a common assessment |
|  | Team analyzes unit learning results |
|  | Team reports results to principal |
|  | Principal discusses results with team |

8. *Arrange for high-quality feedback on lessons for teachers.* Once a principal has made the shift to short, frequent classroom visits followed by face-to-face feedback and is looking at unit plans and successfully orchestrating teacher teams to focus on student results, who will give teachers feedback on full-period lessons? The principal won't have time but might arrange for instructional coaches or other teachers to do longer observations and follow-ups on lessons. Colleagues and coaches can give valuable feedback to teachers, especially when their input is part of a "lesson study" process. But there's a potential problem with peers observing one another—*the culture of nice.* It's hard to give critical feedback to people you eat lunch with every day. Videotape is a better medium for taking an unsparing look at a lesson. There's no better way to see the flaws in one's teaching (and appreciate the strengths) than to watch a videotape with a critical friend. Videotaping also requires much less skill than writing up a lesson observation.

The goal of all supervision, whether it comes from the principal's short visits or from a more lengthy peer or video observation, is to foster a real openness to feedback, install the supervisory voice in teachers' heads, and breed an acute consciousness of student learning results. We want individual teachers and teacher teams to be thinking constantly about whether students are learning and what can be done to get better results.

9. *Create a professional learning culture in the school.* Teachers and principals need preparation and support to improve their skills at observing classrooms; giving frank and honest feedback; and assessing unit plans, tests, and data on student learning. The principal needs to be the "chief learner" in this regard, reaching out to the knowledge base and orchestrating study groups, article and book groups, peer observations, and lesson videotapes. The goal is

to create a culture in which nondefensive analysis of student learning is "the way we do things around here."

The nine steps above could be carried out within most collective bargaining agreements. The last three would probably require waivers or contract changes.

10. *Use short observation visits to write teachers' final evaluations.* Dispensing with elaborate, announced evaluations is a huge time-saver, and once a trusting climate has been established, it's the ideal scenario. When I was principal of the Mather School in Boston, teachers became so comfortable with my short visits and personal feedback that virtually all of them agreed (via individual sign-offs with the assent of the union representative) to allow me to skip formal observation visits entirely and use my 12 or so short classroom visits-with-feedback to write their final evaluations. (For teachers who were in danger of getting overall unsatisfactory ratings, I went by the book.) The Littleton Public Schools in Massachusetts are in their second year of a negotiated agreement that gives tenured teachers the choice of being evaluated using the traditional approach or using evaluations based on at least 10 short visits.[13]

11. *Include measures of student learning gains in teachers' evaluations.* Teachers could be asked to submit evidence of changes in student learning from the beginning to the end of the year, using before-and-after assessment results or an analysis of portfolios and student work.

12. *Use a rubric to evaluate teachers.* Scoring guides are being used successfully to evaluate student writing and other open-ended work, and a few school districts, including Alexandria, Virginia, and the Aspire Charter Schools in California, have begun to use them for teacher evaluation. Rubrics have several advantages over conventional evaluation instruments: they are more clearly "judgmental," forcing the principal to give the teacher clear feedback with respect to a standard; they are more informative, telling teachers where they stand on a 4-3-2-1 scale with a detailed description of what performance looks like at each level of proficiency; they counteract "grade inflation," if it's clear that very few teachers will be at the advanced level; and they take much less time.

## CONCLUSION

Let's return to the vignette of the teacher who wept after being told that she had mistaught an important math concept. It's a true story; I was the principal. Looking back, I've done a lot of thinking about what went wrong in that situation. The teacher was clearly putting on a special lesson for my announced visit. Her nervousness about the biennial evaluation may have thrown her off her game, and the high-stakes nature of our conference undoubtedly contributed to her feeling of devastation when, in her view, I played "gotcha." She had been working in isolation from other teachers at her grade level and was probably more focused on impressing me than on bringing her students to proficiency on a fair assessment. The lesson she drew from my criticism—to "never take a risk"—seems like the wrong one, but given the supervision and evaluation process that we were using, it was understandable.

Had this teacher been working in the kind of professional learning community I have advocated in this article, things might have gone differently. She and her teammates would have planned the math unit together, caught the error early on, and figured out a classroom strategy for teaching the concepts. The teachers would have been less concerned about what I thought, if I happened to drop in on a lesson, than on whether the kids were getting it and how they would do on their interim assessments and on the rigorous Massachusetts math test. If I did catch a teaching error during a classroom visit, I would have corrected it in an informal conversation. When their students did well on the end-of-unit assessment, the team teachers would have reported the results to me and their colleagues with real pride—even, perhaps, with tears of a different kind.

If this scenario is to occur, some changes need to be made. We need to streamline supervision and evaluation so that principals can spend their time doing what will make the most difference: quickly and efficiently keeping tabs on what is really happening in classrooms, giving teachers constant feedback, making fair judgments about teacher performance, and getting teams invested in improving student learning and focused on results. Principals need to be able to shape a creative, low-stakes, professional learning community so that teacher teams can continuously improve their students' chances of succeeding in a high-stakes world.

Principals are ideally situated to start this team-driven "engine of improvement" and keep it humming month after month. A few maverick school leaders are already doing this kind of work on their own. Others need permission from their superiors before they take the leap of faith, let go of the current model of supervision and evaluation, and launch a more powerful learning dynamic. I would argue that liberating principals to do the right kind of work is one of the most important steps a school district can take if it wants to close the achievement gap and get all students achieving at high levels.

# ENDNOTES

1.  The distinction between supervision and evaluation in this article is between formative and summative assessment of teachers' work, between coaching and judging.
2.  James Popham, "A Game Without Winners," *Educational Leadership,* November 2004, pp. 46–50.
3.  Personal communication with John King on 6 January 2005.
4.  Grant Wiggins and Jay McTighe, *Understanding by Design,* expanded 2nd ed. (Alexandria, Va.: Association for Supervision and Curriculum Development, 2005).

5. Graham Nuthall, "Relating Classroom Teaching to Student Learning: A Critical Analysis of Why Research Has Failed to Bridge the Theory-Practice Gap," *Harvard Educational Review,* Fall 2004, pp. 273–306.

6. To reduce principals' evaluation workload, Jon Saphier has suggested adopting a four-year evaluation cycle in which each teacher gets an in-depth principal evaluation once every four years and rotates through other kinds of assessment (e.g., peer evaluation, a study group, self-assessment) in the other three. Jon Saphier, *How to Make Supervision and Evaluation Really Work* (Acton, Mass.: Research for Better Teaching, 1993). This approach sounds promising, but with high rates of staff turnover, it is not without problems.

7. Kim Marshall, "How I Confronted HSPS (Hyperactive Superficial Principal Syndrome) and Began to Deal with the Heart of the Matter," *Phi Delta Kappan,* January 1996, pp. 336–45; and idem, "Recovering from HSPS (Hyperactive Superficial Principal Syndrome): A Progress Report," *Phi Delta Kappan,* May 2003, pp. 701–9.

8. Personal communication with John King on 6 January 2005.

9. Personal communication with Douglas Reeves on 5 January 2005.

10. Wiggins and McTighe, op. cit.

11. Douglas Reeves, *Accountability for Learning: How Teachers and School Leaders Can Take Charge* (Alexandria, Va.: Association for Supervision and Curriculum Development, 2004).

12. Mike Schmoker, *Results: The Key to Continuous School Improvement,* 2nd ed. (Alexandria, Va.: Association for Supervision and Curriculum Development, 1999).

13. For information on the Littleton, Mass., teacher evaluation contract language, contact Littleton High School principal Robert Desaulniers at desrobert@aol.com.

# ISSUE SUMMARY

Performance review has always been a fundamental practice of educational leaders. Through the years administrators have been exposed to a vast array of procedures and forms and for the most part, they have managed the process adequately. Typically, the review process follows an annual cycle of setting performance objectives, gathering and documenting evidence that employees are meeting objectives throughout the year, and discussing the outcomes at a year-end meeting. In unionized settings, annual evaluation processes are built into the terms of a binding contract, which may or may not accurately assess performance.

This is the era of accountability and effectiveness for educational organizations, so it is entirely appropriate that performance review is broader than simply assessing an individual faculty or staff member's accomplishments. As organizations move away from a focus on the *activities* of work to concentrating on the *results* of work, it is inevitable that assessment of performance will also shift. Clearly conventional performance assessment is becoming problematic for leaders who attempt to align mission, strategy, and work. From a systems perspective, this alignment makes good sense. A generic measure of performance that does not encompass the institution's goals and structure—and especially results—will not serve an institution well. Administrators who are systems thinkers acknowledge that the employee performance process is interconnected with every aspect of institutional performance.

A larger question about teacher performance review is whether it should focus on uniformity and standards or initiative and innovation. In business, performance review that concentrates on efficiency and performance-to-regulation is not consistent with the conditions necessary for significant improvement and innovation. Reviewing individuals on a predetermined set of criteria on a prearranged schedule may be appropriate for work that does not vary or that must be done to exact standards. Some educational leaders are grappling with the need for a broader understanding of what constitutes improved teaching and learning.

For educational organizations that value and even thrive on innovation and flexibility, the performance review process must be responsive and fluid. The focus of these organizations is on behaviors that demonstrate creativeness, experimentation, and challenge-seeking. The paradox is that "smart" objectives of normal performance appraisal—specific, measurable, achievable, results oriented, time framed—may not be so smart. Employees who meet smart objectives will demonstrate behaviors that are conforming, predictable, and goal-confined. Again, we consider the business setting by asking whether these are the behaviors needed by schools and institutions in an era when innovation and creativity are critical to the nation's future. An educational organization's capacity to meet these challenges may very well depend on the ability of leaders to shape the right performance review process.

# ISSUE HIGHLIGHTS

- Research shows that principals do a good job of predicting and assessing teachers' effectiveness.
- Merit-pay programs should be based on evaluations by principals and these programs should focus on highest and lowest performing teachers.
- Organizational leaders are conflicted about the effectiveness of project teams.
- A national study concludes that few project teams rate their performance as excellent and many projects are not on time or on budget.
- Project success depends largely on the team leader.
- Some organizations are questioning the effectiveness of 360-degree assessments for improving performance.
- Direct feedback is a simpler, more effective approach to performance review.
- Conventional evaluation processes are inefficient and ineffective and are a poor use of leaders' time.
- Performance review should match collaborative team work processes.

# CRITICAL THINKING

As this book goes to press, a congressional funding cut for state-level performance pay systems linked to student achievement may result in an abrupt end to this type of performance assessment. For some members of Congress and their constituents, this spells doom to what they consider an innovative and effective method for improving student achievement. For others, it will be a relief to lift restrictions on performance assessment of teachers and leaders. Should the funding cut to the Teacher Incentive Fund occur, the impact would be significant for those districts that have implemented merit-pay programs. Would they be able to continue making bonus payments already promised or will they have to default? Is this incentive program built on rigorous criteria for teacher impact on student achievement? Does this federal initiative divert funds from other badly needed resources to meet regulations of NCLB? And what about the role of educational leaders in awarding performance pay?

# ADDITIONAL READING RESOURCES

David L. Cleland and Lewis R. Ireland, Effective project teamwork. *Project Management: Strategic Design and Implementation*. McGraw-Hill, 2006.

Lawrence G. Hrebiniak, Obstacles to effective strategy implementation. *Organizational Dynamics,* 2006.

John Hunt, Impact of the failure to make adequate yearly progress on school improvement and staff development efforts. *Connexions,* National Council of Professors of Educational Administration, November 2006. http://cnx.org/content/m14097/latest/

Bruce S. Cooper, Patricia A. L. Ehrensal, and Matthew Bromme, School-level politics and professional development traps in evaluating the quality of practicing teachers. *Educational Policy,* January–March 2005.

For more information on performance assessment practices, check these sites:

What Is 360 Degree Feedback? www.boothco.com/elements.html#what is360

All Teachers Are Not the Same www.hoover.org/publications/ednext/3251891.html

Performance-Based Pay for Teachers http://digitalcommons.ilr.cornell.edu/cgi/viewcontent.cgi?article=1046&context=key_workplace

These sources are helpful in finding answers to this issue that directly affects leaders:

NEA's Position on the Teacher Incentive Fund: Opposed, www.nea.org/lac/highered/tifoppose.html

U.S. Department of Education's Teacher Incentive Fund, www.ed.gov/programs/teacherincentive/index.html

Forcing a Risky Business Model on Us, www.aasa.org/publications/saarticledetailtest.cfm?ItemNumber=7945

# ISSUE 5

# How Can a Systems Approach Help Educational Leaders Manage Change?

Leaders of educational organizations are continually confronted with issues and problems—it's the nature of the job. The dilemma is how to handle a wide range of organizational issues effectively and proficiently. Because the issues are myriad, complex, and seem unrelated, administrators may not be alert to the fact that a simple problem in one area can be affecting another area negatively. And all the while, performance can be slipping and effectiveness lessens. To stay on top of issues, while ensuring that performance does not suffer, educational leaders are turning to comprehensive approaches to decision making. Over the past few decades, systems thinking has been commended as the best way to approach the full spectrum of organizational issues and problems.

Take a moment to reflect on the fundamental meaning of systems. In biology, an organism is a dynamic, living, complex "system" with parts (literally molecules) that are constantly adjusting to each other to function as a whole. When "system" is applied to an organization, it means much the same thing— parts that interact or influence each other so they can function as a whole.

Systems thinking allows educational leaders to see problems as part of a dynamic whole, with ramifications (both positive and negative) for the entire institution. Rather than making isolated decisions or taking tentative action, the goal is to understand the interconnectedness of processes and procedures, or personnel and students, in order to make better decisions. Systems thinking, based on a higher level of analysis than traditional cause and effect, makes it possible for leaders to gain broad understanding, but the question remains— does this approach make a real difference for an educational organization that is low-performing? The readings for this issue provide different perspectives on the value of systems thinking for an organization.

Systems thinking and systems change have proven useful in educational organizations, as well as in business and industry. The first reading with the interesting title, "Suspending the Elephant Over the Table," explains how systems thinking can prevent administrators from confusing the parts for the whole. Similar to business, school systems are complex operations and require a broad

172

approach to problem solving. The authors use the case of the superintendent who turned around a large school system operation through systems thinking to propose that "a systems approach may be the only way to tackle what has been called the 'toughest job in America.'"

The second reading, "Leading Professional Learning," applies systems thinking to learning communities. Fullan approaches the connection between these two constructs in clear and understandable terms. Learning communities, which many people think of as an innovation, should be recast as a regular way of interaction or "enduring capacities." They should also be endemic throughout a school system, not isolated to individual schools. With this as background, Fullan explains the practical implications for workplace practices—practices that are derived from systems thinking. Six core essentials of learning communities parallel concepts of systems thinking: a focus on learning, a collaborative culture, collective inquiry into best practice, an action orientation, a commitment to continuous improvement, and a focus on results. You might think that by casting learning communities as systemic, Fullan would go on to claim that learning communities are the cure-all for underperforming organizations, but that would be a mistake. This is what he concludes about the value of learning communities from a systems perspective:

> It is the case that politicians and policy makers are likely to under-invest in the strategy as it does not represent a quick fix. Equally problematic are educators themselves . . . when it comes right down to it, many teachers tacitly or otherwise play the privatization card, rather than run the risk of engaging in transparent teaching in order to get at the up-close details of instructional improvement as a new normal modus operandi. Only the latter will result in continuous improvement.

The final roundtable viewpoint is a classic reading that provides a vantage point for systems thinking. Russell Ackoff, one of the pioneers in the field of management systems, is considered the dean of the systems academic community. In "On Learning and the Systems That Facilitate It," Ackoff establishes clear definitions for the content of organizational learning and argues that leaders have mistakenly relied on the wrong content for decision making. His design of a learning and adaptation system is a fundamental construct for systems thinkers. And his premise requires careful thought and reflection:

> An ounce of information is worth a pound of data; an ounce of knowledge is worth a pound of information; an ounce of understanding is worth a pound of knowledge; and an ounce of wisdom is worth a pound of understanding. (p. 14)

In this era of content being equal to data points and information bits, teachers and their leaders will find Ackoff's schema can change the course of learning.

As you consider the readings, keep in mind that systems thinking is not a specific program; it is not total quality management (TQM), the Baldrige award, or Six Sigma. Systems thinking may encompass a quality program or a variety of other initiatives but it is a much larger methodology—it is thinking about an entire organization's operation systemically.

## SOURCES

Nelda Cambron-McCabe and Luvern L. Cunningham, Suspending the elephant over the table. *The School Administrator*, November 2004.

Michael Fullan, Leading professional learning. *The School Administrator,* November 2006.

Russell L. Ackoff, On learning and the systems that facilitate it. *Reflections: The SoL Journal*, August 1999.

# Suspending the Elephant Over the Table

## Nelda Cambron-McCabe and Luvern L. Cunningham

**P**eter Negroni, former superintendent in Springfield, Mass., believes Ron Heifetz's insights about the importance of taking the long view helped save his career in school administration. Negroni was on a quick fix, my-way-or-the-highway approach to school reform in 1994 but sensed he was in trouble.

Brutal and ongoing contretemps around his efforts to close the achievement gap had left him with few allies in the schools or community and feeling increasingly isolated from union leaders and significant elements on the governing school committee.

"I was taking fire from all sides and wondering when the cavalry would arrive," says Negroni, now vice president of the College Board in New York City.

Critics derided him as a brash outsider, a know-it-all from New York who didn't understand how things were done in aging New England industrial towns. Then a candidate for the school committee won election with 17,000 votes. "She'd run a campaign demanding my head," recalls Negroni wryly. "It turned out to be a pretty popular platform."

Angry about the election result, Negroni sensed that a backlash threatened the progress he had made in Springfield. People no longer cared that he'd led successful battles for school levies, imposed order on the structural chaos in the schools or saved money and improved programs for recent immigrants. All of that was greeted with disinterest.

What critics focused on was the loss of privilege for Springfield's well-to-do. It was all vaguely reactionary and racist, worried Negroni, a man who wears his heart on his sleeve, suffers fools lightly and remembers how painful it was to listen to Irish cops in New York spit racial epithets at him and his teenage buddies from Puerto Rico.

Then epiphany struck. "Who does this new board member represent?" asked Heifetz at a meeting Negroni attended of the Danforth Foundation's Forum for the American School Superintendent. "Those 17,000 voters? They stand for something. What's precious to them? What are you threatening?"

## SACRED TEXTS

All of us like quick fixes, even though in education, as elsewhere, they rarely work well, according to Heifetz, a lecturer in public policy at Harvard's Kennedy School of Government, and Peter Senge, senior lecturer in management at the

*Why is it important
for leaders to "take the
long view"?*

Massachusetts Institute of Technology. Taking time to do it right may be a persuasive theory around the ivied quadrangles of Cambridge, but do superintendents enjoy the luxury of a time-consuming systems approach? With the notorious amount of heat mounting under their chairs, can they afford to acknowledge they don't have all the answers—and sometimes aren't sure about the questions?

It's daunting, but a systems approach may be the only way to tackle what has been called the "toughest job in America." That's the consensus of skilled current and former practitioners of the high-wire act of serving as a school superintendent.

Concepts of systems change can improve learning while making the job doable, according to nearly 200 superintendents who helped us develop *The Superintendent's Fieldbook* through the decade-long Danforth Foundation's Forum for the American School Superintendent. Rosa Smith, formerly the superintendent in Columbus, Ohio, and Les Omotani, who has taken the systems approach from West Des Moines, Iowa, to his new assignment in leading the Hewlett-Woodmere district on Long Island, speak of Senge's *Fifth Discipline* and Heifetz's *Leadership Without Easy Answers* as akin to sacred texts.

Tim Lucas, former superintendent in Ho-Ho-Kus, N.J., says the same about using systems thinking. Lucas, now a professor of school practice at Lehigh University, even helped write *Schools That Learn,* a book applying Senge's systems ideas to schools with one of the authors of this article.

## THINK SYSTEMS

"It's not personal." That's what Heifetz reminds us to keep in mind as we struggle to survive, according to Smith, president of the Schott Foundation in Cambridge, Mass. Adds Negroni: "What I realized is that it had nothing to do with me. Sure, my new board member opposed what I stood for, but she wasn't reactionary. She represented an important constituency—voters worried about change. What was happening with their kids? Their community? Their jobs?"

Leaders in education or other fields who confuse themselves with the changes their communities are moving through are asking for trouble, and they will probably get it. Taking resistance personally, they are unable to distinguish their role from themselves.

"I was a real Lone Ranger," says Negroni, who was Springfield's superintendent from 1989 to 2000. "I even found myself lecturing the school committee, announcing that unless my proposals were adopted, they'd need to find someone else."

Omotani finds nothing unusual in Negroni's story. To state the obvious, says Omotani, who moved into the Hewlett-Woodmere superintendency in June, there's a lot involved in turning around a big school district. "We need to think systems, not programs," he says, noting that public discussions of schools isolate discrete issues like standards or assessment. "That promotes a quick-fix mentality—what is often called 'single-loop' thinking. What Senge and Heifetz encourage is in-depth, 'double-loop' thinking that attacks core assumptions, not their manifestations."

At West Des Moines, where he worked for nine years, Omotani learned the value of a systems approach that can be thought of as a dynamic triangle or arrowhead aimed at improving outcomes for kids. This triangle, which guided the overall work of the Danforth Superintendents' Forum, consists of seven related entities that we call the commonplaces of school leadership: leadership itself, at the base, interlocked with governance, standards and assessment, race and class, school principals, out-of-school support for learning and community engagement.

"Heifetz and Senge ask us to keep all this complexity in front of us," says Omotani. "In *The Superintendent's Fieldbook,* my wife, Barbara, referred to this process as suspending the elephant over the table so that we don't mistake the parts for the whole."

In West Des Moines, Omotani reports, the systems approach paid big dividends. The community agreed on a long-term vision for the schools and got behind school goals. "What did it give us?" Omotani asks. "Most importantly, we created a shared vision-driven school system and community around educating children. This was a living, breathing statement that mattered—not just a plaque on the wall."

Omotani points with pride to the community's numerous accomplishments that include an exemplary freshman high school now beginning its 10th year, a new Title I elementary school implementing an "artful" approach to learning, innovative summer intervention programs and initiation of a youth leadership forum that reflects the significant voice of West Des Moines's students.

# ADAPTIVE CHANGE

The easy challenges are technical, says Lucas, who left school administration in 2003 for higher education. For officials outside education, they might involve locating oil or figuring out where to run a highway. In education, technical issues may involve balancing a budget or commissioning architectural plans for a new school. "Technical issues require expertise, which is available. Single-loop thinking is ideally suited to solving technical problems," Lucas says.

The tough challenges are adaptive, requiring transformation of existing structures and practices. They turn on what to do after the wells run dry, communities refuse to let highways cut them in half, voters demand services but balk at the costs, and schools have to be closed in one part of town and built in another.

"Expertise can't resolve these dilemmas, which involve emotions and the loss of inherited ways of doing things," says Lucas. "Communities have to coalesce around solutions that require deep-rooted change and double-loop thinking."

The distinction between technical, single-loop thinking and adaptive, double-loop problem solving appeals to Omotani, a Canadian whose earlier career was spent at the district and provincial levels in Alberta. "I can monitor the technical stuff, sometimes from afar, but with the difficult issues, I need to be deeply engaged in creating a space for the schools and community to tackle tough problems. These always involve changes around things that go to the heart of what people believe and value."

Here's where the leader's skills are sorely tested. What isn't negotiable? What will the community go to the mat over? Leaders can't afford to play games with the things the community holds dear.

It's very hard leadership work. Too frequently, leaders prefer to fall back on old ways of doing things, in the process becoming "one-trick, single-loop ponies."

## TURNING WORK OVER

In Springfield, Negroni found himself reinvigorated by Heifetz's question. Determined to stop hectoring the school committee and abusing union officials, he set about transforming his style. When you're trained in command-and-control, acknowledges Negroni, the formula of "I'm OK. You're OK" does not spring readily to the lips.

But he now found himself worrying about the deep-rooted systems and transformational approaches encouraged by Senge and Heifetz. "I stopped saying, 'This is what I want,' and began asking, 'What do you think we need?'" Negroni remembers. "I went from being the Lone Ranger to being the Lead Learner."

Modeling that behavior in the school district, he started visiting individual schools five days a week, encouraging other administrators and school principals to do the same. "All of us needed to become part of a learning community," he says. "I couldn't do the community's learning for it."

*What are some reasons leaders have trouble turning over work to others?*

The results speak volumes: "These initial efforts at community engagement and learning changed the way we interacted in Springfield," Negroni says. "We engaged parents, businesses, religious groups and social service agencies so that we could all define an explicit covenant with one another. That covenant, which was most visible in our curriculum, then drove our common enterprise." Negroni credits improved student performance directly to the new relationships within the schools and community. These relationships also enabled the district to build or renovate 12 school buildings that led to a building boom in the city.

"Giving the work back" is what Heifetz calls this style. Community members have to do the work themselves; leaders can't do it for them. Still the approach has to be thoughtful. Unless handled deftly, the act of turning the work over can blow up in the leader's face.

That's a lesson that some Danforth Forum superintendents learned the hard way. In one school system, a savage public dispute broke out around a proposed photo exhibit of gay families at an elementary school. The superintendent, determined to push the decision back to the people who were most affected by it, turned the work over to the principal, teachers and parents.

After a raucous public gathering degenerated into a homophobic shouting match, the group agreed on ground rules for the exhibit that satisfied the central office but seemed acceptable to few of the ideologues inside or around the school. Within a year, the principal had transferred, and the assistant superintendent who represented the central office on the issue had left the system, followed shortly by the superintendent.

Turning the work over to others requires leaders to create a process or "holding environment" where they can regulate and contain the stress of working through difficult issues. According to Heifetz, leaders who expect to survive transformational change have to gauge the rate at which the community can handle the work.

## LEADERS' LONELINESS

After decades in schools, including a stint as superintendent in Beloit, Wis., Rosa Smith arrived for her new assignment in Columbus, Ohio, determined to push back at the sense of isolation that envelops many school leaders.

Smith was attracted to the ideas Heifetz advances to help leaders stay alive. "You need to 'get up on the balcony' with some trusted friends," Smith says. "On the balcony you can see the patterns on the floor, who's dancing with whom and how partners change as the music changes."

Before assuming her new role in Columbus, Smith convened a two-day meeting involving several district employees and about 10 outside experts, including prominent superintendents and a few university professors. Spending a half-day on briefings about district challenges, she spent the remaining time with the experts figuring out how to proceed with a systemic approach.

"Was it worth it? You bet!" says Smith, who moved into her foundation post in 2001. "Would I do it again? I have. When I started at Schott Roundation, I convened another 'balcony' group, and I plan to visit with this group regularly."

## MASTERING DISEQUILIBRIUM

Whether it's Heifetz talking about adaptive work or Senge advocating the five disciplines of personal mastery, mental models, shared vision, team learning and systems thinking, what leaders are really called on to do today is master disequilibrium in a complex environment.

*What can a leader see about a school or institution from "up on the balcony"?*

Superintendents and other leaders have to generate some stress to make changes in a big system, according to Heifetz. The system needs to be thrown into disequilibrium. The challenge for the leader is figuring out how to parcel out sufficient stress to get people's attention without overwhelming them.

Sound like a tough order? It is. Nobody said that suspending elephants over tables was easy.

# Leading Professional Learning

## Michael Fullan

I have deliberately selected the term "professional learning" in the title rather than professional learning communities, not because I do not value the latter but rather because I think the more fundamental issues of professional learning will be neglected if we pursue PLCs in a direct manner.

I have three reasons to be worried about the spread of professional learning communities. First, the term travels faster and better than the concept. Thus we have many examples of superficial PLCs—educators simply calling what they are doing professional learning communities without going very deep into learning and without realizing they are not going deep.

This is a kind of you-don't-know-what-you-don't-know phenomenon. So problem one is the danger and likelihood of superficiality.

Second, people make the mistake of treating professional learning communities as the latest innovation. Of course in a technical sense it is an innovation to the people first using it, but the moment you treat it as a program innovation, you run two risks. One is that people will see it as one innovation among many—perhaps the flavor of the year, which means it can be easily discarded once the going gets rough and as other innovations come along the following year.

The other risk is that once you see it as an innovation to be implemented you proceed in a fashion that fails to appreciate its deeper, more permanent meaning. Professional learning communities are in fact about establishing lasting new collaborative cultures. Collaborative cultures are ones that focus on building the capacity for continuous improvement and are intended to be a new way of working and learning. They are meant to be enduring capacities, not just another program innovation.

Third, professional learning communities also can be miscast as changing the cultures of individual schools rather than their deeper meaning that PLCs need to be part and parcel of creating new multiple-school district cultures. I know of more than one superintendent who bemoans the fact that this or that school has a wonderful internal professional learning community but eschews working with other schools.

The work of transforming schools means all or most schools, and this means it is a system change. For system change to occur on a larger scale, we need schools learning from each other and districts learning from each other. We call this "lateral capacity building" and see it as absolutely crucial for system reform. Put another way, individual, isolated PLC schools are verboten in any deep scheme of reform, and the PLC as an innovation can easily slip into this

*How does the systems notion of an organization being densely interdependent apply to a professional learning community?*

trap. The third problem then is how PLCs can unwittingly represent tunnel vision, reinforcing the notion of the school as an autonomous unit.

I am, in effect, arguing we must keep our eye on the more basic purpose to which PLCs are presumably a solution. The basic purpose, in my view, is to change the culture of school systems, not to produce a series of atomistic schools, however collaborative they might be internally.

Without a deeper concern for transforming cultures of all schools, these three problems—superficiality, the PLC as a program innovation and the focus on individual schools—can easily marginalize the value of professional learning communities as part of the movement to transform school system cultures.

## CONVINCING RESEARCH

Richard Elmore, in his 2004 work *School Reform From the Inside Out: Policy, Practice and Performance,* argues that decades of school reform have only touched the surface through structural and curriculum initiatives that have failed to get inside the classroom in any telling way.

The research is very convincing on this score. I recently reviewed this work carefully in completing the 4th edition of my own work, *New Meaning of Educational Change.* Even reform efforts that had millions of dollars and political will behind them, along with focusing on many of the right strategies (standards, assessment aligned with standards, curriculum revision, plenty of professional development for teachers and principals and even professional learning communities) have failed to make much of an impact in the classroom.

The Cross City Campaign for Urban School Reform in 2005 conducted case studies of major districtwide reform efforts in Chicago, Milwaukee and Seattle. While noting the three cases had a lot of positive things going for them, when all was said and done their bottom-line conclusion was this: "The three districts had decentralized authority and resources to the schools in different ways and had undergone significant organizational changes to facilitate their ambitious instructional improvement plans. The unfortunate reality for the many principals and teachers we interviewed was that the districts were unable to change practice on a large scale."

Another case in point, described in *Reform as Learning* by Lea Hubbard and others in 2006, is the revealing account of how San Diego fared under an assertive change strategy with a lot of focus and resource support. The strategy involved a strong focus on instruction with school principals being trained and supervised as instructional leaders, and the role of area superintendents being converted to instructional leaders. The strategy moved too fast and too aggressively until a backlash of cumulative resistance resulted in a change of leadership along with a change of strategy. Some gains were made in literacy and math at the elementary level, but the difficulty of accomplishing widespread change in classroom instruction took its toll in the face of a highly pressurized strategy.

Even a less contentious districtwide reform set of strategies, well designed and pursued over a five-year period in Duval County, Fla., did not accomplish much widespread reform, according to Jon Supovitz in his soon-to-be-published book, *The Case for District-Based Reform.*

# WORKPLACE PRACTICES

What is going on here? We finally get jurisdictions to take the reform literature seriously and we still get halting reform efforts. Here is where I want to turn the corner and indicate what is missing, and correspondingly why it is so difficult to accomplish.

*What are some barriers to teachers engaging in sustained learning about their practice?*

Elmore got it right when he observed: "Improvement is more a function of *learning to do the right things* in the settings where you work." Later he emphasizes: "The problem [is that] there is almost no opportunity for teachers to engage in continuous and sustained learning about their practice in the settings in which they actually work, observing and being observed by their colleagues in their own classrooms and classrooms of other teachers in other schools confronting similar problems of practice. This disconnect between the requirements of learning to teach well and the structure of teachers' work life is fatal to any sustained process of instructional improvement."

Previously Elmore identified what it would take to get substantial change in practice: "People make these fundamental transitions by having many opportunities to be exposed to the ideas, to argue them into their own normative belief systems, to practice the behaviors that go with these values, to observe others practicing those behaviors, and, most importantly, to be successful at practicing in the presence of others (that is, to be seen to be successful). In the panoply of rewards and sanctions that attach to accountability systems, the most powerful incentives reside in the face-to-face relationships among people in the organization, not in external systems."

We have made a similar case for achieving breakthrough results, which means success for 90 percent or more of all students, say in literacy. At the core of *Breakthrough,* we offered the Triple P model—personalization, precision and professional learning. The first two P's are what educators do when they try to get differentiated instruction right. That is to say learning for all requires we address the learning needs of each student (personalization) and do so in an instructional manner that fits their learning needs of the moment (precision).

We also said this has to be done in a way that is manageable. It has to be practical and efficient to the degree that it is feasible. The kicker is that in order to achieve these two P's, the third P is crucial: Every teacher must be learning how to do this virtually every day. Individually and collectively professional learning, getting better and better in the setting in which you work, must be built into the culture of the school in both its internal and external interactions.

What is missing in school cultures then is most schools, structurally and normatively, are not places where virtually every teacher is a learner all the time. This is the missing element in standards, qualifications, professional development and so on. The latter do not by themselves represent continuous professional learning.

We also can see immediately why this is so difficult to accomplish on a large scale. It is a cultural change that is both deep and necessary, and one that needs to occur, not in this or that school, but in all schools and the infrastructures within which they operate. It is a system change that permanently de-privatizes teaching in order to build in continuous improvement. Professional learning communities must be seen in this light, i.e., they must be judged on their effectiveness at creating cultures of professional learning on a system scale.

## PLCs REVISITED

We are now in a position to revisit PLCs. Professional learning communities started as a research phenomenon going back at least to Judith Little's 1981 work on collegiality, "The Power of Organizational Setting," and Susan Rosenholtz's study of "learning enriched" and "learning impoverished" schools. In this research collaborative, schools with a focus on teachers working together to improve instruction were better schools.

*How can technology assist both the structure and culture of a professional learning community?*

The clearest depiction of the key components of professional communities is provided by Sharon Kruse and others in their 1995 article, "Building Professional Learning Communities." They point to five critical elements that underpin effective PLCs: reflective dialogue, deprivatization of practice, collective focus on student learning, collaboration, and shared norms and values.

Then they identify two major sets of conditions. One is structural—time to meet and talk, physical proximity, interdependent teaching roles, communication structures and teacher empowerment and school autonomy. The other condition is what Kruse and her colleagues call "social and human resources" or what we refer to as culture. For Kruse, this includes openness to improvement, trust and respect, cognitive and skill base, supportive leadership and socialization (of current and incoming staff).

They claim, as I do, the structural conditions are easier to address than the cultural ones. Kruse concludes by observing: "Professional community within schools has been a minor theme in many educational reform efforts since the 1960s. Perhaps it is time that it became a major rallying cry among reformers, rather than a secondary whisper."

Twelve years later professional learning communities have become more prevalent, which is exactly why we should take them more seriously. The shift from research (what makes professional learning communities tick) to development (how do we cause more of them to become established) also has been part of recent developments. May I note as well that good development includes and sharpens the research knowledge base because there is nothing like trying to make a complex idea work to learn more deeply about it.

The gold standard for fostering the development of PLCs comes from the activist work of Richard Dufour and his colleagues. Their latest offering, *Learning by Doing: A Handbook for Building Professional Learning Communities,* is a powerful contribution to the field. Having led the development of PLCs in both elementary and secondary schools and now being associated with pockets of successful examples across all levels, Dufour essentially sets out to take all the excuses off the table for policymakers and practitioners alike.

Their guide to action for creating PLCs starts with the definition of six core elements: a focus on learning; a collaborative culture with a focus on learning for all; collective inquiry into best practice; an action orientation (learning by doing); a commitment to continuous improvement; and a focus on results.

In addition to showing how these six elements work in their own right and interdependently, Dufour furnishes a rubric aimed at assessing one's culture in terms of 12 dimensions (more detailed than the six) according to four stages: pre-initiation, initiation, developing and sustaining. Most of all, they go deep into the realities of developing collaborative cultures. They contend conflict is inevitable and show how to confront it constructively. Above all, their hand-book draws two conclusions—developing and maintaining PLCs is extremely hard work and there are no excuses for not getting on with it.

The Dufour model and its six components go a long way in combating many of the worry-list concerns I raised at the outset. The approach certainly eschews superficiality and demands depth. Dufour and his colleagues do not see professional learning communities as an innovation per se but mainly as a means of getting more quickly at the core issue of changing cultures. They are involved increasingly in multischool and districtwide initiatives.

Still the concerns remain—implementation is implementation. The worry list should serve as a constant checklist for any group pursuing PLCs. What strikes me as more troublesome is that it is turning out to be much more difficult than we thought to change cultures. Earlier we saw Elmore's description of what it would take to embed professional learning into every teacher learning.

I also referred to Supovitz's study of Duval County where PLCs were one of the small number of core components of the five-year focused reform strategy in the district. Despite learning communities being an explicit strategy in the district, and despite many structural mechanisms and professional learning opportunities for enacting PLCs (such as strategies for sharing practices and using data for improvement), after five years Supovitz found, "The possibilities created by professional learning communities—rigorous inquiry into the problems and challenges of instructional practice and the support of that practice—seemed to be occurring only in pockets of the district."

We have to conclude then that PLCs are at the early stages of being pursued seriously. It is the case that politicians and policymakers are likely to under-invest in the strategy as it does not represent a quick fix. Equally problematic are educators themselves. Some underestimate what it will take to make the cultural changes at stake. And when it comes right down to it, many teachers tacitly or otherwise play the privatization card, rather than run the risk of engaging in transparent teaching in order to get at the up-close details of instructional improvement as a new normal modus operandi. Only the latter will result in continuous improvement. And the latter is about the personal and collective learning of teachers.

# REAL IMPLICATIONS

The first and obvious implication of pursuing the implementation of a deep professional learning is for leaders to declare the agenda is changing the learning culture of the school. There's also a need to distinguish between structure and culture, noting that cultural change is the more important change and more difficult to achieve. While there's no need to use the term "professional learning community," if you do reference it, be sure to emphasize that the planned changes are fundamental.

Second, position PLCs as a whole-system change in which each and every school is implicated. Moreover, the route to all schools changing means each school must engage in lateral capacity building. Put another way, schools interacting with each other is a strategy to promote intra-school collaboration as educators show to others what they are doing and learn from others. Breaking down the walls of schools is a concomitant part of breaking down the walls of the classroom.

Third, in addition to lateral capacity building, PLC work also means refashioning the relationship between the school and the district. Partly to include interschool strategies coordinated by the district, but also to encompass two-way interaction and mutual influence across the two levels.

Fourth, an even bigger change is at stake when school and district leaders see themselves as engaged in changing the bigger context or system—what I have called "system thinkers in action." As Ron Heifetz and Martin Linsky put it in *Leadership on the Line,* leaders these days must be able to be on the dance floor and the balcony simultaneously.

Fifth, part of the purpose of PLCs is to make schools more accountable to the public. In my experience, as strong PLCs develop they are accompanied by a more proactive outreach to students and parents. I think this occurs because educators in these schools become more confident and more competent and thus become more comfortable in taking the risk to involve others, also recognizing that engagement of students and parents is essential for success.

Sixth and finally, the spread of professional learning communities is about the proliferation of leadership. Henry Mintzberg, in his book *Managers Not MBAs,* captured this when he observed that "leadership is not about making clever decisions. . . . It is about energizing other people to make good decisions and do better things."

Doing better things is all about cultures of professional learning. PLCs need to be seen explicitly in this light or they will go the way of just another innovation that captures the limelight ephemerally.

# On Learning and the Systems That Facilitate It

## Russell L. Ackoff

## INTRODUCTION

The extensive literature on learning deals almost exclusively with sociopsychological aspects of learning, that is, how to learn from others. All learning ultimately derives from experience, however, our own or others. Learning from experience is particularly important in organizations in part because of the continuous flux and turnover of personnel. My focus here is on learning from experience in an organizational context. It is meant to redress a shortage of discussion of experiential learning by and within organizations. This is *not* meant to diminish the importance of interpersonal learning within organizations.

I begin with definitions of what I believe are important distinctions between the different content of *learning: data, information, knowledge, understanding*, and *wisdom*. This is intended to rectify the bias in much of the organizational-learning literature toward consideration of information and knowledge to the exclusion of understanding and wisdom. Since there are no generally accepted definitions of these terms, I use my own, which I have found useful in many applications.

Then I distinguish between *learning* and *adaptation*; the latter can be considered a special case of the former. I have also found confusion in the literature on this distinction (for example, Haeckel & Nolan, 1996). In particular, I will deal with the very important role of *mistakes* in learning and adaptation and also with learning how to learn, what Gregory Bateson (1972) called *deutero-learning*.

Finally, I present a design of a *management learning and adaptation system* that meets the varied requirements formulated earlier in this paper.

## THE VARIED CONTENT OF LEARNING

The learning literature contains very little about the *content* of learning, what is learned. In this article, I try to compensate for this deficiency. What one learns consists of either *data, information, knowledge, understanding*, or *wisdom*. Unfortunately, we tend to use *data, information*, and *knowledge* interchangeably; *understanding* as a synonym of *knowledge*, and *knowledge* all-inclusively. *Wisdom* is treated largely as mysterious and incomprehensible, even untransmittable.

Not only are the differences between the various contents of learning important, but they also form a hierarchy of increasing value, as reflected in the adage: An ounce of information is worth a pound of data; an ounce of knowledge is worth a pound of information; an ounce of understanding is worth a pound of knowledge; and an ounce of wisdom is worth a pound of understanding.

Nevertheless, most of our formal education and most computer-based systems are primarily devoted to the less important types of learning: to the acquisition, processing, and transmission of data and information. There is less effort devoted to the transmission of knowledge, practically none to the transmission of understanding, and even less to wisdom. This allocation of effort is reflected in the popular and persistent preoccupation with information in the press, on television game shows, and in such popular games as "Trivial Pursuits." How appropriate this name!

## Data and Information

Data consists of symbols that represent objects, events, and/or their properties. They are products of *observation*. Observations are made either by people or by instruments, for example, thermometers, odometers, speedometers, and voltmeters. The dashboards of automobiles and airplanes are filled with such devices.

Like metallic ores, data are of little or no value until they are processed into usable forms. Data that have been processed into useful forms constitute *information*. Therefore, information also consists of symbols that represent the objects, events, and their properties. The difference between data and information is their usefulness—functional, not structural.

Information is contained in descriptions, in answers to questions that begin with such words as *who, what, where, when,* and *how many.* Information is usable in deciding *what* to do, not *how* to do it. For example, a list of the films currently playing in movie houses enables us to select one to see, but it does not tell us how to get there. Similarly, the address of a cinema tells us where it is but not how to get there. Answers to *how-to* questions constitute knowledge.

## Knowledge

Knowledge is contained in instructions. Knowledge consists of *know-how*, for example, knowing how a system works or how to make it work in a desired way. It makes *maintenance* and *control* of objects, systems, and events possible. To control something is to make it work or behave *efficiently* for an intended end. The efficiency of a course of action is usually measured either by its probability of producing an intended outcome when a specified amount of resources is used or by the amount of resources required to attain a specified probability of success.

Knowledge can be obtained either from experience—for example, by trial and error—or from someone who has obtained it from experience, their own

# Commentary by William J. Altier

As I read Russ Ackoff's article and reflected on his hierarchy of the content of the human mind—data, information, knowledge, understanding, and wisdom—my mind was quickly drawn to the current fad of more and bigger acquisitions and mergers. I recalled many comments in the business media to the effect that "So many mergers fail to deliver what they promise that there should be a presumption of failure...."

So what's the point? Going back to Dr. Ackoff's hierarchy, no doubt the executives responsible for these acquisitions and mergers go into them with considerable data, information, knowledge, and perhaps even understanding—all related to doing things right. But the question is: Do they go into them with adequate wisdom; do they do the right things?

Ackoff observes that "[g]rowth is an increase in size or number. Development is an increase in one's ability and desire to satisfy one's legitimate needs and desires and those of others." It would appear that the focus of today's merger mania is growth, not development. Perhaps that's the reason why the average life span of today's multinational corporations is between 40 and 50 years. A's Arie de Geus points out in The Living Company (1997), companies that develop themselves can live for centuries.

Many of the travails that organizations experience are, de facto, the result of a lack of wisdom on the part of those who make critical decisions. One factor behind this could be that many executives' mindsets acknowledge the roles of data, information, knowledge, and understanding but stop short of the cognizance of wisdom. It is hoped that Russ Ackoff has shattered that glass ceiling. He makes the case that wisdom—the fifth element in his hierarchy of learning—should be recognized as being at the pinnacle of organizational achievement, just as satisfying the fifth element in Maslow's hierarchy of needs—self–actualization—signifies the pinnacle of personal achievement. Ackoff suggests that "learning is least likely to occur the higher one goes in an organization"; this is precisely the stratum at which errors of omission are most likely to occur and "the decline or demise of organizations is generally more likely to derive from errors of omission."

The pinnacle of learning, wisdom, is the most critical element in successful decision making and in reducing errors of omission. The paradox is that the higher echelons of the organization do possess the decisive elements needed to acquire wisdom. As Ackoff notes. "[T]he acquisition of wisdom....is usually associated with age and experience because it is concerned with the long-run consequences of action."

*Continued*

Ackoff states, "Wisdom is the ability to perceive and evaluate the long-run consequences of behavior." Clearly, this ability does not seem to be overly abundant. It is hoped that the world of management will recognize this shortcoming and make Ackoff's hierarchy of learning its mantra for tomorrow. This hierarchy, particularly its fifth element, will be a boon for those who use it as a model to remedy the void in their organizations' learning.

Speaking as a management consultant, I find it ironic that big companies often pay big bucks to obtain advice dispensed by newly minted MBAs who lack the critical prerequisites for wisdom. What are they getting for what they pay? Could there be a corollary here?

Ackoff has a profound message for another hierarchy—the hierarchy of management. Take heed!

or that of others. When computers are programmed and people are instructed, they are *taught* how to do something. Such teaching is *training*, not *education*. Failure to distinguish between training and education is commonplace and results in a so-called *educational system* that devotes a good deal more time to training than it does to education. The content of education should be understanding and wisdom.

Computer-based *expert systems* are systems that have had the knowledge of an expert programmed into them. They store and dispense knowledge. In addition, at least since Shannon developed his electronic maze-solving rat, computers have been programmed to acquire knowledge, to *learn*. Programs for acquiring knowledge, however, are still very limited.

Intelligence is the ability of an individual to acquire knowledge. Therefore, the proper measure of intelligence is an individual's rate of learning, the ability to acquire knowledge, not how much one knows. Expert systems that do not learn, and most do not, cannot legitimately be said to have intelligence, artificial or otherwise. Unintelligent systems, ones with no ability to learn, can possess knowledge but cannot acquire it on their own.

Management obviously requires knowledge as well as information, but information and knowledge are not enough. Understanding is also required. Management suffers more from lack of knowledge than it does from lack of information and more from lack of understanding than it does from lack of knowledge. Most managers suffer from information overload, not from either an overload of knowledge or understanding.

*How does information overload often prevent leaders from doing the right things?*

## Understanding

Understanding is contained in explanations, answers to why questions. We do not learn how to do something by doing it correctly; in such a case, we already know how to do it. The most we can get out of doing something right is confirmation of what we already know. We can acquire knowledge, however, from doing something incorrectly but only if we can determine the cause of the error and correct it. Mistakes can be corrected by trial and error, but this is often very inefficient. A mistake that can be explained by identifying what produced it is understood. Understanding facilitates and accelerates the acquisition of knowledge.

Understanding is required in any situation to determine the relevance of data and information, understanding why the situation is what it is and how its characteristics are causally related to our objectives. On the other hand, explanations can be, and frequently are, suggested by observations. Theories, of course, embody explanations that are obtained by deductions from them.

Objects, events, or their properties may be explained by identifying their cause or producer, for example: "The boy is going to the store because his mother sent him." The behavior of an entity that can display choice may also be explained by identifying that entity's intended outcome, for example: "The boy is going to the store to buy an ice cream cone." Only purposeful entities have intentions. (A purposeful entity is one that can pursue the same end (1) in different ways in the same environment and (2) the same way in different environments.) Therefore, to say that an apple falls from a tree because it wants to get to the ground is no explanation at all, but to say that a person climbed a tree to avoid attack by an animal is.

It is possible to construct computer-based systems that explain the failures of some relatively simple mechanical systems. For example, some automobile-manufacturing companies have developed sensing devices that can be applied to their engines. The data collected are then processed by a computer to determine whether the engine is defective, and if so, what is the cause of the defect or its location. The Russians developed a number of such systems for application to heavy military vehicles.

Some computerized systems have been developed to diagnose the malfunctioning of organisms, but they are still in relative infancy. The types of malfunctioning that can be explained by computerized diagnostic systems do not involve choice, or purposefulness. As yet, we do not have the ability to program computers to determine the intentions behind, or the producers of, purposeful behavior.

Data, information, knowledge, and understanding presuppose each other. They are acquired and develop interdependently. They form a hierarchy with respect to value, but none is more fundamental than the others. Although computers have made inroads into providing data, information, knowledge, and understanding, I am aware of no computerized wisdom-generating or disseminating systems.

# WISDOM

Peter Drucker once made a distinction between doing things right and doing the right thing. This distinction is the same as that between efficiency and effectiveness. Information, knowledge, and understanding contribute primarily to efficiency, but provide little assurance of effectiveness. For effectiveness, wisdom is required.

# Commentary by Vincent P. Barabba

This article by Russell L. Ackoff is of inestimable value to those interested in understanding the differences between a systemic approach to learning and adaptation and the traditional ways in which we have been taught to manage the use of knowledge. The extent to which the reader can reap these rich rewards, however, is related directly to how well the reader is cognizant of Ackoff's other contributions—particularly related to systems thinking and idealized design. For example, Ackoff, along with Drucker and others, has made significant contributions to illustrating the change that has taken place as we have moved from an industrial-age, mechanistic approach toward a knowledge-age, organismic approach to systems thinking.

The systems thinking approach to knowledge use starts out with the belief that in any enterprise striving to meet its full measure of success, the parts that make up the enterprise, by themselves, are of little value outside their interaction with all the other parts. Familiarity with the writings of Ackoff has led me to believe that concepts such as knowledge management and data warehousing—based on taking an inventory of what is known—are ideas whose value is passing. From a systems thinking perspective, these concepts are replaced by decision support systems that pump a free flow of contextual data, information, knowledge, understanding, and wisdom (as precisely defined by Ackoff in this article) into a series of networked dialogs that take place continuously across the functions within the firm, as well as between the enterprise and its extended alliances, which include the ultimate consumers of its products and services.

A distinction between two metaphors helps illustrate the importance of these differences. The industrial-age mechanistic mind-set encouraged us to think about managing business as if it were made up of replaceable parts—like pieces in a jigsaw puzzle. The metaphor fit reasonably well for that era. When you start a puzzle, you know how many pieces you are supposed to have, and chances are good that they are all there. Each of the parts will interact with only a small portion of the other parts. If you have trouble deciding how to put the pieces together, you have a picture on the box to remind you that there is a single solution to the problem. Finally, though some puzzles are more complex than others, the underlying process of putting them together is always the same.

However, today's business challenges are more complex than this. We operate in a world of complex problems compounded by an accelerating rate of change. It is an environment that consists of constantly changing processes, relationships, and interacting components—more like a DNA molecule than a jigsaw puzzle. Depending on how the pieces come together, we can end up with a different final result than we had any reason to expect. We cannot always know up front exactly what we are creating.

Trying to "manage" this complexity is not necessarily the best approach. In many circumstances, that sort of thinking implies there is a single right way—a correct outcome or a predictable framework—and if we could only get all that we know to fit into that framework, we would come out with the "right" answers.

I believe that many of the current purveyors of knowledge management techniques and practices are anchored in the industrial-age way of thinking, based primarily on the predictable world of the make-and-sell business design. With that mental model, we are encouraged to believe that we can manage knowledge in the same way that we manage the more predictable aspects of our enterprises. These purveyors of knowledge management also bring up the issue of establishing a value for our intellectual assets. I am certainly not opposed to the need to justify expenditures for collecting and using information. I am also not negating the value of the tools that provide the proper information to those who make value-adding decisions for our public and private enterprises. What I *am* concerned about is that the attempt to establish such value forces us to try to separate the components of a system and assign value to them independently when, as Ackoff has stated elsewhere, "a system is a whole that cannot be divided into independent parts."

The experience of beginning to implement the learning and adaptation system here at General Motors leads me to believe that it is of great potential value. For it to work well, however, the enterprise needs to create an environment that stresses the interdependence of information users and providers.

My advice to the readers of this article is to read also, at a minimum, "Our Changing Concepts of the World," the first chapter in Ackoff's book *Creating the Corporate Future,* or, if the reader is truly serious, the recently published *Ackoff's Best.* In that way, readers will increase their chances of gleaning insight from the incredible amount of knowledge, understanding, and wisdom developed by this very thoughtful man, an important portion of which is presented in the article reprinted here.

Wisdom is the ability to perceive and evaluate the long-run consequences of behavior. It is normally associated with a willingness to make short-run sacrifices for the sake of long-run gains.

What one does is clearly the product of the information, knowledge, and understanding one has. The value of information, knowledge, and understanding is *instrumental*; it lies in their ability to facilitate the pursuit of ends—desired outcomes, objectives, and goals. Although one must be aware of the end that is being pursued in order to determine the efficiency of a means for pursuing it, one needs not be aware of the value of that end. Therefore, one can talk about the efficiency of immoral as well as moral acts—for example, the relative efficiency of different ways of breaking the law or harming another.

On the other hand, the effectiveness of behavior necessarily takes the value of its outcome(s) into account. Effectiveness in the pursuit of an end is the product of the efficiency of that pursuit and the value of that end. Therefore, the inefficient pursuit of a valuable end may be more effective than the very efficient pursuit of a negatively valued objective.

*What is an example of a leader doing the right thing wrong . . . an example of doing the wrong thing right?*

Put another way, it is usually better to do the right thing wrong than it is to do the wrong thing right. When one does the wrong thing right, one's error is reinforced, and this encourages further improvement in the pursuit of the wrong end. For example, improving the quality of the current automobile, which is destroying the quality of life in an increasing number of cities, is a conspicuous example of doing the wrong thing *righter and righter*, hence making things *wronger and wronger*. On the other hand, when one does the right thing wrong, identification and diagnosis of the error can lead to improved pursuit of the right end.

Wisdom is normative as well as instrumental. The difference between efficiency and effectiveness, which differentiates wisdom from understanding, knowledge, and information, is also reflected in the difference between *growth* and *development*. *Growth* is an increase in size or number. *Development* is an increase in one's ability and desire to satisfy one's legitimate needs and desires and those of others. A legitimate need or desire is one the satisfaction of which does not reduce the chances of others satisfying their legitimate needs or desires.

Although growth and development can effect each other, they can also occur independently of each other: An entity can grow without developing (for example, a rubbish heap), and a person can continue to develop long after he or she has stopped growing. *Standard of living* is an index of growth; *quality of life* is an index of development. One can grow without wisdom but one cannot develop without it. Growth and increases in standard of living do not necessarily entail increases in the value of what is obtained; but development and increases in quality of life do.

One who seeks to increase wisdom must be concerned with the value of outcomes (long-run as well as short-run) but value to whom? One person's behavior usually effects others. Then, ideally, all our behavior should serve the legitimate needs and desires of all those it effects, its *stakeholders*. This means that effective decisions must be value-full, not value-free. Objectivity, which is usually defined as the absence of value considerations in decision making, is antithetical to effectiveness, hence wisdom. Objectivity is better taken to be value-full, not value-free, that is, as a property of decisions that make them valuable to all they effect, whatever their legitimate values.

Evaluation of outcomes is a product of *judgment*. As yet we do not know how to program the process of making value judgments. In fact, this appears unprogrammable. On the other hand, the determination of efficiency can often be programmed because, among other things, the efficiency of an act is independent of the actor. This is not so for effectiveness. The value of the outcome of an act is never independent of the actor and is seldom the same for two actors even when they act in the same way in the same environment. It may not even be the same for the same actor in different environments or in the same environment at different times. In contrast, the efficiency of an act in a specified environment is constant.

Values are very personal matters. Therefore, wisdom-generating systems are ones that are very likely to continue to require human participation. It may well be that wisdom, which is essential to the effective pursuit of all ends, is a characteristic of humans that ultimately differentiates them from machines and other organisms.

# LEARNING AND ADAPTATION

To learn is to acquire information, knowledge, understanding, or wisdom. Systems that facilitate learning, computer-based or otherwise, can be called learning support systems. The varieties of learning—acquisition of information, knowledge, understanding, or wisdom—can, but need not, take place independently of each other.

Individuals acquire information when their range of possible choices increases over time. To inform someone serves to increase his or her probability of making one or more choices. For example, telling someone that it is raining outside is likely to increase the probability of his or her carrying an umbrella.

Individuals acquire knowledge when their efficiency increases over time. Such increases can take place under constant conditions, as in successive tries at hitting a target with rifle shots. The acquisition of knowledge (learning) can also take place when the conditions effecting the efficiency of one's choice change—for example, a strong cross-wind arises or a distracting noise interferes with shooting. Under such conditions new learning is required to maintain, let alone to increase, efficiency. Such learning is called *adaptation*.

To adapt is to change oneself or one's environment so as to maintain or increase efficiency/effectiveness when changes of internal or external conditions, if they are not responded to, result in decreased efficiency/effectiveness. Therefore, adaptation is learning under changing conditions.

*How do these characteristics of a complete learning system apply to K–12 schools?*

As has been noted above, one does not learn from doing something right, but one can, but does not necessarily, learn from doing something wrong, by making a mistake. In order to learn from mistakes, they must first be detected—this requires information. Then their cause or source must be identified—this requires understanding. Finally, successful corrective action must be taken—this requires knowledge.

Therefore, *a complete learning system* is one that detects errors, diagnoses them, and prescribes corrective action and these activities require information, knowledge, and understanding. The values served by such a system are those of the individuals served by the system, hence reflect their wisdom, or lack of it.

It should be noted that in most organizations mistakes tend to be concealed even from those who make them. The likelihood of such concealment increases with rank or status—the higher the rank, the greater the claim to omniscience. This implies that learning is least likely to occur the higher one goes in an organization.

There are two kinds of mistakes: *errors of commission*, doing something that should not have been done, and *errors of omission*, not doing something that should have been done. Those organizations that reveal mistakes generally reveal only errors of commission, not those of omission. Errors of omission include lost opportunities. Unfortunately, the decline or demise of organizations is generally more likely to derive from errors of omission than from errors of commission. It is much harder to correct errors of omission; these, like Clementine, are usually "lost and gone forever."

In order to accelerate learning, decisions must be made and monitored that will improve the ability to learn continuously. *Learning how to learn* is called *deutero-learning*. Such learning occurs when we identify and correct mistakes made in trying to correct mistakes. Because of the accelerating rate of change in our environment and its increasing complexity, much of what we know becomes obsolete in less and less time. Therefore, learning how to learn is much more important than what we learn.

Most learning by adults and organizations involves replacement of something thought to be known by something new; that is, much learning presupposes *unlearning*. Nevertheless, the literature on organizational learning has virtually ignored the unlearning process until recently when Peters (1994) and Hamel and Prahalad (1994, p. 59), among others, gave it a little attention. The system described below not only facilitates learning (including adaptation), but it also facilitates learning how to learn, and unlearning.

Only entities that can display choice can learn and unlearn, that is, only *purposeful* individuals or systems. Learning and unlearning can only take place in the context of decision making. Therefore, systems that support decision making should facilitate rapid and effective learning and unlearning and, of course, the acquisition and development of information, knowledge, and understanding. In addition, a *learning support system* should facilitate the following aspects of decision making.

Figure 1    Management Learning & Adaptation System.

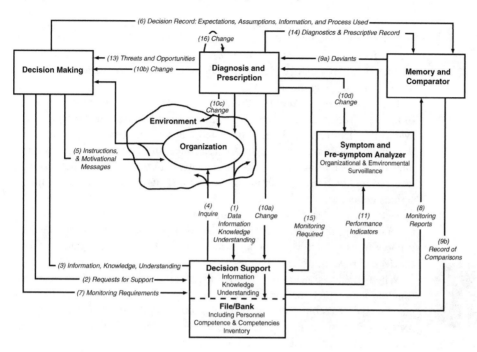

- Identification and formulation of problems
- Making decisions—that is, selecting a course of action
- Implementing the decisions made
- Controlling implementation of the decisions, their effects and the assumptions on which they are based
- Provide the information required to carry out these functions.

# THE DESIGN

The design illustrated in Figure 1 is meant to be treated as a theme around which each organization should write its own variation, one suited to the uniqueness of its structure, business, and environment. No two of its applications have ever been exactly the same. For example, its application in the North American organization of General Motors is very different from its application in one of the divisions of DuPont. It should be noted that the apparent complexity of the design derives from the not-so-apparent complexity of the processes of learning and adaptation. All the functions contained in the model are usually carried out in the mind of an individual who learns from experience, most of them, of course, unconsciously.

Numbers and letters in parentheses below refer to Figure 1. The boxes shown in Figure 1 represent functions, not individuals or groups. As will be seen, they may be performed by individuals or groups or even by computers and related technologies.

Since the support of learning should be continuous, a description of it can begin at any point, but it is easiest to follow if we begin with the generation of *data, information, knowledge*, and *understanding* (1) about the behavior of the organization being managed and its environment. These inputs are received by the *decision support* function.

In another article (Ackoff, 1967), I argued that management suffers more from an overabundance of irrelevant information than from a shortage of relevant information. Therefore, I suggested that a management support system should *filter* incoming messages for relevance and *condense* them to minimize the times required to acquire their content. That these two functions have received relatively little attention in the learning literature is, in my opinion, a serious deficiency.

Data must be processed to convert them into information, knowledge, or understanding; therefore, data processing is a necessary part of the *decision support* function. Information, knowledge, or understanding is transmitted to the *decision-making* function in response to its *request for support* (2).

When the decision makers receive the information, knowledge, or understanding with which they are provided, they do not always find it useful. They may find it unreadable, incomprehensible, doubt its validity, or question its completeness. Therefore, the receipt of information often leads them to additional requests (2). Such requests require two additional capabilities of the decision support function. This subsystem must be able to generate new data—that is, *inquire* (4) into the organization and its environment so that the additional data, information, knowledge, or understanding (1) required can be obtained. It must also have the ability to reuse data, information, knowledge, or understanding previously received or generated. This means that it must be able to store data in retrievable form. A data-storage facility is a *file/bank* whether it resides in a drawer or in a computer. It is a part of the decision support function.

Once the new or old data have been processed to provide the information believed to be responsive to the request received from the decision-making function, it is transmitted back to them. This request-fulfillment cycle may continue until the decision makers either have all the information, knowledge, or understanding they want or have run out of time and must make a decision with whatever they have. In some cases, they may believe that the time and cost of further inquiry is not likely to be justified by the improvement or increase of information, knowledge, or understanding they believe is possible.

The output of a decision to do something is a message that is either *instructive* or *motivational* (5) and is addressed to those in the organization whose responsibility it will be to carry out the instructions or whose motivation is the target. An instruction is a message to others or to oneself that is intended to increase or maintain the *efficiency* of the organization. A motivational message is one intended to effect the organization's, or some of its (internal or

*Compare Ackoff's design for a learning and adaptation system to a SWOT (strengths, weaknesses, opportunities, threats) analysis. What are essential differences between the two approaches?*

Figure 2    An Example of a Decision Record.

**Decision Record**

Issue Identification No.: _____

Prepared by.: _____

Description of issue:_____

_____

_____

_____

Outcome (check one):

_____ No decision       _____ Decision to do nothing

_____ Decision to do something (Describe): _____

_____

_____

Documents pro: _____

_____

_____

Documents con: _____

_____

_____

Expected consequences or effects, and when they are expected: _____

_____

_____

Assumptions on which expectations are based: _____

_____

_____

Information used: _____

_____

_____

Who participated in dealing with the issue? _____

_____

Who is responsible for implementation (if anyone)? _____

_____

_____

Implementation plan: _____

_____

Observations on the decision-making process: _____

_____

Expected consequences or effects, and when they are expected: _____

_____

_____

Upfront learnings, if any, from dealing with this issue: _____

_____

_____

_____

Additional comments: _____

_____

_____

_____

_____

_____

external) stakeholders' values, hence the organization's *effectiveness*. A decision, of course, may be to do nothing as well as to do something. In this case, no instructions are required but a decision record (6) is.

Every decision has only one of two possible purposes: to make something happen that otherwise wouldn't or to keep something from happening that otherwise would. In addition, there is always a time by which the effect of the decision is expected. Therefore, to control a decision, its expected effects and the expected times of their realizations should be made explicit and recorded. All this is equally true of decisions involving the implementation of a decision. If, for example, a decision has been made to build a new factory, there are expectations about when it should be completed, what it should cost, and so forth. Implementation decisions should be separately recorded and tracked. In addition to the expected effects and when they are expected, for each decision a record should be kept of the information, the assumptions on which the expectations are based, and the process by which the decision was reached, by whom, and when.

All this should be recorded in the *decision record* (6) that should be stored in an inactive *memory and comparator*. (An example of a decision record that has been used is shown in Figure 2.) There is more on the comparator below. Because human memories are inclined to modify their content, especially forecasts and expectations, over time, it is important that the memory employed be completely inactive. Inactive storage of information may be the only thing a computer can do that a human cannot do.

A version of the decision record (6), *monitoring requirements* (7), should be sent to the decision support function, which has responsibility for checking the validity of the expectations, assumptions, and information used in making the decision and for its implementation. When obtained, information about the validity of the expected effects, the relevant assumptions, and the information used should be sent to the memory and comparator in the form of a monitoring report (8). Then, using the information on the decision record (6) stored in the memory and the monitoring reports (8), a comparison should be made of the actual and expected effects and the assumptions and relevant occurrences.

When the comparator finds no significant difference between expectations and assumptions and the performance actually observed and reported in the monitoring report (8), nothing need be done other than to enter a *record of comparisons* (9b) in the memory for future reference. This record preserves what is known or believed. Therefore, it should be stored in an easily retrievable form, for example, by the use of key words. If a significant difference is found, however, it is reported as a *deviant* (9a) to the *diagnosis and prescription* function.

Such deviations indicate that something has gone wrong. A diagnosis is required to determine what is wrong and what should be done about it. The purpose of the diagnosis is to find what is responsible for the deviations and to prescribe corrective action. In other words, the diagnostic function consists of explaining the mistake, and therefore, producing *understanding* of it.

There are only a few possible sources of error, each of which requires a different type of corrective action.

1. The information, knowledge, or understanding (3) used in making the original decision was in error, and therefore the decision support function requires *change* (10a) so that it will not repeat that type of error. The information used in decision making can also come from the symptom and presymptom analyzer that is described below. Therefore, it too may require change (10d).
2. The decision making may have been faulty. In such a case, a change (10b) in this subsystem should be made.
3. The decision may have been correct, but it was not implemented properly. In such a case changes (10c) are required for either the behavior of those in the organization who were responsible for the implementation or the communication, instructions and motivational messages (5), to them.
4. The environment may have changed in a way that was not anticipated. In such cases, what is needed is a better way of either anticipating such changes, decreasing sensitivity to them, or reducing their likelihood. Such changes involve changes (10a, 10b, or 10c) in either the decision support function, the decision-making function, or the organization.

Through these types of corrective actions, the diagnosis and prescription function assures both learning and adaptation.

Now consider how threats and opportunities that are not related to previous decisions are identified and formulated. A *symptom* indicates the presence of a threat or an opportunity. It is one of a range of values of a variable that usually occurs when something is exceptionally right or wrong but seldom when things are normal. For example, a fever is an abnormally high body temperature that is seldom associated with good health but frequently associated with illness.

Variables used as symptoms are properties of the behavior of the organization or its environment. Such variables can also be used dynamically as presymptoms or omens: indicators of future opportunities or problems. A presymptom is nonrandom, normal behavior, for example, a trend, a (statistical) run, or a cycle. Therefore, a trend of rising body temperature, each of which is separately within the normal range, is a predictor of a coming fever. There are many statistical tests for non-randomness, hence presymptoms, but the naked eye and common sense can identify many of them.

A complete *management learning and adaptation system* regularly obtains information on a number of internal and external *performance indicators* (11), some of whose values are revealed as *symptoms and presymptoms* (12) by the *symptom and presymptom analyzer*.

When symptoms and presymptoms (12) are found, they are sent to the diagnosis and prescription function. Once a diagnosis is obtained, the *threats and opportunities* (13) revealed are reported to the decision-making function.

Whenever the diagnosis and prescription function prescribes a change, a diagnostic and prescriptive record (14) of it should be prepared. This record is sent to the memory and comparator where its content can be compared with the facts supplied by the decision support function in response to the *monitoring required* (15) issued by the diagnosis and prescription function. Deviants (9a) are then reported to the diagnosis and prescription function where corrective action should be taken. Such corrective action may involve change (16) of the diagnosis and prescription function or making any of the types of change previously referred to. Such changes are what makes possible learning how to learn and adapt.

Finally, information on *threats and opportunities* (17) may be sent directly to the *decision-making* function by a source within the organization or its *environment*, but outside the management learning and adaptation system.

## Implementation

As was noted above, the functions shown in Figure 1 may be carried out by individuals or by organizational units. In a small organization, the entire system can be carried out by one person.

All the functions except diagnosis and prescription (g) can currently be automated to some degree. This ability increases over time with the further development of computers and communication technologies.

Parts of the system can be created separately. Obviously, freestanding management information systems are commonplace, but I believe it is wrong to

*What are some ways a free-standing management information system may not be able to facilitate learning?*

start by building such a system. I think it is wrong because the other parts of the learning support system are seldom added subsequently when an information subsystem is created first. The problems of maintaining such a system are so great that little energy and time are left for extending the system to other functions. In general, it is better to create a complete learning support system for part of an organization than a subsystem for the whole organization. Complete and coordinated systems are more likely to be developed by other parts of the organization than are subsystems to serve the entire organization.

If only one part of a system is to be developed separately, it should be the control subsystem--monitoring decisions made, correcting errors, and detecting changes that require attention in the organization managed or in its environment. There are several reasons for this preference. First, the payoffs come much sooner than they do from constructing an information system and are much more visible. Second, a successful control system in one part of the organization invites other parts to follow suit. Third, the successful operation of a control subsystem leads naturally to inclusion of other subfunctions. Unlike an information system, a control system does not give the impression of being self-sufficient. Finally, without the type of control described here, unlearning is not very likely, and without unlearning, learning is difficult or impossible to achieve.

## Acquisition of Wisdom

We normally do not refer to the acquisition of wisdom as learning perhaps because it is not normally associated with schooling. It is usually associated with age and experience because it is concerned with the long-run consequences of action. Therefore, the acquisition of wisdom tends to be anything but systematic.

Because wisdom involves awareness of the *long-run consequences* of actions and their *evaluation*, it necessarily requires ethical judgments. Such judgments can only take place where choice is possible. (This is why ethics is a distinctively human concern.) Therefore, ethics necessarily requires the preservation and increase of legitimate options available to others as well as to oneself. *Legitimate options* are those that do not reduce the options available to others.

Wisdom must be directed toward the maintenance, if not the increase, of options for two reasons. First, we cannot forecast with accuracy most long-range consequences of choices made today so we must allow for possible error; second, we cannot predict with accuracy what choices we and others will value in the future. Both of these deficiencies are exacerbated by the accelerating rate of change occurring in our environments and their increasing complexity.

To assist in the acquisition of wisdom, a record should be made of the expected long-range effects of decisions, if any, and their ethical evaluations. When the actual consequences become apparent, they should be assessed ethically. The assessment process should be treated much like the diagnostic and prescriptive function in the system described above. Where an unethical consequence occurs, it should be noted and recorded in a memory so that future wrongs of this type can be avoided or made less likely.

# CONCLUSION

I have tried to show how learning and adaptation—the acquisition and preservation of information, knowledge, and understanding—can be facilitated. A good deal of such a system can be computerized, but it need not be. The entire system can be installed in either a single mind or multiple units of a large organization. In addition, I suggested how the acquisition and preservation of wisdom might be initiated in a manner similar to the way information, knowledge, and understanding are treated in the management learning and adaptation system described here. The principal difference in the acquisition of wisdom lies in the amount of lapsed time between decision and evaluation of consequences. This increases the importance of acquiring it whenever and wherever it is possible to do so.

# BIBLIOGRAPHY AND REFERENCES

Ackoff, R. L. "Management Misinformation Systems." *Management Science* 14, no. 4 (December 1967); B-147–B-156.

Ackoff, R. L. "From Data to Wisdom," Journal of Applied Systems Analysis 16 (1989): 3–9.

Ackoff, R. L. et al. *The SCATT Report: Designing a National Scientific and Technological Communication System* (Philadelphia: University of Pennsylvania Press, 1976).

Argyris, C. *On Organizational Learning* (Cambridge, MA: Blackwell Publishers, 1993).

Bateson, Gregory. *Steps to an Ecology of Mind* (New York: Ballantine Books, 1972).

De Geus, A. "Planning as Learning." *Harvard Business Review* 66 (1988): 70–74.

Geranmayeh, Ali. *Organizational Learning Through Interactive Planning: Design of Learning Systems for Ideal-Seeking Organizations* (Philadelphia: University of Pennsylvania Press, 1992).

Haeckel, S. H. and R. L. Nolan. "Managing By Wire: Using I/T to Transform a Business From Make-and-Sell to Sense-and-Respond" in *Competing in the Information Age: Strategic Alignment in Practice*, ed. J.N. Luftman. (New York: Oxford University Press, 1966).

Hamel, Gary, and C. K. Prahalad. *Competing for the Future* (Boston: Harvard Business School Press, 1994).

Peters, Tom. "To Forget Is Sublime," *Forbes ASAP Supplement* (April 11, 1994): 126, 128.

Sachs, Wladimir, Man Machine Design: An Inquiry into Principles of Normative Planning for Computer-Based Technical Systems. (Ph.D. dissertation, University of Pennsylvania, Philadelphia, September 1975).

Senge, P, *The Fifth Discipline* (New York: Doubleday/Currency, 1990).

Stata, R. "Organizational Learning: The Key to Management Innovation." *Sloan Management Review* 30, no. 3 (1990): 63–74

# ISSUE SUMMARY

——————————————————————————————●

Systems thinking is a way of thinking about an organization that takes into account all of its parts. The notion that systems thinking may be the solution to an ailing organization is of particular interest to those who are attracted to this way of thinking. Is systems thinking powerful enough to produce necessary changes to turn a low-performing organization into an effective one? That is what the readings for this issue address. One of the readings states that systems thinking makes sense, but is no panacea. Another claims that concepts of systems thinking make the job of administration doable. And another argues for using systems thinking to facilitate not just data and information but knowledge and wisdom. No doubt, systems thinking (even a mechanistic, Newtonian approach) is helpful, especially in situations that are conflicted or undergoing immense change. By thinking systems, members of an organization are able to view the parts in a holistic manner, not merely as cause and effect or points in time. An organization is not a simple machine and as one of the authors states, it would be "counterproductive" to analyze the performance of a complex entity using linear thinking. Yet it is fairly clear that the power of systems thinking extends only so far. After all, organizational systems are mental models created by people and the only way the power of a mental model can be seen is in positive change, growth, and results. It takes courageous action to move an organization from being low to high performing and action is a matter of will and determination.

Leaders who ask difficult questions, who regard organizational systems as open, and who make every effort to keep processes transparent, are likely to rely on systems thinking. These leaders are able to get comfortable with the discovery process that systems thinking requires. They refrain from jumping to conclusions or prematurely determining strategy while they take the time to understand what is in the system. Brenda Barker Scott, Industrial Relations professor at Queen's University, points out that diagnosis is vital:

> . . . taking time in the diagnosis phase lets you uncover what is going on—and that knowledge yields both the best solutions, and just as important, the energy for change. Deep diagnosis ensures that people will be committed to solving big issues and doing whatever it takes to make change happen. Having a solid appreciation and understanding of *what is* naturally enables people to make good decisions about *what can be.*

The roundtable viewpoints presented in the readings make us aware of how important it is to understand the unit of functioning that people have in mind when they think systems—is it one department or all departments, one group of teachers or everyone, the institution as an isolated entity or all institutions within a system, the system alone or with its surrounding communities? How to define the unit of functioning will continue to be a challenge, particularly as systems thinking is influenced by the sciences of complexity and quantum physics.

## ISSUE HIGHLIGHTS

- Systems thinking provides a useful framework for making decisions in today's complex educational organizations.
- The systems approach enables leaders to identify problems within larger systems rather than arrive at answers solely on the basis of cause and effect.
- Interrelationships, patterns, and feedback loops are more effective than reliance on simple flowcharts.
- Systems thinking, particularly double-loop problem solving, helps solve tough challenges that require transformation of structures and practices.
- Systems thinking is apparent in the six elements of enduring learning communities throughout a school district.
- Systems thinking can incorporate knowledge and wisdom in addition to data and information.

## CRITICAL THINKING

The conventional systems paradigm used in business and industry has been based on outmoded mechanistic thinking and leads to a search for certainty and control. In this form of systems thinking, leaders attempt to analyze the whole by looking at its parts in isolation. While borrowing deep into the details is necessary, it limits leaders' thinking to analysis, which naturally leads to an emphasis on efficiency and outcomes.

For decades, educational organizations have been structured to reflect mechanistic thought; personnel are organized in hierarchies, teaching is done in isolation, and quality is something to be controlled. But this paradigm of the world and its organizations has been changing due to the findings of twentieth-century sciences:

> Quantum physics tells us that the universe actually consists of patterns of dynamic energy, self-organizing wave patterns like so many whirlpools, the boundaries of each interlaced with those of all the others. . . . From chaos theory we learn about the famous "butterfly effect"—the world's physical systems are so interrelated that sometimes the mere flapping of a butterfly's wings in Beijing is enough to cause a tornado to form over Kansas City. (Zohar, 1997, pp. 11–12)

Only recently have we begun to recognize that these features appear in schools and institutions as in all of life. We are coming to understand that a school's operational systems are not separate, but interwoven. The same holds true for a school's human system; employees are interlaced with others, regardless of their position or responsibility. By implication, educational leaders are working within a space that has insignificant boundaries, where everything is interrelated and full of energy.

The question is how new systems thinking that is influenced by complexity sciences can be translated into working principles and strategies for such a space. Are there graphics other than flowcharts and decision maps that would be useful? What kind of infrastructure could educational leaders build to support change and potentiality in an atmosphere of ambiguity and uncertainty?

## ADDITIONAL READING RESOURCES

Russell L. Ackoff, *Transforming the Systems Movement.* Ackoff Collaboratory for Advancement of the Systems Approach, At *www.acasa.upenn. edu/RLAConfPaper.pdf,* May 26, 2004.

Daniel Kim, *Introduction to Systems Thinking.* Pegasus, 1999.

Barry Oshry, *Leading Systems: Lessons from the Power Lab.* Berrett Koehler, 1999.

Barry Oshry, *Seeing Systems, Unlocking the Mysteries of Organizational Life.* Berrett Koehler, 1996.

Peter Senge, *The Fifth Discipline.* Doubleday, 1990.

Margaret J. Wheatley, Leadership lessons for the real world, *Leader to Leader,* Summer 2006.

Danah Zohar, *Rewiring the Corporate Brain: Using the New Science to Rethink How We Structure and Lead Organizations.* Berrett-Koehler, 1997.

For more information on systems thinking, check these sites:

AASA Center for System Leadership www.aasa.org/AASA Center

Society for Organizational Learning www.solonline.org/

Systems Thinking www.thinking.net/Systems_Thinking/systems_thinking. html

Systems Thinking in Schools www.watersfoundation.org/

Systems Thinking in Practice www.centerforcsri.org/webcasts/webcast3/ webcast3.html

What Is System Dynamics www.systemdynamics.org/

Asking the Right Questions: A School Change Toolkit www.mcrel.org/ toolkit/systems/

# How Do Educational Leaders Shape Organizational Culture?

**I**n these days of constant evolution of educational structures and strategies, the culture of a school or institution matters a lot. Organizational scientists would say culture matters to performance. Sociologists would say it matters to the people. Watchdog organizations would say it matters to the public. And new research is proving that culture definitely matters to the success or failure of any improvement initiative. Whether the initiative is AYP (adequate yearly progress), high-performing schools, or successful charters, experts are saying that culture plays a role previously unrecognized.

Some regard a weak organizational culture as the cauldron for low performance, failure to improve, or even ethical lapses. Is the culture of some institutions so powerful that it has such dire consequences? Conversely, is a strong culture the breeding ground for excellent performance, ethical steadiness, or innovation?

The problem with culture is that it is difficult to quantify. In this era of "accountability equals quantifiability," that makes culture the elephant in the room. Granted, many improvement initiatives are holistic efforts and one would assume any of them would be culture changers. However, it is apparent that cultural "best practices" continue to be elusive and no particular initiative is powerful enough to make lasting changes in culture. In fact, it is distressing to learn that new research shows if school culture is left undisturbed, most initiatives are doomed:

> Although the tools and techniques may be present and the change strategy is implemented with vigor, many efforts to improve organizational performance fail because the fundamental culture of the organization—values, ways of thinking, managerial styles, paradigms, approaches to problem solving—remain the same. (Cameron & Quinn, 2006, p. 11)

The roundtable viewpoints selected for this issue of educational culture focus on elements that affect the way teachers and staff work together, express their values, celebrate success, and cope with failure. This is a broader perspective than climate, which typically refers to an institution's effect on students.

A recent issue brief on school culture from the Center for Comprehensive School Reform and Improvement starts our roundtable discussion. In "School

Culture: 'The Hidden Curriculum,'" the author provides a broad perspective on what a strong, positive culture looks like and how it benefits student achievement. This reading summarizes several studies that are instructive for leaders. Culture is a powerful way of sending "unambiguous signals to students and teachers about what their roles and responsibilities are."

Can school culture change? That is the provocative question Kelleher and Levenson ask in the second reading. As new initiatives and reforms escalate, the issue of entrenched culture is even more crucial. From their own experience as superintendents, the authors point out a paradox—successful initiatives by a subgroup of faculty can actually undermine the culture of the institution. A telling lesson in culture backsliding is urban administrators who attempt to use state standards and external pressure to heighten accountability of faculty and staff. The authors argue that it doesn't work because leaders do not have sufficient time or support for building trust and creating team responsibility. Evidently, command-and-control leadership is not very conducive to creating a positive culture.

"The Passive-Aggressive Organization" deals with a dynamic that can make or break an institution's culture. A passive-aggressive organization is not a rarity—in fact, many organizations suffer this syndrome. The authors point to a cluster of factors that identify an organization as passive-aggressive. When the term *passive-aggressive* is applied to a school or institution, a cluster of behavioral dynamics can appear: procrastination, resentment, pessimism, sabotage. As with a passive-aggressive individual, it may not be apparent at first that an organization is passive-aggressive. Only over time, as a pattern of subtle resistance or obstruction becomes obvious, is the behavior understood to be harmful or dysfunctional. Interestingly, such an organization can be conflict-free, friendly, pleasant work environments and still be intransigent.

Does labeling an organization as passive-aggressive imply that the faculty and staff are all passive-aggressive or is something else occurring? Neilson, Pasternack, and Van Nuys contend that flawed processes and policies are the root cause, not an inordinate number of hostile people. Turnaround is difficult, but not impossible when what's "broken" is not people but processes and policies. The authors end with an ominous warning that what is broken must be fixed: "It's only a matter of time before the diseased elements of a passive-aggressive organization overwhelm the healthy ones and drive the organization into financial distress."

Culture can handicap an organization to the point of its demise or it can propel an organization to amazing performance. At the center of an institution's cultural formation are its leaders, not because they will determine the culture but they can certainly enhance it.

# SOURCES

Craig D. Jerald, *School Culture: "The Hidden Curriculum."* The Center for Comprehensive School Reform and Improvement, December 2006.

Paul Kelleher and Marya R. Levenson, Can school culture change? *The School Administrator,* September 2004.

Gary L. Neilson, Bruce A. Pasternack, and Karen E. Van Nuys, The passive-aggressive organization. *Harvard Business Review*, October 2005.

# ARTICLE 6.1

# School Culture: "The Hidden Curriculum"

## Craig D. Jerald

*What school-level factors do you regard as essential for higher student achievement?*

**W**alk into any truly excellent school and you can feel it almost immediately—a calm, orderly atmosphere that hums with an exciting, vibrant sense of purposefulness just under the surface. Students carry themselves with poise and confidence. Teachers talk about their work with intensity and professionalism. And despite the sense of serious business at hand, both teachers and students seem happy and confident rather than stressed. Everyone seems to know who they are and why they are there, and children and staff treat each other with the respect due to full partners in an important enterprise.

Sociologists recognized the importance of school culture as early as the 1930s, but it wasn't until the late 1970s that educational researchers began to draw direct links between the quality of a school's climate and its educational outcomes. Harvard researcher Ron Edmonds, often regarded as the father of the "effective schools" movement, included "safe, orderly climate conducive to learning" on his influential list of school-level factors associated with higher student achievement. "The school's atmosphere is orderly without being rigid," he observed, "quiet without being oppressive, and generally conducive to the instructional business at hand."[1]

Yet despite its importance, organizational culture is possibly the least discussed element in practical conversations about how to improve student achievement. Perhaps that is because factors such as strong leadership, close monitoring of student progress, a common and coherent curriculum, and teacher collaboration all seem like pieces of the puzzle that educators can directly affect. On the other hand, even the synonyms we use to describe a school's culture—terms such as "atmosphere" and "climate"—make it sound more like an environmental condition than an educational one. And much like the weather, school culture seems to exist beyond direct human control.

But educators in highly effective schools, especially those that serve large populations of disadvantaged students, do not seem to regard the organizational culture as beyond their control. They talk about it and work on it as if it were a tool they can shape and wield to achieve outcomes they desire. Gaining a deep understanding of what a strong, positive organizational culture looks like and how it works can help educators become more thoughtful about developing one.

# MORE THAN "SAFE AND ORDERLY"

Too often, educators interpret the effective schools research to mean that the school's climate should be safe and orderly—and *only* safe and orderly. Few would argue that those attributes are unimportant. Beyond the ethical responsibility to provide children with safe surroundings, such conditions help protect instructional time from needless interruptions and distractions. But discussions of school climate that begin and end with classroom management and student discipline miss an important part of the puzzle. A truly positive school climate is not characterized simply by the absence of gangs, violence, or discipline problems, but also by the *presence* of a set of norms and values that focus everyone's attention on what is most important and motivate them to work hard toward a common purpose.

Analyzing an extensive body of research on organizational culture, leadership and change experts Terrance Deal and Kent Peterson contend that "the culture of an enterprise plays the dominant role in exemplary performance." They define school culture as an "underground flow of feelings and folkways [wending] its way within schools" in the form of vision and values, beliefs and assumptions, rituals and ceremonies, history and stories, and physical symbols.[2]

According to Deal and Peterson, research suggests that a strong, positive culture serves several beneficial functions, including the following:

- Fostering effort and productivity.
- Improving collegial and collaborative activities that in turn promote better communication and problem solving.
- Supporting successful change and improvement efforts.
- Building commitment and helping students and teachers identify with the school.
- Amplifying energy and motivation of staff members and students.
- Focusing attention and daily behavior on what is important and valued.[3]

Russell Hobby of Britain's Hay Group suggests, "Viewed more positively, culture can also be the ultimate form of 'capacity'—a reservoir of energy and wisdom to sustain motivation and co-operation, shape relationships and aspirations, and guide effective choices at every level of the school."[4]

One useful concept for understanding how culture performs those functions comes from sociology. W.I. Thomas, a pioneer in the field, observed that individuals consider something he called "the definition of the situation" before they act.[5] To take a very simple example, many people answer the telephone differently depending on whether they are in a professional or casual setting. Very young children impose their own self-centered definitions on most situations, but society gradually suggests or imposes other definitions.

Some schools allow individuals to decide their "definition of the situation"—what the organization is about and how individuals should act in it. Effective schools, however, suggest a clear, common "definition of the situation" for all individuals, sending a constant stream of unambiguous signals to students and teachers about what their roles and responsibilities are. The school does that through its organizational culture.

In some high schools, for example, the organizational culture defines athletic success as paramount. In others, especially where peer cultures predominate, norms and values push social popularity as sacred. And in others, academic effort and excellence are revered or at least valued highly enough to compete for students' attention amid many other claims on it.

The instructive role of school culture is not lost on effective leaders. John Capozzi, the principal of Elmont Memorial Junior-Senior High School near Queens, New York, explains, "In addition to [a] close emphasis on classroom instruction, we have what we call our 'hidden curriculum,' which develops personal relationships between faculty and students and deliberately works at developing character."[6] By identifying school culture as his "hidden curriculum," Capozzi acknowledges that like the academic curriculum, the elements of school culture can be identified and taught. Elmont's 2,000 students, most of whom are African American and Latino, produce impressive outcomes. Ninety-seven percent of entering ninth graders graduate on time with a regular diploma, and 88 percent of its 2005 graduates earned a prestigious Regents Diploma.[7]

At University Park Campus School in Worcester, Massachusetts, students begin learning the "culture curriculum" even before the first day of school. Entering seventh graders are required to attend a three-week August Academy. "It allows students a chance to meet their teachers, meet their peers, and experience school a full three weeks before the school year starts [and] provides them with a comfort level," says Principal June Eressy. "But the most important thing is they get to understand the culture of the school. They get to understand that we are serious about education and that we are serious about them going to college. They need to start thinking about it now to get where they need to be."[8]

Teachers at University Park's August Academy accomplish that goal through a combination of overt messages and subtle lessons that emphasize not only academics but also the values and behaviors the school expects of students. "We work on interdisciplinary units during that time," Eressy explains. "I wanted the kids to be reading a book they could finish in three weeks, because in my experience a lot of urban kids don't finish what they start, so I want them to learn right from the get go: 'You start it, you finish it.'"[9]

University Park establishes a "definition of the situation" that tells students they are capable young people who *will* work hard and go to college. The results are impressive. Although three quarters of University Park's students are low income, compared with only about 30 percent statewide, 90 percent of the school's 10th graders scored proficient or advanced on the Massachusetts mathematics assessment in 2005, beating a statewide 29 percent by a huge margin.[10] And all of its students get accepted to college, with most going on to four-year institutions.[11]

Still, although many effective schools couple an ambitious academic ethos with warm, caring, and supportive relationships, Eressy warns that schools too often focus on nurturing alone. "There are too many schools that have succeeded in building warm and caring and nurturing places for kids but have failed to translate that into a culture of high expectations," she says. "That doesn't do the kids any good."[12] Research bears out her assertion. A large study of middle school climate involving 30,000 students in Chicago Public Schools found that social support has a positive effect on academic achievement but only when coupled with a climate of strong "academic press."[13]

A school's culture sends signals not only to students but also to staff. Teachers and school leaders also must work to build positive norms related to their own work. According to Robert Marzano, this part of a school's culture has to do with professionalism and collegiality—whether teachers believe and act as if they can achieve positive outcomes for students and whether they support each other, working collaboratively to achieve common goals.[14] In a study of social relations in Chicago elementary schools in the 1990s, Anthony Bryk and Barbara Schneider found that one powerful factor affecting school improvement was whether staff in the school trusted each other.[15] Marzano advises schools to take a proactive approach to establishing a professional culture—defining norms and expectations clearly, creating governance procedures that give teachers an active role in decision making, and ensuring that teachers can engage in meaningful professional development focused on improving classroom instruction in the subjects they teach.[16]

Building a strong culture is not an overnight task. According to Bryk and Schneider, "Relational trust is not something that can be achieved simply through some workshop, retreat, or form of sensitivity training, although all of these can be helpful. Rather, relational trust is forged in daily social exchanges. Trust grows over time through exchanges where the expectations held for others are validated in action."[17] Creating and maintaining a strong culture—for students and teachers alike—also depends on their understanding of "the definition of the situation" defined earlier. "For relational trust to develop and be sustained," say Byrk and Schneider, both staff and students "must be able to make sense of their work together in terms of what they understand as the primary purpose of the school: Why are we really here?"[18]

*What can you infer about the right balance of nurture and high expectations for an effective school?*

# MAKING IT "POSITIVE": VISION AND VALUES

As Elmont and University Park illustrate, at the heart of every positive culture is a positive vision for students and staff. But vision can be a very vague and fuzzy concept, leading to vague and fuzzy definitions of the situation. What is vision really, and what are its pieces and parts?

One useful definition of vision comes from James Collins and Jerry Porras, who conducted a research study of "visionary companies" that had sustained successful outcomes over long periods of time. They say that an organization's vision first consists of a well-defined "core ideology." That ideology includes a "core purpose" as well as a set of fundamental values and beliefs, the "essential and enduring tenets" of an organization.[19]

Do effective schools differ *measurably* from other schools in the fundamental values and beliefs shared by their staff members? Two years ago, the Hay Group set out to answer that question. The organization asked several thousand teachers across 134 randomly selected schools to participate in a "culture sort," a group exercise in which participants work together to arrange statements of belief and values in order of priority.

The study found that staff members in both high-performing and low-performing[20] schools ranked "measuring and monitoring results" at the top of their lists. But high-performing schools also prioritized "a hunger for improvement," "raising capability—helping people learn," "focusing on the value added," "promoting excellence—pushing the boundaries of achievement," and "making sacrifices to put pupils first." In contrast, low-performing schools valued statements such as "warmth—humour—repartee—feet on the ground," "recognising personal circumstances—making allowances—toleration—it's the effort that counts," and "creating a pleasant and collegial working environment."[21]

The second component in an organization's vision, according to Collins and Porras, consists of an "envisioned future"—a clear picture of what the organization expects to look like and what it wants to have accomplished five, 10, or even 15 years from the present. In many effective schools, the envisioned future encompasses *graduates* as well as the organization itself. Where does the school staff expect students to be five, 10, or 15 years after they graduate? The answer to that question will shape how teachers work and the messages they send to students.

## MAKING IT "STRONG": ALL ABOUT ALIGNMENT

A school's culture—positive or negative—stems from its vision and its established values. But whether the culture is *strong* or *weak* depends on the actions, traditions, symbols, ceremonies, and rituals that are closely aligned with that vision. In their study of visionary companies, Collins and Porras found that "Many executives thrash about with mission statements and vision statements [. . .] that evoke the response 'True, but who cares?' [. . .] Building a visionary company requires 1% vision and 99% alignment."[22]

Some schools have a generally "positive" culture that is focused on student achievement and success but too weak to motivate students and teachers. For example, school leaders might talk about values and beliefs, but no follow-up actions, traditions, ceremonies, or rituals reinforce those messages. Similarly, a teacher might be told that improving professional practice is a value but find that the school budget provides few resources for professional development or be asked to embrace a more collegial culture only to find that no time is designated for teachers to meet and plan together. In such situations, individuals are likely to arrive at their own definitions of the situation, which makes work toward common goals difficult. Even if the climate is pleasant and orderly, it is likely that teachers quietly disagree on what their primary responsibilities are and what the main purpose of the institution is, making improvement planning and instructional collaboration nonproductive. Students receive little guidance and are left to come up with their own answers to the question, "What am I here for?" Although most follow the rules, academic effort is considered voluntary.

In contrast, effective schools make sure that even the smallest aspects of daily life align with the core ideology and envisioned future. No symbol or ceremony is too minor to be coopted into serving the larger vision. For example, fifth graders who enter Washington, D.C.'s, Key Academy middle school this fall will be asked to identify themselves as members of the "Class of 2018"— the year their teachers expect them to graduate from *college*. Visitors to the school are encouraged to ask students what class they are in, and students invariably provide their intended college graduation date. Teachers talk frequently about what college they attended and their diplomas hang on the walls of the school. Identification cards outside teachers' classrooms list their alma maters along with their names.

*Does the principle of strong alignment work equally for K–12 schools, colleges, other educational institutions?*

To be sure, many middle schools encourage students to begin thinking about college. But Key Academy envelops students in a ubiquitous and infectious set of symbols, ceremonies, and traditions that foster *ambition* and *effort* focused on the unifying vision—preparing every single student to go to college. Not surprisingly, the school's mostly low-income African-American students consistently garner the highest middle school assessment results in the city, and many of its graduates win admission (and sometimes substantial scholarships) to competitive public and private high schools.

Staff members in effective schools also see concrete signs that reinforce the school's professed culture. If the school values raising student achievement, then the most proficient teachers are assigned to the hardest-to-reach students. If family involvement is valued, all staff learn how to engage in partnerships with parents. The core ideology is monitored, reinforced, and supported.

Hobby of the Hay Group lists five kinds of "reinforcing behaviors" as follows that send strong signals about vision and values:

- **Rituals:** celebrations and ceremonies, rites of passage, and shared quirks and mannerisms.
- **Hero Making:** role models, hierarchies, public rewards, and mentors.
- **Storytelling:** shared humor, common anecdotes, foundation myths, and both oral and written history.
- **Symbolic Display:** decoration, artwork, trophies, and architecture.
- **Rules:** etiquette, formal rules, taboos, and tacit permissions.[23]

At Dayton's Bluff Elementary School in St. Paul, Minnesota, for example, teachers post the state academic standards and student writing that meets them on bulletin boards. Many schools do something similar, but Dayton's Bluff teachers take one extra step—translating the standards from educator language into "kid language" in order to ensure that the bulletin boards send signals to students and not just to teachers or parents in the school. Thus, the standard that reads, "By the end of the year, we expect fourth-grade students to be able to produce a narrative account that engages the reader by establishing a context, creating a point of view, and otherwise developing reader interest" bears the translation, "The beginning makes the reader want to keep reading your memoir."[24] In schools that simply post the standards as they are written, the standards are a symbolic display targeting teachers and other staff. At Dayton's Bluff, they are a symbolic display targeting students.

When alignment is tight and the culture is strong, new students and staff members pick up on an organization's true vision and values almost immediately, whether the culture is negative or positive. According to Peterson and Deal, students "know things are different in a positive or negative way—something more than just rules or procedures." Teachers are quick to get the message too. "Within the first hour of a new assignment, teachers begin to sift through the deep silt of expectations, norms, and rituals to learn what it means to become an accepted member of the school."[25]

# CONCLUSION

As educators come under greater pressure to achieve much better and more equitable student outcomes, they will need to leverage every tool available to them, including organizational culture. Of course, no one suggests that changing culture is simple, easy, or quick. As Michael Fullan puts it, "Reculturing is a contact sport that involves hard, labor-intensive work."[26] But it is a sport that must be played more aggressively if our schools are to achieve the kinds of results we now expect of them. The first step is to help educators recognize that having a strong, positive culture means much more than just safety and order.

# ENDNOTES

1. Edmonds, R. (1979, March/April). *Some schools work and more can. Social Policy,* 9(5), 28–32. (p. 32)
2. Deal, T. E., & Peterson, K. D. (1999). *Shaping school culture: The heart of leadership.* San Francisco: Jossey-Bass. (pp. 1–3)
3. Deal, T. E., & Peterson, K. D. (1999). *Shaping school culture: The heart of leadership.* San Francisco: Jossey-Bass. (pp. 7–8)
4. Hobby, R. (2004, March). *A culture for learning: An investigation into the values and beliefs associated with effective schools. London: Hay*

*Group Management.* (p. 6). Retrieved October 3, 2006, from http://www. haygroup. co.uk/downloads/Culture_for_Learning.pdf

5. Thomas, W. I. (1969, March). *The unadjusted girl* (Reprinted.). Glen Ridge, NJ: Patterson Smith. (Original work published 1923).

6. Chenoweth, K. (2006, April 4). Much better than adequate progress. *Washington Post* Online. Retrieved October 3, 2006 from http://www.washingtonpost.com/wp-dyn/content/article/2006/04/04/AR2006040400644.html

7. New York Department of Education. (2006, April). *New York state school report card: Elmont Memorial Junior-Senior High School in Sewanhaka Central High School District, 2004–05.* (p. 3). Retrieved October 3, 2006 from http:// emsc33.nysed.gov/repcrd2005/cir/280252070002.pdf

8. Eressy, J. (2005, September). *The University Park Campus School in Worcester, Massachusetts.* Presentation given at the Alliance for Excellent Education's High School Achievement Forum, Washington, DC. Audio file retrieved October 3, 2006, from http://www.all4ed.org/events/UPCS.html

9. Eressy, J. (2005, September). *The University Park Campus School in Worcester, Massachusetts.* Presentation given at the Alliance for Excellent Education's High School Achievement Forum, Washington, DC. Audio file retrieved October 3, 2006, from http://www.all4ed.org/events/UPCS.html

10. Massachusetts Department of Education. (2006). *2005 MCAS report (school) for grade 10 students.* Retrieved October 3, 2006, from http://profiles.doe.mass.edu/mcas.aspx?mode=school&year=2005&grade=10&student_ code=AL&filterBy =

11. Massachusetts Department of Education. (n.d.). *2004–05 plans of high school graduates report.* Retrieved October 3, 2006, from http://profiles. doe.mass.edu/plansofhsgrads.aspx?mode = school&orderBy=

12. Eressy, J. (2005, September). *The University Park Campus School in Worcester, Massachusetts.* Presentation given at the Alliance for Excellent Education's High School Achievement Forum, Washington, DC. Audio file retrieved October 3, 2006, from http://www.all4ed.org/events/UPCS.html

13. Lee, V. E., & Smith, J. B. (1999, Winter). Social support and achievement for young adolescents in Chicago: The role of school academic press. *American Educational Research Journal, 36*(4), 907–945.

14. Marzano, R. J. (2003). *What works in schools: Translating research into action.* Alexandria, VA: Association for Supervision and Curriculum Development. (pp. 60–61)

15. Bryk, A. S., & Schneider, B. (2002). *Trust in schools: A core resource for improvement.* New York: Russell Sage Foundation. (p. xiv). In 1994, the researches conducted surveys of educators in Chicago public schools and analyzed those findings along with data on student achievement: "A

relatively small number of survey items, on what we began to call relational trust, sharply distinguished schools moving forward under reform from those that were not."

16. Marzano, R. J. (2003). *What works in schools: Translating research into action.* Alexandria, VA: Association for Supervision and Curriculum Development. (p. 65)

17. Bryk, A. S., & Schneider, B. (2002). *Trust in schools: A core resource for improvement.* New York: Russell Sage Foundation. (pp. 136–137)

18. Bryk, A. S., & Schneider, B. (2002). *Trust in schools: A core resource for improvement.* New York: Russell Sage Foundation. (p. 137)

19. Collins, J. C., & Porras, J. I. (1998). Building your company's vision. In *Harvard business review on change* (pp. 21–54). Boston: Harvard Business School Press. (p. 21)

20. Schools were sorted into performance categories based on a "value-added" analysis of three years of student assessment data.

21. Hobby, R. (2004, March). *A culture for learning: An investigation into the values and beliefs associated with effective schools.* London: Hay Group Management. (p. 67). The full report, which includes a step-by-step description of the Culture Sort activity as well as a list of the 30 values statements the Hay Group used in its research, can be found online at http://www.haygroup.co.uk/downloads/ Culture_for_Learning. pdf

22. Collins, J. C., & Porras, J. I. (1998). Building your company's vision. In *Harvard business review on change* (pp. 21–54). Boston: Harvard Business School Press. (p. 49)

23. Hobby, R. (2004, March). *A culture for learning: An investigation into the values and beliefs associated with effective schools.* London: Hay Group Management. (p. 9). Retrieved October 3, 2006, from http://www. haygroup. co.uk/downloads/Culture_for_Learning.pdf

24. Achievement Alliance. (2005). *"Excuses are dream killers."* Washington, DC: Author. (p. 11). Retrieved October 3, 2006, from http://www. achievementalliance.org/files/ DaytonsBluff.pdf

25. Peterson, K. D., & Deal, T. E. (2002). *The shaping school culture fieldbook.* San Francisco: Jossey-Bass. (p. 8)

26. Fullan, M. (2001). *Leading in a culture of change.* San Francisco: Jossey-Bass. (p. 44)

# Can School Culture Change?

## Paul Kelleher and Marya R. Levenson

A t the annual Superintendents Work Conference at Teachers College last summer, we heard Bill Baker, then president of WNET Channel 13 public television station in New York City, make the provocative claim he did not think organizational cultures could improve in nonprofits, including school systems. Large, established organizations, he insisted, are so "transfixed with their internal systems and bureaucracies they are unable to change."

Leaders in these environments, Baker suggested, ought to adapt to prevailing organizational norms and expect their successes to occur "around the edges" by creating new organizational subcultures, for example.

We found ourselves taking Baker's remarks to heart for two reasons. First, Baker has proven himself to be a successful public television executive, in part through his innovative use of smaller units within larger organizations. But more significantly, his remarks challenged a deeply held assumption. In our practice, we have believed that deep, transformative change in school organizations is possible and that it occurs precisely through the kind of culture change Baker sees as impossible.

*How do you view Bill Baker's provocative statement about school systems being unable to change?*

## COMPLEX QUESTIONS

There is an obvious urgency to answer the question of whether and under what conditions school and school district culture can really change. The question, of course, is deceptively simple to state but confoundingly complex to answer.

The question itself raises more questions. What do we mean by culture change? How do we know change has occurred if it happens? What relationship exists between culture change and school improvement? Is there a cyclical relationship in which new actions by teachers bring some results and produce some culture change, which motivates more new actions as the cycle recurs?

Does research help us in answering these questions? Considerable evidence of the intractability of school organizations exists. School reform efforts over the years have had little substantive and enduring impact on school culture. Some experts even have suggested that the clearest outcome of the endless implementation of reform ideas is the next cycle of work for reformers.

Researchers also have suggested a powerful reason for this response. Change efforts often move too far and too fast and threaten to destroy the organization's sense of competence that has taken years to develop. If the organization loses its sense of self, it cannot become successful. Leaders should avoid revolutionary

*What is the theory behind the statement that leaders should avoid revolutionary changes and attempts to import rather than develop culture?*

changes and attempts to import rather than develop culture. Instead, they should learn to live with the tension between maintaining and even protecting the old culture while pushing at the same time to change it.

# PAST SUCCESSES

What about our experience? Together we have more than 30 years in the super-intendency. We each consider ourselves to have been successful superintend-ents. But did we make lasting changes in school districts in which we worked? Did cultures change?

To answer these questions, we first clarified what we mean by culture. Twenty years ago, Terry Deal suggested "culture is what keeps the herd roughly mov-ing west." In Deal's terms, culture relates to the values and norms that underlie action. Characteristics of culture explain "the way we do things around here."

If culture deals with how people perform their work, then changes in culture must involve new patterns of work. For culture to change in a school or school district, teachers, principals and other staff must relate to each other in different ways and actually do something differently.

Moreover, they must continue to do work differently in the future. Teachers and principals will not substantially change how they do things on a temporary basis. Cultural change in work activities is deep and lasting. It requires time and team building, often through recruiting people who have a shared vision and dedication to implement it.

To claim the culture has changed, new ways of doing things must be institu-tionalized. As superintendents looking back on districts that we led, we believe the litmus test is whether the changes survive us and continue.

# ENDURING CHANGES

In applying this definition of culture change and this test of its occurrence, we discovered both bad and good news.

Both of us invested time, energy and personal credibility in efforts to change culture. Such efforts are always fragile at first, subject to variables beyond our control. A group of tenured teachers in a high school academic department may be prima donnas who could substantially improve their practice by col-laboration. But if they are successful in terms of the indicators they and their clients have established, such as Advanced Placement test scores and college admissions, and if they are recognized for that success, they may defeat every effort to foster more collaboration.

In another area, a data-based program assessment process may produce enthusiastic responses from the first groups of teachers involved. However, if the superintendent who helped to put it in place moves on before building a critical mass of teacher and administrative support, the program may founder during the leadership transition.

In contrast, we can confidently point to changes in how teachers work together that we initiated and that continue to this day. One of us, in collaboration with the teachers' union, initiated a sequence of formal courses that exposed teachers to the research base on teaching, provided them with hands-on opportunities to broaden their repertoires of teaching strategies and required them to engage in experiments together in their classroom to apply what they learned and to critique each other's success. For more than 10 years, these courses have continued to be offered by the district. The collaboration that the experiments spawned has continued, too. By our definition, the culture appears to have changed—more collaboration, less isolation.

Our experience suggests it often is easier to change the culture by opening up a school or school district to more shared decision making than it is to confront the challenges of creating a culture of shared accountability. One of us was successful at increasing shared ownership within a district by including faculty and site administrators in decision making, recruiting a stable administrative team with a shared vision of excellence and creating in-house teams for building skills and capacity to implement shared goals with faculty and parents.

On the other hand, we have observed the difficulties of some of our colleagues, especially those in urban districts, who have worked to build shared accountability for student achievement. It is not surprising that much of the support for state standards and accountability has come from urban administrators who have used these external pressures as leverage to confront the culture and lack of student achievement within their schools and district.

Too few urban educational leaders have been given sufficient time or appropriate support to build a team and develop trust. They have been expected to walk on water and turn around a school district within a few years. When this does not occur, a new administrator, hired with great fanfare, repeats the pattern and is often gone within a few years. No wonder many teachers respond cynically to calls for reform by repeating, "This too shall pass."

This kind of resistance to change from large secondary schools has caused several urban superintendents, now supported by foundation grants, to break up large schools in order to create schools within the school. Deborah Meier, Ted and Nancy Sizer and others who have started alternative or charter schools have achieved substantial success by creating new, small subcultures within or outside larger organizational structures, precisely the path to success that Bill Baker recommended at the superintendents conference. Indeed, we would question whether the new reorganizations being mandated in large city secondary schools will work unless the reformers and educational leaders of these new small schools understand how a common culture affects development of a community of learners.

# REALISTIC PROSPECT

Can culture change? Our answer is a qualified yes. Our experience and that of many others provides clear evidence that aspects of culture change. But

*What does your experience tell you about the author's conclusion that organizational culture may be intractable to change?*

many variables affect whether changes endure. These include the ability of the educational leader to build trust and commitment in staff, the length of the superintendent's tenure and the willingness of the district to make a transition to a new leader with a similar set of values and beliefs.

Even with these issues adequately addressed, organizational culture may be intractable to certain changes, especially those conceived on a large scale that would attack the organization's collective identity. The lesson for district leaders is to reaffirm the importance of learning and to develop a healthy respect for those aspects of organizational culture that are deep in the fabric of the institution. We may still decide to confront and attempt to change them. But we will do so with more realistic expectations and a greater likelihood of long-term success than if we act in ignorance.

# The Passive–Aggressive Organization

Gary L. Neilson, Bruce A. Pasternack, and
Karen E. Van Nuys

**H**ealthy companies are hard to mistake. Their managers have access to good, timely information, the authority to make informed decisions, and the incentives to make them on behalf of the organization, which promptly and capably carries them out. A good term for the healthiest of such organizations is "resilient," since they can react nimbly to challenges and recover quickly from those they cannot dodge. Unfortunately, most companies are not resilient. In fact, fewer than one in five of the approximately 30,000 individuals who responded to a global online survey Booz Allen Hamilton conducted describe their organizations that way.1 The largest number—over one-quarter—say they suffer from the cluster of pathologies we place under the label "passive-aggressive." The category takes its name from the organization's quiet but tenacious resistance, in every way but openly, to corporate directives.

In passive-aggressive organizations, people pay those directives lip service, putting in only enough effort to appear compliant. Employees feel free to do as they see fit because there are hardly ever unpleasant consequences, and the directives themselves are often misguided and thus seem worthy of defiance. Making matters worse, senior management has left unclear where accountability actually lies, in effect absolving managers of final responsibility for anything they do. Those with initiative must wait interminably for a go-ahead, and their actions when finally taken are accompanied by a chorus of second-guessing, a poor but understandable substitute for the satisfaction of accomplishing the task at hand. (See the exhibit "What Kind of Company Is Yours?")

When employees' healthy impulses—to learn, to share, to achieve—are not encouraged, other harmful but adaptive conduct gradually takes over. It is no wonder that action of any kind becomes scarce and that erstwhile doers find safety in resisting unpromising efforts. The absence of confrontation at such places is only a disguise for intransigence.

As a general rule, companies that are not healthy suffer from either too much control at the top or not enough. Either can cripple performance: in the former case, by failing to devolve authority, share information, and reward constructive decision making; in the latter, by allowing individuals and business units to work at cross-purposes or do little. The passive-aggressive corporation, due

*Why do the authors single out encouragement as the means to a healthy organization?*

to the peculiarities of its evolution, can exhibit the drawbacks of both too much control and not enough.

In such organizations, people with authority lack the information to exercise it wisely or the incentives to serve the company's strategy and interests or the personnel that will carry out their directives. Conversely, people with the incentives and information necessary to make good decisions lack the authority to execute them or oversee their execution by others. As a result, many in senior positions operate under the false impression that they control things they actually do not. At the same time, many think they cannot control what they actually can.

Of course, there is no such thing as a pure exemplar of the passive-aggressive corporation, any more than there is a firm somewhere that has never suffered from the syndrome. Even high-performing organizations harbor pockets of resistance, while semiautonomous pockets of excellence lift up poorly performing ones. These areas of excellence can be the levers by which good managers show to the rest of the firm that action is possible. Nonetheless, we've found that the passive-aggressive organization is the hardest to change of the seven types we studied because such companies have generally had more time than the others to accumulate and institutionalize dysfunctions, and their people are the most cynical about reform attempts.

Before bursting into full flower, passive-aggressive organizations are dotted with frustrated world-beaters who cannot understand why their most promising projects can't gain traction. After a couple of years, such individuals either quit or become demoralized into ineffectuality by the thanklessness and futility of effort. Still, it would be wrong to say that organizations displaying passive-aggressive behaviour must have lots of passive-aggressive people in them. The passive-aggressive organization is not one where bad outcomes can be attributed to the hostile or perverse intentions individuals bring to the job. It is, in fact, a place where mostly well-intentioned people are the victims of flawed processes and policies.

To some venerable observers, the employees of such companies bear a passing resemblance to the "organization man" of 1950s sociology and literary fiction. In the postwar era, when U.S. corporations dominated their domestic markets and enjoyed stable market shares, personal initiative and risk taking were understandably seen as disruptive rather than opportunity seeking. But what may have been innocuous and even suitable behavior for its time can, in today's world of global markets and unfettered competition, bring a company to the brink of failure. Indeed, some of the companies today that find security and comfort in inertia are the very ones that dominated markets 50 years ago.

Our conception of the passive-aggressive company and the other six organizational types in our seven-part schema grew out of our decades of experience advising firms in a wide variety of industries and locations on organizational issues. Over and over, we saw certain classic behavioral patterns occur, which, we began to notice, correlated with certain objective features of those companies, such as size and age. To explain the emergence of these patterns, we postulated the existence of a limited number of underlying forces in every organization. After isolating what we determined to be the four most basic ones, we studied how each operated and interacted with the others to shape the seven organizational types. As we came to understand what made each type of organization function well or poorly, we were able to refine our definitions. When we tested the soundness of our schema in the online survey, we found that the organizational portraits the responses painted corresponded closely to the seven types we had identified.

## THE SLIDE INTO PASSIVE-AGGRESSIVENESS

Most passive-aggressive organizations don't start out full of entrenched resistance. Problems develop gradually as a company grows, through a series of well-intended but badly implemented organizational changes layered one upon another. Passive-aggressive organizations are, therefore, most commonly large, complex enterprises whose seeds of resistance were often sown when they were much smaller.

*How does the passive-aggressive developmental pattern happen in schools and institutions?*

While each organization takes a unique path, we have seen a particular development pattern recur. A company is founded on a healthy core business. The large amount of cash it throws off finances a series of acquisitions, increasing organizational complexity and confusion. As it grows beyond about $1 billion in revenues, the firm becomes too large and complex to be run effectively by a small, hands-on senior team. So it begins to experiment with decentralization in ways that are ill planned, because it is inexperienced at integration or growing too quickly, and halfhearted, because the founders have trouble genuinely letting go. To regain control, the founders add layers of managers to oversee the line managers whose performance has disappointed them. The additional layers make it difficult for people in the organization to understand who bears responsibility for specific results. Some managers become reluctant to make decisions, and others won't own up to the ones they've made, inviting colleagues to second-guess or overturn them. An already passive-aggressive organization grows increasingly so as its people become more certain of the acceptability of such conduct. Resistance becomes entrenched, and failure to deliver on commitments becomes chronic. . . .

Regardless of how they arrived where they are, passive-aggressive organizations are usually the sum of a series of ad hoc decisions or events that made sense in the moment but have the effect of gradually blurring decision rights. Over time such shotgun arrangements outlive their individual rationales, and the organization loses all vestiges of a coherent overall plan.

**What Kind of Company Is Yours?** Of the seven major organizational types we've observed, the healthiest is the resilient organization, which as its name implies is the most flexible and adaptable. Our online survey shows, unfortunately, that the most common is the far-from-healthy passive-aggressive type, in which lines of authority are unclear, merit is not rewarded, and people have learned to smile, nod, and do just enough to get by.

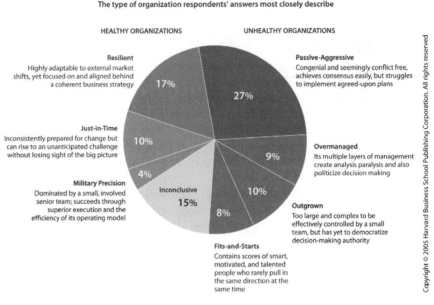

The type of organization respondents' answers most closely describe

HEALTHY ORGANIZATIONS    UNHEALTHY ORGANIZATIONS

**Resilient**
Highly adaptable to external market shifts, yet focused on and aligned behind a coherent business strategy — 17%

**Just-in-Time**
Inconsistently prepared for change but can rise to an unanticipated challenge without losing sight of the big picture — 10%

**Military Precision**
Dominated by a small, involved senior team; succeeds through superior execution and the efficiency of its operating model — 4%

**Inconclusive** 15%

**Fits-and-Starts**
Contains scores of smart, motivated, and talented people who rarely pull in the same direction at the same time — 8%

**Passive-Aggressive** 27%
Congenial and seemingly conflict free, achieves consensus easily, but struggles to implement agreed-upon plans

**Overmanaged** 9%
Its multiple layers of management create analysis paralysis and also politicize decision making

**Outgrown** 10%
Too large and complex to be effectively controlled by a small team, but has yet to democratize decision-making authority

Source: Org DNA data set, 30,000 observations; Booz Allen analysis

# THE ANATOMY OF THE ORGANIZATION

In all unhealthy organizations, dysfunction is rooted in a fundamental misalignment of four basic building blocks of the organization: incentives or, more broadly speaking, motivators; decision rights; information; and organizational structure. In passive-aggressive organizations, the misalignments generally involve complicated interactions among all four, which together conspire to freeze initiative.

**Ineffective motivators** • We define "motivators" to include not just financial compensation but all the factors, explicit and implicit, that affect anything an employee cares about: whether her office has a window, whether he is promoted to a position with greater visibility or a larger number of direct reports, whether she receives a company car or is invited to important meetings

Diagnosing the Passive-Aggressive Organization. People working in passive-aggressive organizations feel strongly that they don't know which decisions they're responsible for, that no decision is ever final, that good information is hard to obtain, and that the quality of their work is not being accurately appraised. People in resilient organizations feel the opposite.

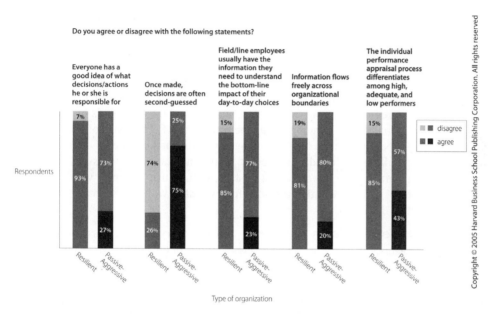

Do you agree or disagree with the following statements?

Source: Org DNA data set, 30,000 observations; Booz Allen analysis

or foreign off-sites. Far surpassing these in influence is some tangible evidence of the impact of one's efforts.

Passive-aggressive organizations are exceptionally poor at providing that evidence, often failing to judge and reward individuals according to their business value to the organization—or even to distinguish better performance from worse. Fifty-seven percent of respondents working at passive-aggressive companies agreed that in their organizations the individual appraisal process fails to differentiate among high, adequate, and low performers. Yet only 15% of respondents from resilient companies agreed with that statement. (See the exhibit "Diagnosing the Passive-Aggressive Organization.") In some cases, the rewards given to certain job titles seem incommensurate with those functions' overall contribution to the firm. People who expect their efforts to go unrecognized or to be inadequately valued put in just enough effort to stay out of trouble, since they have no reason to believe that any extra effort or initiative will lead to additional rewards or superior results.

What's more, incentive systems communicate to the organization as a whole what really matters to upper management. Corporate may send out countless memos about its strategy, mission, and goals, but its true values are embodied in what it is willing to pay for and otherwise recognize, which is one reason that the annual e-mail describing how bonuses will be calculated is the one everybody not only reads but remembers.

Within passive-aggressive firms, privileges and pecking order often loom larger than the realities of the marketplace. Such firms' very size and wealth can insulate employees from competitive pressures, which register as mere symbols—the share price or numbers on a P&L statement—not as forces that will affect the company's success. So, for example, a manager may be rewarded for the number of market studies his department prepared in the past fiscal year, regardless of how many of those studies served as the basis for marketing campaigns that actually enhanced sales. The job of senior management is to remind everyone else of the reality behind those symbols by connecting each manager's standing within the firm—size of office, size of bonus, access to superiors—to the firm's standing within the marketplace.

Still, as profoundly in need of proper motivation as a passive-aggressive organization is, it would be a mistake to think that tinkering with incentives alone, without regard to the other forces at play, will coax such a company out of its doldrums.

**Unclear decision rights •** . . . Nearly everyone in a passive-aggressive organization is unsure about where the limits of his or her own responsibilities end and those of other colleagues begin. In our online survey, only 27% of respondents from passive-aggressive organizations agreed that "everyone has a good idea of what decisions/actions he or she is responsible for," compared with 93% at resilient organizations.

*What are some of the reasons "decision rights" are unclear?*

Vaguely defined roles give their occupants "plausible deniability" when things go badly. The problem can always be said to be the responsibility of the next person, who can likewise shift blame elsewhere. Meanwhile, conscientious employees may hang back for fear of intruding on someone else's turf.

As a consequence, authority becomes fragmented. When everyone has a say in making a decision, everyone thinks he has the right to stymie or reverse it after it has been made. In passive-aggressive organizations, 75% of respondents believe that "once made, decisions are often second-guessed," versus just 26% in resilient organizations. And second-guessing that occurs in the middle of the decision-making process can bring it to a halt. . . .

Of course, it is never possible to specify every decision right a priori. Opportunities and challenges will appear as matters unfold, and any attempt to give a complete accounting of all decisions that can be foreseen would take too long and be too complex to be useful. But in healthy organizations, decisions do not go unmade because no one has been designated to make them. Most of the time, someone will jump in and get the job done. In such places, people take the initiative because they know their efforts will be rewarded. . . .

**The wrong information** • Employees of a passive-aggressive organization are often more interested in learning about what goes on inside their company than about the competitive realities that affect the firm's long-term survival. For example, though never officially, brand managers at one software company were judged on the elaborateness of their forecast presentations. However, forecasts and results differed on average by as much as 25% in that volatile industry, suggesting that spending so much time on documents intended for internal consumption was diverting brand managers from more productive pursuits.

In another case, employees noticed that executives who received frequent promotions spent a lot of their time in meetings at headquarters. Wanting to get ahead, they started seeking invitations to those meetings themselves, whether or not they had anything to contribute. They failed to realize that the high performers were called into meetings because they had important market insights others sought. In a passive-aggressive organization, rituals and routines, even modes of dress, become fetishized, as though they contain the secret to the firm's past successes.

When in possession of information or knowledge of genuine value, employees of passive-aggressive organizations are reluctant to share it, since doing so frequently benefits the recipient more than the sharer. For example, many departments use acronyms and terms of art to abbreviate the information they use internally. When sharing that information with a new department, they neglect to explain what their shorthand means, if not out of a desire to hoard the information for their own benefit then because spending the time required to translate it will not be rewarded.

Finally, in an organization already rife with meddling, many managers find that providing information gives the recipients a pretext to interfere. All these factors explain why only 20% of surveyed individuals in passive-aggressive organizations agree that "information flows freely across organizational boundaries." By contrast, that figure is 81% at resilient organizations.

**Misleading structure** • Because individuals in passive-aggressive companies often lack clear measures of how they add value, they may instead rely on the organization chart as a map of relative status—focusing on how many direct reports they have, how many levels away from the CEO they are, or whether their immediate supervisor is a favorite. Ironically, the org chart rarely conveys much information about how work gets done in these firms because decision rights are unclear or often reside in unexpected places.

# CURING THE PATIENT

Passive-aggressive organizations are, by definition, uniquely resistant to change and are therefore uniquely difficult to rehabilitate. To begin with, it's hard to discern their actual condition from beneath the accretions of earlier failed fixes. What's more, the remedy is bound to be complicated and taxing. Analysis may reveal the need for greater centralization in some areas (to support products that rely on the same basic technology or production process, for instance) and greater decentralization in others (perhaps to serve a market requiring significant product tailoring).

The first order of business is the greatest challenge of all: getting a passive-aggressive organization's attention. A long history of seeing corporate initiatives ignored and then fade away makes employees almost hopelessly jaded. Many people have become so hard-bitten that only a significant business threat can rouse them to action. But because such organizations are also so inward gazing, such a threat remains invisible until it's almost too late. . . .

In addition to these catalysts, elements of successful programs to fix passive-aggressive organizations include the following:

**Bring in new blood** • Outsiders often lead the change in passive-aggressive organizations, for several reasons. First, they send an unmistakable signal to the troops that "things are so badly broken we can't fix them ourselves anymore." Second, outsiders bring new standards they expect the organization to meet; they haven't been worn down by the old habit of making excuses. And third, they often find it easier than incumbents to treat the organization more like a business than a family.

John Thompson was one such outsider when he became CEO of software security firm Symantec in April 1999 after 28 years at IBM. He says of Symantec: "This was a company that had lost its way, and it needed somebody who was not connected to the people or processes or strategy to ask the tough questions and be prepared to act on the answers. The former CEO, Gordon Eubanks, did a terrific job of building the company from nothing. The raw material, the raw attributes, were there. I just brought a different set of eyes, a different set of lenses."

Nevertheless, outsiders like Thompson have certain handicaps. If they alienate middle management by going too fast, they can aggravate its natural tendency to display resistance in classic passive-aggressive fashion. Successful newcomers retain enough senior members of the old guard to enlist the organization's loyalty while purging those who are unlikely ever to get on board.

Because of these hazards, a homegrown CEO who is capable of grasping the urgency of the situation can sometimes be the safer choice. But the message he or she sends that a new day has arrived must be unequivocal.

**Leave no building block unturned** • Passive-aggressive organizations are so fundamentally misaligned that the best way to get their attention is by changing everything at once, so that the magnitude of the problem, and of the effort that will be required to fix it, cannot be denied.

Soon after he arrived at Symantec, Thompson spun off several businesses and product lines, changed the management team, reassigned decision rights, and revised all the incentive systems—in short, "changed almost everything about the company." Thompson explains: "We chopped up all of the old signal paths. It's like what goes on in Florida when the hurricanes hit, one after another. The power lines are down; they're just crackling there on the ground. And somebody's got to reconnect them. We decided to seize the opportunity to reconnect them a different way."

**Make decisions, and make them stick** • Clarifying and articulating decision rights is often the first order of business in fixing a passive-aggressive organization, where decisions have been made, unmade, overturned, and second-guessed so many times that no one really knows who truly decides what any more. In many cases, decision-making authority has become lodged where it doesn't belong. When Thompson took over at Symantec, "the product manager was king. And the regional managers were even more autonomous." Regions were known to redesign packaging and sit on inventory they didn't want to sell.

"We had many people who could say no, but few people who could say yes and make it stick," Thompson explains. So one of the first things he did when he arrived was firmly establish, once and for all, what the respective roles of the regional and product managers should be. "We told the regions, 'Your job is execution. You're going to do what you're told to do. You're not a business unit. You are the sales engine of the company. Your job is to sell what we build, not to decide whether or not you want to sell it and then design your own company campaign around it.'"

Once decision rights are clarified, they must be respected. If they are, people in the organization begin to count on one another and to trust that what is planned will be done.

Early in his tenure, Thompson realized the company could save money by providing computer cables free only to customers who requested them instead of putting them in every box of software. At a meeting on cost reduction, everyone, including the executive responsible, agreed it should be done. But weeks later, the boxes still contained the cables. "We don't make decisions but once," Thompson told the executive. "If you've got a disagreement or a point of view, bring it up when we're going through the discussion. Don't hold back and give me this smiley kind of benign agreement. Go back and get it fixed. We're not shipping cables any more. And if you can't communicate that, I will."

"That was the shot heard around the world," Thompson says. "There was this epiphany, 'Wow, this guy's serious.'"

**Spread the word—and the data** • No organization can make good decisions without having access to the relevant information. But to know what's relevant, people must be clear about which issues deserve the highest priority. This is not just a matter of sending out a memo or two.

At 7-Eleven, for example, bright and early every Monday morning, the eight members of the executive committee and invited guests convene to discuss strategic issues and survey the week that was and the week coming up. They arrive knowing which of the 2,500 products in the 7-Eleven inventory are moving and which are not in its 5,800 stores across the United States and Canada. By 11 AM the senior executive team has determined the week's priorities and

*How could 7-Eleven's priority-setting process be adapted for school leadership teams?*

begins relaying them to all executives down to the vice president level. During the first half of this two-hour national video conference, division VPs go over the updated forecast for the month and the quarter. At noon, department heads, product directors, category managers, and sales and marketing managers discuss issues at the store level that need to be bumped up to headquarters.

On Tuesdays at 11:15 AM, 7-Eleven's nearly 800 field consultants—each of whom oversees a group of stores—are debriefed in another videoconference. The call covers case studies, new merchandising issues, featured products, findings in test markets—everything the field consultants need to educate store owners and associates about that week's priorities. When these consultants head into the field after the call, they know exactly what news to deliver to the stores because they've heard it directly from the top. Clearly, the care in setting and keeping to priorities is paying off: As of July 2005, 7-Eleven had reported 35 consecutive quarters of same-store sales growth.

**Match motivators to contribution** • When Thompson arrived at Symantec, any executive who was promoted to vice president automatically was given a BMW. Senior management's bonuses were paid quarterly and were heavily skewed toward cash rather than stock. "So if the stock didn't do well, they didn't care," Thompson explains. "We [now] have a stock option plan that is broad based but not universal. One of the things we recognized early on was that if we were going to grow at the rate that we were growing, we had to be more selective in who we gave options to so as not to dilute the value of our stock. And so the first thing we did was identify a range of employees who were valuable to the company but didn't need equity to come to work, and we focused their compensation around cash bonuses. Then we increased the equity we gave to the engineers and other people that were critical to our long-term success." By paying the two groups differently, the new compensation scheme recognizes their distinctive importance.

"We changed the alignment throughout the organization," says Thompson. "Now everyone gets paid based upon revenue production as well as profit generation. My view was, 'Most of you don't have anything to do with profit. But all of you have something to do with revenue, so let's rebalance our incentives to reflect that reality.'"

It's only a matter of time before the diseased elements of a passive-aggressive organization overwhelm the healthy ones and drive the organization into financial distress. In fact, our research confirms a link between organizational health and profitability. Respondents who identify their organizations as resilient report better than average profitability nearly twice as often as respondents in passive-aggressive organizations (see the exhibit "Where There's Health, There Are Profits").

A full transformation of a passive-aggressive organization is impossible without the engagement of senior management. But even those in the middle of the organization can make a difference within their own scope of influence. Large organizations are made up of many small overlapping units. Even if

**Where There's Health, There Are Profits.**   In our survey, more than half the respondents from resilient organizations characterized their companies as being more profitable than the average for their industry. But less than a third of the people from passive-aggressive companies said theirs was.

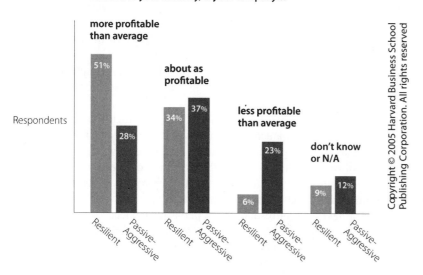

**Relative to your industry, is your company...**

Source: Org DNA data set, 30,000 observations; Booz Allen analysis

they are not entirely independent, most of us can make changes in ours. If you are a brand manager in a passive-aggressive company, for instance, you can make it clear to your team that delivering on promises matters. Then find an opportunity to prove it—not a public hanging, but some signal that things have changed. When, say, your market researchers report in the staff meeting that the focus groups have to be postponed for two weeks, express disappointment that the team contract hasn't been followed. Make the point in the staff meeting so that everyone gets the message.

When such a message is delivered clearly and consistently, it sinks in. Slowly, your division can become a source of initiative in a sea of lassitude. You may not change the whole company overnight, but you just might begin to set a new tone.

# NOTE

1.  In addition to the approximately 30,000 responses to our Web site (orgdna.com), our research also includes about 20,000 responses to the same survey given in the course of client engagements.

# ISSUE SUMMARY

⎯⎯⎯⎯⎯⎯⎯⎯⎯⎯⎯⎯⎯⎯⎯⎯⎯⎯⎯⎯⎯⎯⎯⎯⎯●

Getting a handle on organizational culture is particularly complex because so many aspects are invisible, thus difficult to discern. Characteristics of culture like norms, assumptions, unwritten rules, are implicit and carried in people's minds. Retirees and job changers take the unwritten aspects of culture with them. For educational institutions with frequent turnover, this only exacerbates the difficulty of passing culture along. There are consequences of such gaps in cultural memory. A sort of cultural meltdown can occur when no one is making sure the expectations continue to be translated and norms restated.

It is not that culture doesn't matter; it is simply difficult to quantify. And once quantified, those characteristics are even more difficult for individuals to address and change. Federal and state regulations deal with every aspect of public schools and institutions—with the exception of organizational culture. Leaders in the public sector are left without many resources for dealing with the unwritten facets of everyday work relationships.

On top of the dearth of resources is a pervasive tendency to regard culture as a given, thus impervious to alteration or overhaul. If culture is intransigent, why call for its reform, which many experts are doing these days? Largely it is because so many educational institutions abandon so many well-conceived improvement initiatives. Improvement and reform initiatives are costly, labor intensive, and risky. If faculty and staff live in fear at work—fear of intimidation, of confrontation, of litigation—and none of these fears are addressed, it becomes more apparent why improvement initiatives fail.

For educational leaders, shaping culture is a difficult journey. Wise leaders recognize that the best intended reforms will suffer unless there is a close alignment and compatibility of culture with improvement initiatives.

## ISSUE HIGHLIGHTS

- Organizational culture is an underexamined factor in how to improve student achievement.
- A positive culture is characterized by the presence of norms and values that focus attention and motivate people toward a common purpose.
- A nurturing and supportive culture is not necessarily a culture of high expectations.
- The intractability of school organizations is a serious problem.
- Some experts believe organizational cultures cannot be improved; therefore, they should create new subcultures.

- The ability of the educational leader to build trust and commitment in staff is a critical variable in culture change.
- Many organizations fall in the category of passive-aggressive, an unhealthy condition that is resistant to change.
- Rehabilitation of passive-aggressive organizations requires use of systematic steps and often complete realignment throughout the organization.

## CRITICAL THINKING

Culture is a complex social system. It consists of processes, patterns, and events. The tendency is for educational leaders to focus on the events themselves; however, a systems approach requires taking a "balcony view." Looking at the processes and patterns rather than the events per se is what Peter Senge refers to as personal mastery of the situation: "continually clarifying and deepening our personal vision, of focusing our energies, of developing patience, and of seeing reality objectively" (1990, p. 7). When leaders have clarified the big picture, they can then form a mental image of the culture: "Mental models are deeply ingrained assumptions, generalizations, or even pictures or images that influence how we understand the world and how we take action" (p. 8).

Any participant in an organization can reach this stage in systems thinking yet still not influence the culture, but leaders take the next step by sharing their mental model: "If any one idea about leadership has inspired organizations for thousands of years, it's the capacity to hold a shared picture of the future we seek to create" (p. 9).

For Senge, shared vision is necessary to culture change, but it is not sufficient. The way to change a culture is through a group approach: "Team learning is vital because teams, not individuals, are the fundamental learning unit in modern organizations" (p. 10). It is a simple strategy, but often ignored in educational settings—through dialogue, shared understandings emerge and the culture is changed.

## ADDITIONAL READING RESOURCES

Kim S. Cameron and Robert E. Quinn, *Diagnosing and Changing Organizational Culture: Based on the Competing Values Framework.* John Wiley & Sons, 2006.

Terrence E. Deal and Kent D. Peterson, *Shaping School Culture: The Heart of Leadership.* Jossey Bass, 1999.

Michael Fullan, *Leading in a Culture of Change.* Jossey-Bass, 2001.

James L. Gibson, John M. Ivancevich, James H. Donnelly, Jr. and Robert Konopaske, Organizational Culture, *Organizations: Behavior, Structure, Processes.* McGraw-Hill, 2003.

Steven Jay Gross, *Promises Kept: Sustaining School and District Leadership in a Turbulent Era.* Association of Supervision and Curriculum Development, 2004.

Peter Senge, *The Fifth Discipline.* Doubleday, 1990.

For more on improvement of organizational culture, check these sites:

School Culture http://education.gallup.com/content/default.aspx?ci=22156

Institutional Formation www.novalearning.com/html/institutional_formation.htm

Managing the Climate of a TQM Organization http://cqmextra.cqm.org/cqmjournal.nsf/reprints/rp09100

The Culture Audit http://cnx.org/content/m13691/latest/

School Culture Triage www.nsdc.org/library/publications/jsd/wagtools233.pdf

# What Do Educational Leaders Need to Understand about Organizational Improvement and School Reform?

Reform and improvement are garnering an enormous amount of attention these days. Not that this is news—the education community has been embroiled in series after series of reforms for several decades. Large-scale reforms tend to polarize, resulting in winner-take-all battles. The basic premise of reform may not be an issue—who could disagree with the notion that education should lead to achievement and improvement? What polarizes the community are methods, measures, assessment, environment, curriculum, school choice, and numerous other elements of the educational enterprise. Chief among current reform issues are measures and assessment— particularly in math and reading—and for some experts, a narrow focus on these areas leaves little room for dealing with other important elements.

> The notion that we can and should use data to guide school practice is spreading and is an important and positive trend. The issue of what we measure, however, is still up in the air. Evidence-based research guidelines tend to push practitioners and evaluators to focus on experience that can be operationally defined in behavioral terms alone. However, there are many important social, emotional, and ethical dimensions to interpersonal and school life that are not simple to define operationally. (Jonathan Cohen, Social, emotional, ethical, and academic education: Creating a climate for learning, participation in democracy, and well-being. *Harvard Educational Review,* Summer 2006)

Some defenders of current federal policy (the No Child Left Behind Act of 2001) would respond that instructional programs must be scientifically based— how else will we know whether educational programs are effective? And while social, emotional, and ethical dimensions may be important, math and reading are far more critical to America's competitiveness around the globe.

What are leaders to make of the plethora of reforms that divides teachers, communities, and researchers? Foremost, leaders must understand the nature of the reforms themselves, particularly those stipulated by legislation:

> School leaders who depend on federal funding are now required to be aware of the nature of the research that guides their programs and practices. In particular,

federal funding decisions will be determined in part by whether programs and practices have a basis in "scientific research." (Beghetto, 2003)

Leaders also need to gauge whether an organization can handle reform initiatives. In this decade, improving student performance is the driver of reforms and not every organizational structure or model will result in improvement, no matter how hard everyone tries. Some institutions—as currently structured—are incapable of incorporating new initiatives. Think of it like this—a business attempts to offer new products and services only to discover their structure is incapable of supporting necessary changes in production. Determining whether a structure is able to reform is a matter of concern to Phillip Schlechty, CEO of a national center on systemic reform:

> . . . school leaders seldom take capacity issues into account when they are installing innovations. Because of this leadership shortcoming, innovations that might have dramatically improved school performance often end up being labeled as failures. (Phillip C. Schlechty, Creating the capacity to support innovation. *Schlechty Center for Leadership in School Reform*, 2005)

A bad fit between a traditional institutional model and reform innovations causes a dilemma for leaders. If new initiatives cannot be accommodated in the current model, then it doesn't make sense to install them, much less assume improvement will occur. To be successful in making systemic changes, leaders need to ensure that certain capacities are in place first. Research by organizations such as the American Association of School Administrators and the Stupski Foundation is showing that it is crucial for leaders to consider implications of reform before an initiative even gets underway. What's becoming clear is that answering the capacity question ahead of time will help school reformers succeed.

But what should leaders do when it becomes evident that internal reforms are still not sufficient and larger social and economic reforms are needed? Richard Rothstein, author of a policy perspective titled "Reforms That Could Help Narrow the Achievement Gap," maintains the United States will never close the gap without implementing vital societal reforms. Rothstein believes educational institutions should not be left alone to take the rap for failure to substantially close gaps in achievement between lower-class and middle-class children. Wise leaders understand how social policies and investment in health care, housing, and after-school programs can complement internal reforms.

When leaders take up questions of curriculum, instruction, and assessment reform, they must recognize what is at stake. According to the author of the third viewpoint, an excerpt from a report commissioned by the National Center on Education and the Economy, the implications of reforming key aspects of the educational process are profound. The author has scathing criticism for the direction No Child Left Behind legislation has taken assessment:

> It is somewhat ironic that in the context of rising expectations about what all students should learn—and, by implication, what they should be assessed on—we

have moved in the opposite direction with respect to the types of assessments that now drive the educational system . . . states have been driven to put in place assessment systems that seriously undermine high achievement standards and quality instructional practices. (p. 6)

Understanding this cleavage involves taking a step back to grapple with the nature of learning. Only through deep dialogue can leaders and faculty choose valuable curricular goals and effective assessment approaches that are the heart of worthwhile reforms. The report of the New Commission on the Skills of the American Workforce provides a bold framework for leaders to use in analyzing what reforms are crucial. Make no mistake; this is not just another reform diatribe. The report calls for the largest changes in the educational system in a century. According to the commission, without these changes the American standard of living will be in serious jeopardy. Educational leaders be aware.

The final reading is based on the premise that schools are so intertwined, it is impossible for one school to be a model of reform without crippling other schools. The title, "The Ripple Effect," may make it sound like simple cause and effect, but the impact of stand-out or star schools on other schools is complex. The authors tackle reform as a matter of sustainability and social justice.

These readings on reform and improvement of educational organizations point to underlying forces that are political, social, and economic. All of these forces, while unpredictable, play a significant role in how schools and institutions function. One thing is certain, reform is ever present. To prosper in this time, educational institutions and their leaders need critical skills in discerning links between reform initiatives and structure, internal and external reform, workforce skills and curricular reform, and reform and social justice.

# SOURCES

Richard Rothstein, Reforms that could help narrow the achievement gap. *WestEd,* 2006.

James W. Pellegrino, Rethinking and redesigning curriculum, instruction and assessment: What contemporary research and theory suggests. *National Center on Education and the Economy,* November 2006.

Andy Hargreaves and Dean Fink, The ripple effect. *Educational Leadership*, May 2006.

# Reforms That Could Help Narrow the Achievement Gap

## Richard Rothstein

*Policymakers almost universally conclude that persistent achievement gaps must result from wrongly designed school policies — either expectations that are too low, teachers who are insufficiently qualified, curricula that are badly designed, classes that are too large, school climates that are too undisciplined, leadership that is too unfocused, or a combination of these. This exclusive focus on schooling is wrong. Without complementary investments in early childhood preparation, health care, housing, after-school and summer programs, and other social and economic supports, the achievement gap will never be closed.*

*What is the theory behind linking social class differences with gaps in achievement?*

Americans have concluded that the achievement gap is the fault of "failing schools" because it makes no common sense that it could be otherwise. After all, how much money a family has, or a child's skin color, should not influence how well that child learns to read. If teachers know how to teach and if schools permit no distractions, children should be able to learn these subjects whatever their family income or skin color.

This common sense perspective, however, is misleading and dangerous. It ignores how social class characteristics in a stratified society like ours may actually influence learning in school. It confuses social class, a concept which Americans have historically been loathe to consider, with two of its characteristics, income and, in the United States, race. For it is true that low income and skin color themselves don't influence academic achievement, but the collection of characteristics that define social class differences inevitably influences that achievement.

If as a society we choose to preserve big social class differences, we must necessarily also accept substantial gaps between the achievement of lower-class and middle-class children. Closing those gaps requires not only better schools, although those are certainly needed, but also reform in the social and economic institutions that prepare children to learn in different ways. It will not be cheap.

What follows is a series of reforms, in addition to school improvement, that could help narrow the achievement gap.

# GREATER INCOME INEQUALITY

Low-income families have seen their incomes grow far less than those of middle-class families in recent years. As a result, too many families have inadequate incomes to provide security for children. Doing something about the wide income gap between lower and middle-class parents could be one of the most important educational reforms we could consider.

The lowest fifth of families with children in the national income distribution saw after-tax income decline by 1.2% per year from 1979 to 1989. These families had gains in the early 1990s (up 2.5% annually from 1989 to 1995), largely because of improvements in the Earned Income Tax Credit. But after-tax income growth for low-income families was just 1.1% per year in the boom of the late 1990s. Then recession reduced their incomes by 5.8% from 2000 to 2002.[1] Thus, over the entire 1979–2002 period, after-tax incomes of the lowest fifth of families with children rose by just 2.3%, and during much of this period, these families' already low incomes were declining, placing them (including their children) under great stress.

In contrast, middle-income families saw after-tax income rise by 17% during this period, even after a 3% decline in the recent recession.[2] Thus, the last few decades has seen a widening income gap between those in the bottom and those in the middle.

A more positive development is that the ratio of Black to White median family income increased from 57% a quarter century ago to about 64% today. This still leaves Black family incomes far behind those of Whites. The ratio of Black to White median family wealth has improved at an even greater rate, from 7% to 12%. Yet these trends still leave a far greater disparity in wealth than in income.[3]

Many families, especially minority families, have incomes that are too low to adequately support children. In 2000, 11% of Americans had incomes below the poverty line, no different from the poverty rate in 1973.[4] The racial disparity has diminished, as Black poverty has dropped from 31% in 1973 to 23% in 2000, while White poverty has risen from 8% to 10%. This still leaves the Black poverty rate more than twice as great as the White rate. A third (33%) of Black children under age 6 were poor in 2000, as were 13% of young White children.[5]

Further, the official poverty line (roughly $18,000 for a family of four in 2001) sets too low a threshold to describe the income needed to assure minimal stability. A more realistic basic family budget is about twice the poverty line. Using such a standard, half of all Black and one fifth of all White families have inadequate incomes.[6]

To narrow the Black-White achievement gap and the gap between all lower- and middle-class children, supporting the incomes of low-wage parents can make an important contribution. In real dollars, the value of the minimum wage has plummeted by 25% since 1979.[7] While few parents of school children work for the minimum wage, many work in industries whose wages are affected by the minimum wage.[8] A wage increase could well have an impact on student performance, comparable to that of within-school educational reforms. Other reforms to labor market institutions, such as making it easier for workers to seek and obtain collective bargaining (as the law was intended to facilitate), would also lift wages of low income workers who are trying to support children.

In the 1990s, the federal government moved to offset trends toward growing income inequality, primarily by expansion of the Earned Income Tax Credit, a subsidy to low-income working parents with children. It had an impact. In 2000, low-income single mothers earned, on average, about $8,000, but after the tax credit and other public assistance, their average income nearly doubled.[9] However, this income, at about the poverty line, is still not enough to enable their children to have a reasonable chance to achieve, on average, at the level of middle-class children.

A commitment to low unemployment would be particularly helpful to low-income families and minorities, groups disproportionately hurt by recessions. The 4% unemployment rate achieved in 2000, if sustained, could have done much to increase the security of low-income families and their children.

## STABLE HOUSING

Also important are reforms, not typically thought of as educational, that help lower-class families afford stable and adequate housing. The high mobility rates in lower-class neighborhoods inevitably result in lower student achievement. When children move in and out of schools, not only does their own achievement suffer but so, too, does the achievement of their classmates whose learning is also disrupted. There are many reasons for the high mobility of low-income families, but one of them is the lack of affordable housing in many urban areas today, as housing prices accelerate faster than wages and inflation. A serious commitment to narrowing the academic achievement gap should include a plan to stabilize the housing of working families with children who cannot afford adequate shelter. A national housing policy that reduced the mobility of low-income families might also do more to boost test scores of their children than many instructional reforms.

One federal program to subsidize rents of such families is the "Section 8" voucher program. It is under constant political attack and never fully funded.[10] The average annual cost of a Section 8 voucher is now about $6,700.[11] The federal government spends about $14 billion annually on Section 8 vouchers for about two million families, only about one fourth of those eligible.[12] If vouchers were provided to all eligible families, the cost could rise to $56 billion. Considered as an expenditure that contributes to an adequate education, it would be equivalent to about $1,000 on a per pupil nationwide basis.[13] Even with a commitment to such spending, the money could be appropriated only very gradually because there is now insufficient housing stock to accommodate the families who need it.

An experiment to test whether housing policy could affect student achievement (as well as other outcomes) was stimulated initially by a housing desegregation suit in Chicago. A settlement required the Chicago Housing Authority to provide federal housing vouchers that would help public housing residents (mostly Black) to move to rental units in desegregated neighborhoods. This "Gautreaux" program (the name is that of the plaintiff in the original lawsuit) seemed to show that families who moved to suburbs had better employment outcomes than comparable families who used vouchers for rental units in the city. Adolescent children of suburban movers also apparently fared better than their urban counterparts, having lower dropout rates and better achievement. Although grade point averages of suburban and city movers were nearly identical, similar grades probably represented higher achievement in suburban than in urban high schools because suburban schools had higher standardized test scores.[14]

These results whet the appetites of housing experts for a true experiment, and in 1994 Congress appropriated funds for the Department of Housing and Urban Development to implement a "Moving to Opportunity" (MTO) experiment to determine whether low-income families benefit from living in communities where fewer families were poor.[15] Such experimentation is rarely possible in social science because the denial of a benefit to a control group presents difficult ethical problems, but these problems are mitigated if the benefit is scarce due to no fault of the experimenters, and the experimental pool from which both treatment and control groups are drawn can be comprised entirely of volunteers. The benefit can then be allocated in some random fashion lending itself to observation of an experiment.

These conditions were met in MTO because there are long waiting lists for Section 8 vouchers, and demand for private apartments whose owners are willing to participate in the program far exceeds the supply.[16] So establishing a control group whose members do not receive subsidies does not withhold a benefit from those who otherwise might receive it.[17]

The MTO experiment established lists of families with children who presently live in high-poverty neighborhoods. To get on the lists, families had to express interest in using vouchers to move to private apartments in low-poverty communities. MTO officials then randomly selected families from these lists for three groups: the main treatment group that received vouchers for subsidies to rent private apartments in low-poverty communities (the families were given counseling and assistance in locating such apartments); a comparison group that received vouchers for subsidies to rent private apartments wherever they could find them without counseling and assistance; and a third group, the controls, that received no vouchers for private housing. Scholars were invited to track the experiment over a 10-year period.

Although it was generally expected that the mover children would benefit, this was not certain. Effects on children of associating with higher-achieving peers should be positive. But there is also some evidence that placing lower-class children in middle-class communities can lead these children to withdraw from academic competition due to feelings of inadequacy.[18]

At this point, MTO evidence is mixed. One study found that younger children in mover families had higher test scores than the controls, but outcomes for adolescents were more ambiguous. Teenagers from mover families were more likely to be disciplined in school and to drop out than those in the control group. This might be because the disciplinary and academic standards in the suburban high schools were higher than the standards in the neighborhoods where the controls resided.[19]

*What might account for positive peer influence in an integrated education?*

While the results of the MTO experiment are mixed, we can still only speculate about how important such efforts might be in narrowing the achievement gap.[20] It seems reasonable, though not certain, that if funds spent to stabilize housing were included in a broader program that facilitated the movement of low-income families to mixed neighborhoods, the achievement gap might be further narrowed as children benefited from the positive peer influences that characterize more integrated educations. Along with rental subsidies and assistance to families in finding rental units in mixed neighborhoods, such a broader program, to be effective, should also include changes in local zoning laws that now prevent low- and moderate-income rental units from being located in many middle-class neighborhoods, and better enforcement of fair housing laws that prohibit racial discrimination by realtors and landlords. These should all be considered educational, not only housing, programs.

## SCHOOL–COMMUNITY CLINICS

Without adequate health care for lower-class children and their parents, there is little hope of fully closing the achievement gap. A high priority should be establishing health clinics associated with schools that serve disadvantaged children. Because many lower-class children have health problems that impede learning, quality education cannot be delivered to these children without adequate medical care. Because parents in poor health cannot properly nurture children, a quality education also requires that lower-class parents get the means to achieve good health themselves.[21] These goals require the establishment of school clinics that serve children through their high school years, and their parents as well.

A school-community clinic should include services that middle-class families take for granted and that ensure children can thrive in school. Clinics associated with schools in lower-class communities should include: obstetric and gynecological services for pregnant and post-partum women; pediatric services for children through their high school years; physicians to serve parents of all school-age children; nurses to support these medical services; dentists and hygienists to see both parents and children semi-annually; optometrists and vision therapists to serve those who require treatment for their sight; social workers to refer families to other services; community health educators to instruct young women in proper health habits during pregnancy, or to organize smoking reduction campaigns; and psychologists or therapists to assist families and children who are experiencing excessive stress.

For elementary and secondary schools, the nation currently spends over $8,000 per pupil, on average.[22] Health clinics with a full array of services, associated with schools serving lower-class children, would add another $2,500 per pupil to the annual cost of educating the children in these schools.[23] Some of this money is not new public spending. The costs for some of these services are eligible for Medicaid or other public reimbursement. However, because some children and their parents who should get Medicaid and other public health services do not presently receive them, either because the application is cumbersome or because parents fear applying or do not know to apply, only guaranteed access through a school-based clinic can ensure that children will be healthy enough to learn to their full capacities.

Several small programs could be implemented relatively cheaply. Putting dental and vision clinics in schools serving low-income children would cost only about $400 per pupil in those schools. This is less money than is often proposed for school reforms like teacher professional development or class size reduction. Schools might get a bigger test score jump from dental and vision clinics than from more expensive instructional reforms. Designing experiments to evaluate this possibility would not be difficult.

# EARLY CHILDHOOD EDUCATION

Low-income and minority children can benefit fully from good schools only if they enter these schools ready to learn. Narrowing the achievement gap requires early childhood programs, staffed with professional teachers and nurses, and with curricula that emphasize not only literacy but social and emotional growth. Social class differences in vocabulary and conceptual ability develop by age 3.

Lower-class children's early childhood experiences should provide an intellectual environment comparable to what middle-class children experience—rich in language, where well-educated adults are companions, instructors, and role models. Lower-class children should hear more sophisticated language, be exposed to books at an early age, and experience the excitement of stories read, told, and discussed.

To achieve in school, toddlers who don't gain these experiences at home will have to gain them in formal programs that differ from typical day care settings in lower-class communities where children may be parked before television sets and rarely taken on interesting excursions or guided in exploratory play. Typical day care staff for lower-class children are poorly paid and often have educations that are no greater than the children's parents'. Because of the low wages, the educational background of caregivers for low-income children declined in the 1990s.[24]

Adequate early childhood programs also differ from Head Start, which typically does not serve children until the age of 3 or 4, too late to fully compensate for their disadvantages.[25] But there are nonetheless exemplary aspects of Head Start. Although the Bush administration is attempting to shift the balance of Head Start instruction toward more academic activities, most Head Start programs have addressed not only academic skills alone but also children's health, dental, nutritional, social, and emotional needs. Head Start also includes a role for parents, and staff members are required to visit parents to instruct them in "middle-class childrearing skills."[26]

To narrow the achievement gap later in life, lower-class toddlers should begin early childhood programs at six months of age, and attend for a full day. Three and four-year-olds should attend preschool, also for a full day, year-round.[27]

This would be costly. Programs for infants from six months to one year of age should place teams of two caregivers with groups of no more than eight children, or an adult-to-child ratio of 1:4. As toddlers mature to two years of age, this group size should increase to 10 children, a ratio of 1:5.[28]

To provide an intellectual environment similar to one that gives middle-class children a boost, preschool teachers (for four-year-olds) should have a bachelor's degree in early childhood education. Each should be assisted by a paraprofessional, in groups of 15, resulting in an adult-child ratio of 1:7.5. This permits adequate supervision of group work and play, reading aloud, and less formal instruction.[29] . . .

An adequately staffed early childhood center should also have professionals who help bridge the gap between lower-class parents and schools. A home-school teacher can offer parent workshops on appropriate play activities and discipline. She can visit children's homes, observe regular classrooms, and consult with regular teachers, then help parents, to the extent they are able, support teachers to aid instruction. Such a professional can prepare parents to meet with teachers, help them to interpret school documents (like report cards), and connect parents with others who have similar problems and concerns.

An adequate early childhood program for lower class children would also employ visiting nurses. Home nurse visits to pregnant women and those with newborns should monitor mothers' and infants' health as well as teach health-related parenting skills that affect children's ability to learn. Educating new mothers and all women of childbearing age about the effects on children of smoking and alcohol would be an obvious role.

Where such programs have been tried, there is evidence of their value. In one randomized controlled experiment, nurses visited low-income unwed mothers during their pregnancies and continued these visits during the first two years of the newborns' lives. The researchers continued to track the children through adolescence. The youngsters who, along with their mothers, received the nurse services had less crime, sexual activity, cigarette and alcohol use, and associated behavioral problems, compared to a control group that received no such services. The visiting nurses also affected the mothers' behavior: The mothers had less closely spaced subsequent unplanned pregnancies and less alcohol and drug abuse themselves. Mothers' behavioral changes of this kind are known to reduce anti-social behavior in children. In the experiment, children of mothers who were visited by nurses during pregnancy had higher I.Q. scores at ages 3 and 4, attributable solely to nurses' success in getting mothers to reduce smoking.[30] Added positive effects flowed from other behavioral changes.

Adding the cost of such early childhood programs to regular education finances would boost average annual costs of elementary and secondary schools for lower-class children by another $2,500 per pupil.[31]

# AFTER SCHOOL

After-school and summer programs are also necessary contributions, organized to provide not only added opportunities for academic work, but also the non-academic activities that enhance students' personal skills. When middle-class children leave school in the afternoons, they may go to Girl or Boy Scouts, religious groups, Little League, or soccer practice, or take art, dance, or music lessons. Lower-class children are more likely to play informally or watch television.[32]

Structured after-school activities contribute to academic proficiency. Children with broader experiences can empathize with literary characters, and this enhances the incentive to read. After school, privileged children are more likely to practice social responsibility in church or youth organizations, and develop the organizational skills and discipline that make them more effective adults.

Every child has a somewhat different collection of skills, abilities, and interests. Children who may not excel in math may get a chance to do so in soccer, drama, or piano. Self-confidence gained may carry over to academics. It is foolish to think that lower-class children can achieve, on average, at middle-class levels without similar opportunities. Although some lower-class students have these opportunities at the YMCA, Boys and Girls Clubs, the Children's Aid Society, or publicly funded after-school programs, many do not.

Adolescents need such activities not only for what they provide but what they prevent. Students without supervision are at greater risk for truancy, stress, poor grades, and substance abuse. They are most likely to be perpetrators or victims of crime in the first few hours after school.[33]

An adequate after-school and weekend program for lower-class children would add another $5,000 per pupil annually to the cost of these children's elementary and secondary schools.[34]

# SUMMER PROGRAMS

The achievement gap between Black and White children grows the most during summer vacations, when middle-class children have experiences—reading books, going to camp, visiting museums, and traveling—that reinforce their school-year learning, while lower-class children fall behind. An education that hopes to narrow the achievement gap, therefore, should provide comparable summer experiences—not only extra drills in reading and math and not even a summer school only of more advanced academic skills. Art, music, drama, dance, and physical education teachers should be more numerous in summer than in the regular year.

A summer program that truly provides lower-class children with such "middle-class" experiences would add another $2,500 to annual per-pupil costs of the schools lower-class children attend.[35]

# THE DANGERS OF FALSE EXPECTATIONS AND ADEQUACY SUITS

*How does the cost of added services compare with the total annual cost of public schools?*

All told, adding the price of health, early childhood, after-school, and summer programs, this down payment on closing the achievement gap would probably increase the annual cost of education, for children who attend schools where at least 40% of the enrolled children's families have low incomes, by about $12,500 per pupil, over and above the $8,000 already being spent. In total, this means about a $156 billion added annual national cost to provide these programs to low-income children.[36] Even such an expenditure will not fully close the gap, but it might increase the overlap in outcomes of Black and White, lower- and middle-class children.

There would be some offsetting savings. If lower-class children had adequate health care and intellectually challenging experiences in an early childhood program, their later placement in special education programs would decline. Experiments that tested high-quality preschool programs showed that children in these programs were less likely to require special education when they got to regular schools.[37] Similarly, vision therapy, adequate prenatal care, reduction in adult smoking and alcohol use, and other health interventions also reduce the placement of children in special education. For 35 years, special education has been the fastest-growing category of education spending, consuming about 40% of all new money given to schools.[38] A significant part of this growth is attributable to the learning difficulties and mental retardation of lower-class children whose disabilities result disproportionately from inadequate health care and inappropriate early childhood experiences.

Education policymakers often say that higher salaries are needed for teachers in general, and even higher salaries than these are needed to attract the most qualified teachers to take jobs in schools where children are most in need. Teaching lower class children who come to school not ready to learn is difficult, and even if dedicated teachers volunteer for the task, they often wear down and leave for easier assignments after a few years. But if lower-class children came to school ready to learn, in good health, and with adequate early childhood experiences, teachers would find more success and fulfillment in working with them. Less of a salary increment would be needed to attract teachers to work with such children.

Another often recommended policy is smaller class sizes, especially in elementary schools that mostly serve children from lower-class families. These smaller class sizes have had a demonstrable effect on life-long achievement but are expensive. In the Tennessee experiment, for example, class sizes in kindergarten through third grade were reduced from 24 to 15. If this reduction were implemented for lower-class children only, average spending for these children would go up by about $500, not including the cost of building new classrooms to house the added classes.[39] But if teachers of lower-class children had the opportunity to build on the academic and social achievements of an adequate early childhood program, higher achievement could be generated without so drastic a decrease in primary grade class size. . . .

Many lawsuits around the country involve plaintiffs, usually representing minority children or school districts in which they are numerous, who demand "adequate school funding." The most prominent recent case is one in New York State where the Court of Appeals found the state's school financing system unconstitutional because it does not give lower-class children the opportunity to achieve at middle-class levels. Such lawsuits, if successful, can improve education for minority and low-income youth. But advocates of this litigation should not raise expectations that even significantly more new dollars in schools alone will close the academic gap. In New York, the plaintiffs have proposed an added $4,000 per pupil for schools in New York City, a 24% increase in per-pupil spending. The plaintiffs say these new funds should mostly be used for smaller classes and higher teacher pay. Such new spending will certainly improve education for New York City youngsters. But advocates for the plaintiffs have gone further, and say that such an increase could close the achievement gap and enable all students to achieve at high enough levels to qualify for admission to academic colleges.[40] This expectation is bound to be disappointed. If social class differences in readiness for learning are unaddressed, such a goal can only be met if high school graduation and college admissions standards are diluted to unrecognizability.

Funds sought in adequacy cases, while substantial, are tiny compared to what is truly needed for adequate outcomes. Schools, no matter how good, cannot carry the entire burden of narrowing our substantial social class differences.

# TEACHER MORALE

In American education today, policymakers and educators frequently invoke slogans like "no excuses," or "all students can learn to the same high standards," proclaiming what they say is their commitment to close the achievement gap between lower-class and middle-class children. Some say that these incantations are harmless, and, even if they are hyperbolic, serve the useful purpose of spurring teachers, principals, and other school officials to greater efforts to raise the achievement levels of minority and other disadvantaged students.

Such whips can serve this useful purpose. But they can also do great damage. They de-legitimize good and great teachers who dedicate themselves to raising minority student achievement in realistic increments. They drive out of the teaching profession decent teachers who feel inadequate to the task of reaching utopian goals, or who resent the cynicism of politicians and administrators who demand that such goals be attained. If this disconnect continues between what is realistically possible and the goals we establish for educators, the nation risks abandoning public education only to those willing to pander to political fashion by promising to achieve in schools what they know, in their hearts, is not possible. And in the polity, "no excuses" slogans provide ideological respectability for those wanting to hold schools accountable for inevitable failure.

# REFERENCES

Allgood, Whitney C., and Richard Rothstein. Forthcoming. *At-Risk Adequacy Calculations.* Washington, DC: Economic Policy Institute.

Barnett, W. Steven. 1995. "Long-Term Effects of Early Childhood Programs on Cognitive and School Outcomes." *The Future of Children: Long-Term Outcomes of Early Childhood Programs* 5(3): 25–50.

Barnett, W. Steven, Kenneth B. Robin, Jason T. Hustedt, and Karen L. Schulman. 2004. *The State of Preschool: 2003 State Preschool Yearbook.* New Brunswick, NJ: National Institute for Early Education Research. http://www.nieer.org/yearbook

Bernstein, Jared, and Jeff Chapman. 2002. *Time to Repair the Wage Floor.* Washington, DC: Economic Policy Institute.

Bernstein, Jared, Chauna Brocht, and Maggie Spade-Aguilar. 2000. *How Much is Enough: Basic Family Budgets for Working Families.* Washington, DC: Economic Policy Institute.

Boushey, Heather, Chauna Brocht, Bethney Gunderson, and Jared Bernstein. 2001. *Hardships in America: The Real Story of Working Families.* Washington, DC: Economic Policy Institute.

Brooks-Gunn, Jeanne, and Greg J. Duncan. 1997. "The Effects of Poverty on Children." *The Future of Children* 7(2): 55–71.

CBO (Congressional Budget Office). 2003, May 15. *Effective Federal Tax Rates for All Households, by Household Income Category,* 1979 to 2000. Washington, DC: CBO. ftp://ftp.cbo.gov/45xx/doc4514/08-29-Report.pdf

Center on Budget and Policy Priorities. 2003. *Introduction to the Housing Voucher Program.* Washington, DC: Center on Budget and Policy Priorities.

Citizens for Tax Justice. 2003. *Details on Bush Tax Cuts So Far.* http://www.ctj.org/pdf/gwbdata.pdf

Currie, Janet, and Duncan Thomas. 1995. "Does Head Start Make a Difference?" *American Economic Review* 85(3): 341–364.

Donohue, John J. III, and Peter Siegelman. 1998. "Allocating Resources Among Prisons and Social Programs in the Battle Against Crime." *Journal of Legal Studies*, 27 J. Legal Stud. 1.

Dreier, Peter, and David Moberg. 1995. "Moving From the 'Hood'." *American Prospect* 24 (Winter): 75–79.

Garces, Eliana, Duncan Thomas, and Janet Currie. 2000. *Longer Term Effects of Head Start.* NBER Working Paper W8054, December. Cambridge, MA: National Bureau of Economic Research.

Gordon, Larry. 1997, September 23. "A Social Experiment in Pulling Up Stakes." *Los Angeles Times*.

Hacsi, Timothy A. 2002. *Children as Pawns. The Politics of Educational Reform.* Cambridge, MA: Harvard University Press.

Janofsky, Michael. 1999, March 7. "The Dark Side of the Economic Expansion. The Poor Wait Longer for Affordable Housing, Government Finds." *New York Times*.

Jencks, Christopher, and Susan Mayer. 1990. "The Social Consequences of Growing Up in a Poor Neighborhood." In Laurence E. Lynn and Michael G. H. McGeary, eds., *Inner-City Poverty in the United States.* Washington, DC: National Academy Press.

Kaufman, Julie E., and James E. Rosenbaum. 1992. "The Education and Employment of Low-Income Black Youth in White Suburbs." *Educational Evaluation and Policy Analysis* 14(3): 229–240.

Kling, Jeffrey R., and Jeffrey B. Liebman. 2004. *Experimental Analysis of Neighborhood Effects on Youth.* Working Paper 483, Industrial Relations Section, Princeton University, Princeton, NJ.

Krueger, Alan B., and Pei Zhu. 2003. *Another Look at the New York City School Voucher Experiment.* Working Paper 470, Industrial Relations Section, Princeton University, Princeton, NJ.

Lareau, Annette. 2002. "Invisible Inequality: Social Class and Childrearing in Black Families and White Families." *American Sociological Review* 67 (October): 747–776.

Lee, Valerie, Jeanne Brooks-Gunn, and Elizabeth Schnur. 1988. "Does Head Start Work? A 1-Year Follow-Up Comparison of Disadvantaged Children Attending Head Start, No Preschool and Other Preschool Programs." *Developmental Psychology* 24(2): 210–222.

Lippman, Laura, Shelley Burns, and Edith McArthur. 1996. *Urban Schools, The Challenge of Location and Poverty.* NCES 96-184. U.S. Department of Education, Office of Educational Research and Improvement.

Ludwig, Jens, Helen F. Ladd, and Greg J. Duncan. 2001. "Urban Poverty and Educational Outcomes." *Brookings-Wharton Papers on Urban Affairs, 2001.* Washington, DC: Brookings Institution.

MacDonald, Heather. 1997. "Comment on Sandra J. Newman and Ann B. Schnare's "'. . . And a Suitable Living Environment': The Failure of Housing Programs to Deliver on Neighborhood Quality." *Housing Policy Debate* 8(4): 755–62.

Mishel, Lawrence, Jared Bernstein, and Heather Boushey. 2003. *The State of Working America 2002 / 2003*. Ithaca, NY: Cornell University Press.

NAEYC (National Association for the Education of Young Children). 1998. *Accreditation Criteria & Procedures of the National Association for the Education of Young Children—1998 Edition*. Washington, DC: Author.

NCES (National Center for Education Statistics). 2003b. *Digest of Education Statistics—2002*. NCES 2003-060. Washington, DC: U.S. Department of Education, Office of Educational Research and Improvement.

Neuman, Susan B. 2003. "From Rhetoric to Reality: The Case for High-Quality Compensatory Pre-Kindergarten Programs." *Phi Delta Kappan* 85(4): 286–291.

NIOOST (National Institute for Out of School Time). 2000. *Fact Sheet on School-Age Children's Out-of-School Time*. http://www.wellesley.edu/WCW/CRW/SAC/factsht.html

Olds, David L., et al. 1997. "Long-Term Effects of Home Visitation on Maternal Life Course and Child Abuse and Neglect: Fifteen-Year Follow-Up of a Randomized Trial." *Journal of the American Medical Association* 278 (8): 637–643.

Olds, David L., et al. 1999. "Prenatal and Infancy Home Visitation by Nurses: Recent Findings." *Future of Children* 9(1): 44–65.

Rosenbaum, James E. 1991. "Black Pioneers: Do Their Moves to the Suburbs Increase Economic Opportunity for Mothers and Children?" *Housing Policy Debate* 2(4): 1179–1213.

Rothstein, Richard. 1997. *Where's the Money Going? Changes in the Level and Composition of Education Spending, 1991–96*. Washington, DC: Economic Policy Institute.

Rothstein, Richard. 2000b, October 18. "Better Than a Voucher, a Ticket to Suburbia." *New York Times*.

Rothstein, Richard, with Karen Hawley Miles. 1995. *Where's the Money Gone? Changes in the Level and Composition of Education Spending*. Washington, DC: Economic Policy Institute.

Sard, Barbara, and Will Fisher. 2003, September 23. *Senate Committee Bill May Avert Cuts to Housing Vouchers Despite Inadequate Appropriation*. Washington, DC: Center on Budget and Policy Priorities.

Sanbonmatsu, Lisa, Jeffrey R. Kling, Greg J. Duncan, and Jeanne Brooks-Gunn. 2006. *Neighborhoods and Academic Achievement: Results from the Moving to Opportunity Experiment*. NBER Working Paper No. 11909, January. Cambridge, MA: National Bureau of Economic Research.

Vandell, Deborah Lowe, and Barbara Wolfe. 2000. *Child Care Quality: Does it Matter, and Does it Need to be Improved?* Washington, DC: U.S. Department of Health and Human Services. http://aspe.hhs.gov/hsp/ccquality00/index.htm

Vinovskis, Maris A. 1995. "School Readiness and Early Childhood Education." In Diane Ravitch and Maris A. Vinovskis, eds. *Learning From the Past. What History Teaches Us About School Reform.* Baltimore, MD: Johns Hopkins University Press.

Winter, Greg. 2004, February 5. "$4 Billion More Is Needed to Fix City's Schools, Study Finds." *New York Times.*

# ENDNOTES

1. CBO 2003. Data from 2003 are not yet available.
2. The most spectacular contrast, of course, is with the highest 1% of families, who had income growth exceeding 230% over the 1979–2002 period. However, the focus here is on the contrast between low- and middle income families because this is the relevant comparison for the educational achievement gap between lower- and middle-class children.
3. The data on income are from 1979 to 2000. Mishel, Bernstein, and Boushey 2003, Table 1.4. The data on wealth are from 1983 to 1998. Mishel, Bernstein, and Boushey 2003, Table 1.4. These are the most recent comparable data.
4. Mishel, Bernstein, and Boushey 2003, Table 5.2.
5. Mishel, Bernstein, and Boushey 2003, Table 5.3.
6. Bernstein, Brocht, and Spade-Aguilar 2000; Boushey et al. 2001, Table 3.
7. Mishel, Bernstein and Boushey, Table 2.41.
8. Bernstein and Chapman 2002.
9. Low-income single mothers are defined here as those whose earnings were below the median for all single mothers. Mishel, Bernstein, and Boushey 2003, Figure 5M.
10. A widely promoted reform, claimed to raise the achievement of lower-class children, is the provision of vouchers to pay private school tuition for such children. However, such vouchers usually only enable these children to attend private schools that are similar in social class composition to the public schools that voucher recipients would leave. The result is that such voucher programs have no meaningful effect on lower-class children's achievement. Krueger and Zhu 2003. Housing vouchers, however, permit lower-class children to attend middle-class schools where their achievement can rise. Rothstein 2000b.
11. Sard and Fisher 2003.
12. Center on Budget and Policy Priorities 2003.

13. There are presently about 50 million children enrolled in public elementary and secondary schools.

14. Rosenbaum 1991; Kaufman and Rosenbaum 1992.

15. MTO differs from Gautreaux in that MTO tests the effect of moving out of predominantly low-income communities, whereas analyses of Gautreaux test the effect of moving out of predominantly minority communities. In practice, there is considerable overlap.

16. Janofsky 1999.

17. In other respects, however, the program has still been controversial. Particularly in Baltimore, groups claiming to represent suburban residents complained that moving poor families into the suburbs would raise crime rates and reduce property values in these suburbs. As a result of these complaints, the federal government delayed commencement of the experiment, and then scaled it back (Dreier and Moberg 1995; Gordon 1997). Some conservative social critics attacked the program, claiming that recipients of vouchers who move to the suburbs will include not only the victims of inner-city social disorganization, "but the perpetrators as well, who may then spread social problems to marginal but stable working-class neighborhoods" (MacDonald 1997).

18. Jencks and Mayer 1990.

19. Ludwig et al. 2001.

20. Subsequent to the initial publication of the book, *Class and Schools,* from which this article is drawn, a new review (Sanbonmatsu et al. 2006) of all MTO studies finds less reason for encouragement, and wonders why the experiment's results were so much less favorable than the experimenters had expected.

21. Brooks-Gunn and Duncan 1997 cite evidence that low-income parents have worse physical and mental health than middle-class parents, and that parental mental health has an adverse effect on child outcomes.

22. NCES 2003b, Table 167. The average per-pupil amount for 1999-2000, the most recent year reported, was $8,032.

23. This is based on a cost estimate of $2,600 per pupil in schools that had such clinics. The bases for this and subsequent estimates in this chapter, with program models and descriptions of service assumptions, will be published in a forthcoming working paper by Allgood and Rothstein. The numbers are still subject to revision. If we assume that these clinics should be placed in schools where at least 40% of the enrolled students were eligible for free and reduced lunch, clinics should be placed in schools serving 26% of all students; see Lippman et al. 1996, Table 1.7, p. A-9. This would increase the per-pupil spending, averaged for all children, rich and poor, by about $700.

24. Vandell and Wolfe 2000.

25. Lee, Brooks-Gunn, and Schnur 1988; Currie and Thomas 1995.

26. Garces, Thomas, and Currie 2000; Currie and Thomas 1995.

27. Barnett 1995.
28. NAEYC 1998.
29. NAEYC 1998. The recommendation for professional qualifications for preschool teachers was recently reinforced by Barnett et al. 2004.
30. Olds et al. 1997; Olds et al. 1999.
31. It would increase average per-pupil costs nationwide by another $700 per pupil. See note 23, above.
32. Lareau 2002.
33. NIOOST 2000.
34. It would increase average per-pupil costs nationwide by another $1,400 per pupil. See note 23, above.
35. It would increase average per-pupil costs nationwide by another $700 per pupil. See note 23, above.
36. Enrollment in public elementary and secondary schools in 2001 was about 48 million (NCES 2003b, Table 37). Spending an additional $12,500 on 26% of these children would cost about $156 billion a year.
37. Barnett 1995.
38. Rothstein 1997; Rothstein and Miles 1995.
39. This rough estimate assumes that average per-pupil spending is currently about $8,000 per pupil, that teacher salary and compensation represents 56% of that amount (NCES 2003b, Table 164), and that a class size reduction of 37% (from 24 to 15) would be applied to the first 4 of the 13 grades of elementary and secondary education. This calculation does not adjust for the fact that not all students finish high school, and it does not take account of the fact that costs are not identical at each grade level (i.e., it assumes that grades K-3 represent 4/13 of total costs).
40. Winter 2004. The plaintiffs have proposed funding that, they claim, would enable all students to pass New York State's "Regents" exams, which signify the satisfactory completion of a college preparatory academic curriculum.

# ARTICLE 7.2

# Rethinking and Redesigning Curriculum, Instruction and Assessment: What Contemporary Research and Theory Suggests

James W. Pellegrino

## THE CONFLICT BETWEEN RISING EXPECTATIONS AND CONTEMPORARY ASSESSMENT PRACTICES

It is somewhat ironic that in the context of rising expectations about what all students should learn—and, by implication, what they should be assessed on—we have moved in the opposite direction with respect to the types of assessments that now drive the educational system. Under the No Child Left Behind legislation, states have been driven to put in place assessment systems that seriously undermine high achievement standards and quality instructional practices. In addition to the many conceptual and operational weaknesses of these assessments as indicated below, there is little awareness on the part of the public concerning the tremendous amount of money that is being spent by each state separately on designing and administering these tests as well as by the federal government in monitoring the separate states assessments and enforcing the provisions of the NCLB legislation. These are dollars that would be far better spent on quality assessment that was much more closely linked to important curricular and instructional goals such as those outlined in the New Commission Report.

At least four sets of concerns exist about the quality and efficacy of the current assessment systems that many states have produced in their attempt to comply with the NCLB regulations:

- **Effectiveness of measurement.** Do the most widely used assessments effectively capture the complex knowledge and skills emphasized in contemporary standards and deemed essential for success in the information-based economy? Probably not. Limits on the kinds of competencies currently being assessed also raise questions about the inferences one can therefore draw from test results. If scores go up on a test that measures a relatively narrow range of knowledge and skills, does that mean student learning has improved, or has instruction simply adapted to a constrained set of outcomes? If there is explicit "teaching to the test," at what cost do such gains in test scores accrue relative to acquiring other aspects of knowledge and skill that are valued in today's society? This is a point of considerable controversy with regard to the so-called "miracle in Texas" but also for the periodic ups and downs in state assessment results more generally.

- **Utility for improving teaching and learning.** How useful are current assessments for improving teaching and learning—the ultimate goal of education reforms? Not very. Most current large-scale tests provide very limited information that teachers and educational administrators can use to identify why students do not perform well, or to modify the conditions of instruction in ways likely to improve student achievement. The most widely used state and district assessments provide only general information about where a student stands relative to peers or whether the student has performed poorly or well in certain domains (for example, that the student performs "below basic" in mathematics). Such tests do not reveal whether students are using misguided strategies to solve problems or fail to understand key concepts within the subject matter being tested. They do not show whether a student is advancing toward competence or is stuck at a partial understanding of a topic that could seriously impede future learning. In short, many current assessments do not provide strong clues as to the types of educational interventions that would improve learners' performance, or even provide information on precisely where the students' strengths and weaknesses lie. Nor is information provided in a timely manner.

*Why is alignment of curriculum and assessment difficult to achieve?*

- **"Snapshots" versus progression over time.** Can we tell how much a student has progressed in a year? Not really. Most assessments provide "snap shots" of achievement at particular points in time, but they do not capture the progression of students' conceptual understanding over time, which is at the heart of learning. This limitation exists largely because most current modes of assessment lack an underlying theoretical framework of how student understanding in a content area develops over the course of instruction, and predominant measurement methods are not designed to capture such growth.

- **Fairness and equity.** Are tests fair and equitable? Perhaps not. Much attention is given to the issue of test bias—whether differences occur in the performance of various groups for reasons that are irrelevant to the competency the test is intended to measure. Standardized-test items are subjected to judgmental and technical reviews to monitor for this kind of bias. However, the use of assessments for high-stakes decisions raises additional questions about fairness. If the assessments are not aligned with what students are being taught, it is not fair to base promotion or rewards on the results, especially if less advantaged students are harmed disproportionately by the outcome.

If current assessments do not effectively measure the impact of instruction or if they fail to capture important skills and knowledge, how can educators interpret and address gaps in student achievement? One of the main goals of proposed reforms is to improve learning for all students, but especially low-achieving students. If this goal is to be accomplished, assessment must give students, teachers, administrators and other stakeholders information they can use to improve learning and inform instructional decisions for individuals and groups, especially those not performing at high levels.

One of the most important things to recognize is that assessments need to be designed to satisfy specific purposes (e.g., formative, summative, or program evaluation) and that different assessment purposes demand different assessment designs. The current accountability tests developed by states to comply with NCLB are ostensibly designed to fulfill multiple purposes. However, in attempting to do so most states have created sub-optimal designs. If the goal is to monitor the overall status of educational achievement then assessment approaches of the type used in the National Assessment of Educational Progress are far better suited to this purpose especially with respect to valued curricular outcomes. If, however, the goal is to monitor the attainment of individual students with respect to specific curricular goals and standards then one needs assessments designed to meet that purpose. In this regard, the recommendation of the New Commission Report for periodic, standards-based exams in specific curricular areas is a far better investment of resources than the mass standardized testing approach that now dominates the educational landscape across K-12. Not only would students and teachers have a clearer sense of the content and criteria on which performance would be evaluated but the assessments would serve the needs of the individual and they would be motivated to perform well as opposed to the current situation of meeting the needs of a bureaucracy and not the individual tested. In addition to developing high quality, standards-based exams in critical instructional areas, considerably more investment is needed in ways to make the assessment process more supportive of teaching and learning through effective formative assessment materials and practices. In the material that follows, consideration is given to what it might take to build a far better system of assessments that would help meet the goals articulated in the New Commission Report.

# OUTMODED THEORIES AND UNDERUTILIZED TECHNOLOGIES

Whether we realize it or not, every educational assessment, whether used in the classroom or large-scale policy context, is based on a set of scientific principles and philosophical assumptions. First, every assessment is grounded in a conception or theory about how people learn, what people know, and how knowledge and understanding progress over time. Second, each assessment embodies certain assumptions about which kinds of observations, or tasks, are most likely to elicit demonstrations of important knowledge and skills from students. Third, every assessment is premised on certain assumptions about how best to interpret the evidence from the observations in order to make meaningful inferences about what students know and can do.

Current assessment systems are the cumulative product of various prior theories of learning and methods of measurement. Although some of these foundations are still useful for certain functions of testing, major change is needed. The most common kinds of educational tests do a reasonable job with certain limited functions of testing, such as measuring knowledge of basic facts and procedures and producing overall estimates of proficiency for restricted parts of the curriculum. But both their strengths and limitations are a product of their adherence to theories of learning and measurement that are outmoded and fail to capture the breadth and richness of knowledge and competence. The limitations of these theories also compromise the usefulness of the assessments. Assessment systems need to evolve to keep pace with developments in the sciences of learning and measurement if we are to achieve the learning goals embedded in current and future standards.

# RETHINKING THE FOUNDATIONS OF ASSESSMENT: THE MERGER OF COGNITION, MEASUREMENT AND TECHNOLOGY

As described above, several decades of research in the learning sciences have advanced our knowledge about how children develop understanding in areas of the curriculum, how people reason and build structures of knowledge in academic subject areas, which thinking processes are associated with competent performance, and how knowledge is shaped by social context. As noted earlier, studies of expert-novice differences in subject domains have illuminated many critical features of proficiency that should be the targets for assessment. Experts in a subject domain not only "know a lot"—more importantly they organize knowledge into schemas that support the rapid retrieval and application of such knowledge. Experts also use metacognitive strategies—ways of guiding one's thinking—for monitoring understanding during problem-solving and for performing self-correction.

These and many other findings on how people learn and the differences in what novices and experts know suggest directions for revamping assessment practices to move beyond a focus on component skills and discrete bits of knowledge. Assessment should encompass the more complex aspects of student achievement. To aid learning, we need to have access to better information about students' levels of understanding, their thinking strategies and the nature of their misunderstandings. This also suggests the need for a serious investment in high quality assessments that are domain specific and that take into account the richness of knowledge that we associate with high levels of competence in a domain. These could well be the types of periodic exams recommended in the New Commission Report. It will, however, take a serious investment to design and validate such assessments but the investment should be well worth it in terms of utility within the educational system. It also makes sense for this to function as a collaborative activity among states rather than a series of separate investments by individual states in much inferior assessment products.

During the last few decades significant developments have also accrued in measurement methods and theory. A wide array of statistical measurement methods are currently available to support the rigor we want in testing while simultaneously enabling the kinds of inferences about student knowledge that cognitive research suggests are important to pursue when assessing student achievement. In particular, it is now possible to characterize students in terms of multiple aspects of proficiency, rather than a single score; chart students' progress over time, instead of simply measuring performance at a particular point in time; deal with multiple paths or alternative patterns of valued performance; model, monitor and improve judgments based on informed evaluations; and report performance not only at the level of students, but also at the levels of groups, classes, schools and states. Nonetheless, many of the newer models and methods are not widely used because they are not easily understood or packaged in accessible ways for those without a strong technical background.

Technology offers the possibility of addressing this shortcoming. For instance, by building statistical models into technology-based learning environments for use in classrooms, teachers can assign more complex tasks, capture and replay students' performances, share exemplars of competent performance, and in the process gain critical information about student competence. Without question, computer and telecommunications technologies are making it possible to create powerful learning environments and simultaneously assess what students are learning at very fine levels of detail, with vivid simulations of real-world situations, and in ways that are tightly integrated with instruction.

Research has already shown that assessments that inform teachers about the nature of student learning can help them provide better feedback to students, which in turn can significantly enhance learning. Many of the most effective examples of the use of assessment to inform learning and instruction in the classroom rely on technology-based task presentation and information management systems.

If well-designed and used properly, assessments based on contemporary scientific knowledge could also promote more equitable opportunity to learn by providing better-quality information about the impact of educational interventions on children. More informative classroom assessments could result in earlier identification of learning problems and intervention for children at risk of failure, rather than waiting for results from large-scale assessments to signal problems. Students with disabilities could also benefit from this approach. At the same time, it is necessary for educators and researchers to continuously monitor the effects of their practices to ensure that the new assessments do not exacerbate existing inequalities.

Assessments based on contemporary theories and data on how competence develops across grade levels in a curriculum domain could also provide more valid measures of growth and the value added by teachers and schools. Such assessments could also enhance community dialogue about goals for student learning and important indicators of achievement at various grade levels and in different subject areas. Comparisons based on attainment of worthwhile learning goals, rather than normative descriptions of how students perform, could enhance the public's understanding of educational quality. New forms of assessment could also help provide descriptive and accurate information about the nature of achievement in a subject area and patterns of students' strengths and weaknesses that would be more useful than existing data for guiding policy decisions and reform efforts.

It is no surprise, then, that collective advances in the study of thinking and learning, in the field of measurement, and in the deployment of powerful technologies for learning have stimulated many people to think in new ways about educational futures. New information technologies provide substantial opportunities to advance the design and use of assessments based on a merger of contemporary scientific knowledge of cognition and measurement. Focus is needed on ways to bring together the knowledge of how students learn, what they know and what is therefore worth assessing, with knowledge of how to do this with technical rigor, and ways to harness technology to make the merger feasible. Several intriguing implications arise from projecting what could happen from the coupling of advances in cognition, measurement and technology.

# VISIONS OF THE FUTURE

Within the next decade, extremely powerful information technologies will become as ubiquitous in educational settings as they are in other aspects of people's daily lives. They are almost certain to provoke fundamental changes in learning environments at all levels of the education system. Many of the implications of technology are beyond people's speculative capacity. At the time of issuing the Commission's first report, for example, few could have predicted the sweeping effects of the Internet on education and other segments of society. The range of computational devices and their applications is expanding exponentially, fundamentally changing how people think about communication, connectivity, information systems, educational practices and the role of technology in society.

While it is always risky to predict the future, it appears clear that advances in technology will continue to impact the world of education in powerful and provocative ways. Many technology-driven advances in the design of learning

*What are some barriers to the use of technology for integrating assessment with instruction?*

environments, which include the integration of assessment with instruction, will continue to emerge, and will reshape the terrain of what is both possible and desirable in education. Advances in curriculum, instruction, assessment and technology are likely to continue to move educational practice toward a more individualized and mastery-oriented approach to learning. This evolution will occur across the K-16+ spectrum. To manage learning and instruction effectively, people will want and need to know considerably more about what has been mastered, at what level, and by whom.

Consider the possibilities that might arise if assessment is integrated into instruction in multiple curricular areas and the resultant information about student accomplishment and understanding is collected with the aid of technology. In such a world, programs of on-demand external assessment such as state achievement tests might not be necessary. Instead, it might be possible to extract the information needed for summative and program evaluation purposes from data about student performance continuously available both in and out of the school context.

Technology could offer ways of creating, over time, a complex stream of data about how students think and reason while engaged in important learning activities. Information for assessment purposes could be extracted from this stream and used to serve both classroom and external assessment needs, including providing individual feedback to students for reflection about their learning strategies and habits. To realize this vision, additional research on the data representations and analysis methods best suited for different audiences and different assessment objectives would clearly be needed—and is certainly doable.

We can therefore imagine a future in which the audit function of assessments external to the classroom would be significantly reduced or even unnecessary because the information needed to assess students, at the levels of description appropriate for various monitoring purposes, could be derived from the data streams generated by students in and out of their classrooms.

A metaphor for such a radical shift in how one "does the business of educational assessment" exists in the world of retail outlets, ranging from small businesses to supermarkets to department stores. No longer do these businesses have to close down once or twice a year to take inventory of their stock. Rather, with the advent of automated checkouts and barcodes for all items, these enterprises have access to a continuous stream of information that can be used to monitor inventory and the flow of items. Not only can business continue without interruption, but the information obtained is far richer, enabling stores to monitor trends and aggregate the data into various kinds of summaries. Similarly, with new assessment technologies, schools would no longer have to interrupt the normal instructional process at various times during the year to administer external tests to students. Nor would they have to spend significant amounts of time preparing for specific external tests peripheral to the ongoing activities of teaching and learning.

Extensive technology-based systems that link curriculum, instruction and assessment at the classroom level might enable a shift from today's assessment systems, which use different kinds of assessments for different purposes, to a balanced design in which the three critical features of *comprehensiveness, coherence,* and *continuity* would be ensured. In such a design, assessments would provide a variety of evidence to support educational decisionmaking (*comprehensiveness*). The information provided at differing levels of responsibility and action would be linked back to the same underlying conceptual model of student learning (*coherence*) and would provide indications of student growth over time (*continuity*).

Clearly, technological advances will allow for the attainment of many of the goals that educators, researchers, policymakers, teachers and parents have envisioned for assessment as a viable source of information for educational improvement. When powerful technology-based systems are implemented in classrooms, rich sources of information about student learning will be continuously available across wide segments of the curriculum and for individual learners over extended periods of time. This is exactly the kind of information we now lack, making it difficult to use assessment to truly support learning. The major issue is not whether this type of data collection and information analysis is feasible in the future. Rather, the issue is how the world of education anticipates and embraces this possibility, and how it will explore the resulting options for effectively using assessment information to meet the multiple purposes served by current assessments and, most important, to enhance student learning.

# A CONCLUDING COMMENT

It has been noted that the best way to predict the future is to invent it. Without doubt, multiple futures for curriculum, instruction and assessment could be invented on the basis of synergies that we know exist among information technologies and contemporary knowledge of cognition and measurement. While we are a considerable distance away from implementing the types of fully integrated instructional and assessment systems envisioned above, there are steps that can be taken now that would put us on the path to such a future. That future is certainly a critical component of realizing the sweeping transformation of the American educational landscape advocated by the New Commission Report.

# REFERENCES

Bransford, J. D., Brown, A. L., Cocking, R. R., Donovan, S., & Pellegrino, J. W. (Eds.) (2000). *How people learn: Brain, mind, experience, and school (Expanded Edition)*. Washington, D.C.: National Academy Press.

Donovan, S., & Bransford, J. D. (Eds.) (2005). *How students learn history, science, and mathematics in the classroom.* Washington, DC: National Academy Press.

Donovan, S., & Pellegrino, J. W. (2004). *Learning and instruction: A SERP research agenda.* Washington, DC: National Academy Press.

Kilpatrick, J., Swafford, J., & Findell, B. (Eds.) (2001). *Adding it up: Helping children learn mathematics.* Washington, DC: National Academy Press.

National Research Council (1996). *National science education standards.* Washington, DC: National Academy Press.

National Research Council (2002). *Learning and understanding: Improving advanced study of mathematics and science in U.S. high schools.* Washington, DC: National Academies Press.

National Research Council (2003). *Assessment in support of learning and instruction: Bridging the gap between large-scale and classroom assessment.* Washington, DC: National Academies Press.

Pellegrino, J. W., Chudowsky, N., & Glaser, R. (Eds.) (2001). *Knowing what students know: The science and design of educational assessment.* Washington, DC: National Academy Press.

Wilson, M., & Bertenthal, M. (2005). *Systems for state science assessment.* Washington, DC: National Academy Press.

# The Ripple Effect

## Andy Hargreaves and Dean Fink

The fates of schools are increasingly intertwined. What leaders do in one school necessarily affects the fortunes of students and teachers in other schools around them; their actions reverberate throughout the system like ripples in a pond. As exemplary or high-profile institutions draw the most outstanding teachers and leaders, they drain them away from the rest. For every magnet or lighthouse school that attracts most of the local resources and attention, dozens of surrounding schools may operate more like outhouses—low status places in which districts dump their difficult students and weaker staffs. The more school systems run on the market principles of competition and choice, the tighter these interconnections become (Powell, Edwards, Whitty & Wigfall, 2003; Wells, 2002).

There's a better way to think about school reform. Sustainable education leadership is about being responsible to and for all the schools and students that your leadership actions affect. Sustainability is ultimately and unavoidably about social justice.

## FATAL ATTRACTION

With its downtown location in a depressed Northeast rust belt city, Barrett Magnet High School has been through a lot.[1] But as a result of its magnet status and dynamic leadership, Barrett stands proud in *U.S. News and World Report's* national high school rankings as one of the top 150 schools in the United States.[2]

Barrett Magnet sits in one of its city's most concentrated areas of poverty. In the 1970s, lower-income African American students represented 95 percent of the school's population; student violence, poor attendance, low academic performance, and discipline problems were life. As a result of pressure from the neighborhood association, the district renamed the school, assigned it a charismatic new principal, and eventually granted it magnet status in fall 1981.

With heightened outside interest and a new, inspiring identity, Barrett and its principal were able to attract talented and motivated faculty and administrators. Under Presidents Reagan and Bush Sr., magnet schools were encouraged to compete against other schools for students. Students at Barrett who didn't like the discipline or who couldn't keep up with the pace were assigned to other schools or asked to leave.

*What do you think of the decisions the leader of Barrett made?*

The school became a showcase. Its adoption of the prestigious International Baccalaureate program heightened its image of excellence. Local newspapers wrote glowing reports about it. President Bush Sr. made a high-profile visit in 1989, and many other visitors came from far and wide to discover the secrets of the school's success.

When Barrett's founding principal resigned in 1986 because he refused to accept a transfer to another school, the district appointed a new principal, whom most of the staff liked because she put students and instruction first. She believed in and perpetuated the school's magnet mission as well as its International Baccalaureate program. She was successful in raising funds and buffering staff from unreasonable district demands. She emphasized student achievement, the importance of standards, and the need for measurable results. She praised teachers who got good results; she panned those who didn't.

Not all teachers were followers of the new principal, however. Those who taught the special education students, whom the school was required to include because of open enrollment and federal legislation, quickly learned that their students were not part of the principal's or the school's mission. These students and their teachers were assigned to the basement. If the special education teachers questioned the elitist atmosphere, complained about their students' marginalization, or advocated for them too strongly, they were quickly targeted—given the most difficult classes, reassigned to undesirable rooms on the periphery of the school, or banished from the school altogether.

Barrett's magnetic attraction ended up damaging its lower-status students as well as teachers who didn't enhance the school's image or mesh with its mission. But that wasn't all: Barrett's fatal attraction harmed students and teachers in neighboring schools as well.

## A STAR EXTINGUISHED

Sheldon High School is in the same city and district as Barrett Magnet. Change and the geography of competition have set the schools on two different paths, propelling them past each other in opposite directions. In the 1960s, Sheldon was the shining star of the district. Teachers lived locally. Although desegregation and school busing in the early 1970s led to white flight to the suburbs and even to some race riots in the school's cafeteria, teachers were still able to maintain Sheldon's status as the top high school in the city. They did this by providing 10-week electives and thematic courses on such topics as Vietnam, science fiction, slavery, sports literature, and black figures in U.S. history. These programs engaged student interest, connected with students' lives, and catered to an increasingly diverse student body.

All this changed in the 1980s. Further desegregation, the establishment of magnet schools, and the introduction of enrollment policies that allowed parents to rank order the schools that they preferred for their children led to a second "white and bright" flight from neighborhood schools like Sheldon to the magnets around them. Losing its best students to Barrett and to the other magnets, Sheldon also had to contend with the many poor African American students who were bused from a school on the opposite side of town that had closed down as a result of the magnets. By the late 1980s, white students in the school were in the minority, and the number of students in poverty was rapidly on the rise. By the mid-1990s, the schools special education department, which had previously been the smallest unit in the school, had become its largest unit, with 25 special education teachers.

With Sheldon's lost reputation went its ability to attract outstanding staff. As student achievement deteriorated, veteran teachers became demotivated and nostalgic for the 1960s and 1970s. Six superintendents—often with contradictory agendas—rolled in and out of the district within a 15-year period; autocratic and iron-fisted principals gave teachers little opportunity for leadership. In 1986, when the district sought to reverse the decline by transferring Barrett's charismatic African American principal to Sheldon, the principal promptly resigned and moved out of the district altogether.

By the late 1990s, Sheldon's teachers found themselves teaching in extremely difficult circumstances. Meeting the state standards was much harder at Sheldon than in the magnets, and the school's staff didn't have the curriculum flexibility that Barrett enjoyed. Standards turned into standardization. Innovative teachers became demoralized as they were deprived of the freedom to adjust to student needs. "I'd much rather be teaching a book or a story or something they might enjoy," one English teacher said, "but we've got to prep them for the tests." Teachers who taught by the book, meanwhile, found that the standardization process enabled them to become more tradition-bound still. By the early stages of No Child Left Behind, Sheldon's downward trajectory was moving it toward designation as an underperforming school. Its major challenge now was survival: avoiding being turned over to the state or a private company, being replaced by a charter school, or being closed down altogether.

## SOCIALLY JUST LEADERSHIP

The Barretts and Sheldons of this world are not unfortunate coincidences or historic accidents. They are interconnected and indivisible alter egos—like Dr. Jekyll and Mr. Hyde. The fortunes of one are perversely linked to the failures of the other.

*How important is socially just leadership across a district when federal legislation rates schools individually?*

The challenge of education leadership, therefore, is not just to care for the private good of one's own students and their parents, but to commit to the public good, caring for students and teachers in neighboring schools whom your leadership choices affect. Responsible leadership[3] is synonymous with socially just leadership and requires that school leaders ask themselves some tough questions: What imprint does your leadership leave on the surrounding community's scarce resources of motivated students and talented teachers and leaders? Does your district lure talented teachers and leaders away from the inner cities with higher salaries and other rewards? Does your oversubscribed school, with its selective strategies, deprive other schools of student talent? Do you take your fair share of emotionally disturbed or socially disadvantaged students compared with schools around you—and do you serve those students well?

# BECOMING MORE JUST

Socially just education leaders stretch beyond their individual schools, distributing their leadership and its effects across many different schools—strong and weak, black and white, rich and poor. By promoting practical and positive strategies, socially just leadership can have an actively restorative effect on neighboring schools.

## Paired Schools

Successful schools can coach struggling schools to help them improve. This is most effective when the schools serve similar students and communities. Under the leadership of coordinator Dave Blackburn, Virginia's Newport News School District has pioneered just such a model of paired schools (Blackburn, 2003). With district support, underperforming schools choose a higher-performing partner. The high performer doesn't just send in a small administrative team to evaluate and turn around its underperforming peer in a quick-fix way. Instead, this model promotes shared and distributed leadership: Leaders coach leaders; counselors coach counselors; departments coach departments. Peer assistance is the key principle. And the learning runs in both directions; even underperforming schools have pockets of excellent practice from which their higher-performing partners can benefit.

Paired schools, peer assistance, and shared leadership have raised student performance on standardized achievement tests in the Newport News School District. With the support of the Hope Foundation and its professional development model, these practices have spread to dozens of school districts across the United States as well as to other parts of the world.[4]

## Networked Districts

Under England's Specialist Schools and Academies Trust, which includes more than 1,000 specialist secondary schools, almost every school has its own emphasis, be it sports, technology, arts, or the environment (Wilce, 2004). For some communities, this kind of niche marketing will encourage schools to hunt for the best students, leaving secondary schools in poorer communities with lower achievers who have not been chosen elsewhere.

To ensure social justice, we need to break the assumption of the essential bond between one student and one school. Instead of establishing specialist schools in isolation or in competitive relationships to one another, Knowsley Education Authority (equivalent to a U.S. school district) near Liverpool, England, is creating interrelated and networked centers of learning (Whittaker, 2004). Although students will have one school as their base, they will have access to varied learning resources across the district. For example, students based in one school might attend another one in the afternoon for a specialized sports or technology program with concentrations of teachers who have expertise in these areas. These networked learning communities use choice and diversity to discourage rather than promote elitist competition and thereby bring about greater social justice.

## Community Consultation

Schools of choice, purpose-built innovative schools, and charter schools should actively consult, contribute to, and avoid harming the wider communities in which they are located. One charter school we know avoided raiding the best talent from nearby urban public schools by ensuring that it advertised its teaching positions far beyond the district. Actively considering the needs of the community not only contributes to social justice and the public good but also benefits the long-term reputation, viability, and sheer endurance of the newly established schools.

Blue Mountain Secondary School in Ontario, Canada, was established as a learning organization and community in 1995, with the license to handpick its leaders and teaching community. The school had seen other innovative schools fade over time because they failed to involve the surrounding communities, which became suspicious of them, or to consult neighboring schools, which subsequently envied and resented them. Blue Mountain therefore took great care not to lure all the best teachers, leaders, and students from nearby schools. In consultation with the school district and with other high school principals, Blue Mountain's principal operated a quota system to ensure that the school would not draw disproportionately from any one school or from any one age group of teachers in the district, be they beginners or veterans.

## Collective Accountability

In early 2004, a number of schools in England's Birmingham Education Authority became concerned that individual school accountability was making them compete with one another, undermining their collective capacity to learn and improve. These schools lobbied the government to pool their standardized achievement scores. The collective accountability would encourage schools of greater and lesser performance and advantage to work together to narrow achievement gaps and improve their overall performance—directly benefiting the entire community (Reed, 2005).

Similarly, in Melbourne, Australia, in the 1990s, a group of contiguous high schools had been spending their budgets on advertising for students in a system of competitive school choice. The principals discovered that their advertisements were almost identical. In response, rather than frittering away the rest of their resources on enhancing their individual images, they courageously decided to work together as a federation of schools dedicated to shared improvement for the entire community (Hargreaves, 2003). Federated schools, rather than fragmented and competitive ones, offer a positive and creative way to achieve greater social justice for our students. This approach might be a more equitable and inclusive option for U.S. school districts and school networks in the future.

### Environmental Impact Assessment

In many countries, before starting a construction project or creating a new business, the developers are legally required to undertake an environmental impact assessment of the project's effect on the surrounding community. We propose that all newly established schools—charters, magnets, or schools that have moved into new buildings—do the same. They should examine the effects that this new venture will have on surrounding schools and on the community at large, including the effects of the school's physical design and policies for selecting students and staff. In this way, schools will avoid harming their communities and make an active and socially just contribution to the wider public good.

## LEARNING TO SEE

As sociologist Arlie Hochschild reminds us, we are all connected in chains of care, not only to friends and family around us, but also to other people whom we cannot see (Hochschild, 2000): the exploited children who make our clothes, the impoverished communities that live amidst our exported waste, and the disadvantaged students in neighboring schools whose best teachers and peers have been taken from them.

The hardest part of sustainable leadership and improvement is the part that provokes us to think beyond our own schools and ourselves. We need to perform not merely as managers of organizations or as professionals who produce performance results, but also as community members, citizens, and human beings who lead to serve and promote the good of all.

## ENDNOTES

1. This article draws on research from *Change Over Time? A Study of Culture, Structure, Time, and Change in Secondary Schooling* (Andy Hargreaves and Ivor Goodson, principal investigators). The project was funded by the Spencer Foundation. Barrett Magnet and Sheldon High School are pseudonyms.
2. Although these rankings no longer apply, they were in evidence during the time period to which this article refers.

3. For more information about responsible leadership, see R. J. Starratt's *Ethical Leadership* (Jossey-Bass, 2005).

4. For more information about the Professional Learning Communities of HOPE model, visit the HOPE Foundation Web site at www.communitiesofhope.org.

# REFERENCES

Blackbum, D. (2003). *School leadership and reform: Case studies of Newport News paired-school model* [Occasional paper]. Newport News, VA: Newport News Schools.

Hargreaves, A. (2003). *Teaching in the knowledge society.* New York: Teachers College Press.

Hochschild, A. (2000). Global care chains and emotional surplus value. In T. Giddens & W. Hutton (Eds.), *On the edge: Globalization and the new millennium* (pp. 130–146). London: Sage Publishers.

Powell, S., Edwards, T., Whitty, G., & Wigfall, V. (2003). *Education and the middle class.* London: Open University Press.

Reed, J. (2005, April 8). Sense and singularity. *The Times Educational Supplement.* Available: www.tes.co.uk/search /story/?story_id=2088555

Wells, A. S. (2002). *Where charter school policy fails.* New York: Teachers College Press.

Whittaker, M. (2004, Oct. 15). Take a risk and talk to heads. *The Times Educational Supplement.* Available: www.tes.co.uk/search/story/?story_id=2042414

Wilce, H. (2004, Nov. 19). Prophet of the specialist schools. *The Times Educational Supplement.* Available: www.tes.co.uk/search/story/?story_id=2053058

# ISSUE SUMMARY

───────────────────────────────●

School reform. If you google on these two words, more than a million results will appear. Among the Web sites are national centers or local institutes that focus on a particular model of reform. Several clearinghouses provide catalogs of current models, with charts comparing features and goals. Plenty of sites are for leaders of school reform but very few are designed to explain school reform to families or communities. Some school reform efforts are grassroots movements, others are research-based, and a few are the result of state takeovers.

A decade ago, Richard Elmore used the term *cottage industry* to define local reforms and innovations that have been a tradition in education. Typically an innovation was tried out by a small group of teachers and if it proved effective, it might be attractive enough for others to adopt. Adoption was iffy though:

> These cottage industry innovations in instructional practice seldom apply to schools other than the ones in which they are developed and tested, and, if they do, they are often adopted in an eviscerated, watered-down form that bears little resemblance to the original. (Elmore, 1997, p. 248)

Richard Elmore's characterization of school reform as a cottage industry is no longer accurate. Reform is now a full-size industry of comprehensive innovations that are being adopted schoolwide or even districtwide. This is an anomaly for a system that has been thought of as "loosely-coupled" (Weick, 1976). Traditionally, education has been relatively regulation free; teachers have autonomy.

But political, economic, and business factors are driving the way education reform is conceived and adopted and tight coupling is now being tried in a loosely coupled environment. Organizational theorists would posit that education is moving from a loose system to one that is more tightly coupled. In 2002, as reforms escalated, Lance Fusarelli wrote about what can happen when tight policies are imposed on loose systems in "Tightly Coupled Policy in Loosely Coupled Systems: Institutional Capacity and Organizational Change."

And today the multilayered reforms of some districts are too complex to be characterized as "loose-tight." An example is the takeover reform in the School District of Philadelphia:

> Frustrated by a history of low student achievement and financial crises, the state of Pennsylvania took charge of the Philadelphia public schools in 2002. Within months of the takeover, a newly created School Reform Commission had launched the nation's largest experiment in the private management of public schools. The commission, which replaced the local school board, turned over 45 elementary and middle schools to seven private for-profit and nonprofit managers. In addition, the school district, under a new CEO, implemented wide-ranging and ambitious reforms in district-managed schools. (Gill, Zimmer, Christman, & Blanc, 2007, p. iii)

We live in an age of sophisticated, comprehensive reforms that come in different sizes and shapes. Some districts are attempting multiple comprehensive reforms at once, many of which are privatized. Taking these viewpoints on school reform and improvement into consideration, the larger issue is how leaders position an organization in terms of people, structures, and processes. In determining the shape of reform that will be most suitable, leaders also must come to terms with issues raised in the readings: How important is capacity-building prior to implementing a reform? What do the trends say are the most effective reforms? What are the reform's collateral effects on social justice, choice, and sustainability?

## ISSUE HIGHLIGHTS

- Ignoring large social class differences means accepting substantial gaps between achievement of children.
- In addition to school improvement, complementary reforms of income, housing, early childhood education, and community support systems are needed.
- Under NCLB legislation, states are using assessment systems that undermine high achievement standards and quality instructional practices.
- New assessment systems are needed that merge cognition, measurement, and technology, resulting in a balanced design that ensures comprehensiveness, coherence, and continuity.
- With more school systems operating by market principles of competition and choice, sustainability and social justice become problematic.
- School leaders face the challenge of committing to the public good in systems that decentralize through charter schools and isolated initiatives.

## CRITICAL THINKING

With the rapid expansion of the education reform movement, it is evident that the nature of decision making is changing. Instead of long-term planning, organizations must plan and adapt quickly. Yet, leaders of educational organizations are often stymied in their ability to make decisions. They may be inundated with data or their data analysis capability may be deficient. This is a paradox of educational organizations in the information age. Do institutions have robust analytic tools that keep up with the pace of decision making in reform initiatives?

Accompanying inadequate analysis tools is the need to produce quick results. This aspect of high-stakes reform can lead to ethical lapses, as seen in leaders' decisions to disaggregate certain students from the data set or inflate scores in order to show spectacular results on standardized achievement tests. What drives some leaders to report misleading results?

Private education organizations that are run for profit can be susceptible to the need to produce quick results. Some EMOs develop their own proprietary assessment systems for student learning. While these systems may be reliable and valid, the modes of data presentation and assessment methods can vary from the regular district assessment system. In this case comparisons of students may be unreliable. Should districts require EMOs and non-reform programs to use identical assessments?

Changing schools for the better is the whole point of educational reform. Regardless of the shape and scope of the reform, the burden falls on leaders to maintain transparency in implementation and evaluation of the initiative's success.

# ADDITIONAL READING RESOURCES

Ron Beghetto, Scientifically based research: ERIC Digest 167. *Clearinghouse on Educational Policy and Management*, April 2003.

Richard Elmore, Getting to scale with good educational practice. *Harvard Educational Review,* Spring 1996.

Lance Fusarelli, Tightly coupled policy in loosely coupled systems: Institutional capacity and organizational change. *Journal of Educational Administration*, December 2002.

Brian Gill, Ron Zimmer, Jolley Christman, and Suzanne Blanc, *State Takeover, School Restructuring, Private Management, and Student Achievement in Philadelphia.* RAND Corporation, 2007.

Karl Weick, Educational organizations as loosely coupled systems. *Administrative Science Quarterly*, 1976.

Joe Williams, Breaking the mold. *Education Next,* Spring 2006.

For more information on reform and improvement, check these sites:

American Association of School Superintendents www.aasa.org

Baldrige Criteria for Performance Excellence www.quality.nist.gov/ Education_Criteria.htm

Catalog of School Reform Models www.nwrel.org/scpd/catalog/index.shtml

New Commission on the Skills of the American Workforce http://skills commission.org/

Restructuring: What We Know About the NCLB Options (PPT) www. centerforcsri.org/pubs/CSRConference/BryanHassel.pdf

Schlechty Center for Leadership in School Reform www.schlechtycenter.org/

The Stupski Foundation www.stupski.org

# U N I T 3

# Challenges of Educational Leaders

Education is a task that always embodies utopias, looks toward the future, and requires the exercise of our full imaginations.

—Adriana Puiggros

Despite our attempts to cast education as utopia, some matters are persistent challenges for educational leaders. Two of these challenges have been selected for this unit: sustaining diverse and socially just organizations and the impact of accountability legislation. But one challenge is ever-new—the specter of the future and the leader's role in it. Systems theory is germane to challenges addressed in Unit 3. In systems terms, leaders who understand an educational organization's adaptive skill, its commitments, and its response to external demands will be better able to handle challenges like diversity, compliance with legislation, and the future.

We live in an era when schools and institutions are more *diverse* than ever. And the need to close the achievement gaps among diverse students is more pressing than ever. America's school leaders can ill afford to ignore the challenges that have arisen because of changing demographics. In such a high-stakes environment it could be tempting to treat diversity as a problem instead of an asset. The readings look at diversity issues from several angles—creating cultural competency, complying with law, managing age-diverse faculty and staff, and designing diversity initiatives.

There are very real risks for educational institutions that fail to meet *accountability* regulations. Students fail, teachers and administrators lose their jobs, the public loses trust, and the state takes over the system. But what if the accountability legislation itself is failing? The readings for this issue explore this question from a variety of viewpoints. It's possible that current federal regulations and America's new competitiveness agenda are on a collision course. It's also possible that tinkering with the legislation will correct current flaws. Another viewpoint is that tinkering isn't sufficient—the "bright lines" or fundamental principles are seriously flawed and regulations need in-depth revamping. Still another viewpoint is that it is possible to limit regulations and let market models loose in America's school districts.

This book ends with a very compelling issue—the shape of educational *leadership in the future.* Whether the future brings dramatic shifts in accountability systems, in global demands of education, in women's ways of leading, or in school structures, there's no way to really know. But the readings for this issue provide valuable insights into how educational leaders will be working. The readings for this issue are by authors who have the future in their bones. At this point in time here's what we *do* know: The future calls for smarter, more connected educational leadership. An informed citizenry, a knowledge economy, and a globalized world will demand it.

**Issue 8:** How Can Educational Leaders Sustain Diverse and Socially Just Educational Organizations?

**Issue 9:** What Is the Impact of Accountability Legislation on Educational Organizations?

**Issue 10:** How Will Educational Organizations Be Led in the Future?

Quote: Adriana Puiggros, Neoliberalism and education in the Americas. *Comparative Education Review*, August, 2000.

# How Can Educational Leaders Sustain Diverse and Socially Just Educational Organizations?

**D**iversity is a fact of life in America's workplaces. The range of differences among employees can be quite amazing. Employees in a particular workplace can vary by age, gender, national origin, physical appearance, race, religion, sexual orientation, to name a few factors. Whether these differences are considered a given, a goal, a problem, or a strength depends on the organization. For decades, workforce diversity in business was a matter of assimilation. Through the years initiatives and programs were created to cope with increasing diversity, mainly to ensure that employees adapted. Compliance became the measure of workforce diversity. Now however, instead of attempting to homogenize employees, there is another way that leaders are handling workplace diversity. Today the focus is on leveraging or capitalizing on diversity. Some regard diversity as good business; others regard it as good values. The point is diversity can be used strategically to create a more effective business organization. But how do educational organizations regard diversity?

For institutions with educational aims rather than business aims, diversity could appear to be a rather simple matter. After all, public education has been under integration orders by federal law. And private education isn't blind to the nation's increasing diversity. But anyone paying closer attention sees that America's schools and institutions are not diverse, despite decades of court cases. Inequality and inadequacy, more than equity and sufficiency, are the hallmarks of American education. While many may disagree about the details, it is up to leaders to commit to finding a way forward.

In 2004, to commemorate the fiftieth anniversary of the most famous integration/segregation case—*Brown vs. Board of Education*—a group of prominent education, community, and policy leaders convened in New York City. The outcome of their deliberations is a monograph titled " 'With All Deliberate Speed': Achievement, Citizenship and Diversity in American Education" (New York University, 2005). The monograph begins with a wake-up call:

> The fact that so many public schools in the United States are segregated by race, ethnicity and income stands in sharp contrast to the integration of the American workplace, our armed forces and the many civic and religious communities that make up our society. This is a vexing problem that we cannot ignore. (p. 4)

The readings for this issue present a range of viewpoints, yet each has been influenced by *Brown vs. Board of Education*. Two of the readings deal with diversity in terms of race, ethnicity, and income levels—arguably the most apparent and pressing for educational organizations. But generational diversity also merits attention, as does the key to an effective diversity initiative. Leaders also need to consider the notion of how to develop culturally competent schools—an acknowledgment that diversity extends throughout the educational enterprise and cannot be left to chance. As with all areas of achievement like math or science, schools must set goals for culturally sensitive education, according to the author of the first reading, "Culturally Competent Schools." Mary Beth Klotz, director of IDEA Projects for the National Association of School Psychologists, makes the case that leaders play a central role in ensuring that the institution is culturally competent. More than making sure the curriculum is multicultural, leaders should consider how the organization of the institution, its policies and procedures, and its community involvement are culturally responsive. To this author, an educational institution that regards diversity as permeating every aspect of its operations is a culturally sensitive learning organization.

Another way to take sustaining action is by implementing specific strategies to enhance diversity. Judd Sills, the author of the second reading, advocates for a radically different approach to diversity initiatives than merely assimilating differences into a common culture. He maintains that traditional diversity programs have forced people to "restrain behavioral diversity" with negative emotional results. Instead, if leaders begin with John Kotter's eight steps for organizational transformation, their initiatives have a greater chance of being sustained. According to Sills, the most important steps are the initial ones—creating and instilling a sense of urgency throughout the institution.

The third reading is about how organizations handle a workforce that includes four generations. "Managing Generation Y" explains why faculty and staff who differ widely in age may be having disputes at work. Author Susan Eisner believes that "intergenerational differences may become a foremost aspect of diversity in the U.S. workplace." If so, what do leaders need to know about these four generations, typically called Traditionalists, Baby Boomers, Generation X, and Generation Y? Eisner proposes that strategies are needed that are intentionally intergenerational. While age differences should be built into strategies, age stereotypes need to be avoided. Of particular value to leaders is a summary table defining the four generations at work.

School diversity cases that reach the U.S. Supreme Court can alter national policy and local procedures. The final reading, "The Diversity Test," provides a perspective on what happens when the Supreme Court accepts school diversity cases. The potential consequences of two pending cases are staggering. This reading was chosen as an example to be instructive for leaders. By the time you read this selection, the Supreme Court will have ruled on whether districts can consider race and ethnicity when assigning students to school buildings.

In a postscript to a national report of the National Association of State Boards of Education titled *A More Perfect Union: Building an Education System that Embraces All Children* (Brenda Lilienthal Welburn, National Association of State Boards of Education, 2002), leaders are warned that diversity must be approached with great sensitivity:

> How schools promote individual achievement, national unity, collective interests, and cultural diversity in a balanced way is one of the most profound issues policymakers will face in the years to come. (Welburn, 2002, p. 44)

Leaders of some institutions believe designing a balanced and sustainable approach to diversity is too important to achieve alone, so they are turning to other organizations for help. NTL Institute is one such nonprofit group. Their goals are ambitious: to strengthen relationships and organizations by fostering self-awareness and interpersonal, group and system effectiveness. And their values are inclusive: "Social justice manifested through inclusion, equity, access and opportunity for all people and the elimination of oppression." The increasing number of support groups with similar missions, ready to assist schools and institutions, shows that we have moved very far from the days of diversity as an issue of integration/segregation.

# SOURCES

Mary Beth Klotz, Culturally competent schools: Guidelines for secondary school principals. *Principal Leadership,* March 2006.

Judd Sills, Experts weigh in about what makes diversity initiatives effective. *The Diversity Factor,* Fall 2005.

Susan P. Eisner, Managing Generation Y. *SAM Advanced Management Journal*, Autumn 2005.

Edwin C. Darden, The Diversity Test. *American School Board Journal*, October 2006.

# ARTICLE 8.1

# Culturally Competent Schools: Guidelines for Secondary School Principals

## Mary Beth Klotz

> The highest result of education is tolerance.
>
> —Helen Keller

*Does culturally responsive education also have disadvantages?*

As the number of students from diverse backgrounds continues to grow in U.S. schools, the role of culturally responsive education gains increasing importance. Currently there are 5.5 million English Language Learners (ELLs) in U.S. public schools who speak more than 400 different languages (U.S. Department of Education, 2004). The 2000 census estimated that 65% of school-age children are non-Hispanic White and that 35% are from other racial and ethnic backgrounds.

It is estimated that by 2040, no ethnic or racial group will make up the majority of the national school-age population. Adding to the complexity, many students of diverse cultures come from families in poverty, do not speak English well, have parents who are not well-educated, and move and change schools frequently. In fact, 39% of children in the United States live at or near the poverty level (National Association of State Boards of Education, 2002).

To create culturally sensitive educational environments, schools must set goals for success. These goals for culturally competent schools are to establish settings where all students are made to feel welcome; are engaged in learning; and are included in the full range of activities, curricula, and services. As the leaders of their schools, principals must work collaboratively with school staff members, parents, and the community to accomplish goals that include closing achievement gaps and promoting prosocial behaviors. The benefits of culturally competent schools are numerous and include preventing academic failure, reducing drop-out rates, and engaging students and their families in the school community.

## WHAT IS A CULTURALLY COMPETENT SCHOOL?

A culturally competent school is generally defined as one that honors, respects, and values diversity in theory and in practice and where teaching and learning are made relevant and meaningful to students of various cultures. In *A More Perfect Union: Building an Education System that Embraces All Children*, the

National Association of State Boards of Education (2002) discusses culturally competent schools. The report describes the nation's growing diversity among schoolchildren, the challenges and opportunities this diversity presents, and the need to teach all students to high standards while providing a common set of core values. The report urges state policymakers to counter intolerance and inequity in their education systems through culturally competent practices.

The report also offers the following key recommendations for school leaders:

- Use high academic standards as the basis of instruction for all students
- Adopt a curriculum that fosters cultural competency
- Demonstrate respect for students' identities and welcome a diverse community to participate in schools

## Roadblocks to Future Opportunities

It is important for principals to consider the unforeseen roadblocks to graduating and transitioning to college that many undocumented students encounter. Doris Páez, the director of the Metropolitan Studies Institute of University of South Carolina Upstate and a culturally competent education expert, advises secondary school principals to investigate the various obstacles that undocumented students face in school. School leaders should be asking themselves, "What opportunities are denied to my undocumented students, and how can our school keep these students motivated to achieve high standards in school and in the community?"

Páez notes that because students who are undocumented are frequently denied access to higher education, there often is little motivation to achieve in high school. In most instances, students interested in attending college who are not U.S. citizens will be asked to submit documentation of citizenship status, such as the permanent resident card (i.e., a green card); hold the U.S. refugee travel document; or apply as an international visa-holding student. Further, to qualify for in-state tuition, students must hold one of the accepted forms of documentation no matter how long they have been living in-state.

Another frequent roadblock to success for students who are English language learners is passing mandatory high school exit exams. Principals, along with ESL and general education teaching staff members, should plan the steps and supports needed to ensure that students who are learning English will be able to pass the exit exams well in advance of graduation dates. The goal for secondary school principals is to provide a setting where all students are given the same access to educational opportunities and experiences.

## Programs and Strategies That Contribute to a Culturally Responsive High School

Herndon High School in Fairfax County, Virginia, offers a number of programs and initiatives to help create a culturally responsive school setting. These successful programs include:

- Elective courses designed to help students from diverse backgrounds get along, such as Combating Intolerance
- Peer mediation to allow students from diverse backgrounds an opportunity to talk about potentially divisive issues
- Student clubs that help large groups of students retain cultural identity (e.g., Muslim Student Society)
- Openness to starting new clubs to reflect the interests of the student body
- Parent liaisons who are paid to work with families who would not otherwise have a traditional involvement with the school
- Home visits by parent liaisons
- Telephone tree in multiple languages
- Minority parent committee that organizes evenings for minority parents to come to school in smaller groups and learn about the college admissions process, SAT prep classes, scholarship and grant opportunities, and so forth
- Letters sent home and phone contact with parents from culturally and linguistically diverse backgrounds to ensure a good turnout at parent meetings
- Open communication with students
- Quarterly meetings between a randomly selected group of students from each grade level and their administrator to obtain feedback on how school is going for them and what specific things can be improved or changed
- Effort awards honor breakfast for students who have had trouble but who have raised their grades; each teacher nominates two students from his or her class
- Establishment of a Hispanic PTSA with business discussion and programs in Spanish
- Initiation of a "challenge" program to invite promising students to enroll in honors and Advanced Placement classes.

*Source:* Jan Leslie, the director of the Office of High School Instruction and K-12 Curriculum Services and the former principal of Herndon High School, Fairfax County (VA) Public Schools.

- Acknowledge students' diverse learning styles
- Ensure qualified personnel for all students
- Provide extra help for schools and students who need it.

# BUILDING A CULTURALLY COMPETENT SCHOOL

As with many aspects of establishing a positive school climate and setting high academic standards for all students, the principal plays a key role in ensuring that his or her school is culturally competent. In the practitioner brief *Addressing Diversity in Schools: Culturally Responsive Pedagogy* (Richards, Brown, & Forde, 2004), the authors outline three specific areas that must be addressed

---

## A New Twist on Professional Development Opportunities

Deborah Crockett, a program consultant for School Psychological Services of Fayette County (GA) Public Schools, recently initiated a creative solution to the language barrier felt between the school psychology staff and Hispanic parents in her school district. Through the use of grant and professional development funds, the School Psychological Services Department will be offering an intensive yearlong introductory Spanish language class. The class will be taught by one of the district's ESOL teachers and will be open to school psychologists as well as to the administrators and support staff. School Superintendent John DeCotis and ESOL Coordinator Ann Richardson supported the initiative as an exciting new endeavor to help build community relations and improve the cultural sensitivity of school personnel. Goals of the voluntary program are to:

- Increase sensitivity and understanding of the process of second language acquisition that the students experience by going through the process personally

- Help staff members acquire basic language and communication skills in Spanish to work more effectively with Spanish-speaking parents

- Improve the ability of school psychologists to work effectively with translators and interpreters by having some basic knowledge of Spanish

- Increase collaboration and teamwork between the School Psychological Services and the English as a Second Language Departments of Fayette County.

*What are some administrative challenges related to cultural competence?*

to ensure that a school is culturally responsive: organization of the school, school policies and procedures, and community involvement.

The organization of the school includes the administrative structure and the way it relates to diversity. The principal might consider such details as the assignment of classrooms, the hours the building is open, whether the building and the staff are accessible, and whether the building's physical appearance is respectful of different cultural groups.

School policies and procedures refer to practices that affect the delivery of services to students from diverse backgrounds. Principals must ask questions about their school's special education referral rates and identification procedures and access to honors and AP classes. Principals must also examine which students get instruction from the most experienced teachers and how school resources are allocated.

Community involvement encompasses neighborhood and community outreach efforts and the outcomes of these initiatives. These outreach efforts might include hiring parent liaisons or a staff member who speaks the language of a student group and who understands their cultural background. The parent liaison would work with parents to bring them into the school process.

# CULTURALLY COMPETENT CHECKLIST FOR SUCCESS

Principals of culturally competent schools encourage understanding and respect for individual differences and strive for high educational standards and levels of achievement for all students. Students' problems are examined within the context of environmental factors, including prior educational experiences, instruction, second language acquisition, and culture. The following tips are reminders of strategies and procedures that are essential to creating a culturally competent school environment.

## Staff Development

- Ensure that all professional development opportunities are culturally sensitive and inclusive
- Teach all staff members the distinction between the second language acquisition process and language differences and learning disabilities
- Recruit qualified school personnel who represent the cultural and ethnic makeup of the communities being served.

## Early Intervention and Assessment

- Use a team problem-solving model to address student achievement or behavior problems and provide early intervention support

- Match students with appropriate mentors or life coaches from similar cultural backgrounds
- Include ESL teachers and other staff members who have a background in cultural differences and second language acquisition issues on the general education problem-solving team
- Use assessments that are unbiased, culturally sensitive, and advocacy-oriented
- Use outcome-based data for decision making and planning.

## *Instruction and Curriculum Selection*

- Give all students the same enriching, evidence-based educational opportunities
- Offer a culturally inclusive curriculum that encourages cultural inquiry

---

# Resources

**National Association for Bilingual Education (NABE)**
Determining Appropriate Referrals of English Language Learners to Special Education: A Self-Assessment Guide for Principals.
www.cec.sped.org/law_res/doc/resources/files/NABEguide.pdf

**NASSP**
Promoting School Completion
*Principal Leadership Magazine,* 4(5), 9–13.
www.naspcenter.org/principals/nassp_completion.html

**National Association of School Psychologists (NASP)**
Culturally Competent Practice
www.nasponline.org/culturalcompetence/index.html

Portraits of the Children: Culturally Competent Assessment
video and CD-ROM
The Provision of Culturally Competent Services in the School Setting
www.nasponline.org/culturalcompetence/provision_cultcompsvcs.html

**National Center for Culturally Responsive Educational Systems (NCCRESt)**
www.nccrest.org

**National Center for Educational Statistics (NCES)**
The Nation's Report Card: 2005 Assessment Results
http://nces.ed.gov/nationsreportcard/nrc/reading_math_2005

- Encourage teachers to hold cultural sensitivity discussions with students when literary selections or references present negative stereotypes
- Explicitly teach and model important values and appropriate classroom behavior.

### *Community and Parent Involvement*

- Ensure that communications from the school are available in languages other than English, as appropriate
- Have childcare available at parent meetings
- Help students develop a sense of civic responsibility toward their immediate community, the nation, and the world
- Collaborate with parents and other community members and invite them to share their home cultures with the school.

## FINAL THOUGHTS

Daniel Domenech, the former superintendent of Fairfax County (VA) Public Schools, said, "Look at diversity as an opportunity to learn, and not as a problem in your school." By defining the challenges of educating students from multicultural and multilingual backgrounds as an opportunity to learn, rather than as a problem, principals can begin to shape thinking and collaborative efforts in positive ways.

## REFERENCES

National Association of State Boards of Education (2002). *A more perfect union: Building an education system that embraces all children.* Retrieved from www.nasbe.org/Educational_Issues/Reports/More_Perfect_Union. PDF

Richards, H., Brown, A., & Forde, T. (2004). *Practitioner brief: Addressing diversity in schools: culturally responsive pedagogy.* Retrieved from www.nccrest.org/Briefs/Diversity_Brief.pdf

U.S. Department of Education. (2004). *Fact sheet: NCLB provisions ensure flexibility and accountability for limited English proficient students.* Retrieved from www.ed.gov/print/nclb/accountability/schools/factsheet-english.html

# Experts Weigh in about What Makes Diversity Initiatives Effective

Judd Sills

Few initiatives reach as deep into a company's soul and encounter as much resistance—stated and unstated, overt and covert—as diversity initiatives. The oft-maligned diversity initiative promises access to untapped productivity, yet is sometimes the most poorly executed change initiative companies undertake. If media headlines and the Department of Labor caseload are meaningful indicators, companies have a lot riding on successfully accomplishing culture change, yet many rely on instinct about how to best initiate change.

The idea that companies should value differences has been around a long time, but leaders often focus on assimilating differences into a common corporate culture and restraining behavioral diversity that should instead be nurtured in the resultant gender, racial and ethnic mixture. Virtually guaranteed to evoke strong feelings no matter what your ethnicity, race or gender, and no matter where you reside on the organization chart, diversity initiatives fly in the face of emotions and memories of everyone involved, promising an uphill climb for any diversity change effort.

Successful turnarounds of unhealthy cultures do happen, but how can a leader keep momentum moving forward and anchor long-lasting change? To gain insight into this puzzle, I interviewed diversity experts, leadership gurus and change experts. In this article, we consider their advice.

## THE IMPETUS FOR DIVERSITY

Diversity remains a hot button subject at American workplaces. The Equal Employment Opportunity Commission reports racial bias filings alone are up 125 percent since the mid-1990s and monetary settlements of all their cases have more than tripled over the same period. Executives and HR professionals won't forget the landmark 1996 $176 million settlement between Texaco and minority workers, since eclipsed by a $192.5 million settlement between Coca-Cola Co. and black workers in 2000.

Organizations everywhere are investing in diversity initiatives intended to address the underlying issues and drive change toward healthier organizational environments. According to Reuters, Harvard University recently designated $50 million "to promote diversity on its faculty and reform the way women in

*Do schools and institutions need diversity initiatives for faculty and staff if the education is culturally responsive?*

science and engineering are treated." Other institutions and companies, often prompted by lawsuits or crises, are investing millions of dollars in diversity initiatives as well.

Settlements and diversity program investments represent only the obvious costs of an unhealthy organizational culture. Unreported are the hidden costs due to erosion of trust between executives and workers, loss of well-earned reputations in the marketplace, and public skepticism and scorn. Increasingly, companies have begun to discover that diversity, when managed and valued as a key cultural aspect and strategy, offers clear competitive advantages. The business case for diversity, which has been widely accepted in corporate America, addresses these advantages and benefits.

M. Elizabeth Holmes, senior vice president and chief learning officer of Roosevelt Thomas & Associates says, "If you make diversity part of your business strategy, then there is a strong case for it. Simply having demographic diversity won't translate to results. Most organizations focus strongly on representation at a time when they aren't yet prepared, as a company, to cope with the changes that real diversity brings. You have to take the time to manage the diversity you have. Diversity needs to be part of your strategy, and supported by systems, strategies, policies, practices and behaviors.

"Executives must treat a diversity initiative as an important cultural change," says Holmes. "In short, looking at the organization and applying the principles that you would for any initiative . . . to create an environment where everyone can contribute and have a voice."

## LEADERSHIP, VISION AND COMMUNICATION ARE KEY

It is not uncommon for diversity transformations to take as long as ten years to establish. In my own company, someone coined a phrase based upon a quote by motivational author Ben Sweetland: "Diversity is a journey not a destination." I couldn't have said it better myself.

Because organizational change is at the heart of any successful diversity initiative, I talked with longtime leadership professor John Kotter at Harvard Business School.[1] Kotter, who outlines eight steps for organizational transformation (see sidebar I), believes that several of these steps are particularly important to a winning diversity initiative. First, he believes that raising a feeling of urgency is the first and most critical step in any successful change effort. "I know a lot of programs where you have a sense of urgency among about ten people, all of whom have formal roles associated with diversity, and not much urgency among the other 10,000 people. When that's the case, well, you're dead."

Second, he makes a big case for the role of senior executives to instill that sense of urgency. If the CEO and the board don't care about diversity, the workforce certainly can't be expected to either. The importance of diversity to the welfare of the company must be evident to everyone by the level and quality of the people assigned to the initiative, and by the energy that the executives devote to shepherding the change.

"If you have a CEO who is a great leader, he or she will be out there slipping in a little something as part of all their meetings and talks. It doesn't have to be a big thing. It can be five percent of a meeting or speech. This is their personal conviction and you've got to, got to, do something about it," says Kotter. "All too often in the diversity efforts I've run into, the team consists of two outside consultants and two lower-level managers. Nope, it won't work," he says, warning, "they don't have the credibility, don't have enough power and don't have enough of anything."

Holmes takes ownership even further into the management structure. "It would help," she says, "if managers took an interest in what employees were learning and each participant had to identify and share some action they will take following the session. Their bosses should be accountable for providing support and feedback on the learning efforts. Unfortunately, organizations have not taken this training seriously enough to actually expect and support real change."

*Why is there a tendency for internal breakdowns in diversity initiatives?*

Pat Zigarmi, vice president of business development for the Ken Blanchard Companies[2] points to a common risk for leadership teams. "Nothing could diffuse a diversity initiative faster than people looking for internal breakdowns between senior leaders and resistance to changing their own behavior. People are looking for cracks in the alignment between senior leaders. This is more about getting people to really own the change initiative."

Kotter's third point is the importance of building and communicating a clear vision, but he is wary of training as the only means to accomplish that. "You need some clarity of vision about where you're trying to drive this and you might say that's pretty simple," he says, "but more often than not, the visions don't exist, don't make sense or are just blurry. The strategy for getting there is very often to throw in some training programs, which is a bad strategy. Then it's communicating all of that out and getting enough people to buy in; I've never seen a company do a good job of that."

The next step in the process is empowering people to act on the vision, and to help them believe in it, says Kotter. In her practice, Zigarmi refers to a vital process she calls "exploring possibilities." "What would it be like if we continued on the path we are on, or what would it be like if we were to change the path that we're on?" she asks, discussing the importance of allowing people to consider the future described by the vision and how it's likely to affect them.

She works with an adaptation of Frances Fuller's Concerns-Based Adoption Model,[3] which anticipates people experiencing predictable and sequential stages of concern when an organization is adopting large-scale change. Listening to people talk about the change and determining where they sit on the scale of six stages helps nail down how to best help individuals progress, support them in collaborating with change agents and ultimately to further refining the change on their own in order to anchor it.

# DIVERSITY ISN'T JUST ABOUT WOMEN AND MINORITIES

White males, in particular those in leadership roles, often find themselves struggling with tough questions about the need for diversity change. Kay Iwata, president of K. Iwata Associates[4] acknowledges these troubling questions. "When we have questions around the dilemma that the current culture works for us, we have to ask, 'what is it going to take to convince me that the system that works for me needs to change?' Going beyond political correctness, these leaders are going to have to give up some of the strategy that has worked for them."

One company, White Men as Full Diversity Partners (WMFDP), sees this as an obstacle for any diversity initiative and, in 1996, began offering workshops to address what they saw missing—the active role of white heterosexual men in those efforts. Michael Welp, a founding partner of WMFDP, believes it is essential to engage everyone, in particular those who have benefited the most from the longstanding system of male advantage in business.

"There's a lot at stake for me," he says. "There are a lot of privileges that go with being a white man. Things I don't have to think about, and there isn't much that's going to happen to me if I don't think about it. I also need to learn what the impact of my privilege is on women and people of color." Welp sees the importance of broadening the definition of diversity to include everyone, and to welcome the differences among all of us.

WMFDP has advanced this idea to the point of encouraging white men to recognize they also belong to a specific culture. "White men tend to feel that diversity is not us," he says. "But upon closer examination, what this means is that so long as other people act like white men, there isn't a problem: if they don't, then there's a problem, but it's not my problem. What this really means is other groups need to assimilate into the dominant white male culture. Yet, we don't think of ourselves as having a culture."

Welp sees serious restraint to the spirit from unquestioned acceptance of behaviors associated with membership in the herd. "This white male culture in the U.S. is a rugged individualist culture," he comments. "There is a silent, closed-off nature associated with white men. We can talk about sports and unimportant issues, but we can't really talk about feelings." He contrasts this with what is available through inclusive relationships at work.

"Part of what diversity offers me, as a white man, is some additional freedom to make choices about who I want to be," he says. "I can step outside of that white male cultural box with the behaviors that I'm expected to follow. This allows me to have deeper relationships with others. Through diversity and being a full partner, I actually gain a lot."

Another opportunity Welp sees for white men willing to partner in diversity change is in the area of nurturing their own leadership skills, skills difficult to develop in life or in leadership development programs; "Things like courage, tolerating ambiguity, having difficult conversations," he says. "The process of building diversity partnerships really catapults our leadership skills."

# STEADY WINS THE RACE

Kotter says that once you achieve buy-in to the vision, and empower people to act, it's important to offer up some easy, short-term wins to help the initiative gain some credibility and momentum. "Then, it's just going at it *again and again and again* until you get the place operating in a new way that fits the new diversity vision. Then make sure it gets nailed to the floor and doesn't fly back to tradition through a variety of mechanisms that anchor it in the culture."

Holmes sees the definition of success in terms of the new skills people acquire to face diversity challenges. "From an educational standpoint," she says, "a diversity program is successful if people leave with an understanding of specific skills they can use when faced with a diversity challenge. People typically work from an 'unconscious level' and don't know what to do when they have to think about it.

"In essence, we want to instill a high degree of self-management skills in people and develop the ability to see beyond their own perspective and share and understand someone else's views," adds Holmes. "In a successfully diverse organization, people are comfortable with a high level of diversity tension. This tension is the ability to pursue common objectives despite a large number of differences and similarities among the people on the team. We believe that if you have real diversity, people willing to own their differences, you will have tension."

# MAKING THE GRADE

Kotter is humble about his advice to those undertaking diversity change efforts, but unyielding on the need to stick to basics. "Very often you have a core group of people who care enormously and who recognize, for all kinds of legal, moral and strategic reasons, that this is the right thing to do. But they haven't had a single experience in producing a big leap, they're not getting any help from anyone else and so they're just struggling out there trying to do the best they can."

What makes some diversity initiatives successful when so many others are struggling as Kotter has witnessed? Call it what you will, what it amounts to is applying strategic human resource management and using the tools of effective organizational change. Knowing what to say might be important, but it just isn't as crucial as knowing when to say it, who should say it and how often they need to address the subject of diversity. Context is critical.

A diversity initiative should reflect the needs of the company. A detailed project strategy for every step with high visibility and executive blessing should be developed and communicated at every opportunity through every available channel. Celebrate even the smallest achievements to reinforce the importance and positive direction of the change. Once the change is in progress, monitor its progress and measure its effectiveness. Accountability to the changes at all levels serves to reinforce the change and anchor it in the company's culture.

In all of the interviews I conducted, one unassailable point was universal. Successful initiatives are the ones with executive leaders firmly behind them and, most importantly, in front of people expressing the importance of diversity to the welfare of the company.

Communicated effectively, the diversity initiative should bring people to the realization that executives aren't just paying lip service to diversity; that conviction is behind their words and deeds. The realization, says Kotter, is fundamental. "We've got to get off our fannies and do something about this. If we don't it's a problem, and if we do, it could be an opportunity."

*How could Kotter's eight steps be modified for K–12 schools?*

# SIDEBAR I
# John Kotter's Eight Steps of Successful Large-Scale Change

## Step 1: Creating a Sense of Urgency Among Relevant People

This means examining market and competitive realities, identifying and discussing crises, potential crises or major opportunities. In smaller organizations, the "relevant" people are more likely to number 100 than five, in larger organizations 1,000 rather than 50. The less successful change leaders aim at five or 50 or zero, allowing what is common nearly everywhere—too much complacency, fear or anger, all three of which can undermine change. Sometimes developed by very creative means, a sense of urgency gets people off the couch, out of a bunker and ready to move.

## Step 2: Forming a Powerful Guiding Coalition

This step translates to assembling a group with enough power to lead the change effort and encouraging the group to work together as a team. The less successful rely on a single person or no one, weak task forces and committees, or complex governance structures, all without the stature, skills and power to do the job.

## Step 3: Creating a Vision

To help direct the change effort the business must create a vision. This means developing strategies for achieving that vision. In less successful cases, there are only detailed plans and budgets that, although necessary, are insufficient. Or there's a vision that is not very sensible in light of what is happening in the world and in the enterprise, or a vision that is created by others and largely ignored by the guiding team. In unsuccessful cases, strategies are often too slow and cautious for a faster-moving world.

## Step 4: Communicating the Vision

To communicate the new vision and strategies, leadership must use every vehicle possible to communicate. This often means teaching new behaviors by the example of the guiding coalition. In the less successful cases, there is too little effective communication, or people hear words but don't accept them. Remarkably, smart people under communicate or poorly communicate all the time without recognizing their error.

## Step 5: Empowering Others to Act on the Vision

To change systems or structures that seriously undermine the vision, leadership must get rid of the obstacles to change while encouraging risk taking and nontraditional activities and actions. Change leaders then focus on bosses who disempower, on inadequate information and information systems, and on self-confidence barriers in people's minds. In less successful situations, people are often left to fend for themselves despite impediments all around. So frustration grows and change is undermined.

## Step 6: Planning for and Creating Short-Term Wins

To create short-terms wins, leadership must plan for visible performance improvements. Once improvements are created, employees involved need to be recognized and rewarded. Without a well-managed process, careful selection of initial projects and fast enough successes, the cynics and skeptics can sink any effort.

## Step 7: Consolidating Improvements and Producing Still More Change

By using increased credibility to change systems, structures and policies that don't fit the vision, leaders press forward in the change process. These systems include hiring, promoting and developing employees who can implement the vision, and reinvigorating the process with new projects, themes and change agents. In less successful cases, people try to do too much at once. They unwittingly quit too soon. They let momentum slip to the point where they find themselves hopelessly bogged down.

## Step 8: Institutionalizing New Approaches

Articulating the connections between the new behaviors and corporate success. Developing the means to ensure leadership development and succession.

A new culture—group norms of behavior and shared values—develops through consistency of successful action over a sufficient period of time. Here, appropriate promotions, skillful new employee orientation and events that engage the emotions can make a big difference. A great deal of work can be blown away by the winds of tradition in a remarkably short period of time.

# SIDEBAR II
# Keys to Effective Diversity Initiatives

- Involve the executive team as the change champions; more than mere support is needed. They are critical to communicating the importance of the effort to the welfare of the company and its workers.
- Put your "A-Team" on the project and ensure that they have access to the resources and people necessary.
- Choose consultants with care. Ensure that there is a good fit between consultants, the company and the project team. This is not an effort to turn over to a consultant for turnkey execution. Buy-in must be unilateral and the company's commitment must be highly visible.
- Perform a comprehensive analysis of the needs and issues driving the change. Study barriers, beliefs and points of resistance opposing the change and reflect these in project design.
- Articulate a clear vision of the desired culture and outcomes expected. Be frank about the support and behavior needed from executives and management throughout the initiative. Listen and respond to concerns.
- Get everyone involved. An effective diversity effort affects all the people in the company, not just women and minorities. Show everyone that there is something in it for him or her and for the company.
- Give the effort the attention it deserves, start-to-finish. Develop and execute a detailed change strategy.
- Communicate, communicate, communicate—up, down and across the organization. Use creative training to teach new behaviors and to explain the vision, but keep the effort visible to the workforce at all times via every available communication channel (e.g., company newspapers, speaking engagements, meetings, advertisement, recruitment, etc.).
- Measure the effectiveness of the effort throughout and fine tune where needed.
- Celebrate early wins to demonstrate progress.
- Anchor the change and hold executives, management and supervisors accountable to the new behaviors and initiatives.

# ENDNOTES

1.  John Kotter is author of two bestselling books on successful change, "Leading Change," Harvard Business School Press, 1996, and "The Heart of Change," Harvard Business School Press, 2002.
2.  Pat Zigarmi is coauthor with Ken Blanchard of "Leadership and the One Minute Manager: Increasing Effectiveness Through Situational Leadership," William Morrow, 1999.
3.  Hall, G. E., A. A. George, and W. L. Rutherford, "Measuring Stages of Concern about the Innovation: A Manual for the Use of the SOC Questionnaire," University of Texas at Austin, 1979.
4.  Kay Iwata is the author of "The Power of Diversity: Five Essential Competencies for Leading a Diverse Workforce," Global Insights Publishing, 2004.

# Managing Generation Y

## Susan P. Eisner

### INTRODUCTION

With the entry of Generation Y to the working world, the workforce for the first time contains four generations: *Traditionalists* (also called Veterans, Silents, or Greatest Generation; 75 million born before 1945; 10% of the workforce), *Baby Boomers* (80 million born 1945–1964, 45% of the workforce), *Generation X* (46 million born 1965–1980, 30% of the workforce), and *Generation Y* also called Echo Boomers, Millenials, Internet Generation, or Nexters; 76 million born after 1980; 15% of the workforce) (Paul, 2004; Francis-Smith, 2004; Johns, 2003; Martin and Tulgan, 2004; Raines, 2002). Despite some variations in the way the literature names these generations and classifies start and end dates, there is general descriptive consensus among academics and practitioners regarding these generations.

More important, there appears to be agreement that this confluence of generations has immediate consequences for managers. Over the next 10 years, the U.S. population older than 65 will increase by 26%, those 40–54 will fall by 5%, and those 25–30 will increase by 6% (Connelly, 2003). By 2006, two experienced workers will leave the workforce for every one who enters it (Piktialis, 2004). Already, nearly 60% of HR professionals in large companies report conflict between younger and older workers (Work Ethic Primary Conflict, 2004), and cite impending labor shortages as increasing the value of every employee (Southard and Lewis, 2004; Dealing With Your New Generation Mix, 2004). Against this backdrop, intergenerational differences may become a foremost aspect of diversity in the U.S. workplace. . . .

### FOUR GENERATIONS AT WORK

The literature is remarkably consistent in its descriptions of the four generations now in today's workforce. On the whole, it describes the coexistence of age-diverse workers in a transitioning workplace once characterized by long-term, mutually loyal, employer–employee relations that produced work through command and control management. That workforce is moving toward a 21st century workplace characterized by free agency. There, workers no longer expect long-term rewards, but instead negotiate each new job seeking the best overall working environment including opportunities for training and work-life balance (Connelly, 2003; Tulgan, 2004).

The most senior generation at work today is frequently termed Traditionalists. Children of Depression and World Wars, Traditionalists were socialized through scarcity and hardship. They tend to value family and patriotism, have had a parent at home to raise children, prefer consistency, and use a top-down management style. They are inclined to inform on a need-to-know basis, be satisfied by a job well done, remain with one company over time, and have amassed wisdom and experience (Allen, 2004). Traditionalists are likely to be loyal and self-sacrificing employees who prefer a traditional, hierarchical management structure (Francis-Smith, 2004). When in command, they tend to take charge. When in doubt, they tend to do what is right (Martin and Tulgan, 2004).

The Traditionalists' children were socialized in the 1950s and 1960s feeling prosperous, safe, and that anything was possible. The largest generation in history, these Baby Boomers believe in growth, change, and expansion. Their numbers alone made them competitive. Baby Boomers tend to want it all and seek it by working long hours, showing loyalty, and being ruthless if necessary; many do not plan to retire. They are likely to respect authority, but want to be viewed and treated as equals (Allen, 2004). Baby Boomers tended to be the center of their parent's attention and redefined many social norms, especially family, in which their generation increased divorce rates. They tend to be driven to succeed and to measure that success materially. Like their parents, they are inclined to lack technological skills but to be social beings; networking works well for them in career building (Johns, 2003). Baby Boomers tend to be optimistic and confident and to value free expression and social reform (Francis-Smith, 2004).

In the workplace, Baby Boomers tend to seek consensus, dislike authoritarianism and laziness, and micro-manage others (Francis-Smith, 2004). They have paid their dues and proactively climbed the corporate ladder making new rules along the way. But now they tend to find themselves reactive in an era of downsizing and reengineering. The sink-or-swim survival mode they are accustomed to becomes more difficult as they reach a life stage in which keeping up a nonstop pace becomes an ever-greater challenge (Martin and Tulgan, 2004).

Gen X is the child of the workaholic Baby Boomer. Socialized as latch-key kids in a downsizing work world where technology was booming, Gen X tends to lack the social skills of its parents but to have strong technical ability (Johns, 2003). It is likely to be self-reliant, individualistic, distrustful of corporations, lacking in loyalty, and intent on balancing work and personal life. Independent, entrepreneurial Gen X lives on the edge and embraces change; it produced the 1990's dot-com stars. Gen X tends to be outcome-focused, and seeks specific and constructive feedback (Allen, 2004). It is skeptical but loves freedom and room to grow (Francis-Smith, 2004).

At work, Gen X is not likely to prioritize long-term employment with a single company or value long hours. It tends to respond well to competent leadership and to be educated and technically skilled enough to move into management more quickly (Francis-Smith, 2004). Gen X is likely to value developing skills more than gaining in job title and to not take well to micromanaging. Reflecting its lack of social skills, Gen X tends to be reluctant to network and is attracted more by ads and recruitment (Johns, 2003). It pioneered the free-agent workforce and believes security comes with keeping skills current. This generation is likely to find a way to get things done smartly, fast, and best even if it means bending the rules. It tends to respond well to a coaching management style that provides prompt feedback and credit for results achieved (Martin and Tulgan, 2004).

Gen Y is the most recent cohort to enter the workforce. Far larger than the generation before it, much of Gen Y was raised in a time of economic expansion and prosperity. But Gen Y is coming of age in an era of economic uncertainty and violence. Though it is the most affluent generation (Allen, 2004), some 16% of Gen Y grew up or is growing up in poverty (Raines, 2002). In its post-Columbine, post-9/11, 24-hour media world, this latest generation has seen more at an earlier age than prior generations have seen (Sujansky, 2004). It is not surprising that Gen Y reflects some values held by Traditionalists. Like that "greatest generation," Gen Y tends to have a strong sense of morality, to be patriotic, willing to fight for freedom, is sociable, and values home and family. But Gen Y's large size, level of education, and technical skill position it to echo the Baby Boomers' impact on business and society (Allen, 2004).

Having worked throughout high school while continuing to live with parents in a 24/7 digitally connected and globalizing world, Gen Y is the most technically literate, educated, and ethnically diverse generation in history and tends to have more discretionary income. It tends to want intellectual challenge, needs to succeed, seeks those who will further its professional development, strives to make a difference, and measures its own success. Meeting personal goals is likely to matter to Gen Y, as is performing meaningful work that betters the world and working with committed co-workers with shared values. Making a lot of money tends to be less important to Gen Y than contributing to society, parenting well, and enjoying a full and balanced life (Allen, 2004).

Gen Y was socialized in a digital world. It is more than technically literate; it is continually wired, plugged in, and connected to digitally streaming information, entertainment, and contacts. It has so mastered technology that multitasking is a habit it takes into the workplace, where it tends to instant message its contacts while doing work (Lewis, 2003). A recent study found Gen Y consuming 31 hours of media (through multi-tasting) within a 24-hour period (Weiss, 2003).

Gen Y has been told it can do anything and tends to believe it (Martin, 2004). It has lived with strong social stressors ranging from pressure to excel in school to parental divorce and one-parent homes. It is accustomed to being active in family decisions and is likely to expect to contribute to decisions in employer organizations (Johns, 2003). Overall, Gen Y is inclined to be positive, polite, curious, energetic, and respectful of its parents and grandparents (Francis-Smith, 2004).

In the workplace, Gen Y tends to favor an inclusive style of management, dislike slowness, and desire immediate feedback about performance (Francis-Smith, 2004). It is a truly global generation, socially conscious and volunteer-minded and positioned to be the most demanding generation. If treated professionally, it is likely to act professionally. Gen Y is likely to perform best when its abilities are identified and matched with challenging work that pushes it fully. Speed, customization, and interactivity—two-way nonpassive engagement—are likely to help keep Gen Y focused (Martin and Tulgan, 2004). Technically able, highly informed and confident, but lacking direction, Gen Y is more likely to "rock the boat" than any prior generation (Johns, 2003). . . .

*How many generations are typically working together in schools and institutions?*

## GEN Y: OPPORTUNITY AND CHALLENGE

Gen Y has been deeply affected by several trends of the 1990s and 2000s: a renewed focus on children, family, scheduled and structured lives, multiculturalism, terrorism, heroism, patriotism, parent advocacy, and globalization. Coincidentally, Gen Y has been socialized with several core messages: be smart—you are special, leave no one behind, connect 24/7, achieve now, and serve your community (Raines, 2002). It tends to ignore traditional media and advertising channels, play video games, and watch DVDs rather than listed TV programming. Those in Gen Y tend to live with their parents before college, plan to return to their parents' home after college, and are less at home in the real world than in the virtual world—in which they spend more than six hours a day online. One-third of 21-year olds are not Caucasian. A similar number is being raised by single parents, and three-quarters have working mothers. Perhaps reflecting 9/11/01, Gen Y tends to want to connect with its parents rather than rebel. As consumers, Gen Y is likely to be independent and not brand loyal. Traditional at home, it tends to be nontraditional and sophisticated in the marketplace (Weiss, 2003).

Gen Y's entrance into the workplace would seem to present many opportunities in today's ever-more competitive organizations in which high-performing workers are an asset, and demographic shifts point to impending labor shortages. Gen Y workers would seem to be a timely addition. They tend to be goal-oriented (Southard and Lewis, 2004) and interested in self-development and improvement (Dealing With Your New Generational Mix, 2004). They are likely to have high expectations of personal and financial success, feel that hard work pays off, and have a get-it-done result-producing attitude (Breaux, 2003). They are inclined to plunge into work they find interesting and important even when they know little about it (Lewis, 2003).

Some of Gen Y's characteristics may make it easier to manage than Gen X. Gen Y tends to value teamwork and fairness and is likely to be more positive than Gen X on a range of workplace issues including work-life balance, performance reviews, and availability of supervisors (What You Need to Know, 2003). Moreover, Gen Y descriptors include attributes predictive of high performance. Gen Y workers are inclined to be sociable, hopeful, talented, collaborative, inclusive, and civic-minded. In addition to being well educated and technically savvy, they tend to be open-minded, achievement-oriented, and able to work on parallel tasks (Raines, 2002). Cautiously optimistic and enthusiastic about the future, Gen Y is likely to have a solid work ethic and entrepreneurial bent. At the same time, it tends to acknowledge and admire authority, especially Traditionalists. Strength, cooperation, energy, conformity, virtue, and duty tend to be among Gen Y's values (Pekala, 2001).

A recent Work and Education survey by the Gallup Organization also suggests that Gen Y will not be harder to manage than workers from other generations. Like workers in the 30–49 and 50+ age groups, Gen Y has a strong sense of company loyalty, is at least as satisfied with supervisors as are older workers, is as content as the others with the amount of praise received, and is as satisfied as the others with amount of vacation time and work flexibility or hours required. Additionally, Gen Y feels no more workplace stress than the other workers and is as satisfied as the others with retirement and health benefits (Saad, 2003).

At the same time, Gen Y's entrance to the workforce seems to present some challenges. Although Gen Y workers tend to be more positive than Gen X about working in general, Gen Y tends to be less satisfied than Gen X with their jobs and employers. The survey described earlier in this paper pinpoints several dimensions of that dissatisfaction. Further, Gen Y is more open than Gen X to leaving for something better (What You Need to Know, 2003). Gen Y is likely to equate job satisfaction with a positive work climate, flexibility, and the opportunity to learn and grow more than any prior generation. Compared with other generations, Gen Y tends to have less respect for rank and more respect for ability and accomplishment. It is likely to trade more pay for work it feels is meaningful at a company where it feels appreciated (Alati, 2004). Gen Y tends to value respect and wants to earn it. Acknowledgement and freedom to perform as it finds best tend to matter to Gen Y, too (Dealing With Your New Generational Mix, 2004).

Additionally, Gen Y workers are likely to dislike menial work, lack skills for dealing with difficult people, and be impatient (Raines, 2002). Less than half of this youngest generation describe themselves as confident or prepared to enter the workforce. Their strong technical skills are not matched by strong soft skills such as listening, communicating, independent thinking, being a team player, and managing time (Pekala, 2001). Mercer Human Resource Consultant's 2002 People at Work Survey found Gen Y rating employers lower than other employees do on being treated fairly, getting necessary cooperation from others, and having opportunity to do interesting and meaningful work (The Next Generation, 2003).

Moreover, Gen Y workers tend to look for instant gratification rather than long-term investments of time and effort (Southard and Lewis, 2004). In addition to demanding immediate rewards, they are likely to prefer special projects rather than "dues-paying chores." They often prefer being given time off to receiving money; putting in face time tends to puts them off. Accustomed to coming, going, and staying as needed, and being involved when present, Gen Y workers tend to be constant negotiators and questioners. As one author describes it, "The forty hour workweek doesn't apply . . . (and) 'how' meetings become 'why' meetings" (Lewis, 2003). Intergenerational management expert Bruce Tulgan describes the resulting challenges of Gen Y workers this way: "Gen Y'ers are like X'ers on steroids . . . They are the most high-maintenance generation to ever enter the work force" (Breaux, 2003).

# RECOMMENDATIONS: MANAGEMENT STRATEGIES

Presenting both challenges and opportunities, Gen Y is entering the workforce in ever-increasing numbers. What management strategies are likely to be most effective for achieving high performance in today's intergenerational workplace? Experts suggest that managers apply messages and strategies deliberately tailored to the characteristics of each of the four generations. They recommend identifying and addressing the motivational needs of each generation, and training each generation mindful of its learning styles. Age stereotypes should be avoided, and age differences should be built into diversity training. Team building should include intergenerational pairing based on complimentary strengths. Open and ongoing discussions for discussing intergenerational needs should become corporate culture norms (Piktialis, 2004).

What strategies should resonate with Traditionalists? Members of this longest-working generation should respond well to being told that their experience is respected and important to the company and that their perseverance is valued and will be rewarded. They should be encouraged to share their knowledge of what has and has not worked in the past. They are likely to welcome training that is offered in formats consistent with their more traditional learning style (Kogan, 2001). Also, Traditionalists should be encouraged to respectfully assert their authority and demonstrate their track records. Engaging them as teachers is recommended. Rehiring them as part-time team leaders and coaches when they retire is also suggested (Martin and Tulgan, 2004).

On the other hand, Baby Boomers should respond well to being told that they are important to the organization's success, are valued for their unique and important contributions, and are needed. They should be provided feedback with sensitivity. Change should be presented to them in a way that minimizes conflict (Kogan, 2001). What's more, Baby Boomers should be encouraged to become facilitating coaches rather than authoritarian figures dictating expectations and methods. They should be offered flexibility, authority, and respect. Additionally, Baby Boomers should be challenged to keep on growing (Martin and Tulgan, 2004).

For its part, independent Gen X should respond well to being told to do things its own way, with minimal rules and bureaucracy. This first techno-savvy generation should be provided with current hardware and software (Kogan, 2001). Its growth-oriented nature should be managed with a coaching style. At the same time, this outcome-focused generation should be asked to learn just-in-time for each new assignment (Martin and Tulgan, 2004).

The newest entrants to the workplace, the Gen Y group, are largely uncharted territory for many managers. Gen Y workers tend to have unbridled energy, endless enthusiasm, and the skills and experience of those much older. They too, then, should be managed with a coaching style (Sujansky, 2002). Gen Y should respond well to being told that it will be working with other bright and creative people, and that the boss is over 60. Hearing that, together with peers, they can turn the company around, and that they can be heroes at the company, should also resonate with Gen Y workers (Kogan, 2001). Flexibility and voice, access to co-workers and company information through technology, and project-centered work are recommended (Allen, 2004). Expectations should be explained to Gen Y from the outset, including the big picture and how they fit into it. Gen Y should be given a sense of belonging (Hansford, 2002).

Leaders would do well to model expected behavior for Gen Y workers and interact with them, creating a sense of enjoyment and challenge. Candid talk without hype and with a sense of humor should help reach Gen Y. Movement toward cultural openness and transparency is recommended, as is investment in programs encouraging teamwork and flexibility. At the same time, roles and responsibilities should be defined and written for Gen Y. Task lists and time-lines should suggest how and when to reach goals (Dealing With Your New Generation Mix, 2004).

Job conditions that cannot be attained should not be promised, as doing so will leave Gen Y feeling disappointed and betrayed. Instead, Gen Y workers should be given the chance to contribute to a greater good and to work for a socially responsible company (Loughlin and Barling, 2001).

*How can Gen Y faculty and staff be provided space they need for collaboration in a traditional school building?*

Spaces, processes, and practices tailored to Gen Y should be well worth the cost. Office spaces set up to facilitate the exchange of ideas with others are recommended. Goal accomplishment in Gen Y team projects should be evaluated as a whole. Reverse mentor programs in which Gen Y's technical skills can be recognized and shared are also suggested (Raines, 2002).

Furthermore, it is advisable to meet the high expectations of Gen Y workers with respect and positivism (Raines, 2002). Digital-based training programs should resonate with Gen Y, for whom work and play are blended and achievement and winning matter. Training for Gen Y workers should focus on strategic areas and not be trivial. Optimally, it will engage them experientially, allow for practice, and provide a valued pay-off at the end (Salopek, 2003).

Some companies are tackling the challenges of recruiting and retaining Gen Y using innovative strategies tailored to Gen Y characteristics. These techniques include providing on-site leadership academies, creating formal mentoring programs to maximize Gen Y access, and giving early chances to do meaningful work. To better reach Gen Y, some are streamlining the recruitment process and providing longer vacations after shorter service. For similar reasons, some are building comprehensive intranet sites, allowing conversion of unused administrative leave into cash, and permitting conversion of health benefits into deferred compensation accounts (Southard and Lewis, 2004).

Some companies are literally going where Gen Y workers are, connecting with them through the media and locations such as Internet cafes and video game stores. Or they recruit Gen Y through on-site career-day seminars in which ranking personnel share their own success stores. Some companies are using their Gen Y employees as the first outreachers to peer Gen Y candidates in an effort to quicken the pace of recruitment. In this way, the companies aim to both engage their Gen Y employees more fully and to create a workplace ally for the Gen Y candidate (Employing Generation Why, 2004).

# WIDER HORIZONS?

A 2001 article by Loughlin and Barling provides solid foundation for understanding the context within which today's intergenerational workforce operates. It reports that almost 80% of North American high school students worked part-time for pay before graduating from high school. Coinciding with this unprecedented rate of employment is the conclusion Gen Y has drawn from their parents' work experience. Gen Y workers tend to distrust long-term job security and seek immediate payoffs from employers as a result. Many have developed a work-to-live rather than live-to-work mindset that spills over into valuing the quality of the work environment as well as work-life balance. Moreover, an increasing number of jobs awaiting Gen Y are "non-standard;" 30% of North American and European jobs are temporary, part-time, or contract. Under-employment is an additional reality. Some 75% of the labor force in most industrial countries is doing little more than simple, repetitive tasks. The level of skilled jobs available is far less than the skill levels of the employable population (Loughlin and Barling, 2001).

In 2003, intergenerational expert Bruce Tulgan reported the results of a comprehensive 10-year study that interviewed more than 10,000 people and studied management practices of more than 700 companies to explore the contemporary U.S. workplace. The study found generational shifts amounting to significant and lasting workplace changes. Tulgan states, "Between 1993 and 2003, a profound revolution has taken place in the values and norms of the U.S. workforce; the impact has been felt throughout the world . . . the new economy is a far cry from dot-coms with magical business models, and rather has created a very challenging environment for most workers today" (Tulgan, 2004).

In that study, Tulgan identified several core dimensions of the workplace transformation. First, work has become more demanding. Second, the employer–employee relationship has become less hierarchical and more

Table 1    Summary (1) — Four Generations at Work

| | Traditionalists<br>*75 million born<br>pre-1945; 10% of<br>workforce* | Baby Boomers<br>*80 million born<br>1945–1964;<br>45% of workforce* | Generation X<br>*46 million born<br>1965–1980;<br>30% of workforce* | Generation Y<br>*76 million born post-1980;<br>15% of workforce* |
|---|---|---|---|---|
| **Formative<br>Events** | Great depression<br>World war | Post-war prosperity<br>Largest generation | Globalization<br>Downsizing<br>Technology boom | Prosperity/uncertainty<br>Violence/terrorism<br>Outsourcing/under-employment |
| **Socialization** | Scarcity/hardship<br>Parent at home | Prosperous/safe<br>Anything is possible<br>Parent's focal point | Latchkey kids | Strong social pressure<br>Structured life/live at home<br>Nontraditional families<br>Active role in family<br>Fallout from work<br>Nonstandard word<br>Multiculturalism |
| **Imprint<br>Made** | Greatest<br>generation<br>Dual incomes | Free generation<br>Redefined norms<br>Civil rights | Me generation<br>Dot.com stars<br>Free agency | We generation<br>Wired/switch/populist<br>Work at early age/worldly |
| **Pattern** | Stay with<br>company | Loyal<br>Workalcoholic<br>Sink or swim | Live on edge<br>Embrace change<br>Devalue long hours<br>Job hop<br>Will find a way | Expect to make decisions<br>Need to achieve/self-reliant<br>Curious/energetic/question<br>Distrust job security<br>Dislike face time/menial job |
| **Qualities** | Loyal<br>Self-sacrificing | Pro-growth/change<br>Competitive<br>Optimistic/confident<br>Paid dues/climbed<br>Want it all | Independent<br>Individualistic<br>Distrust companies<br>Lack loyalty<br>Entrepreneurial | Large size/diverse/loyal<br>Skilled/energetic<br>Polite/positive/leave none<br>Socially conscious/hopeful<br>Sophisticated/demanding |
| **Value** | Family<br>Patriotism | Success/materially<br>Free expression<br>Reform<br>Equity | Skill more than title<br>Work-life balance | Heroism/patriot/virtue/duty<br>Elderly/family/home/time<br>Service/respect more than $ Work<br>to live; shared norms |

transactional. Third, employers have moved away from long-term employment relationships. Fourth, employees have less confidence in long-term rewards and greater expectations for short-term rewards. Fifth, immediate supervisors have become the most important people in the workplace. Sixth, supervising employees now requires more time and skill at the very time when there are fewer managers (Tulgan, 2004).

Tulgan's study depicts a 21st century workplace in which traditional career paths and management techniques, long-term employment, and cookie cutter approaches to employee relations are disappearing. What replaces them? Employees take responsibility for their own success and failure. Employees make their own way by attaining and marketing cutting edge skills that they

Table 2    Summary (2) — Four Generations at Work

| | | | | |
|---|---|---|---|---|
| **Assets** | Wisdom<br>Experience<br>Perseverance | Social skills | Technology skills<br>Education<br>Fast track to manage | Educated/experienced<br>Sociable/technical/perform<br>Work ethic/multitask |
| **Lack** | Technology skills | Technology skills | Social skills | Direction/focus/confidence<br>Interpersonal/soft skills |
| **Style** | Top-down<br>Directive<br>Inform as needed<br>Take charge<br>Do what's right | Respect authority<br>Network<br>Micro-manage<br>Proactive<br>Work hard | Skeptical<br>Reluctant to network<br>Outcome-focused<br>Achieve well/fast<br>Bend rules as need | Get done/produce/negotiate<br>Plunge right in/fast-paced<br>Open and civic minded<br>Blend work and play<br>Measure own success |
| **Strategy for** | Respect experience<br>Share past lessons<br>Reward staying<br>Teach to assert<br>Match learning style<br>Use as teachers<br>Rehire to coach/lead | Give important roles<br>Value contributions<br>Show respect<br>Minimize conflict<br>Sensitize feedback<br>Be flexible<br>Challenge to grow<br>Have coach/facilitate | Recruit traditionally/ad<br>Manage by coach<br>Don't micro-manage<br>Reduce rules/layers<br>Allow innovation<br>Update technology<br>Feedback quickly<br>Specify and help<br>Credit for results<br>Train just in time | Treat fairly/professionally<br>Give meaningful/fun work<br>Challenge intellectually<br>Meet growth/personal goals<br>Model expected behavior<br>Manage inclusively/belong<br>Provide importance/voice<br>Have positive/open environ<br>Don't over-promise/hype<br>Assign projects/teams/tasks<br>Allow freedom to try/access<br>Focus by speed/target/win<br>Train strategically/digitally<br>Clarify big picture/timeline<br>Specify roles/responsibilities<br>Use to reverse mentor<br>Streamline/target recruiting |

leverage through networking into career opportunity. Managers are pressured to hire the best person for every opening. Managers aggressively push each person to unleash the highest productivity (Tulgan, 2004).

The result? Tulgan's study projects an inevitable push-pull between the employer's need to squeeze the employee and the employee's need for quality of work life. To resolve this, the employee is likely to become more assertive about exacting short-term transactions in return for meeting the employer's goals. Tulgan describes that transforming 21st century workplace this way: "Managers will have to discard traditional authority, rules, and red tape, and become highly engaged in one-on-one negotiation and coaching with employees to drive productivity, quality, and innovation" (Tulgan, 2004).

To older workers, that description may seem like a brave new world in which the culture shock is unpalatable and even incomprehensible. But younger workers may have a leg up. The following summary of this paper shows that, to Gen Y, the workplace Tulgan describes seems very much like the one it expects to enter. . . .

Because the managerial implication of Gen Y's entrance to the contemporary workplace is still largely uncharted territory, it may be helpful to present some recurring comments from such discussions. First, some say that generational labels tend to be determined by marketers, and should not be allowed to create differences between people that might otherwise not exist. A second point some raise is that managers should be careful not to oversimplify workplace differences, but should see intergenerational differences as one of several aspects of diversity. A third set of comments contemplates the consequences of management failure to manage intergenerational realities and projects the resulting possibility of further erosion of psychological contract between manager and employee. This is a particularly interesting line of thought given the free agent, quality of work life, and inclusive mindset of newer entrants to the workplace. If these workers are alienated by managerial strategies that do not resonate with them, will managers be able to retain them, let alone unleash their potential? The relevance of that question is underscored by a final line of comment, expressed repeatedly by those of Gen Y: Will managers recognize intergenerational workplace factors and begin to use responsive strategies that optimize this aspect of diversity?

*What strategies should a leader consider in successfully dealing with age diversity in a K–12 school?*

## REFERENCES

Alati, D. (2004, May). Retention race. Incentive, 178(5), 6.

Allen, P. (2004, September). Welcoming Y. Benefits Canada, 28(9), 51(3).

Breaux, J. (2003, November 19). Face of American workplaces is changes, human resource professionals say. *Knight Ridder/Tribune Business News*.

Connelly, J. (2003, October 28). Youthful attitudes, sobering realities. *The New York Times*.

Dealing with your new generation mix. (2004, August). *Accounting Office Management & Administrative Report*, 4(8), 5–7+ (4).

Employing generation why? (2002). *Workforce Management*. Retrieved on November 2, 2004, from http:// www.workforce.com

Francis-Smith, J. (2004, August 26). Surviving and thriving in the multigenerational workplace. *Journal Record*, 1.

Hansford, D. (2002, June). Insights into managing an age-diverse workforce. *Workspan*, *45*(6), 48–54.

Johns, K. (2003, April 11). Managing generational diversity in the workforce. *Trends & Tidbits*. Retrieved on October 10, 2004, from http:// www.workindex.com

Kogan, M. (2001, September 1). Talkin' 'bout four generations. Govexec. Retrieved on October 29, 2004, from http:www.govexec.com

Lewis, K. R. (2003, November 3). Managing multiple generations in the workplace can be a challenge. *Newhouse News Service*.

Loughlin, C., and Barling, J. (2001, November). Young workers' work values, attitudes, and behaviours. *Journal of Occupational and Organizational Psychology*, 74(4), 543–558.

Martin, C., and Tulgan, B. (n.d.) Managing the generation mix—part II. *Top Echelon, Employers*. Retrieved on October 29, 2004, from Pekala, N. (2001, November/December). Conquering the generational divide. *Journal of Property Management*, 66(6), 30–38.

Piktialis, D. (2004, August). Bridging generational divides to increase innovation, creativity, and productivity. *Workspan*, 47(8), 26–41.

Raines, C. (2002). Managing millenials. *Generations At Work*. Retrieved on October 29, 2004, from http:// www.generationsatwork.com

Saad, L. (2003, October 14). Are young employees harder to manage? *The Gallup Organization*. Retrieved on February 11, 2005, from The Gallup Brain database.

Salopek, J. (2003, June). Going native: cross the generation gap by learning to speak. T+D, 57(6), 17 (3).

Southard, G., and Lewis, J. (2004, April). Building a workplace that recognizes generational diversity. Public Management, 86(3), 8(5).

Sujansky, J. (2002, May). The critical care and feeding of generation Y. *Workforce*, 81(5), 15.

Sujansky, J. (2004, April). Leading a multi-generational workforce. *Occupational Health and Safety*, 73(4), 16–18.

Thtulgan, B. (2004, Winter). Trends point to a dramatic generational shift in the future workforce. Employment Relations Today, 30(4), 23–31.

Weiss, M. J. (2003, September 1). To be about to be (Generation Y). *American Demographics*, 25(7).

Work ethic primary conflict among different generations. (2004, August 25). *PR Newswire*.

# ARTICLE 8.4

# The Diversity Test

## Edwin C. Darden

In many places across the United States, a child can complete 13 years of public school and never encounter a youngster who speaks another language at home.

That same child also might never sit next to a fellow student with a dramatically different skin tone—or one who has lived through starkly dissimilar life experiences or contrasting family circumstances that color his or her view of the world.

The key question is this: Does it really matter?

While the social debate might go on forever, the legal answer about taking intentional steps to accomplish diversity will be forthcoming in the next few months. The U.S. Supreme Court will decide two cases by June 2007 that will give guidance on whether districts can consider race and ethnicity when assigning students to school buildings. More specifically, can officials take extraordinary measures to make sure an ideal racial blend is achieved?

An example: a high-achieving elementary school has an overabundance of black children. Because of its stellar reputation, everybody wants to enroll there. Citing educational reasons, district policy forbids any additional black children to transfer in, but would admit white, Asian, or Native American children for balance.

Advocates say there are concrete learning benefits and research-based evidence to prove that both academic achievement and long-term prospects for success increase in a diverse learning climate. They say the power rests with school boards and superintendents to pursue those educational advantages. Opponents say that balancing children by racial designation is another form of stereotyping; it perpetuates the race-conscious history of our country, and overrides personal choice, since families generally move to a neighborhood with school boundaries in mind.

*What are possible impacts of the Supreme Court ruling within a school district?*

The job of the nine Supreme Court justices will be to examine the 14th Amendment's Equal Protection Clause. That provision guarantees that government entities—like public schools—treat all citizens the same, forsaking attributes that might interfere with that goal. Both school policies were upheld by federal circuit courts in their jurisdiction.

The outcome could have an impact of titanic proportions. With demographers predicting that within 15 years the nation will consist of a non-white majority, this ruling will set the backdrop for school policymaking deep into the 21st century.

# WHAT ARE THE CASES ABOUT?

The court accepted one case from Louisville, Ky., and one from Seattle. In Louisville, the schools were historically segregated by law, while Seattle's schools were segregated due to housing patterns.

In 2001, Louisville's Board of Education adopted a "managed choice" school diversity policy. The action came shortly after the system was released from more than two decades of court oversight of a desegregation case. Every school must seek an enrollment of at least 15 percent black students and no more than 50 percent. A mother whose kindergarten son was denied a transfer is challenging the policy.

Seattle's "open choice" plan applies only to the city's 10 high schools. Admission is based on a variety of factors, including proximity to the school and whether a sibling already attends. Race is used as a "tie breaker" when all else is even.

By policy, the student population of Seattle high schools cannot deviate by more than 15 percent from the racial makeup of the total district. The student population is about 60 percent non-white. This challenge is led by a group of parents whose children missed out on their first choice due to the policy and other factors.

The importance of the cases is underscored by the uncommon way in which the justices responded. According to *New York Times* reporter Linda Greenhouse, the cases "evidently provoked a vigorous internal debate among the justices, who considered the Seattle case six times and the Louisville case seven times before issuing the one-line order accepting both. Prolonged review of this sort is unusual."

*How does Louisville's "managed choice" differ from previous desegregation strategies?*

# PUTTING IT IN PERSPECTIVE

From a legal standpoint, these cases are "tweeners." They do not fit neatly into a category that can be analyzed, boxed, and rendered.

The constitutional legal standard by which the policies will be examined is likely to be "strict scrutiny," which requires the court to apply its most skeptical and searching probe. Measured by that yardstick, the court will ask whether the districts have a compelling interest in pursuing diversity policies, and whether the programs are narrowly tailored to accomplish that goal.

Some analysts and news reporters refer to the duo as desegregation cases, saying they really seek simple integration, like the lawsuits of days gone by. But there are important differences both in the motivation and the result. Desegregation cases were built on the idea of being a remedy for laws that kept black and white students in separate learning facilities. The result was a court order or a government-enforced consent decree that legally required school districts to put the populations together.

By contrast, the Seattle and Kentucky cases are based on voluntary policies adopted by school boards with educational aims—and their implementation goes well beyond black and white students. Observers are tempted to call these affirmative action cases and compare them to the 2003 University of Michigan cases of *Grutter v. Bollinger* and *Gratz v. Bollinger.* The former dealt with using race as an advantage in admission to law school and the latter to Michigan's undergraduate campus.

Again, the comparison seems to fall short, since the K-12 policies do not give any particular student a leg up based on race/ethnicity. The two policies can be applied to the benefit or detriment of a student of any race, depending on the circumstances, such as when a black student would be denied his/her choice placement.

Last, the higher education cases dealt with adult students, while K-12 involves children in their formative years. What is hard to say is whether the justices will view the cluster of distinctions as constitutionally significant.

## WHAT ARE THE BENEFITS?

Louisville officials say their program goes to the heart of the district's mission. It has several aims:

- A better academic education for all students
- Better appreciation of political and cultural heritage for all students
- More competitive and attractive public schools
- Broader community support for all Jefferson County public schools
- Substantially uniform educational resources for all students
- Teaching basic skills and critical thinking skills "in a racially integrated environment"

Yet race-sensitive programs bring distinct challenges. As more schools use choice programs, the same self-selection criteria that led to racially segregated neighborhoods could be repeated. True marketplace choice could be dampened by diversity policies.

Racial and ethnic classifications also remain a tricky proposition. Children with parents of different races, for example, often chafe at attempts to place them in a single group for any purpose.

Some school folks look at the two cases and cluck their tongues, saying both are anomalies. Big-city school populations are generally so far tipped toward non-white that a racial diversity policy is unworkable, they contend. The same practicality argument arises with rural school districts.

Yet all districts might experience boundary-line changes, or have special admission academies, or manage magnet or charter schools. Decisions on those issues are potentially affected by the Supreme Court ruling to come.

Board members and superintendents should be mindful that much ado in these cases stems from parents competing to get their children into what they see as a superior placement. Thus, part of the solution could lie in equalizing the quality of offerings across the district, so citizens are content that school

---

## Policy Questions to Consider

Has your school district adopted a policy stating its beliefs about students, diversity, and learning circumstances?

Is race a part of the equation (outwardly or quietly) when considering attendance zone changes, transfer standards or admission criteria for special academies?

Has your central office staff produced population projections for the next 10 years, and have the superintendent and board discussed potential legal questions that flow from any shifts?

Do your policies reflect 21st century sensitivity to race and ethnicity? For instance, do you permit children of interracial parentage to check "multiracial" or "check all that apply"?

Is your board conscious of equity, as seemingly routine votes on building repairs, teachers, special programs, etc., make certain buildings more desirable than others, and trigger competition for quality programs that lead to challenges?

---

assignments are fair. Another part of the solution may be time, as the rapidly rising demographic diversity in the United States redistributes students of all descriptions to all locations, making the policy goal unnecessary.

Before then, however, the Supreme Court will have its say.

# ISSUE SUMMARY

O n April 9, 2007, the lead story on *Good Morning America*, Fox News, WFAN, and DiversityInc (among many other news services) was whether an MSNBC shock jock's racially offensive comments would get him fired, despite his apology. He called his own remarks idiotic and stupid. Immediately, social and professional groups decried this individual's crass comments and some demanded that he not be allowed to broadcast on airwaves monitored by the Federal Communications Commission.

But what is the connection to educational leadership? Isn't this just another example of an individual who doesn't get it—an incident we shake our heads over? There are some, perhaps many, within the educational community who will see this recent diversity-clueless issue as another powerful reason that leaders must find the way forward in sustaining diverse and just educational organizations.

In this age of sophisticated diversity initiatives prompted by layer upon layer of federal guidelines, the insensitivity of a single but highly visible individual proves again that diversity is not solely a matter of policy and procedure. Enlightened admissions policies and anti-discrimination statements and inclusive application procedures may be the right things to do but diversity is less about forms and policy and more about education and shared understandings. Above all, it is about relationship-building and affirmation. Creating an educational setting where diversity is honored is hard work. The approach needed to sustain a diverse and just learning environment is nothing short of transformational and it begins with leaders. With a multitude of diversity models, initiatives, reports, guidelines, resolutions, and legislation available to educational leaders, there is much to consider before making decisions about how to sustain a diverse and just learning environment. In the end, it comes down to a matter of commitment and will.

## ISSUE HIGHLIGHTS

- Culturally competent schools honor and respect diversity in theory and in practice.
- Building culturally competent schools means more than multicultural curriculum; it involves policies, administrative structure, and community involvement.
- Leadership, vision, and communication are key to successful diversity initiatives.
- Diversity isn't solely about race and ethnicity; it is about differences of every kind.

- The presence of four generations in the workforce has definite consequences for leaders of organizations.
- Some management strategies will be more effective than others for different generations of employees.
- Current school desegregation cases accepted by the U.S. Supreme Court will likely set policy well into the twenty-first century.
- School leaders should be cognizant of equity, sensitivity to race and ethnicity, and adequacy in all district policies.

# CRITICAL THINKING

Diversity of the workforce is a good thing for educational organizations. But are leaders convinced of that? When times are good economically, diversity programs thrive. However, studies show that when times are bad, diversity programs are the first to be reduced or cut. The issue for educational leaders is what drives diversity approaches. For diversity to be on the agenda in good times, but off again in an economic downturn is an indication that diversity is not being sustained.

The problem could well be that leaders are not applying systems thinking to the diversity question. If leaders intend to sustain diversity, any initiative must be related to the institution's vision of the future and shaped through group dialogue. It's about moral, not market, values according to the author of an perceptive article in the Chronicle of Higher Education:

> If we value difference, we should do so not as an antidote to tedious homogeneity, but as the stuff of critical thinking. We should value difference, not because it is a successful marketing ploy that draws student dollars, but because it reflects our commitment to overcoming the historical legacies of institutional discrimination and privileges that we all live with and benefit from. If diversity is our value, then our practices will emerge in ways that are natural and integral to our institutions. (Pierce, 2007, p. C2)

This perspective leads back to the issue of diversity as quotas, affirmative action, and policies. It is apparent that making the market case for diversity is less appropriate for educational organizations if they desire to sustain their commitment. Diversity sustainability must be a matter of values and conscience for educational organizations.

# ADDITIONAL READING RESOURCES

Jean Anyon, *Radical Possibilities: Public Policy, Urban Education, and a New Social Movement.* Routledge, 2005.
Judith H. Katz and Frederick A. Miller, Redefining the imperative for leveraging diversity and inclusion: A fresh look. *The CEO Refresher*, 2004.

Jonathan Kozol, *Shame of the Nation: The Restoration of Apartheid Schooling in America*. New Three Rivers, 2006.

Leo Parvis, Diversity and effective leadership in multicultural workplaces. *Journal of Environmental Health*, March 2003.

Lori Pierce, It's about moral, not market, values. *Chronicle of Higher Education,* April 13, 2007.

Joel Spring, *Decentralization and the Struggle for Equality: A Brief History of the Education of the Dominated Cultures in the United States*. McGraw-Hill, 2007.

Edward Stevens, Jr., George H. Wood, and James Sheehan, *Justice, Ideology and Education*. McGraw-Hill, 2002.

Joanne Sujansky, Leading a multi-generational workforce. *Occupational Health and Safety*, April, 2004.

For more information on sustaining diversity, check these sites:

Achieving Diversity: Race-Neutral Alternatives in American Education www.ed.gov/about/offices/list/ocr/edlite-raceneutralreport2.html

Appleseed www.appleseednetwork.org/

Coalition for Community Schools www.communityschools.org

Diversity Inc www.diversityinc.com

National Association for Multicultural Education www.nameorg.org/

NTL Institute www.ntl.org

The Civil Rights Project www.civilrightsproject.harvard.edu

# What Is the Impact of Accountability Legislation on Educational Organizations?

It was a simple notion that prompted creation of the No Child Left Behind Act early in President Bush's first term of office: *every child can learn.* This simple notion has now resulted in sweeping, unprecedented reform of accountability systems in a short span of time. For the past five years, public schools in the United States have been operating under what some would say is a test-based accountability system built on politically volatile values. The scope of impact is spelled out in a single sentence at the top of the federal government's Web landing page for NCLB:

> The law helps schools improve by focusing on accountability for results, freedom for states and communities, proven education methods, and choices for parents. (ed.gov/nclb)

Nothing in recent years has brought together *and* divided more administrators, teachers, unions, legislators, researchers, business leaders, and journalists. Compliance with NCLB has spawned an industry of resources, conferences, and consultants. Despite all this attention and expertise, the realities of implementing NCLB remain daunting as the years go by. This accountability legislation is so far-reaching that implementation has been difficult at best. Any legislation that calls for radical changes in structure and accountability is bound to be a struggle to apply at the local school level. Yet the results, when fully implemented, will be quite spectacular—all American children will learn and succeed.

With such an immense goal at stake, consequences of failing to meet NCLB are dire:

> If a school fails to meet performance objectives for two consecutive years, then in the third year, it must receive technical assistance from the district to help it improve, and its students will have the option to transfer to another public school in the district.
>
> After the third consecutive year of failure students will also have the option of using their share of Title I funds to pay for tutoring and other supplemental educational services either from their own school or from a state-approved outside group, such as a for-profit company or a private non-profit entity.

After the fourth consecutive year, technical assistance, public school choice, and supplemental services will continue, but the failing school must also change its staffing or make another fundamental change.

After the fifth consecutive year, the governance of the failing school must be changed—for example, by converting it to a charter school, turning it over to a private management company, or having the state take it over. (Center for Educational Policy, *A New Federal Role in Education,* September 2002, p. 4)

To monitor progress and consequences, a report card on each state is available to the public. The report includes test results of students in reading and math and a school-by-school comparison of each district in the state. Scores are separated into four subgroups: children with disabilities, limited English proficiency, racial and ethnic minorities, and different economic backgrounds. Schools that are in need of targeted improvement are listed separately.

It is another simple notion that is behind the reauthorization of NCLB in 2007: Every child *does* learn. Numerous changes are slated for reauthorization, all of which revolve around the singular goal of students reading and doing math at grade level by 2014. Among the proposed changes are:

- Creation of a Teacher Incentive Fund that allows states and districts to reward teachers who "demonstrate results for their students"
- Improved options for parents that allow them more transfer options and scholarships to private or religious schools
- Tighter high school requirements, early testing of high school students and expansion of Advanced Placement classes

Taken together, the proposed changes reinforce the original regulations and tilt attention more toward high-achieving students. Driving the newest version of NCLB is the need to ensure that the United States will continue to compete successfully in the global economy. Innovation, competition, and entrepreneurship require universal proficiency in math, science, and language, a monumental goal still not met under NCLB.

Frederick Hess, resident scholar at the American Enterprise Institute, sees this new emphasis on competitiveness as clashing with NCLB regulations. As Hess explains in "NCLB and the Competitiveness Agenda: Happy Collaboration or a Collision Course?", incompatibility is caused by a fundamental difference of intent between the two initiatives. NCLB is about equity, as seen in the simple notion—every child can learn. But equity is not the intent of the American Competitiveness Initiative announced by the White House in 2006. The notion behind ACI is competitiveness. It is disheartening to realize that this clash is more than ideological—there is a significant disparity in funding of ACI and NCLB, with NCLB at the bottom of the pile.

"Fixing the NCLB Accountability System" is an analysis of fundamental problems in the law. This roundtable viewpoint delves into problems within the legislation itself, chief of which is the unrealistic expectation of universal (100% of students) proficiency in math and reading by 2014. Through a series of simple tables and charts, Robert Linn explains how current discrepancies in state definitions of proficiency complicate the problem. For Linn, a positive feature of NCLB is its emphasis on groups of low-achieving students. However, he points out that this focus on equity is actually hampered by disaggregation reporting requirements that penalize schools.

In 2006, a group of fifteen prominent education leaders formed The Commission on No Child Left Behind, with the sole purpose of improving the law. These bipartisan leaders believe NCLB as currently designed has not been able to ensure that all students are successful. After a year of gathering evidence, they prepared a widely distributed report outlining dramatic improvements. Their basic criticism is that compliance regulations and sanctions do not go far enough:

> Accountability is only the first step on the road to student and school success. . . . It is what happens after a school is labeled "in need of improvement" that is most important. (United States Department of Education, *Building on Results: A Blueprint for Strengthening the No Child Left Behind Act,* January 2007)

Education leaders who are wondering *what happens next* will find this commission's report enlightening.

In the final reading, "Next-Generation Models of Education Accountability," the authors present the case for an alternative model of school regulation and accountability. While such a model is not specifically linked to NCLB, leaders should be aware of the theory and structure of forward-looking models. In business, a market-based accountability model de-emphasizes bureaucratic rules in order to foster innovation and entrepreneurship. The same premise can apply to education. While schools would still be regulated, they would operate from a more flexible, assertive stance than mere compliance. In a market-based model, accountability is on the basis of performance objectives and incentives, with the local school or district in the central role. Under NCLB, the federal government plays the central role in accountability by using oversight and sanctions as the mechanisms for compliance. The authors argue that this generation's model of accountability—NCLB—is by no means a market model. And with several elements in the system in conflict, it's not surprising that performance is not meeting expectations.

Whether you believe the federal accountability system is flawless or full of flaws, you cannot escape the fact that NCLB is having an impact on public schools. Yet the question remains whether this system can fulfill its stated purpose—to focus accountability on results rather than compliance.

# SOURCES

Frederick M. Hess and Andrew J. Rotherham, NCLB and the competitiveness agenda: Happy collaboration or a collision course? *The American Enterprise,* January, 2007.

Robert L. Linn, Fixing the NCLB accountability system. *National Center for Research on Evaluation, Standards, and Student Testing*, Summer 2005.

The Commission on No Child Left Behind, Beyond NCLB: Fulfilling the promise to our nation's children. *Aspen Institute*, February 2007.

Jacob E. Adams, Jr. and Paul T. Hill, Next-generation models of education accountability: The regulated market model. *Education Commission of the States*, July 2003.

# NCLB and the Competitiveness Agenda: Happy Collaboration or a Collision Course?

Frederick M. Hess and Andrew J. Rotherham

American Schools have spent the last five years under the spotlight of No Child Left Behind (NCLB). The statute's relentless push to close the racial achievement gap and pursue universal proficiency in reading and math has focused unprecedented attention on basic instruction.

However, this push has also raised concerns about a slighting of high-achieving students and about inattention to advanced instruction and the dictates of national "competitiveness." These concerns have taken on a more pressing cast in the past three years, a period backlit by Thomas Friedman's best seller, *The World Is Flat,* and by the growing recognition that modern communications, transportation, and financial markets have created an increasingly global economy in which high-level science, math, and language skills are crucial to national well-being.

Of course, for all the popular attention that Friedman has garnered, his point is hardly new. Robert Reich, secretary of labor under President Bill Clinton, made many of the same arguments in his influential 1992 book, *The Work of Nations.* The fears about China and India today are more than a little reminiscent of—and tinged with the same hysteria as—discussions of "Japan, Inc." in the 1980s. Nonetheless, the shrinking American manufacturing sector and the accelerating "off-shoring" of service jobs—including a growing number of white-collar positions—have sparked much concern about the rate at which America is producing engineers, scientists, and graduates conversant in multiple languages.

In 2005 the National Academy of Sciences reported, "Having reviewed trends in the U.S. and abroad, the committee is deeply concerned that the scientific and technical building blocks of our economic leadership are eroding at a time when many other nations are gathering strength."[1] In 2006 ETS reported that 61% of opinion leaders identify math, science, and technology skills as the most important ingredients in determining whether the United States will continue to compete successfully in the global economy.[2]

Addressing such concerns, the Bush Administration launched its "American Competitiveness Initiative" (ACI) in early 2006. The Administration announced at the time:

> The President has launched the ACI to help our students do better in math and science. We will train 70,000 high school teachers to lead Advanced Placement

courses in math and science, bring 30,000 math and science professionals to teach in classrooms, and give early help to students who struggle with math. If we ensure America's children have the skills they need to succeed in life, they will ensure America succeeds in the world.[3]

What does this new emphasis on competitiveness mean for schooling? Is it consistent with the requirements of No Child Left Behind that have so thoroughly dominated education policy for the past five years? Are the two agendas on a collision course? And what are the implications for the future of federal education policy?

# A BIT OF HISTORY

Historically, there always has been an unavoidable tension between efforts to bolster American "competitiveness" (read: efforts to boost the performance of elite students, especially in science, math, and engineering) and those to promote educational equity. Champions of particular federal initiatives tend to argue that the two notions are complementary, but history shows that the ascendance of one tends to distract from attention paid to the other. For instance, the great investment of energy in high achievers in math, science, and language by the National Defense Education Act (NDEA) of 1958 largely dissipated when the Johnson Administration and the Washington education community turned their attention to the Elementary and Secondary Education Act (ESEA) and the equity agenda of the Great Society.

Congress enacted the NDEA at the height of the Cold War as a hurried response to the Soviet Union's 1957 launch of Sputnik I. Intended to ensure the U.S. an adequate supply of scientists, engineers, and individuals with specialized training, the law included money for college loans and graduate fellowships; funds for improving science, math, and foreign language instruction, especially in elementary and secondary schools; and resources for expanded vocational and technical training.

Seven years later, in 1965, ESEA signaled a new direction in federal policy. Specifically, it aimed to expand and improve opportunities for America's "educationally disadvantaged children" through compensatory programs for the poor.[4] ESEA did not provide blanket grants to all schools; instead, it allocated extra funding to districts with the highest proportion of low-income students. This focus on bridging the achievement gap between the "haves" and "have-nots" was central to the Johnson Administration's War on Poverty, and it couldn't have been more different from the dictates of "national defense" that had shaped NDEA seven years earlier.

Johnson claimed that ESEA, through its Title I provision, would help "five million children of poor families overcome their greatest barrier to progress: poverty."[5] ESEA provided funding to develop school library resources, buy textbooks and instructional materials, establish after-school programs of enrichment and remediation, enhance professional development, recruit and train personnel, and improve the health and safety of urban schools.

By the 1980s the zeitgeist had once again shifted. Amid concerns that "Japan, Inc." was consigning the U.S. to history's dustbin, policy makers picked up the competitiveness banner. In 1983 *A Nation at Risk* challenged states to raise achievement across the board and reinvigorate programs for high-achieving students. This influential report fretted that the U.S. had engaged in "unilateral educational disarmament" while competing for markets against other industrial, educated nations. In 1984 President Reagan declared, "Strengthening values also demands a national commitment to excellence in education. . . . [America's schools] need tougher standards, more homework, merit pay for teachers, discipline, and parents back in charge."[6] In the 1980s the standards movement was born in answer to this challenge.

*What are the obstacles to a dual focus on equity and achievement in public education at the national level?*

In 1989, at the Charlottesville Summit, the first President Bush and the nation's governors assembled to map out a set of ambitious goals that embraced both equity and achievement. In doing so, they gave a national platform to contemporary notions of standards and accountability. The dual focus on equity and achievement did not last long. The end of the Cold War and the rapidly receding threat posed by Japan led federal policy makers to put the competitiveness agenda on the back burner and turn their attention to more salient concerns, particularly the desperate condition of urban schooling. The "rigor-centric" reforms of the 1980s were dropped or defanged in all but four or five states, while "adequacy" lawsuits and growing attention to "achievement gaps" elevated the equity agenda.

That push for equity culminated in 2001 with congressional enactment of No Child Left Behind (the reauthorization of the old ESEA), a law marked by its relentless attention to elementary and middle school math and reading achievement, race- and income-based achievement gaps, and "universal proficiency." Today, once again, there is concern that we are failing to attend to the dictates of competitiveness.

## NCLB AND ACI

In some form or other, NCLB was a necessary and inevitable development. For too long, inadequate instruction in essential skills and abysmal performance by poor, black, and Latino children have been tacitly accepted as the status quo. At the same time, in 21st-century America it's more than a little unfortunate that NCLB has largely reduced the education debates to questions of proficiency in reading and math, testing, and achievement gaps. It's worth noting, however, that this unfortunate development has as much to do with questionable school and district management as with the law itself.

NCLB was largely the product of frustration. It was crafted by Washington policy makers fed up with the seeming refusal of educators to accept responsibility for mediocre performance or to concede the need to address schools that were massively failing black, Latino, and poor children. As analysts have explained,

> Democrats and Republicans grew increasingly angry with state and local officials whom they saw as endlessly demanding more money, committed to explaining all the reasons why high expectations were unrealistic, and overly occupied with explaining why standards, testing, pay-for-performance, and accountability systems were incredibly difficult to implement. In a real sense, NCLB was a mighty yawp of frustration uttered by Washington policy makers tired of nicely asking educators to cooperate—and ready to ruffle some feathers.[7]

On the strength of its bipartisan support, NCLB passed the U.S. House on a 381–41 vote and the U.S. Senate, 87–10.[8]

The Bush Administration's assertive stance on NCLB was defined by the President's fervent embrace of test-based accountability, his denunciation of the "soft bigotry of low expectations," and his declaration at the signing ceremony that the law would set America's schools "on a new path of reform, and a new path of results." Bush's enthusiasm was equaled on the other side of the aisle, where such leading Democrats as Massachusetts Sen. Ted Kennedy and California Rep. George Miller echoed the President's rhetoric and hailed the law as a signal victory for poor and minority children.

Aside from the inclusion of science in NCLB, this mighty congressional "yawp" swamped sensible concerns that NCLB might shift attention from or undermine support for advanced instruction. Today, 71% of adults think that U.S. high schools are falling behind when it comes to helping students compete for scientific and engineering jobs against students from other countries, and 64% reportedly think that education reform is necessary if America is to remain globally competitive in the next decade.[9] Sen. Kennedy has declared, "Perhaps nowhere is it more obvious that we are falling behind than in math and science. For a nation that prides itself on innovation and discovery, the downward slide is shocking."[10]

*Why has the American Competitiveness Agenda focused exclusively on research agencies instead of public education?*

Amidst this atmosphere of urgency, President Bush unveiled his American Competitiveness Initiative in January 2006. The plan called for $5.9 billion in new spending in fiscal 2007 and more than $136 billion in spending over the course of the next decade. Despite the rhetorical centrality of education in the policy debate on "competitiveness," the vast majority of this new money would fund not K-12 schooling or teacher preparation but research agencies and R&D. Over 10 years, the Administration proposed $50 billion in new spending for the National Science Foundation, the Department of Energy's Office of Science, and the National Institute of Standards and Technology; $86 billion to fund the research and development tax credit; and $380 million to support math, science, and technological education in K-12 schooling.

While the push for math, science, and engineering has proved popular, the long-term agenda has proved to be a tough sell. The Administration has had trouble winning support for even the modest new expenditures it has proposed.

The ACI has fallen prey to political infighting among various members of Congress, and the initial bipartisan support that surrounded the legislation has waned amid quarrels over jurisdictional issues, funding, and specific provisions.

In fact, doubts have emerged regarding the Administration's commitment. Although President Bush has repeatedly touted the legislation, he has made it only a limited priority on his wide-ranging education agenda and has earned criticism for a lack of leadership as Congress has failed to enact the plan's major components. Today, as politicians, scientists, and concerned citizens struggle to rekindle interest in ACI, many are worried about the seeming indifference of key officials. As Sherwood Boehlert (R-NY), former chair of the House Committee on Science, has remarked, "I'm concerned about this. We must push, push, push the American competitive agenda. We simply can't out-sweat the low-wage countries. We have to outthink them."[11]

# DIFFERENT DIAGNOSES

Is meeting the "global competitiveness" challenge to train elite scientists and engineers compatible with No Child Left Behind? The preferred line for school reformers—both Right and Left—is to deny any real conflict between the NCLB and competitiveness agendas. The popular refrain is that addressing the education "pipeline" will both promote social equity and bolster the national economy. Advocate Charles Kolb, president of the Committee for Economic Development, explains:

> We can no longer afford the inequities that have long characterized our system of education. As our need for educated workers grows, the American work force is going to come increasingly from the ethnic groups that have been least well served at all levels of American education. By 2020, some 30 percent of our working-age population will be African-American or Hispanic, nearly double the percentage in 1980.[12]

The claim is that continuing NCLB's focus on equity will ultimately strengthen the economy. However, for all those who have argued that ACI is the natural next step to "build upon" NCLB, neither history nor recent experience supports such rosy scenarios. A skeptic may well wonder whether the twin projects are likely to create serious conflict over priorities and resources.

The equity camp postulates that America's biggest source of untapped talent resides in its cities and that it is the poor, generally minority students who fall out of the education pipeline before they ever get a chance to see what they can do. By giving these students a solid education and then providing them with access to college, equity-based reformers argue, the nation will dramatically broaden the extent of the nation's development of human capital. They suggest that focusing on affluent students fails to address the crux of the problem because, unless a substantial number of these students are failing to choose math, science, or engineering careers for want of proper inducements, the scarce resources devoted to new scholarships and similar programs of the competitiveness agenda may well reward people of means for choices they would have made anyway.[13] It is notable, though, how narrowly the equity camp has focused on urban and minority achievement in the past decade and how this focus has tended to dictate strategies geared to minority and urban students (e.g., disaggregation, school choice) rather than their rural counterparts. This has marked a sharp departure from the Great Society's dual focus on urban and rural poverty and illustrates just how readily an effort to tackle one social ill can push another to the back burner.

The competitiveness camp is less explicit about its theory of action, but it goes something like this. There are many kids in the U.S. who lose interest in math and science or who never develop the essential skills necessary for advanced study because of inadequate programs or poor teaching. Consequently, there is a need to invest in better curricula, better math and science teachers, and better programs and schools, so as to attract students to and prepare them for these fields. Such an approach obviously can benefit from the larger pool of students that a successful equity approach would provide, and low-achieving students may benefit as well. But the approach is focused on dealing with the ranks of "potentially high-achieving math and science" students rather than on figuring out how to increase their numbers.

The tension between the equity and competitiveness agendas is made more poignant because influential state level actors—including key governors, such powerful philanthropies as the Gates Foundation, and such business-oriented groups as Achieve, Inc.—have prioritized high school standards and math and science education. So, while the federal pressure is focusing on bringing up the bottom in K-8 reading and math, these state-level actors are focusing on raising the level of high school achievement. The implication is that policy can do both, but, in practice, the emphasis on gap-closing necessarily shifts attention from higher-end skills, at least in the short term.

In this context, it's worth noting the meager dollars attached to the ACI. Not only does the proposal call for relatively small outlays, but there is little evidence in this fiscal environment that others are eager to up the Administration's bid. The new Democrat-led Congress might focus on fulfilling pledges to "fully fund" NCLB and other commitments, leaving it unclear how many resources it would be prepared to devote to competitiveness. After all, it was President Clinton's work force and economic "investments" that got slashed by 50% or more in his 1993 and 1994 budgets, even with a Democratic Congress.

## THE POLITICAL TENSION

While major national voices from the Citizens' Commission on Civil Rights to the Education Trust to the Business Roundtable are unanimous in preaching the happy gospel that NCLB and ACI fit hand in glove, the reality is that inevitable tension is already present if barely visible—in Washington and across the land.

On one side is the marker that many policy makers and educators have placed on gap-closing and the moral authority of equity-oriented groups like the Education Trust and the Citizens' Commission on Civil Rights. These parties will seek to maintain a focus on the achievement gap, which will—despite protests to the contrary—ensure that high-achieving students remain a secondary concern.

Meanwhile, although business and civic leaders offer rhetorical nods to the gap-closing agenda, they may instead prefer to focus on the real, more readily addressed problems of advanced math and science than on the endlessly frustrating, politically contentious, and seemingly intractable problems of equity. Frankly, the most straightforward and effective solution to the practical needs of the American economy and its hyper-competitive technology, investment, and engineering interests is to dramatically relax restrictions on H1-B visas, permitting a wealth of European, Indian, and Pacific Rim engineers and scientists eager to work in America to be hired.

From any short- or even medium-term perspective, K-12 schooling is a flimsy tool for addressing competitiveness in science and engineering. It is akin to signing promising preschoolers to a baseball team's farm system rather than bringing in top-tier free agents—even when those free agents make it clear they're eager to sign with your team at a discounted price. The reality is that today's third-graders won't be receiving their first Ph.D.s in engineering until about 2025.[14] Consequently, the ability of NCLB to gradually broaden the pipeline is more relevant to our competitiveness in 2030 than to our standing in the next decade or two. This helps explain why even those most ardently focused on America's "economic well-being" sometimes see the K-12 debate as less than urgent.

Nonetheless, whatever the substantive merits of the strategy to pursue competitiveness through the schools, it has immense political appeal. First, investing in high-achieving students, advanced math and science courses, foreign languages, and Advanced Placement programs allows politicians to cater to the demands of educated, high-income, suburban families. This demographic group is both politically active and ambivalent about or hostile to NCLB-style reform, which focuses on boosting performance in low-achieving schools through increased testing, standardized curricula, and other measures that may alienate high-achieving communities.

Second, whereas NCLB-style accountability requires reformers to challenge existing routines, identify low-performing schools, and force change upon resistant educators, STEM (Science, Technology, Engineering, and Mathematics) proposals are more manageable and engender less conflict. Rather than trying to change the way schools serve overlooked students, the pursuit of competitiveness focuses on improving the quality of advanced instruction for a subset of high-achieving students. Rather than demanding that teachers do a better job of boosting performance among the hard-to-educate, the competitiveness agenda calls for giving more resources and training to teachers who instruct students who are already highly successful. A competitiveness strategy focuses on augmenting the status quo rather than remaking it, and this is an easier task—substantively and politically—for legislators, governors, superintendents, and school boards.

Third, while raising the performance floor can be a grudging and thankless task, addressing science, math, and engineering may produce more tangible and visible rewards. A handful of successful classes, programs, or curricula can yield contest winners, Ivy League admissions, prestigious scholarships, or a bump in AP results—in short, a public relations bonanza. Targeting the needs of high achievers has the virtue of being easier to do and more popular. In light of the challenges, it's surprising how effectively the redistributive focus of NCLB has dominated the agenda in the past five years. This dominance is a testament to the Bush Administration's efforts, the moral power of the declaration to educate the children "left behind," the odd coalition of Left and Right that has resolutely supported the law, and the frustration of the public and policy makers with the seemingly intractable troubles of low-performing schools and districts.

This debate is playing out in an environment in which federal spending on K-12 education rose sharply over the past six years. Massive federal budget deficits, coupled with a bipartisan refusal to rein in entitlement programs and public resistance to tax increases, mean there is little likelihood of significant new federal spending on education. Meanwhile, at the state level, continued growth in Medicaid is squeezing state budgets, an aging population looms, and concerns about college affordability are competing with K-12 spending. Consequently, school spending in the coming decade is unlikely to grow at a rate that exceeds the familiar trend.

This means that expenditures for competitiveness will have to come at the expense of ongoing NCLB efforts and in an environment where critics argue that schools lack funds to achieve the performance targets set by the law. As the equity and competitiveness agendas joust for resources in a tight fiscal environment, it's going to be increasingly difficult for partisans of education reform to merely endorse both. Will middle-class voters and business leaders support tax measures intended to devote more resources to schooling, and will they acquiesce to having the majority of those resources fund the NCLB agenda?

## WHERE THE PUBLIC STANDS

Efforts to rally the public behind NCLB and the equity agenda must contend with the fact that NCLB's public appeal is mixed, at best. NCLB has been a source of much unrest among teachers and principals. It has prompted nine states to engage in some form of statutory resistance, though none of those states has actually refused to accept federal education dollars and the accompanying conditions.

The general public endorses the ambitious goals of NCLB and the effort to shrink the racial achievement gap but is less enamored with key provisions of the law. In fact, the public is uncertain that schools are really responsible for the existence of the gap. The PDK/Gallup poll has reported that 67% of the public believes it is "very important" to close the achievement gap between white students and black and Latino students and that 88% think it "very" or "somewhat" important.[15] Given this concern with equity, one that has been aggressively pushed by leaders on the Left and Right, there are political difficulties in making the case for putting new dollars into programs that will predominantly aid more advantaged students from more educated families.

At the same time, 81% of adults believe the achievement gap can be "narrowed substantially" even while maintaining high standards for all children. Just 17% doubt that this can be done.[16] Such responses constitute massive support for the "no tough choices" strategy. Unanswered is whether the public is right and, if so, whether it is willing to support the actions necessary to narrow the gap. For instance, just 19% of respondents think the racial achievement gap is "mostly related to quality of schooling," while fully 77% believe it is primarily due to "other factors."[17] This suggests a public open to arguments that schools cannot and should not focus relentlessly on achievement gaps and one that may not welcome painful reforms designed to address those gaps.

*What are the implications for school leaders of negative public reaction to schools' relentless focus on achievement gaps?*

Moreover, Americans are persistently skeptical about the importance of academic excellence. For instance, when asked whether they would prefer that their oldest child get "A grades" or make "average grades and be active in extracurricular activities," just 29% of Americans opted for A grades.[18] That figure has been static over the past decade. This preference is an inconvenient reality for those promoting an "excellence" agenda.

Both the NCLB and ACI agendas call for more work, more discipline, and more rigor in schooling. However, a substantial portion of the population is skeptical of such pleas and sympathetic to critics, such as Alfie Kohn, Nel Noddings, and others, who argue that America's children are already overworked and overtested. For instance, 26% of adults oppose requiring students in their local public high schools to take four years of math, 30% think elementary students are required to work too hard today, 49% reject proposals to extend the school year or school day in their community, 39% think there is currently too much testing in their community's schools, and 67% think more testing will lead teachers to teach more to the test (which three out of four respondents think is a bad thing). These figures suggest that a quarter or more of voters may resist calls for more intensive schooling, longer school days, extended school years, more homework, or beefed-up accountability—whether for closing the achievement gap or for competitiveness.[19]

## 2008 AND BEYOND

What does all of this mean for the future of federal policy and its effect on America's students, teachers, and schools?

For NCLB, reauthorization looms. In theory, it is scheduled for reauthorization in 2007. Practically speaking, it's an open question whether the Administration and congressional leaders will ram it through as an exhibit of bipartisan comity this year or whether it will ultimately sit and await the Administration that takes office in 2009. In the interim, the Bush Administration is gearing up to hold its ground on the law, with the President asserting that reauthorization is a priority and Education Secretary Margaret Spellings insisting, "I like to talk about No Child Left Behind like Ivory soap. It's 99.9% pure. There's not much needed in the way of change."[20]

Meanwhile, both the Democrats and Republicans number among their ranks competing factions on the equity and the competitiveness agendas, putting this issue very much in play within the parties, as well as between them. As NCLB comes up for reauthorization and as both parties face open fields for their 2008 Presidential nominations, this will be an opportunity to sort through and influence thinking in both parties.

Among Democrats, there are two primary coalitions. The first is the generally pro-NCLB coalition made up of centrist reformers or "New Democrats" and liberal reformers like Rep. George Miller (D-Calif.) of the House Committee on Education and the Workforce. This coalition believes that NCLB-like accountability is the most effective equity strategy that the federal government can pursue. The pro-NCLB Democrats are more fragmented on the competitiveness agenda, though both the moderates among them and most Democratic governors, who generally have closer ties to business groups, are more likely to regard it as a priority.

There also exists a liberal anti-NCLB coalition, one united by the belief that NCLB-like policies are damaging to teachers, schools, and students. Some members are simply following the lead of the National Education Association, parroting the union's resistance to testing, accountability, and disruption. Others believe the argument put forward by Richard Rothstein and others that it is folly to hold schools accountable for closing the academic achievement gap absent massive changes in social policy. Inattention to such issues as health care, they say, invalidates the NCLB policy, whatever its other merits might be. And some members of this group have an aversion to federal testing requirements that dates back to the 1994 debates about ESEA. Though often more antagonistic toward business interests, this coalition reads Tom Friedman, too, and its members are not uniformly hostile to the competitiveness agenda—especially if supporting it means dropping the current emphasis on universal testing and coercive accountability.

Republicans are split as well. While the GOP let President Bush plant the party's flag on closing the achievement gap through No Child Left Behind, many Republicans only grudgingly supported the President's strategy of expanding the federal role in education. For instance, former Majority Leader Tom DeLay, a Republican from Texas, confessed to Rush Limbaugh that he "voted for that awful education bill" only to support President Bush. He explained to

Limbaugh, "I came here to eliminate the Department of Education, so it was very hard for me to vote for something that expands [it]."[21]

As President Bush recedes from the national political scene, three factions are likely to emerge within the Republican Party with regard to education policy. Business-oriented Republicans who have championed the President's education policies since he was a governor are likely to be squeezed by the tension between the competing agendas. And while they have strongly backed NCLB, they may benefit more—at least in the short term—from ACI. Then there are the more traditionally conservative Republicans. In the wake of the rough 2006 midterm election, which many on the Right are interpreting as the comeuppance for undisciplined spending and "big-government" Republicanism, these small-government conservatives are likely to reemerge as a force demanding a reduction, rather than an expansion, of the federal role in education. Finally, religious Republicans, particularly the evangelical Right, may see an opportunity to draw attention to such issues as prayer in school and school vouchers, which have been largely sidelined by the gap-closing and competitiveness agendas.

The politics at work resemble the politics of the late 1990s more than those of the first few years of the Bush Presidency. Consequently, moderates in both parties—and perhaps especially the New Democrats—may again emerge as a fulcrum of education policy making if stark Left/Right divides again stymie reform efforts. Which agenda the moderates embrace most enthusiastically could prove decisive. In 2009 the new President may have a sufficient mandate to advance his or her own agenda on education.

*Given the current national political scene, do you think a new president will make significant changes in NCLB?*

For the foreseeable future, elected officials will continue to be cross-pressured by the two agendas. Business interests, notably the U.S. Chamber of Commerce, the Business Roundtable, and such coalitions as Achieve, Inc., and TechNet will continue to work to keep competitiveness on the policy-making agenda. Meanwhile, the equity coalition is unlikely to give an inch of ground in its efforts to keep the focus of public policy on gap-closing.

However, NCLB is at its core an attempt to transform the provision of schooling and to ensure that more attention is paid to low-performing students—meaning that its benefits are diffuse and targeted upon a disorganized and frequently voiceless population, while its costs are concentrated among potent constituencies, particularly teachers, school administrators, and high-achieving communities.[22] Consequently, for the same reason that inefficient agricultural subsidies persist—namely, pressure from the constituencies that are most directly affected—it's a safe bet that some of NCLB's sharp edges will be dulled over time. Considering the appeal of the competitiveness agenda, the gloomy fiscal picture, and the inability of policy makers to stay focused for long, proponents of the equity agenda ought not take recent gains for granted. This does not mean, as some hope, the imminent repeal of NCLB. Rather, it is more likely to portend accommodations that weaken the parts of the law that energetic special interests find most objectionable. Conveniently for lawmakers, the competitiveness agenda could provide ideal cover for such efforts.

# CONCLUSION

For schools, teachers, and students, this rhetorical confusion and the ongoing debate about goals and strategies, coupled with the continued drumbeat of support for NCLB from the Bush Administration and its allies, are likely to produce a frequently frustrating parade of mismatched goals, expectations, and rhetoric. Through NCLB, the overwhelming emphasis of federal policy will remain gap-closing and focusing on students in the lowest-performing schools. Meanwhile, prominent members of the business and political communities will continue to fret that schools are failing to prepare America for the competitive challenges we face. It is a confused state of affairs, one that is understandably frustrating for America's educators.

Ultimately, the seeming inability to settle on a coherent agenda is due to a simple truth: schools exist to serve both these agendas and many others besides. Our desire to ignore this banal reality, to "fix" the equity problem and then to "solve" the competitiveness problem, fosters grandiose ambitions and hyperbolic claims that will inevitably come up short. Schools exist to serve a staggeringly diverse population of students and a raft of competing needs. Buckling down somewhere will almost inevitably mean easing up elsewhere. The best we can hope for is an incremental, awkward stagger toward meeting a stew of public and private objectives.

But would-be reformers routinely ignore or forget this fundamental truth, inviting confusion, mixed messages, and facile talk. The ugly truth is that we cannot do everything; this means we must choose what we can and should do at a given time. It means accepting disagreement and abandoning the tempting dream that we might reach consensus on what needs to be done if only good-hearted souls would examine the right data. And it means acknowledging that every policy decision will yield both winners and losers. What we need in 2007, 2008, and beyond is not bland reassurance or misguided efforts to paper over real divides, but honest and informed debate about whose needs take precedence at a given moment, what to do about it today, and what to leave for tomorrow.

# ENDNOTES

1. Committee on Prospering in the Global Economy of the 21st Century, *Rising Above the Gathering Storm: Energizing and Employing America for a Brighter Economic Future* (Washington, D.C.: National Academies Press, October 2005), Executive Summary, p. 2.
2. Peter D. Hart Research Associates, Inc., and The Winston Group, "Keeping Our Edge: Americans Speak on Education and Competitiveness," survey conducted for ETS, Washington, D.C., June 2006, p. 2.
3. "The American Competitiveness Initiative—Strengthening Math and Science Education," White House press release, 26 April 2006.

4. Gerald L. Gutek, *Education and Schooling in America* (Englewood Cliffs, N.J.: Prentice-Hall, 1983), pp. 93–94.

5. Lyndon B. Johnson, "Remarks Following Enactment of the Elementary and Secondary Education Bill," 9 April 1965, available through University of California-Santa Barbara American Presidency Project at www.presidency.ucsb.edu/ws/index.php?pid=26883.

6. Ronald Reagan, "Remarks at the National Conservative Action Conference Dinner," Ronald Reagan Presidential Library, 2 March 1984, available online at www.reagan.utexas.edu/archives/speeches/1984/30284g.htm.

7. Frederick M. Hess and Michael J. Petrilli, "The Politics of No Child Left Behind: Will the Coalition Hold?," *Boston University Journal of Education*, vol. 185, no. 3, 2004, pp. 13–25.

8. Frederick M. Hess and Michael J. Petrilli, *No Child Left Behind: A Primer* (New York: Peter Lang, 2006).

9. Peter D. Hart Research Associates, Inc., and The Winston Group, op. cit.

10. Sen. Ted Kennedy, "Senator Ted Kennedy on Globalization," Kennedy for Senate 2006.

11. David Hess, "Bush's 'American Competitiveness Initiative' Push Languishes," *National Journal's* Congress Daily, 4 August 2006.

12. Charles E. M. Kolb, "Cracks in Our Education Pipeline," *Education Week*, 12 July 2006.

13. Andrew J. Rotherham and Kevin Carey, "Expand the Pool of America's Future Scientists," *Christian Science Monitor*, 20 April 2006.

14. Today's third-graders will be graduating from high school in about 2016, graduating from college in 2020, and, among those who pursue an engineering Ph.D. directly after college, finishing in about 2025.

15. Lowell C. Rose and Alec M. Gallup, "The 38th Annual Phi Delta Kappa/Gallup Poll of the Public's Attitudes Toward the Public Schools," *Phi Delta Kappan*, September 2006, p. 46, table 18.

16. Ibid., p. 47, table 19.

17. Ibid., p. 44, table 9.

18. Lowell C. Rose and Alec M. Gallup, "The 37th Annual Phi Delta Kappa/Gallup Poll of the Public's Attitudes Toward the Public Schools," *Phi Delta Kappan*, September 2005, p. 53, table 39.

19. Rose and Gallup, "38th Annual Phi Delta Kappa/Gallup Poll," pp. 46, 48–49.

20. Ben Feller, "Education Secretary Says Little Change Needed in No Child Left Behind," Associated Press, 30 August 2006.

21. Andrew J. Rotherham, "How Bush Stole Education," *Blueprint: Ideas for a New Century*, March/April 2002, pp. 41–42.

22. Frederick M. Hess, "Refining or Retreating? High-Stakes Accountability in the States," in Paul Peterson and Martin West, eds., *No Child Left Behind?* (Washington, D.C.: Brookings Institution Press, 2003), pp. 55–79.

# ARTICLE 9.2

# Fixing the NCLB Accountability System

## Robert L. Linn

*What prompts national groups like CRESST to address "fundamental problems" in federal legislation?*

The No Child Left Behind (NCLB) Act is praiseworthy for the special attention it gives to improved learning for children who have been ignored or left behind in the past. The emphasis on closing the achievement gap is certainly commendable, as is the encouragement given to states to adopt ambitious subject matter standards and enhance teacher quality. NCLB's focus on students with low achievement seems to have had some short-term positive effects. The percentage of schools meeting Adequate Yearly Progress (AYP) targets increased in 2003–04 from the year before in most states, and the recently released National Assessment of Educational Progress (NAEP) long-term trend scores have shown some narrowing of achievement gaps.

Given the positives, we might conclude that NCLB is working, and hence no changes are needed at this point. Unfortunately, the accountability system has some fundamental problems that threaten to undermine its central goals over the next few years. Dissatisfaction with some of the accountability provisions led the U.S. Department of Education to make some changes in NCLB accountability requirements last year, with more on the way this year.[1] The changes, however, are what Jim Popham calls "edge-softening" and do not deal with NCLB's fundamental problems,[2] which include expectations, targets, state proficiency levels, reporting, and the safe harbor provision. The remainder of this policy brief describes each problem and offers proposals for improvement.

## FUNDAMENTAL PROBLEMS AND PROPOSALS FOR IMPROVEMENT

### Expectations

The most serious problem is that the NCLB expectations for student achievement have been set unrealistically high, requiring that by the year 2014, 100% of students must reach the proficient level or above in math and reading. Based on current improvement levels and without major changes in the definition of adequate yearly progress (AYP), almost all schools will fail to meet NCLB requirements within the next few years.

Using test scores from the National Assessment of Educational Progress (NAEP) as an example, we note that in 2003, no state or large district had anything close to 100% of their students performing at the basic NAEP achievement level, much less the NAEP proficient level, in either Grade 4 or Grade 8 in either reading or mathematics. In 2003, New Hampshire, traditionally one of the highest performing states, still had 25% of its students performing at the below basic achievement level in fourth-grade reading (see Figure 1). On the same assessment, the District of Columbia reported 69% of its students at the below basic level. California, with the largest student population of any state, had just 21% of its students at or above the proficient level in 2003.

Furthermore, the law requires unrealistically rapid rates of improvement when compared to incremental improvements on earlier NAEP assessments. In fourth-grade mathematics, for example, the percentage of students at the proficient level or above on NAEP would have to have an annual improvement rate 3.9 times faster than the rate of increase between 1996 and 2003 (Figure 2). For eighth-grade mathematics, the rate of improvement would need to be 7.5 times faster. Such rapid acceleration of math achievement is unrealistic.

In reading, the rate of increase would require an even more unlikely jump. In fourth grade, 31% of the students scored at the proficient level or above on the 2003 reading NAEP assessment compared to 29% in 1998. At Grade 8, 32% were proficient or above in both 1998 and 2003, representing no increase in 5 years. To reach NCLB goals by 2014, student performance would need

Figure 1   2003 New Hampshire 4th-Grade NAEP Reading Achievement Levels

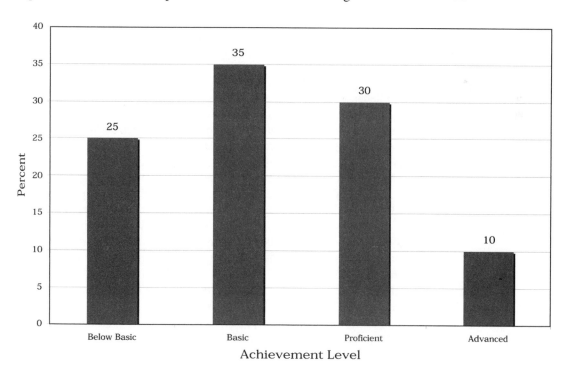

Figure 2   NAEP Mathematics Percent Proficient or Above Trends and Projections (Grades 4 and 8)

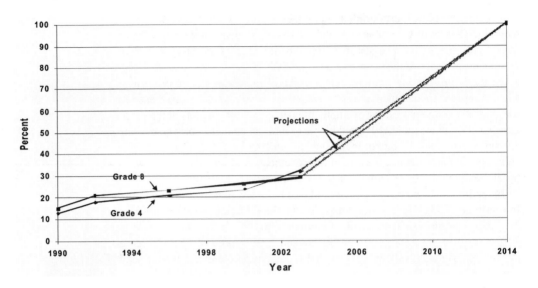

*Why are varying proficiency levels on state assessments a problem?*

to increase from essentially a flat line to at least 7 percentage points every year for 9 years.

Further complicating the high expectations problem is that proficiency levels on state assessments vary substantially. Some state proficiency levels are similar to NAEP, others are more lenient, and a few states are more stringent. Missouri, for example, is more stringent. In 2003, 21.3% of Missouri's eighth-grade students scored at the proficient level or above on the Missouri mathematics assessment. In the same year and grade level, 28% of Missouri students scored at the proficient level or above on NAEP mathematics. The Missouri 3-year trend of percentage proficient or above on its own Grade 8 mathematics test is virtually flat, 21.1% in 2002, 21.3% in 2003, and 22.9% in 2004. Reaching 100% proficient or above by 2014 is not realistic.

California achievement levels are somewhat more lenient than NAEP. In 2003, 31% of California's eighth-grade students scored at the proficient level or above on the California English-language arts test, whereas only 22% scored proficient or above on the 2003 NAEP reading assessment. As with Missouri, eighth-grade California students' language arts performance was virtually flat. Scores for 2001, 2002, 2003, and 2004 were 32, 32, 31, and 33 percent proficient or above respectively. Flat-line performance does not augur well for reaching 100% by 2014.

I've previously argued that performance goals "mandated by the accountability system should be ambitious, but also should be realistically obtainable with sufficient effort."[3] At the very least, there needs to be an existence proof.

That is, there should be evidence that the goal does not exceed one that has previously been achieved by the highest performing schools. For example, if the top 10% of schools in a state improved an annual average of 3% proficient or above each year in the past 5 years, then 3% might be the annual state goal. That would be a major challenge to the vast majority of schools, but might be a target that is within reach with sufficient effort.

## Fixed Targets

Although the "P" in AYP stands for progress, it is important to recognize that, with the exception of the "safe harbor" provision discussed later, the comparison of performance in a given year to a fixed target—known as the annual measurable objective (AMO)—is the sole determinant of whether a school or district makes AYP. For example, Nevada's elementary school annual measurable objective in 2004–05 is 45.4% proficient or above in mathematics. A low-performing school that made a dramatic improvement in the prior year, let's say increasing from 30% proficient or above to 40%, would still fall below the state objective and be placed on a watch list. Meanwhile, a higher performing school whose scores had actually dropped, say from 65% proficient or above to 55%, would still meet its annual measurable objective because it remained above the 45.4% proficient level or above (see Figure 3). While setting fixed targets makes goals easy to understand, it may produce distorted results and does not necessarily treat schools fairly, especially those that are making substantial

Figure 3   Two Schools vs. Fixed Target (Proficient or Above)

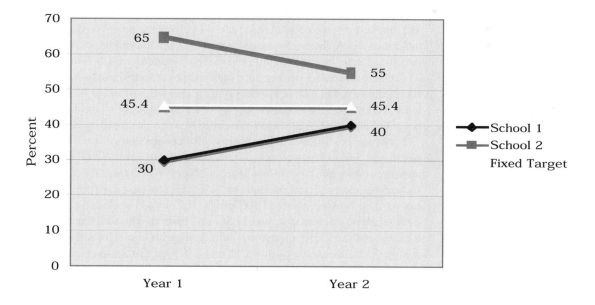

progress. Indeed, schools that make substantial progress yet fail to reach ever increasing fixed targets may lose incentive to make further improvements.

Solutions to this problem are quite simple. Indeed, many state accountability systems already use both status and improvement to measure progress. A typical method is to compare successive groups of students, for example, fourth-grade students in 2005 compared to fourth-grade students in 2004. With the NCLB requirement to test students in Grades 3 through 8 every year, some states are measuring changes longitudinally, tracking improvement from one grade to the next grade, for example, from third grade to fourth to fifth grade and beyond. Tennessee has used the longitudinal method for a number of years, and their "value-added" approach to evaluating schools has attracted a great deal of attention.

Either successive or longitudinal approaches, or both, should be included in determination of AYP.[4] U.S. Secretary of Education Margaret Spellings has indicated that she is open to the possibility of using growth in the determination of AYP. This is a step in the right direction; however, allowing growth to determine AYP will be of limited value if the expectation of 100% proficient or above by 2014 is maintained.

## Definition of Proficient

NCLB requires states to set "challenging student academic achievement standards." The problem is that states have set the achievement standards in ways that vary greatly in stringency, especially compared to NAEP. Figure 4 shows this variation, arbitrarily using reading results from the first four states in the alphabet, Alabama, Alaska, Arizona, and Arkansas. Note the very large differences in achievement level scores between NAEP tests and state tests in 2003. The smallest difference is in Arkansas, 34 percentage points, and the largest difference is in Alabama, 55 percentage points. Gaps are similar for most states, in both mathematics and reading, and in eighth grade as well as fourth.

Compared to NAEP performance standards, most states have set very lenient standards, such that a large majority of their students perform at the proficient level or above on their assessments. Figure 4 also suggests that most states will be far below the 100% proficient goal in 2014 when measured by NAEP.

Performance standards differ substantially between states as well. For example, Figure 5 shows only modest differences in eighth-grade NAEP mathematics scores between Colorado and Missouri students. In 2003, 34% of Colorado students scored proficient or above on NAEP compared to 28% for Missouri.[5] But on their own state tests in 2003, 67% of Colorado students scored proficient or above compared to just 21.3% in Missouri. The difference between the 67% and the 21.3% clearly has more to do with how rigorously states set their performance standards than with real differences in achievement between students. With each state setting its own performance standards and without an external, independent test, the word "proficient" loses meaning.

Figure 4   Achievement Level Differences: 2003 Reading/Language Arts 4th-Grade NAEP vs. 4th-Grade State

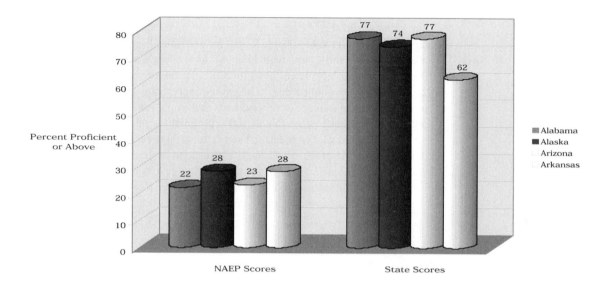

Figure 5   Different State Performance Standards

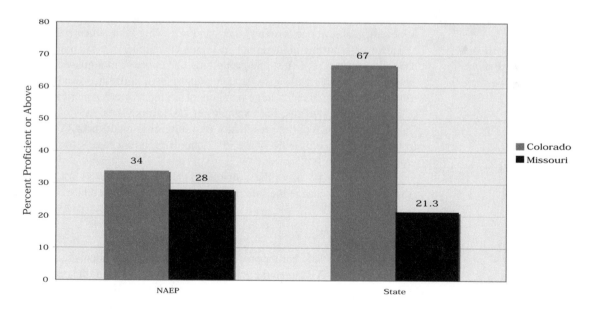

Fortunately, there are several preferable approaches to reporting results in terms of percent proficient or above. One simple approach is to define the standard or cut score on a state assessment to be equal to the median score in a base year, presumably 2002. The percentage of students scoring above that constant cut score would then be used to monitor improvement in achievement with target increases set at reasonable levels, for example, 3% per year. Let's say the median score in fifth-grade mathematics was 50% for a state in 2002. In 2003, the target would have been 53%; in 2006, the target would be 62%; and in 2014, the target would be 86%. This would represent a gigantic improvement in the achievement of the state's students, but might not be totally unrealistic, and surely is not as implausible as 100% proficient or above.

Another alternative would be to use what Jim Popham has called grade-level descriptions.[6] "At-grade-level" might correspond more closely to the "basic" than the "proficient" level in most states. Using past experience, targets could be set that would bring the achievement of an ever increasing percentage of students up to the "at-grade-level" standard.

## Disaggregation

As stated earlier, a positive feature of NCLB is its emphasis on groups of low-achieving students who have too often been ignored in the past. The accountability system attempts to assure adequate attention to these groups of students by requiring the separate reporting of results for economically disadvantaged students, students with disabilities, limited English proficient students, and by race/ethnicity. Such disaggregated reporting of results provides a mechanism for monitoring the achievement of lower performing groups and narrowing achievement gaps.

*Is there a downside to disaggregating scores for groups of low-achieving students?*

However, reporting more groups increases the number of ways that schools can fail to meet AYP. If just one group fails, the entire school misses its goal. This places schools with many student subgroups at a distinct disadvantage, usually urban schools with large numbers of Latino, African American, ELL, or special needs students. For example, in 2003, more than 75% of the 937 California schools reporting results for two subgroups made their AYP target. In the same year, only 39% of the 291 schools reporting results for six subgroups made their AYP target.[7]

A straightforward fix to the over-identification of schools as not meeting AYP would be to change the safe harbor provision as discussed next.

## Safe Harbor

NCLB includes a safe harbor provision. If a subgroup of students in a school falls short of the AYP target, the school can still meet AYP if (a) the percentage of students who score below the proficient level is decreased by 10% from the year before, and (b) there is improvement for that subgroup on other indicators. In application, the safe harbor provision helps very few schools because the bar is set so high. The 10% decrease in students scoring below proficient far exceeds progress even in schools with exceptional achievement improvements. Not surprisingly, only a tiny fraction of schools have met AYP through the safe harbor provision since NCLB's inception. A more realistic criterion is a 3% reduction in the below proficient category. Resetting the safe harbor provision to a more realistic rate would solve many of the problems caused by expanded subgroup reporting, yet still promote significant achievement increases.

# CONCLUSION

NCLB has the potential to make substantial contributions to the achievement of students who have lagged behind and been ignored in the past. Some features of the NCLB accountability system, however, need to be modified if the praise-worthy goals of NCLB are going to be achieved. I offer three suggestions.

1. The most important modification is to set realistic performance targets for adequate yearly progress, rewarding effort with success. The need for more realistic goals applies to both the safe harbor provision of the law and to the annual performance targets.
2. AYP should be determined by a consideration of growth in achievement and not just status in comparison to a fixed target.
3. The current definitions of proficient achievement established by states lack any semblance of a common meaning. Alternatives to defining proficiency should be considered that would provide more meaningful and comparable achievement targets.

# ENDNOTES

1. See Olson, L. (2005). Requests win more leeway under NCLB. *Education Week, 24*(42), p. 1.
2. Popham, W. J. (2004). Shaping up the 'No Child' Act: Is edge-softening enough? *Education Week, 23*(38), p. 40.
3. Linn, R. L. (2003). Accountability: Responsibility and reasonable expectations. *Educational Researcher, 32*(7), 3–13.
4. See Hoff, D. J. (2005). States to get new options on NCLB Law. *Education Week, 24*(31), pp. 1, 38. Olson, L. (2005). States hoping to grow into AYP success. *Education Week, 24*(37), pp. 15, 20.
5. Colorado uses the partially proficient level for state reporting as the proficient level for purposes of NCLB.
6. Popham, W. J. (2004). *Ruminations regarding NCLB's most malignant provisions: Adequate yearly progress.* Retrieved August 8, 2005, from http://www.ctredpol.org/pubs/Forum28July2004
7. Based on Novak, J. R., & Fuller, B. (2003). *Penalizing diverse schools?* (PACE Policy Brief 03-4). Berkeley: University of California, Policy Analysis for California Education.

# Beyond NCLB: Fulfilling the Promise to Our Nation's Children

## Commission on No Child Left Behind

## MOVING BEYOND THE STATUS QUO TO EFFECTIVE SCHOOL IMPROVEMENT AND STUDENT OPTIONS

Accountability is only the first step on the road to student and school success. The goal is not simply to label schools but to ensure that achievement improves. It is what happens *after* a school is labeled "in need of improvement" that is most important.

The implementation of NCLB has shown the need to do a better job in providing interventions, such as public school choice and supplemental educational services (SES or free tutoring), designed to help students in low-performing schools. We must move more effectively and decisively in turning around consistently struggling schools.

### Maximizing Student Options While Improving Quality

*Is it possible for federal legislation to make good on the promise that all children will achieve to high standards in every state?*

Nothing is more important than getting struggling students the help they need to improve their academic performance. But low levels of participation in both NCLB's SES and public school choice options show that students are not getting the support they are entitled to in the numbers envisioned by the authors of the law.

We believe both of these options can enhance and support student achievement and overall school performance. However, both options have to result in genuine improvements in achievement for the children using them. SES in particular, largely due to its relatively short four-year existence, has been difficult to assess and evaluate.

### *Recommendation*

Therefore, the Commission recommends a comprehensive approach to expanding the availability and quality of options for students in schools that do not make AYP. This approach should include the following:

- Schools that make AYP must make available a number equal to 10 percent of their seats for transfers from schools in which students are eligible for choice
- An annual independent audit of the space available for public school choice transfers
- If a school district is unable to accommodate all of its requests for public school choice (as demonstrated in an annual audit), the school district must offer SES to eligible students
- Schools should be required to offer space in school facilities for private providers of SES if those schools offer the use of school facilities to other non-school-affiliated entities
- Districts must provide enrollment periods several times a year to ensure that all eligible children have the opportunity to participate in SES
- Districts must identify and publicize a person of office that would operate as a point of contact for assisting parents in learning about options available for their children

## *Recommendation*

However, simply increasing access to these options without improving their quality would not help children succeed. In addition to a focus on increasing the utilization of these options, we recommend the U.S. DOE use a portion of Title I funding to study the nationwide effects of SES on student achievement and that states evaluate the impact of their SES providers on the achievement of children.

Too often parents select these options without having the information necessary to make the best decision for their children. Too often states, as part of their SES oversight responsibilities, do not identify which providers are producing achievement gains and which are failing to help children. There must be effective monitoring of the quality of these services to ensure that children in struggling schools get the assistance they need.

## Providing More Aggressive and Effective Interventions for Schools

The real work of improving academic achievement at a struggling school happens when schools, districts and states implement instructional strategies and interventions to address the school's shortcomings. When schools fall into corrective action status, NCLB presently requires them to pick one of a menu of options to address academic challenges. Unfortunately, quick fixes and continuing down the path of least resistance won't cut it—schools need to undertake proven, comprehensive reforms designed to improve instruction and learning.

*What are the implications of the recommendation that schools in corrective action have one school year to implement comprehensive interventions?*

### Recommendation

Therefore, we recommend that schools in corrective action be required to select a comprehensive set of interventions designed to have a systemic impact, rather than the one option presently required. We also recommend that schools in corrective action have a full school year to implement such interventions before facing more serious sanctions. These recommendations will ensure that instructional interventions conducted by schools are significantly more likely to improve academic performance.

### Recommendation

We also recommend strengthening the capacity of states and districts to help chronically low-performing schools by increasing the amount of federal funds set aside by states for schools improvement and by allowing districts to focus their restructuring efforts on the lowest-performing 10 percent of their schools.

### Recommendation

Additionally, we recommend boosting research and development on school improvement by doubling the research budget for elementary and secondary education at the U.S. DOE's main research arm—the Institute of Education Sciences.

Without the tools, knowledge and will to do what is necessary to turn around schools, we cannot consistently produce significant improvements in performance. Yet as shown in the testimony before the Commission and in other work we have done, states and districts too often lack one or more of these important precursors—tools, knowledge and will—for taking effective action in their communities for every child. NCLB has had significantly more success in assessing student performance than in improving it.

## FAIR AND ACCURATE ASSESSMENTS OF STUDENT PROGRESS

The assessment provisions of NCLB have been closely watched. Tests are highly visible to students, parents, teachers and the general public. They are essential to the success of NCLB's teacher quality, accountability and school improvement provisions. And they often are credited—or blamed—for many of the improvements or ills, real or perceived, associated with the law.

Assessment results are crucial in systems designed to hold schools accountable for performance; without objective measures to determine how students are performing, there would be no way to know if schools are succeeding or need additional help. In addition, assessment results provide parents and communities with indications of school quality that they can use in making judgments about the performance of their school or districts.

# Improving Assessment Quality

NCLB helped establish a strong foundation for strengthening assessments by requiring them in each grade from 3 through 8 and once in high school and by providing resources to states for building and expanding their assessment systems. Most states have implemented new systems, but there is more work to be done to ensure that all states have in place sound, high-quality assessments that provide valid and reliable information about a broad range of student capacities, particularly for student with disabilities and English language learners.

## *Recommendation*

Therefore, the Commission recommends maintaining existing federal support for assessment development and targeting those funds to several new assessment priorities such as:

- Improving the quality assessments
- Providing alternate assessments for students with disabilities and English language learners
- Developing science assessments currently required under the law and the 12th grade assessment recommended by the Commission
- Improving test delivery and scoring technology

# Linking Assessment and Instruction

The annual assessments required under NCLB have created a desire for even more information that can show how students are progressing. Teachers need detailed information throughout the school year so that they can make adjustments to their instruction and provide additional help to students who are struggling before they face an end-of-the year assessment. Parents deserve regular information on their children's performance to ensure they are on track and achieving. Students deserve to know how they are performing so they can identify areas on which they need to focus.

## *Recommendation*

Therefore, the Commission recommends that districts be permitted to use a portion of their Title I funds to develop or acquire and implement high-quality formative assessments and be required to use such assessments in schools that are identified for school improvement. Such assessments should be aligned to state standards to provide teachers and parents with meaningful information on student progress throughout the year. These assessments would not be used for accountability purposes but rather as tools to improve instruction to better address individual student needs.

*What are formative evaluations, and why are they an improvement over summative assessment currently required by NCLB?*

# HIGH STANDARDS FOR EVERY STUDENT IN EVERY STATE

Standards-based reform is the backbone of NCLB. Standards indicate what all students are expected to know and be able to do. In the past, such expectations were seldom explicit, and they varied widely; some students were expected to learn more than others.

NCLB, by allowing states to set their own content and achievement standards, has respected the long-standing tradition of local control over education. However, this has resulted in unacceptable variations in what constitutes proficiency. The disparities in proficiency definitions have fueled suggestions that some states are "gaming the system" by setting standards arbitrarily low to avoid sanctions under NCLB. And there are growing concerns that state standards do not match what students need to know and be able to do to succeed in college and the workplace. Clearly, many states are demanding too little of their students.

## Aligning State Standards with College and Workplace Readiness Expectations

Over the past decade, as states have implemented standards for student achievement, expectations for all students have been increasingly clarified. Unlike in the past, when only a few students were expected to learn challenging academic content, we now expect all students to achieve to high standards.

But international comparisons show that the level of performance of American students is consistently surpassed by that of students in other countries. And large numbers of employers and college professors say that expectations for students do not match what they need to succeed after high school. It is a travesty for students to meet the expectations set out for them, only to need remediation in college or to be unable to land an entry-level job in their chosen field. States need to take a hard look at whether the standards they are setting for their students will truly prepare them for a future filled with meaningful opportunities.

### *Recommendation*

Therefore, we recommend that states assess their reading or language arts, mathematics and science standards against requirements for success in college and in challenging jobs. All states must complete this process within one year of enactment of a reauthorized NCLB in order to participate in a national summit to be convened by the U.S. Secretary of Education. This summit would provide a forum for states to take a fresh look and report to the American people on whether the expectations they have set are sufficient to ensure that their students have the opportunity for success after high school.

## Creating Model Standards at the National Level

Comparisons of student proficiency on state standards and student proficiency on the National Assessment of Educational Progress (NAEP) show vividly the wide variations in expectations for students across states. For whatever reason, some states have clearly set the bar for students far lower than other states. Not only does this shortchange the students in those states, it also sends misleading messages to parents and taxpayers. Can citizens and businesses in a state where nearly all students are proficient on state tests—but where far fewer are proficient on NAEP—really have confidence in the strength of their education system?

In 2007, when young people in Milwaukee and Atlanta are competing with young people in Beijing and Bangalore, it is difficult to understand why Wisconsin's definition of proficiency should be different from Georgia's and why both would differ significantly from NAEP's definition. It is troubling that many states may not be preparing our children to compete with their peers around the world.

### *Recommendation*

Therefore, we recommend the development of voluntary model national content and performance standards and tests in reading or language arts, mathematics and science based on NAEP frameworks. A distinguished national panel, including members of the National Assessment Governing Board (NAGB), should be commissioned to create the standards and tests, extrapolating from the form and content of NAEP frameworks for grades 4, 8 and 12, and mapping the additional grades appropriately. In addition, the panel would ensure that any standards and assessments it produces would be aligned with college and workplace expectations.

For NCLB accountability purposes, states could adopt the resulting national model standards and tests as their own, build their own assessment instruments based on the national model standards frameworks or continue to keep their existing or revamped standards and tests. However, the U.S. Secretary of Education would periodically issue reports that compare the rigor of all state standards relative to the national model standards using a common metric.

Aiming higher should be non-negotiable. We must not label our children as proficient while leaving them unprepared. The steps outlined above will result in significantly raising the level of expectations for all American children.

# ENSURING HIGH SCHOOLS PREPARE STUDENTS FOR COLLEGE AND THE WORKPLACE

There is a growing sentiment that the American high school is "obsolete," as Microsoft Founder Bill Gates put it at an education summit in 2005. In response, high school reform has rapidly risen on the national education agenda. States and districts are hastening to redesign existing high schools and create new ones.

Concern over high schools partly stems from findings that too many students are dropping out of school. At the same time, there are rising concerns that those who do graduate from America's high schools are leaving without the knowledge and skills they need to succeed in college or the workplace.

## Strengthening Accountability and Support for High Schools

Current efforts across the country to redesign and strengthen high schools are encouraging. But the persistence of low achievement among high school students suggests that much more is needed.

Efforts to improve our high schools cannot—and should not—rest solely on the shoulders of the schools themselves. Low-performing high schools cannot go it alone; they often lack the resources and capacity to bring about meaningful change. We believe that districts can and should play a crucial role in turning around struggling high schools.

### *Recommendation*

Therefore, we recommend requiring districts with large concentrations of struggling high schools to develop and implement comprehensive, districtwide high school improvement plans. These high schools need the leadership and support of the district to spur significant reform and increased student achievement.

## High School Assessments

The requirement for assessments in each grade from 3 through 8 and once in high school has enhanced the quality and reliability of information about school performance. Yet the requirement for assessments in only a single grade in high school has meant that student progress cannot be tracked through the end of high school. In short, we simply don't have the data we need to identify and assist struggling high schools under the current NCLB assessment system.

To make matters worse, a great deal of research shows that far too many of those students who do graduate from high school are unprepared for college and the workplace. As the system currently stands, we have no way to gauge whether schools hold high expectations for students after 10th or 11th grade. We need a stronger assessment and accountability system in high schools, one that would help spur continuous student growth through graduation and ensure that our graduates are adequately prepared for what lies ahead.

### *Recommendation*

Therefore, the Commission recommends creating complete assessment systems by requiring states to add an additional assessment in grade 12 to enable measures of student growth in high school. The 12th grade assessment would provide information on student and school performance at a critical year in students' careers. This assessment should be designed to measure 12th graders' mastery of content they will need to be college and workplace ready. However, we recommend that this assessment not be used as the sole determinant for graduation purposes. This assessment, along with current 10th grade tests, would also make possible the inclusion of growth calculations in AYP for high schools and HQET/HEP measurements for high school teachers and principals.

*What are some of the controversies about a 12th grade test?*

# DRIVING PROGRESS THROUGH RELIABLE, ACCURATE DATA

The information revolution that has transformed the way Americans live, work and play has been slow to reach education. Sophisticated data systems offer tremendous potential for educators at every level. Teachers can use data on student progress to adjust lesson plans. Principals can look at classroom data to gauge the effectiveness of teachers and curriculum. Superintendents can examine school data to make better decisions about professional development and resource allocation. State officials can determine district needs and target assistance more efficiently.

## Developing and Strengthening Data Systems

To implement the recommendations in this report—in particular, the proposals to include student growth in calculations of AYP and to determine whether teachers are "effective"—the federal government and states must partner to create more sophisticated data systems that can track individual student achievement over time and provide critical information to parents, teachers and school administrators. Some states have begun to develop such systems, but all states need to pick up the pace to ensure that needed information is collected and available.

### Recommendation

Therefore, we recommend requiring all states to design and implement a high-quality longitudinal data system within four years of the enactment of a reauthorized NCLB. These systems must have common elements (described in detail in our report), and the federal government should provide formula grants to assist states in their development and implementation.

# ENSURING TEACHER EFFECTIVENESS

The Commission believes that it is time to ask all teachers to demonstrate their *effectiveness* in the classroom rather than just their *qualifications* for entering it.

This is a significant change and must be implemented in a way that is fair to teachers. Teachers who are held to this higher standard need and deserve more support.

### *Recommendation*

Therefore, the Commission recommends requiring all teachers to be Highly Qualified Effective Teachers (HQET)—teachers who demonstrate effectiveness in the classroom. Under HQET, states would be required to put in place systems for measuring the learning gains of a teacher's students through a "value-added" methodology, using three years of student achievement data, as well as principal evaluations or teacher peer reviews.

The new HQET measure will, for the first time, trigger guaranteed, quality professional development for teachers who need it most. Those who are not initially successful in producing measurable learning gains in the classroom must be given access to effective professional development to help them succeed. Those who are unable to demonstrate effectiveness in the classroom after receiving support for a reasonable period of time should no longer teach those students most in need of help.

## CITATIONS

Lekme, M., Sen, A., Pahlke, E., Partelow, L., Miller, D., Williams, T., Kastberg, D., Jocelyn, L. (2004). *International Outcomes of Learning in Mathematics Literacy and Problem Solving: PISA 2003 Results From the U.S. Perspective*, NCES 2005–003. Washington, DC: National Center for Education Statistics.

Alliance for Excellent Education (2007). *The Crisis in America's High Schools*, Retrieved from http://www.all4ed.org/whats_at_stake/crisis.html (on January 7, 2007).

# Next-Generation Models of Education Accountability: The Regulated Market Model

## Jacob E. Adams, Jr. and Paul T. Hill

## ARGUMENTS FOR MARKET ACCOUNTABILITY IN EDUCATION

Market accountability assumes good schools will achieve success through freedom of choice by families, educators and school operators. In the spirit of capitalism, market accountability assumes that competition will result in schools providing good instruction for students and a positive working environment for teachers. Under market accountability, schools are not subordinate to bureaucracies but rather enterprises that succeed or fail depending on whether they can attract families and teachers. It also assumes that competition will reward schools that use money efficiently, thereby serving the interests of citizens and taxpayers. Market accountability de-emphasizes rules, whether set by politics, professional norms or expert standard-setting bodies, thus leaving a school to determine its own success or failure.

Market-based accountability in education argues that focusing resources on family-school connections instead of community-school linkages results in greater efficiencies in achieving education goals. By pushing decision making down to families and allowing schools to respond independently to the variety of family interests, market approaches claim to be more responsive and therefore produce greater accountability and public satisfaction. The logic of regulated market accountability in education is that family choice and school entrepreneurship operating within governmental boundaries can best ensure the interests of families, school providers and the public at large.

*Do you agree or disagree with the logic that focusing resources on family-school connections instead of community-school linkages results in greater efficiencies in achieving education goals?*

## A REGULATED MARKET MODEL

While the market accountability model argues for competition in its purest sense with no regulation whatsoever, market-based education reform proposals generally call for a mix of markets and government or a *regulated* market. A regulated market would put rules and barriers into place to protect children and parents, ensure equality for the disabled, and monitor legitimacy and credibility of school management. To illustrate, the following rules would fall under the regulated market model:

- Schools would have barriers to entry to protect children against schools run by corrupt managers.
- Teachers would be licensed to screen out those with criminal records.
- Parents would be protected from fraudulent claims by school operators.
- Parents would be informed of school choices and public issues.
- Parents' choices would be subject to some constraints to ensure their children are enrolled in competent schools.
- Parents' choices would be subject to some constraints to avoid collusion creating segregated student bodies.

*In what ways can families operate as principals?*

# SPECIFYING A REGULATED MARKET MODEL

Any accountability system comprises 10 components (See Table 1):

- (1) Principals and (2) Agents. Principals establish performance objectives and are owed an account; agents act and report. Knowing who are the principals and agents in accountability systems answers the question: Who is accountable to whom? Agents are accountable to principals. In a regulated market, *families* operate as principals and *schools* run by independent parties but funded and regulated by government act as their agents.
- (3) The Referee. Because *state governments* possess constitutional authority and responsibility for public education, the duty of refereeing (regulating) educational markets would fall primarily to them. The primary function of regulation is to protect the public interest in education while promoting family choice and school freedom of action.
- (4) Performance Objectives. Performance objectives define the tasks that agents must accomplish. Determining performance targets for an accountability system answers the latter clause of the question: Who is accountable to whom *for what?* The standards movement of recent years has emphasized student performance rather than compliance with regulations, as the central objective. This is compatible with accountability expectations in regulated markets.
- (5) Authorizations and (6) Accounts. There must be some transparent means for principals and agents to agree on the work to be done and to establish different actors' obligations. In a market model, *enrolling a child in school* establishes a contract between family and school that serves as an authorization. The account submitted by the school to the family and referee, such as a *school report card,* reporting results and activities, explanations and justifications, becomes the basis for a family's evaluation of school performance and its choice to remain there or enroll elsewhere, and for the state to renew or revoke a school's license.
- (7) Incentives and (8) an Accountability Mechanism. Incentives and accountability mechanisms, respectively, represent the inducement for

Table 1   Components in General and Regulated Market Models
of Educational Accountability

| Components in a General Model | Corresponding Components in a Regulated Market Model |
| --- | --- |
| 1. Principal[a] | Families |
| 2. Agent[b] | Schools |
| 3. Referee[c] | State government[d] |
| 4. Objective[e] | Student performance[f] |
| 5. Authorization[g] | Enrollment |
| 6. Account | Two-tier requirement: basic criterion-reference measures of school safety, equity, and student performance needed for a license to operate and fuller measures of student and school performance needed for family selection of school[h] |
| 7. Incentive/consequence | Patronage of school |
| 8. Accountability mechanism | Choice among schools |
| 9. Agent action | Freedom of action within license, bounded causality[i] |
| 10. Principal support | Tuition payment required, family-based social capital investments allowed[j] |

[a] The principal party, namely, the one who defines the performance objective and the one to whom an account is owed.

[b] The accountable party, that is, the one who accomplishes the objective.

[c] Neither the principal nor agent, the referee establishes conditions in which principal-agent transactions occur.

[d] Based on their constitutional assignment of authority and responsibility for public education.

[e] The task that the agent must accomplish.

[f] An education accountability system in practice must define specific performance objectives for students, specifying the types and levels of knowledge and skills they must learn. A regulated market model assumes variation in performance objectives commensurate with parental preferences, just as it recognizes a public interest in educational performance. Hence, a state government might demand one level of literacy from all schools, reflecting the public's interest in a competent citizenry, while allowing family preferences to dictate performance objectives above this level.

[g] The mechanism that authorizes an agent to act on behalf of a principal.

[h] The actual accounts used must be tailored to specific performance objectives. Nevertheless, all accounts should be useful, valid and reliable in capturing the full story—results and explanations—of an agent's effort. Accounts may serve evaluative purposes only, or they may also contribute to improving an agents' performance over time.

[i] Recognizing that schools do not control all the factors influencing student performance.

[j] Tuition payments always include the needs-based government subsidy, however structured, and may include additional payments from parents to purchase "advanced studies" but not to screen out less wealthy families.

agents to act and the means through which this inducement is allocated. In markets, the incentive is *customer patronage*; the accountability mechanism is *choice*.

- (9) Agent Actions and (10) Principal Supports. Principals (families) authorize and evaluate the work that agents (schools) perform and report. Principals also provide resources to facilitate the work and consequences based on an evaluation of that work. For their part, agents contribute the special knowledge, skills, time, and effort that enable the work, plus an account of their actions and results. In the market model, families direct need-based governmental *subsidies* to schools of their choice and schools provide an *instructional program* designed to attain the family's and public's learning goals.

# HOW ACCOUNTABILITY WORKS IN A REGULATED MARKET MODEL

In theory, accountability systems are designed to ensure that an agent will work diligently on behalf of a principal. In the case of the American education system, it means that schools will serve families in the best way possible. The accountability problem is evident in the too-common occurrences of fraud, malfeasance and lack of competence in both public and private affairs. How do accountability systems address this problem?

Accountability uses resources to manage the principal-agent relationship so that both parties can benefit. Accountability in a regulated market model works by ensuring incentives, accounts and consequences induce agents to act diligently; it enables principals to know the result and to respond in kind. In this way, accountability uses resources to manage the principal-agent relationship so that both parties can benefit. This use of resources represents the nub of accountability's underlying theory. Its logic is thus: if incentives are targeted and sufficient; if accounts are complete, informative and accurate; and if consequences, too, are targeted and commensurate with performance; then agents will act diligently and principals will accomplish their goals.

How does this theory apply to improving the quality of teaching and learning? Accountability concentrates resources of policy, administration and practice on teaching and learning in order to ascertain the best possible performance. These resources may include defining performance goals, allocating authority, managing incentives, building capacity, measuring progress, reporting results, and enforcing consequences, all related to educational performance, however defined. The organization of these particular resources represents the nub of how this model of accountability works in education.

The issue now before policymakers, educators and community members is which type of accountability, or what combination of approaches, best promotes the performance goals now prevalent in public education.

# SUPPORTING CONDITIONS

Four sets of conditions enable a regulated market model of education accountability to function: conditions related to accountability functions, market structure, regulatory boundaries and investments in educational capacity.

## 1. The Ability of Its Constituent Parts to Function as Intended

Questions that must be addressed:

- Does the accountability system clearly define principals and agents?
- Is the role of the referee agreed?
- Is the performance objective adequately specified?
- Is the incentive sufficient to command an agent's attention?
- Does the authorization focus agents' actions?
- Is the account meaningful?
- Does it appropriately make the performance objective operational?
- Are performance indicators valid and reliable? Does the accountability mechanism operate freely?
- Do agents have discretion and other resources they need to act?
- Is the principal appropriately supporting agents' actions?
- Are consequences commensurate with causal responsibility?

If the answer to any of these questions is no, then the system design is flawed and its operations cannot match its potential. Market-based accountability would clarify some of the issues confronting accountability designers but would continue to grapple with others.

## 2. Attributes That Enable a Market to Function

Markets work most effectively when there are large numbers of providers and customers, none of whom is sufficiently influential to manipulate prices or quality. They require free entry and exit for providers and customers with complete information that supports those decisions. Markets also require freedom of action for providers and customers, with providers who are willing to sell to all customers. Finally, markets require that all the costs and benefits of production and consumption appear in the transactions between providers and customers, such that no one else benefits or suffers from externalities.

Market-based accountability defines community in terms of affinity and preference rather than geography. For example, providers could establish schools designed to serve a particular community such as a school for dropout youth, not necessarily a whole geographic area.

To date no one has fully analyzed the preconditions for a full supply response in market-based accountability. It is safe to say that equal real-dollar

*If market-based accountability defines community in terms of affinity and preference rather than geography, what are the equity and social justice implications?*

funding, equitable access to pupil transportation and other publicly funded services, equivalent access to facilities (meaning either that all schools get facilities free, or all pay market rents) and uniform regulatory oversight and renewal structures are essential. New schools will require some investments, of time by founders and of money from nonprofits, foundations or government venture capital funds. Such investments are unlikely if new schools are subject to unequal treatment, or if the rules under which they operate are subject to abrupt changes. State governments probably need to play a supply-monitoring role in a market system, identifying the localities with the weakest supply response and investigating whether the weak response is due to inadequate funding or to anticompetitive actions by local groups. States might also need to offer start-up funds for schools in localities experiencing weak supply responses. There must be a mechanism to create new alternatives, to ensure both that families have multiple options and that all schools are constantly facing new competition.

## 3. Structure of Governmental Regulation

The scope of regulation must be broad enough to ensure the public takes an active role in education and in its community, thus ensuring the legitimacy of market results, but sufficiently constrained to allow the market to function in the competitive framework that was intended.

What do families and communities demand of their education system and schools? Ultimately this is a question for public debate. Three elements of public interest include:

- Student and staff safety
- Equality of educational opportunity
- Student performance at a level required for civic participation.

Through the regulatory process, government would guarantee that all schools in this market operated in safe buildings, conducted their admissions and other procedures without prejudice and produced a level of student literacy sufficient to support students' future economic and civic endeavors. Such a process enables the public to determine the amount and quality of education that reflects its interest and a corresponding level of financial support, regardless of who provides the service. Beyond this level of accomplishment, however, family aspirations and resources would dictate educational choices, just as they do a family's selection of cars and restaurants.

What of the state standards developed to support the standards movement? The main function of state standards could vary in a regulated market where government acts as referee and where families are the principal parties. Under market arrangements, if states use current standards to define the public interest in education, then those standards would establish thresholds for school licensure. Schools that fail to teach certain core skills effectively would not receive public funds. Threshold standards would require external validation, a requirement that is demanding. They should also be parsimonious, with the burden of proof on those wishing to expand them. While all schools would be required to meet threshold standards, aspirational standards could be set to spark competition among schools and distinguish different school performance profiles. Current standards could define an "advanced studies" standard of school accreditation. Advanced studies accreditation would advertise to families that they will find an expanded level of service at schools bearing this mark.

No matter how public and private interests are defined, an accountable education market still should provide families with choices based on at least four dimensions:

- **Provider** – reputation
- **Service Level** – public interest versus advanced studies
- **Instructional Method** – Montessori versus Core Knowledge, etc.
- **School Characteristics** – proximity, climate, amenities

## 4. Investments in Educational Capacity

Specifically, this refers to investments that can improve the overall quality of educational services to children within the market. Ample research needs to be conducted to determine the factors that best serve the children, families and staff in this market environment. Such investments in research could examine how different incentives or school structures influence family selection and student performance, what conditions cause providers to enter and exit the market or which accounts alter family choices among schools. Research could also explore what kinds of outreach enable less motivated families to participate effectively in market transactions and what basis exists for discrepancies in cost across schools. For government itself, a key issue will be deciding how much investment in the infrastructure of education—buildings and buses—is necessary to support the market, or what unconventional mechanisms, such as real estate trusts, may be able to assume a portion of government's traditional role. . . .

# IMPLICATIONS FOR GOVERNANCE, FINANCE AND TEACHER QUALITY

Governance issues are different under market-based accountability than under bureaucratic accountability. Individual school providers make key decisions about who shall operate schools, what variety of schools will be offered in a locality, who will teach in or lead a particular school, what methods of teaching will be used and how teacher effort will be matched with technology. Similarly, parents decide what school a child will attend or whether a child will transfer from one school to another.

Yet, neither providers nor parents are ungoverned: providers' choices are constrained by issues including the availability of school facilities and teachers to the willingness of parents to enroll their children. Parents are constrained by the availability of schools in areas accessible to them. Moreover, parents are constrained by schools' reasonable demands on attendance, effort and deportment unless schools are required to admit and keep absolutely any child, regardless of that child's behavior or willingness to do assigned work.

Educators gain great freedom of action but their entry to the profession, pay, placements and career progression are also governed by the market. Educators from unconventional sources can seek jobs, but whether they are hired, and whether they keep jobs once hired, depends on whether they perform well enough to maintain the confidence of school operators and parents. Similarly, conventionally qualified teachers will compete for jobs and pay on the basis of their personal reputations. As in other professional fields, individuals with the highest pay expectations will need to maintain reputations for high productivity. Moreover, because schools will have fixed budgets, no school will be able to afford a large number of highly paid teachers.

Market-based accountability retains some centralized governance roles. These roles will not be directive as they are now requiring schools to use time in certain ways, maintain certain class sizes or provide individual students with particular services. Yet a variety of government actions will still constrain the actions of people in the market in many important ways. For example, elected officials, primarily state legislators, would retain control over public spending. It would be up to them to adjust the value of subsidies if some geographic areas fail to attract school providers. Additionally, legislators, or administrative agencies under their control, might create and administer start-up funds for new school providers and incentive programs to encourage teachers to become trained in skills for which demand exceeds supply.

State government would also constrain the supply of school providers via licensing. Inevitably, the licensing function will involve discretion and become a focus of political debate. Similarly, government might create parsimonious systems of standards and achievement exams, which could be used to compare schools, inform parents and eliminate providers whose performance is so low as to invalidate their licenses. Government might also perform important services that would constrain the market's operation. For example, performing background checks on potential principals and teachers, providing school specific information and sponsoring research on different schools' long-term consequences for students.

Some of these functions might be delegated from the state to local or regional organizations, including re-designed school districts. However, if school districts continue operating some schools, either as providers of last resort or as competitors in a market, their legitimacy as regulators would be negated. These roles might be assigned to an independent regulatory body. Alternatively, school districts could be allowed to provide schools, but only via contracts with independent organizations.

# MARKET CONTRIBUTIONS TO STANDARDS-BASED REFORM

Under standards-based reform, school-level initiative is the engine of reform. Even in low-performing schools, standards-based reform eschews command-and-control solutions in favor of school-managed improvement efforts. It makes sure that schools that can improve with reasonable amounts of external help are able to get it. Accountability is the critical link between statewide standards and individual school improvement. Standards-based reform regards testing and publication of results as necessary, but not as sufficient conditions for school improvement.

Standards-based reform needs four things that market-based accountability provides:

1. Definite performance incentives for schools as organizations, making it clear that all the adults in a school have a stake in the school's success (or failure) in educating students.
2. School freedom of action, allowing school staff to use their time and money in the ways they believe are likely to have the greatest effect on student learning.
3. Investments in school capacity, enabling schools to invest in effective methods, materials, staff training and recruitment.
4. Parental freedom of exit from schools that evolve in ways that are not appropriate for particular children.

It is not that market accountability provides these resources where other accountability systems cannot, but rather that market accountability specifies them and gives them practical effect to a degree that other systems have not.

Both standards and market accountability make individual schools accountable for student performance. Both put the adults who work in schools—teachers, administrators and support staff—into the same boat. If schools perform well, all stand to benefit; if schools perform poorly, all can suffer.

*What are the implications of market-based accountability for leaders of low-performing schools?*

Market-based accountability is much more explicit about the good and bad consequences of school performance. Parents and teachers are empowered to abandon schools that do not perform. Educators in schools that teach effectively have reason to be confident about their futures. Staff members may also build on their school's good reputation by "hiving" off new schools of their own and by advising schools that would imitate them. In short, market-based accountability provides the performance incentives, freedom of action and investments in the capacity that standards based reform originally intended.

# IMPLICATIONS OF THE NO CHILD LEFT BEHIND ACT

As states move toward full implementation of standards-based reform laws, increasing numbers are recognizing the need to release students from failing schools and to create good alternatives for such schools where none exist. The federal No Child Left Behind Act (NCLB) underlines the urgency of this need, allowing families with children in persistently failing schools to choose another school. The choice, however, extends only to more successful public schools or to public charter schools. Thus, within the regulated market framework developed here, it is fair to say that NCLB introduces choice but not markets into the accountability equation.

A quick comparison based on accountability components demonstrates other differences between the regulated-market (Table 1) and NCLB approaches to accountability. The federal law:

- Places the federal government in the principal party role, with states, school districts and schools as its agents
- Relegates refereeing functions to the occasional involvement of administrative or general law courts, which act when parties seek redress for specific grievances
- Defines performance objectives as state content standards in math, reading and science and as "adequate yearly progress" toward proficiency on those standards based on universal testing
- Uses oversight as the accountability mechanism
- Uses legal mandates to authorize action
- Mandates agent actions, in part, regarding teaching methods and teacher standards; also reaches beyond Title I schools to encompass all schools
- Provides for supplemental services to students and greater local agency flexibility regarding the use of federal monies, but does not provide substantial new resources to carry out its mandates.

The regulated-market and NCLB models are more similar in their use of reporting requirements (the "account" in accountability) and incentives tied to loss of school revenue (the government tuition subsidy in the market versus Title I funds in NCLB).

In short, NCLB represents a legal model of accountability. It is grounded in the relationship between policymakers and policy implementers, expects compliance with legal mandates, uses oversight to ensure accountability and wields the threat of legal sanction leading to loss of program funding as the primary incentive. In this regard, NCLB follows the same pattern as state accountability systems. NCLB differs from market-based approaches to accountability insofar as it favors government over families, disregards family preferences for schooling, favors regulation over freedom of action and rests incentives and sanctions with government. It does, however, provide an "escape" from failing schools.

NCLB's theory of action is consistent with the general theory of accountability, including incentives, accounts, and consequences and particularly educational accountability involving resources concentrated on teaching and student learning. It diverges from the market approach in its assumption that community-school linkages are more efficient than family-school linkages for accomplishing educational goals. It also differs in its reliance on governmental oversight and regulation rather than family choice and school entrepreneurship to ensure stakeholder interests.

NCLB represents an extension of standards-based reform. It federalizes the standards movement, bringing all states and schools, not just Title I schools, under a uniform accountability system based on content standards, universal testing, public reporting and consequences for poor performance. States are responsible for developing the operational components of the system consistent with federal regulations, which may require states to restructure their existing accountability systems. NCLB is in no sense a market model, as it disregards family choice or entrepreneurial opportunity.

# THE IMPORTANCE OF POLICY DESIGN AND ITS EFFECTS ON ACCOUNTABILITY POTENTIAL

As with any public policy, educational accountability's effect depends on sound theory and good practice. The sound design of accountability systems identifies principals and agents and it authorizes action while maintaining control through mandatory accounts. Sound design explicitly defines performance expectations, aligning accounts with these expectations. It manages agent productivity by focusing, alternatively, on behavior, performance, or capacity and it also induces agents' actions through the use of incentives sufficient to redirect their behavior. Finally, sound design matches causality to consequences while also revealing the parties' mutual responsibilities, whenever and however they arise. Together these functions enable productive work while protecting the interests of principals and agents alike.

The biggest challenge in design challenge in educational accountability is to assemble ten components that will operate successfully together amidst the often conflicting interests of education's multiple stakeholders and conflicts of interest. Threats to accountability design include missing elements, weak or conflicting elements and stakeholder resistance. Threats to educational accountability as a policy strategy include public disillusionment and the withdrawal of support.

There is reason to take caution with this model. Because accountability operates as a system of decisions and elements, compromise internal to its design may greatly diminish its chance of success. The multiple decisions and elements that constitute accountability policy cannot tolerate much internal incoherence without failing outright. It is vastly different than an individual policy intervention, such as new highway speed limits or income support rules, where marginal changes in the amount of intervention usually correlate with marginal changes in its impact. In this sense, an accountability system is analogous to an automobile engine, where one element out of whack can stop the whole operation. If accounts do not represent performance objectives, if consequences do not match causality, if principals and agents are not clearly identified, if incentives are not sufficient to alter agent behavior, then performance probably will not match expectations. This restriction does not preclude choices among accountability systems, performance expectations or similar system-orienting decisions. It does mean that, once selected, the parts of a system's internal structure must work together.

# ENDNOTES

1. For options, see Education Commission of the States. (1999) *Governing America's Schools: Changing the Rules.* Report of the National Commission on Governing America's Schools, GV-99-01W, Denver, CO: ECS.

2. Direct financial support for families raises two issues. First, states must devise ways to assign subsides to families and ways for families to redeem them. Second, in the process of moving from state-to-district financing to state-to-family financing, states must revise tax policies to by-pass local agencies. Because educational finance involves a mix of state and local taxes, market system would require finance structures that either (a) move all education-related property tax receipts to the state for redistribution—in effect, 100% recapture—or (b) allow states to assume the full burden of education support, while rebalancing the mix and effort of state and local taxes to ensure that overall tax burdens do not rise. States could accomplish this by trading lower property taxes for higher state income or sales taxes, at the same time prohibiting local governments from making new claims on the "freed" property tax capacity. Because it would remove local wealth from the calculation, direct state payments to families would improve funding equity. At the same time, direct state payments would remove local decisions regarding desired levels of educational support, replacing collective choices with family choices.

3. On standards for accountability systems, see Baker, E.L., Linn, R.L., Herman, J.L. and Kortez, D. (2002) *Standards for Educational Accountability Systems*, Policy Brief 5. Los Angles: University of California, National Center for Research on Evaluation, Standards, and Student Testing.

# ISSUE SUMMARY

———————————————————————————————————————————————●

Judging from the attention being given to No Child Left Behind, accountability for student achievement is no longer a local issue for each school to deal with in isolation. Accountability is taking the prominent place in institutions, trumping quality, finance, and governance, which are other important systems of any organization. And judging from the increase in resources for accountability measures, public schools will continue to be judged on the basis of test scores. But will all of this ensure that accountability becomes part of the DNA of an educational organization? Some say even standards-based testing is not sufficient; it is a matter of individual, family, and local school commitment and no amount of federal oversight or enforcement can make high achievement universal.

The report of the Commission on No Child Left Behind ends by taking this stand:

> A high-achieving education system includes . . . teacher and principal quality and effectiveness, strong accountability, increased and high-quality student options, significant school improvement, accurate assessments, high standards for all students and more. (p. 14)

The question is whether this is a strong enough stand. Although the commission declares its recommendations are more than tweaking, to some critics their work is just that—simple modifications of current regulations.

Other groups are beginning to reach another conclusion—that the NCLB accountability system has been seriously compromised over the past five years and needs a complete overhaul. A recent report, "The Unraveling of No Child Left Behind," reveals numerous ad hoc, isolated changes negotiated with all fifty states that have weakened the integrity of the national system.

> Since the number and kinds of changes that states have adopted are not uniform across states, with each state requesting its own configuration of amendments, accountability no longer has a common meaning across states or even within states. Accountability now depends on which subgroups are included in the system, how each state calculates adequate yearly progress, and which district, school, or subgroup benefit from the various changes states adopted. (p. 10)

Apparently NCLB has not only failed to fulfill its spectacular goal of success for all but has been reduced to just another compliance mechanism with uneven, unreliable results. Not content to lurk at the edges of the law, this report fearlessly recommends that the "bright lines" of the law—its core principles—be reexamined.

These roundtable viewpoints point to the inevitable outcome of any sweeping legislation that tackles dual ambitious goals of equity and achievement—there will have to be adjustments in the law. Just how far the adjustments go in remedying the nation's accountability issues is still an open question as we await reauthorization of No Child Left Behind.

## ISSUE HIGHLIGHTS

- A new national emphasis on competitiveness has implications for the requirements of No Child Left Behind.
- Goals, strategies, and support for NCLB center on closing of the achievement gap, with concentration on lowest-performing schools.
- The American Competitiveness Initiative focuses specifically on math and science with global implications.
- The NCLB accountability system has fundamental flaws that undermine its own goals, including setting expectations for achievement unrealistically high.
- One complication of NCLB is proficiency levels on state assessments vary substantially.
- Annually adjusted but fixed targets for adequate yearly progress may produce distorted results and cause some schools to lose incentive.
- The Commission on No Child Left Behind has uncovered shortcomings in the statues and offers recommendations to remedy problems in the law.
- Recommendations for change to NCLB include more reliable data through state-level longitudinal data systems, providing more aggressive interventions for schools, and aligning state standards with college and workplace readiness expectations.
- Alternative models of school regulation and accountability should be considered.
- One alternative—the regulated market model of accountability—fits well with standards-based education reform.

## CRITICAL THINKING

At its root, *accountability* is an ethical construct, with close conceptual ties to responsibility, answerability, and liability.

We tend to think that national accountability legislation should be the impetus for enabling local accountability efforts to succeed. But here's the rub—accountability comes at the end of the initiative, not during the effort. Accounting for something once the data has been collected is quite different from transparency that calls for precision throughout the process.

When No Child Left Behind was first approved, the Education Commission of the States was charged with tracking and reporting state policy actions related to the seven components of the new law: standards and assessments, adequate yearly progress, teacher quality, safe schools, supplemental services, school improvement initiatives, and national reporting.

In a series of leadership briefs during the first two years of NCLB, ECS touted new opportunities and resources for increasing leadership through Title II training and recruiting funds:

- Reform principal licensure and certification
- Establish, expand or improve alternative routes to principal certification
- Target efforts at recruiting highly qualified principals
- Develop merit-based performance systems
- Provide professional development to principals (2002, p. 3)

The new law was supposed to grant states and districts more money and flexibility in choosing how and where to build leadership, design effective programs, and create appropriate accountability systems.

It's time for reauthorization of NCLB or as some would say, it's time for account-giving of NCLB. Have the regulations lived up to their intended purpose? Are the NCLB standards of accountability in sync or at odds with the inherent goals of leadership?

# ADDITIONAL READING RESOURCES

Katy Anthes, *No Child Left Behind Policy Brief: School and District Leadership*. Education Commission of the States, 2002.

William J. Erpenbach and Ellen Forte Fast, *Statewide Educational Accountability Under the No Child Left Behind Act: A Report on 2005 Amendments to State Plans*. Washington, DC: Council of Chief State School Officers, October 2005.

National Conference of State Legislatures, *Delivering the Promise: State Recommendations for Improving No Child Left Behind*. Author, 2005.

Gail L. Sunderman, *The Unraveling of No Child Left Behind: How Negotiated Changes Transform the Law*. The Civil Rights Project at Harvard University, 2006.

U.S. Department of Education, *Spellings Announces New Special Education Guidelines, Details Workable, "Common-sense" Policy to Help States Implement No Child Left Behind*. At http://ed.gov/print/news/pressreleases/2005/05/05102005.htm, May 10, 2005.

For more information on accountability legislation, check these sites:

A Guide to Standardized Testing: The Nature of Assessment
www.centerforpubliceducation.org/site/c.kjJXJ5MPIwE/b.1460713/apps/s/content.asp?ct=2040961
Center on Educational Policy www.cep-dc.org/
Center for Equity and Excellence in Education ceee.gwu.edu/
Fact Sheet on NCLB Reauthorization: www.whitehouse.gov/news/releases/2006/10/20061005-2.html

National Association of Black School Educators Legislative Agenda www.nabse.org/legislativeagenda.htm

Next-Generation Accountability Models www.ecs.org/accountability

Statewide Accountability Systems www.ccsso.org/projects/Accountability_Systems/

# How Will Educational Organizations Be Led in the Future?

W e live in anxious times and our educational institutions are showing the strain. The authors of *America's Perfect Storm* (Irwin Kirsch, Henry Braun, Kentaro Yamamoto, and Andrew Sum, *America's Perfect Storm*. Princeton, NJ: Educational Testing Service, 2007) make this point vividly:

> Our nation is in the midst of a perfect storm—the result of the confluence of three powerful forces—that is having a considerable impact on our country. If we maintain our present policies, it is very likely that we will continue to grow apart, with greater inequity in wages and wealth, and increasing social and political polarization. If, however, we recognize the power of these forces as they interact over the years—and we change course accordingly—then we have an opportunity to reclaim the American dream in which each of us has a fair chance at sharing in any future prosperity. (p. 3)

The three forces causing the storm—divergent skill distributions among U.S. population groups, a changing economy, and demographic trends of a growing, more diverse population—have a direct bearing on schools and institutions.

In the midst of this perfect storm, we pause to consider how the education organization of the future will cope with such strong forces. Will its fundamental shape change? Is continuous improvement the way of the future? Will competition be a critical factor? Is standardization or personalization of learning more important? How will technology change teaching and learning? Given the fluctuating nature of the global economy, leaders know that the transformation of schools is occurring at a fast pace. What they do not know is the exact shape of the organization in the future—but they know it will impact their role.

No amount of environmental scanning can give a sure answer to how education leaders will be functioning in days ahead. But there are plenty of indicators that make the shape of leadership fairly clear:

> Leaders in the 21st century will need to be highly adept in their specialties. At the same time, they will be expected to be generalists, eager to connect a broad range of people and ideas. The successful ones will constantly and enthusiastically seek to build a connecting web in what is too often a vacuum between disciplines, and they'll enjoy every minute of it. In a fast-moving world, these

thoughtful and exemplary leaders will wrest coherence from growing turbulence and complexity.

As generalists and as education leaders, they will help students learn across disciplines. They will constantly scan the environment, seeking opportunities to bridge the divides between bodies of knowledge, cultures, ideologies, languages, and political divisions. By poking their heads above the specialization of their industries, institutions, or professions, leaders in any field are in a better position to discover common threats, and, better yet, common opportunities. (Gary Marx, *Future-Focused Leadership: Preparing Schools, Students, and Communities for Tomorrow's Realities*. Association for Supervision and Curriculum Development, 2006).

There is no doubt that leaders will need to poke their heads above their own institution to stay in touch with a fast-moving world. In a wired world, the Web becomes a primary way for leaders to access external information. But accessing information is just the start—leaders need to strategically analyze trend data. This is the focus of the first reading, "Using Trend Data to Create a Successful Future for Our Students, Our Schools, and Our Communities." Marx, president of an organization that focuses on future-oriented leadership, argues that scanning the environment is a necessary task of education leaders.

The second reading deals with the question: What is needed to move into the future when the impact of reforms since the 1990s is continually underwhelming. Evidently despite some indications of long-term improvement in student achievement, it will take much more to move the entire system of education. The author of "What's Next? Our Gains Have Been Substantial, Promising, But Not Enough" contends that performance-accountability requirements must be altered because they clash with standards-based education. In other words, the system is not aligned. Fifty states set different standards for proficiency, making comparison useless despite uniform federal requirements. The author proposes four steps that leaders should take to increase the overall quality of education in the future.

One thing that has been undervalued for decades is women's role in educational leadership. That's not to say that women have not been leaders, just not at the top of the system. Recognizing the difference between women leaders and women's leadership is the focus of the third reading, "Echoing Their Ancestors, Women Lead School Districts in the United States." The author, a leader in women's roles in educational leadership, argues that while women have been leading, it is not always regarded as leadership. The image of superintendent with tight control has conflicted with the way women superintendents do their work and the result is the women are overlooked. But as the number of women in superintendency increases, their way of working begins to reshape the role. In essence, the author's message is that the future of schools in America will be impacted by women in the highest levels of educational administration.

The author of the final reading contends that the future of educational organizations is tied closely to global realities and tensions. Leaders who take an ecological role by incorporating an understanding of the world in their work can better position their institutions. At the same time that leaders are adopting an external viewpoint, they also need to keep a focus on internal matters by distinguishing managerial tasks from true leadership. Once those differences are understood, the next hurtle is changing the accountability context: "Educational leaders . . . need to work towards developing proactive and reflexive forms of accountability, ones which are not simply of the form which are 'done' to them, but to whose definition and scope they contribute" (p. 18). Bottery ends his set of priorities with a call for educational leaders in a globalizing world to build trust within the institution and with stakeholder in the broader community.

## SOURCES

Gary Marx, Using trend data to create a successful future for our students, our schools, and our communities. *ERS Spectrum*, Winter 2006.

Marshall S. Smith, What's next? Our gains have been substantial, promising, but not enough. *Education Week*, January 5, 2006.

Margaret Grogan, Echoing their ancestors, women lead school districts in the United States. *International Studies in Educational Administration*, November 2, 2005.

Mike Bottery, Educational leaders in a globalising world: A new set of priorities? *School Leadership and Management*, February 2006.

# ARTICLE 10.1

# Using Trend Data to Create a Successful Future for Our Students, Our Schools, and Our Communities

Gary Marx

*In a fast-changing world, looking at tomorrow and seeing it only as a little bit more or a little bit less of today won't cut it as we move into the future. As educators and community leaders, we need to use powerful trends data, coupled with imagination, as we plan ahead. A challenge will be to not only develop a plan but to turn it into a living strategy—a strategic vision that will help us lead our students, schools, and communities into an even more successful future.*

*All of us are in a constant, unrelenting, and exciting race to lay the groundwork for an even brighter future for our children and ourselves. Much of what happens as we shape the road ahead, however, will come at us out of the blue. That's why we need to stay in touch with a fast-moving society. We need to be ready to deal with what some people aptly call "discontinuities." In essence, all of us need to be environmentalists, adapting the organization to the needs of the environment at the same time we're adapting the environment to the needs of the organization.*

*This article discusses the general necessity of studying trend data and identifies 16 major trends that are already having an impact on our society, and thus our education system. Studying these trends and considering their overall implications will put us in the best possible position to prepare our students today for what can be an even more promising tomorrow.*

All organizations, especially education systems, are *of* this world, not separate from it. To earn their legitimacy, they need to be connected with the communities, countries, and world they serve. Unless they are constantly scanning the environment, educators will soon find themselves isolated . . . and out of touch.

Getting a bead on political, economic, social, technological, environmental, educational, and other forces that are sweeping across the landscape is essential.

---

## What Are Trends?

Howard Chase, the father of issue management, described trends as "detectable changes which precede issues."[1] *Webster's Dictionary* has another take. This venerable definer of words refers to them as "a line of general direction or movement, a prevailing tendency or inclination."[2]

A free and open discussion of these societal forces is a first step in tapping the ingenuity of people around us. While we're listening, we might come across fresh ideas. We'll also be able to identify possible wildcards and reveal both intended and unintended consequences of our actions.

---

Understanding these forces is the key to unlocking rigidity and reshaping our schools, colleges, and other institutions for the future.

How can we maintain a 24/7 connection with the environment? One way is to constantly identify local, statewide/provincial, national, and international issues and sort them according to their probability and potential impact. If an issue is high in probability and high in possible impact, we'd better figure out how to manage it, or it will manage us.

There are other ways to scan. Engaging the wisdom of staff, community, and other constituents, we can pinpoint gaps between where we are today and where we'd like to be tomorrow. We can develop statements describing an organization that is capable of adjusting to a fast-changing world and then use the descriptions as part of a scale to rate our flexibility—our ability to innovate.

Frequently, in looking to the future, organizations are eager to explore strengths, weaknesses, opportunities, and threats. We can also involve diverse groups of people in envisioning the characteristics of the organization we want to become, in weighing our assumptions, and in exploring possible scenarios that describe alternative futures. Bottom line: One of the most far-reaching and effective ways of staying in touch with the environment is to identify and consider the possible implications of trends.

*Why is it advantageous for educational organizations to scan the environment?*

## SEISMIC SHIFTS THAT ARE SHAPING THE FUTURE

As we scan the environment, nothing stands out more than massive, unrelenting trends. Like the movement of tectonic plates beneath the surface of the earth, they are a signal of seismic shifts.

This article identifies 16 of those landscape-shaping trends. Each has implications for schools, school systems, colleges, universities, and other institutions, including communities, nations, and the world. Studying and considering the implications of these and other trends enable us to, among other things:

- Get connected to forces affecting the whole of society.
- Keep our organization fresh, energized, and open to new ideas.
- Encourage creativity and imagination.
- Give us the tools to identify problems or crises far enough in advance that they don't become catastrophes.
- Offer an opportunity for us to stay in tune with possible tipping points.[3]
- Identify opportunities we otherwise might not have considered.
- Provide us with an indication that far-reaching trends go beyond today's issues, such as class size, standards, accountability, and testing, but also may have a direct impact on all of them.
- Overcome the isolation of our disciplines, disagreements, and other differences to find the connective tissue that unifies us.[4]
- Help us and those we serve forecast possible futures and even become trendsetters.
- Turn our institution into an even more indispensable, relevant force.

## CONNECTED LEADERSHIP

Anyone involved in education is, or should be, a leader, by virtue of the crucial role they play in society.

*Connected* leadership is in. Isolation is out. Just as we ask students to learn across disciplines, we also need to *lead* across disciplines. That means, if we're specialists, we should try to be the very best specialists we can become. As desperately as we need depth, it is not a substitute for breadth. Context is crucial. Everything we do affects everything else. The program that guarantees unprecedented benefits for some might bring devastating side-effects for others.[5] The expansive needs of our community and the world should guide us as we strive to serve.

How can we connect people? How can we bring them together in common purpose? How can we tap the diversity and richness of thinking in an organization? How can we create a rallying point and ultimately a sense of ownership for what we want to accomplish? How can we stir a sense that "We're all in this together"?

The answer is not that complicated. We simply need to acknowledge the political, economic, social, technological, environmental, demographic, and other forces that are affecting the whole of society. Then, we need to ask key questions, such as:

- What are the implications of these trends for our education system?
- What are the implications of the trends for what students need to know and be able to do—their academic knowledge, skills, behaviors, and attitudes?

**Figure 1    Sixteen Trends . . . That Will Profoundly Affect U.S. Education and the Whole of Society**

*From your perspective, which of Marx's sixteen trends have the most profound affect on education?*

- For the first time in history, the old will outnumber the young. (Note: This aging trend generally applies to developed nations. In underdeveloped nations, just the opposite is true: the young will substantially outnumber the old.)
- Majorities will become minorities, creating ongoing challenges for social cohesion.
- Social and intellectual capital will become economic drivers, intensifying competition for well-educated people.
- Technology will increase the speed of communication and the pace of advancement or decline.
- The Millennial Generation will insist on solutions to accumulated problems and injustices, while an emerging Generation E will call for equilibrium.
- Standards and high-stakes tests will fuel a demand for personalization in an education system increasingly committed to lifelong human development.
- Release of human ingenuity will become a primary responsibility of education and society.
- Continuous improvement will replace quick fixes and defense of the status quo.
- Scientific discoveries and societal realities will force widespread ethical choices.
- Common opportunities and threats will intensify a worldwide demand for planetary security.
- Polarization and narrowness will bend toward reasoned discussion, evidence, and consideration of varying points of view.
- International learning, including diplomatic skills, will become basic, as nations vie for understanding and respect in an interdependent world.
- Greater numbers of people will seek personal meaning in their lives in response to an intense, high-tech, always-on, fast-moving society.
- Understanding will grow that sustained poverty is expensive, debilitating, and unsettling.
- Pressure will grow for society to prepare people for jobs and careers that may not currently exist.
- Competition will increase to attract and keep qualified educators.

Compiled by Gary Marx, president, Center for Public Outreach, Vienna, Va. (From *Sixteen Trends: Their Profound Impact on Our Future,* published by Educational Research Service).

- What are the implications of the trends for economic growth and development and quality of life in our community, state, or nation?

In the process, we might ask some additional questions, such as:

- Do we have a short-range view or a long-range perspective?
- Are we so intently focused on the bottom line that we've taken our eye off the future?

- Do we accept the status quo, or do we challenge it?[6]
- Are we doing things well?
- Are we doing the right things?
- What even greater benefit could result from our efforts?
- Do we have the right answers?
- Are we asking the right questions?

Richard Feynman, a fellow educator who won the 1965 Nobel Prize for Physics, said in his own challenging way, "I can live with doubt and uncertainty and not knowing. I think it is much more interesting to live not knowing than to have answers that might be wrong."[7]

This philosophy should not be confused with herd mentality or "groupthink." In *The Wisdom of Crowds*, James Surowiecki warned against giving "too much credence to recent and high profile news while under estimating the importance of longer-lasting trends and less dramatic events."[8] Instead, we need to open our minds to the knowledge, experience, and ideas of diverse groups of people, turning them loose to consider possibilities, to learn from each other, and to help us, across all disciplines, as we think about and plan for the future. (See "12 Guiding Principles for Leaders Capable of Creating a Future" in Figure 2.)

# THRIVING IN AN AGE OF RENEWAL

The world is changing at warp speed. Education systems are expected to prepare their students for the future. They answered the call to get students ready for an agricultural society. Schools and colleges were transformed again as we moved into an industrial age. Today, we are entering what seems like the rarified atmosphere of the global knowledge/information age.

Our education systems, often working against great odds, have traditionally been among the most consistently successful institutions in our society. While schools and colleges continue their heroic efforts, often against a backdrop of higher expectations and limited resources, a sense of urgency is growing. An exhibit at the National Building Museum in Washington, D.C., carried this caption, "Companies come and go with the lightning speed of a computer's delete button."[9] That could apply to more than companies—all the more incentive for us to stay ahead of the curve.

Many schools and colleges are discovering that industrial-age schools are fighting an uphill battle in trying to prepare students for life in a whole new era. "Change" can be a nasty word to some. Say it, and someone is likely to respond, "Are you telling me I'm not doing a good job? Change makes me uncomfortable."

Rather than talk about change, then, let's focus our energies on developing descriptions of the system we need to help create an even more effective future for our schools and our students. It's one of the most uplifting things we could ever do and will become a part of our legacy.

Figure 2    12 Guiding Principles for Leaders Capable of Creating a Future

*How does systems thinking fit with Marx's guiding principles for leaders?*

---

*Sixteen Trends . . . Their Profound Impact on Our Future*, published by ERS, and *Future-Focused Leadership: Preparing Schools, Students, and Communities for Tomorrow's Realities*, published by the American Society for Curriculum Development (ASCD), are companion publications. In *Sixteen Trends*, we directly address massive trends and consider their implications for education and the whole of society. In *Future-Focused Leadership: Preparing Schools, Students, and Communities for Tomorrow's Realities*, we zero in on future-focused leadership and communication and provide an in-depth look at the many ways we can scan the environment and develop a vision for the future. In that book is a chapter devoted to "12 Guiding Principles for Leaders Capable of Creating a Future." Here is a brief listing of those items.

- Curiosity, persistence, and genuine interest are the main power sources for futures thinking.
- Breadth and depth are both important.
- Leaders connect the dots and seek common ground.
- There are more than two sides to most issues.
- The future is not necessarily a straight-line projection of the present.
- Enlightenment and isolation are becoming opposites.
- Peripheral vision can help us avoid being blind-sided.
- A belief in synergy can spark knowledge creation and breakthrough thinking.
- Collateral opportunity and collateral damage both deserve our attention.
- Bringing out the best in others is basic.
- Courage and personal responsibility need to overcome fear and self-pity.
- The role of strategic futurist is part of everybody's job.

(Source: *Future-Focused Leadership: Preparing Schools, Students, and Communities for Tomorrow's Realities*, Gary Marx, published by the Association for Supervision and Curriculum Development, 2006.)

---

Considering the 16 trends and 12 guiding principals for leaders mentioned in this article is just the tip of an iceberg. There are many other trends that will have an impact on education and society. Our hope is that this list will stimulate an expansive discussion and get us on a superhighway toward creating an even brighter future.

# ENDNOTES

1. Chase, H. (1984). *Issue management . . . Origin of the future.* Stamford, CT: Issue Action Publications, 38.
2. Merriam-Webster Inc. (1983). *Webster's new collegiate dictionary.* Springfield, MA: Author, 1,258.

3. Gladwell, M. (2002). *The tipping point . . . How little things can make a big difference.* (First Back Bay paperback ed.) Boston, MA: Little, Brown, 7–9.

4. Wilson, E.O. (1998). *Consilience . . . The unity of knowledge.* New York: Borzoi Book, Alfred A. Knopf, 8–12.

5. Marx, G. (2006). *Future-Focused Leadership: Preparing Schools, Students, and Communities for Tomorrow's Realities.* Alexandria, VA: Association for Supervision and Curriculum Development.

6. Bennis, W., & Goldsmith, J. (2003). *Learning to lead.* New York: Basic Books, 8–9.

7. Feynman, R. (2004). Other Feynman quotes. *The Feynman Webring.* Retrieved from the Bill Beaty Science Hobbyist Web Site, http://www.amasci.com/feynman.html

8. Surowiecki, J. (2004). *The wisdom of crowds.* New York: Doubleday, a division of Random House, 229.

9. Caption at an exhibit devoted to "The History of the American Office" at the National Building Museum in Washington, DC, opened 2000.

# What's Next? Our Gains Have Been Substantial, Promising, but Not Enough

## Marshall S. Smith

In 1994, only a handful of states embraced standards-based reforms. Seven years later, *Quality Counts 2001* reported: "The vast majority of states have been working diligently on policies related to standards-based changes. Almost all now have standards for what students should know in core subjects, tests to measure student learning, and at least the beginnings of an accountability system to hold schools responsible for results." In the fall of 2001, Congress, in the No Child Left Behind Act, reaffirmed the basic structure of the state reforms, while simultaneously reducing state prerogatives, particularly in the area of accountability.

How are we to judge the effects of all of this? *What do we know?*

The adoption by almost all states of standards-based reforms in the mid- and late 1990s appears to have established a long-term governance trend in most states that is leading to greater coherence in state and local policy. At the state and district levels, standards-based reforms provide a structure that shapes resource allocation, professional development, assessment, rewards, and sanctions. The language of reform is dominated by talk about standards.

While the reforms appeared to be becoming increasingly sturdy in 2001, this may not now be the case. Standards have never escaped criticism. With the passage of the No Child Left Behind law, the intensity of the criticism has increased, especially over the rigidity of the law's accountability requirements.

As this edition of *Quality Counts* makes clear, there also are clear indications of long-term trends in student achievement, and promising signs about the achievement gaps. Taking the results as a whole, the evidence appears strong on the side of a conclusion that the nation, and especially its least-advantaged minority groups, is making substantial gains in student achievement, as measured by state and national assessments. Not enough, but substantial and promising.

We need to retain the state standards-based systems. To move the system in a productive direction, we must alter our performance-accountability requirements. Yet there is a lot on the negative side. Many high schools continue to be boring and dysfunctional, and graduation rates are abysmally low, well below those of other nations in the Group of 8. The evidence about the narrowing of the curriculum, particularly in elementary and middle school, is quite strong, a possible unintended consequence of the movement to clear and focused goals

*What does "narrowing of the curriculum" mean?*

and corresponding alignment of resources, and to our emphasis on a rigid and overly focused conception of performance accountability. Union labor and management, at least in California, are downright hostile to each other. Education leaders often make shortsighted, political, and ideological decisions. Great attention is paid to passing laws, and few resources are granted to the hard work of implementing them. Lip service is paid to using evidence, while few ever listen to both sides of an issue.

Most important, of course, are the continuing gaps in opportunity, achievement, and attainment between our students from well-to-do families and those of modest means. There is evidence of improvement, but our nation has a long way to go.

My vision of the future of schooling is not at all radical. The general characteristics of our school systems will be here for a long while. With technology, there may be greater numbers of students who are home-schooled, but the vast majority will go to school buildings for a substantial part of one-half of the days in every year, from age 5 to at least age 16. Adults will continue to do most of the teaching, teachers will not be particularly well paid (unfortunately), states will have constitutional responsibility, local elected school boards and unions will exist in most places, and colleges and universities will continue to train most teachers and administrators.

Schools will continue to look like schools. But inside those schools, there can be great changes that stem partly from different policies and actions of the larger system, but far more from changes in the way that adults behave inside the schools.

As a start, we need to retain the state standards-based systems. All of my suggestions assume that states will continue to sustain and improve these very imperfect systems. We might think about this as the second phase of the standards movement. To move the system in a productive direction, however, we must alter our performance-accountability requirements, for in their current form they constitute a substantial threat to state standards-based systems. We need to retain the transparency created by making openly available to all the aggregated and disaggregated results of the performance assessments.

We do practically everything else wrong. We hold accountable people in schools, but exempt the people who determine what resources the schools have and the quality of those resources. We set arbitrary rather than meaningful performance standards. Why not set a performance standard for 4th grade reading that is validated to show that a student can read and understand a national newspaper, a 5th grade text in science or social studies, or the directions for setting up a computer? Let's put some meaning into the performance requirements. I think we might be surprised at how much that would motivate students. Later on in secondary school, as Achieve Inc. suggests, we might even match the assessment performance level to the capacity to carry out certain jobs or to benefit from college courses.

We accept 50 different arbitrary standards for proficiency, some greatly different, thereby rendering comparisons useless and the uniform federal requirements and sanctions absurd and patently unfair, since they implicitly assume a common standard across the states. Were the federal government to impose substantial sanctions on states that have challenging standards and did not meet their goals, I could easily imagine a strong equal-protection lawsuit challenging the federal action. We choose to select only the "proficient" level for reporting, thereby putting attention toward the upper-middle range of the scale, and often we do not report progress below or above. Why not create a system that measures and reports the growth of all students as well as the progress against the proficiency level? Why not reward success all along the scale? We measure with only one form of outcome measure, generally a standardized, machine-scored assessment, ignoring the guidance of experts in assessment who urge us to have a diversified system to help improve the validity of our judgments.

*What are some barriers to creating national standards for proficiency?*

We have a set of sanctions that ignores the vastly different contexts in the country. What does it mean to provide choice to students in rural Utah, or in areas like parts of Los Angeles, where the schools are hopelessly overcrowded? We require actions of state departments of education and districts without providing the resources for them to do their job. We punish, but do not reward. Ask any psychologist of motivation what he or she thinks about that. Most damaging, in many places, we require performance of people without giving them the resources to succeed. And, after finding them lacking, we do not provide the resources to help. This creates great distrust. We are beginning to see the negative consequences. They are avoidable.

In the future, we need to work tirelessly for high-quality and challenging learning experiences for all students, education environments that motivate students and teachers, and adequate time to help students who need it to reach meaningful standards. Four steps would take us a long way:

- **Broaden our goals for schooling.** Let's listen to what the early Greeks, the business world, developmental psychologists, good teachers, and parents tell us. Our basic goals for content and skills should embrace the language arts, mathematics, science, and history. We should strive to support all students to learn to more challenging standards in these areas, but this is not enough, for our children or our country. Broader goals should include service to our communities, exposure to and participation in the arts, and physical and health education. We need to continue appropriate use of didactic instruction, but move beyond it to achieve a balance that includes involving students in directed problem-solving, creating, and doing—building knowledge and other products with their minds and hands, including in art and music, through use of analysis, the scientific method, structured exploration, and collaboration with other students and adults.

  More attention to creation, service, and teamwork will motivate many of our students to stay in school, as well as help prepare them for work or higher education. If schools expose children only to goals that emphasize self-interest, we will lose our vision of a democracy that supports the common good. Positive motivation is a forgotten term in school policy circles. Schools, like places of work and recreation, should be continuously rewarding.

- **Address inequities and inadequacies in our school finance systems.** This requires state action within states, and perhaps federal support to address inequities in resources among states. State standards-based systems, with clear performance goals, create the opportunity for imagining that we can calibrate finance systems to give students the opportunity to reach desired performance levels. If schools do not have adequate resources to reach mandated performance levels, the accountability systems lose the trust that must exist between those who are accounting and those who are accountable. If we ask schools to do what reasonable people think is impossible, our systems lose all credibility.

  Though this approach to financing schools has been viewed as appropriate and even necessary by a variety of state courts, it is by no means easy to implement. Political and financial barriers have been difficult to overcome in almost all of the states where such an approach has been tried.

  To succeed, we will have to get smarter. In order to gain public trust to increase revenues, we need to address issues of productivity in school systems in tandem with efforts to create fair and equitable financing that is in line with desired performance objectives. We also need to realize that some states have enough money to meet their needs, while others do not. In those states where school systems are well-off, resource-allocation strategies may need to be altered.

- **Create a habit of continuous improvement within our school systems.** In the education system, where stability is critical to overall success, the basic strategy for improvement in almost all of the 14,000-plus districts should not be to "blow up the schools," or "fire a third of the employees and replace them with computers," as some people would have us do. In general, stable systems need calmer improvement strategies with constant flows of information from within and outside to keep them honest. This is not to say that we don't need to shake up a system that is atrophying.

  The improvement approach ought to be one of continuous improvement of internal processes at all levels of schooling. This includes states, county districts, local districts, and schools. Goals and metrics should guide the improvement. All levels should be focused on supporting schools to help students achieve to the district and state goals. The implications of such an approach, if taken seriously, reach into all parts of the system. Think about the large school systems that have made sustained gains. In almost every case, the superintendent was in place for over five years. Sustainable change takes time and persistence.

One component of the continuous-improvement strategy deserves specific treatment. Standards-based reforms have helped spur somewhat higher achievement by aligning resources with clear goals and accountability systems. In addition, these reforms create a major new challenge for teachers: teaching all students to be able to achieve to high standards. But the reforms do not address the practice of teaching. In effect, they, like many reforms in other sectors of the economy, set goals and rationalize management, while leaving the production units untouched.

*What are some reasons reforms have not addressed the practice of teaching?*

Over the past decade or two, we have learned a lot about how students learn and how to improve instruction in the classroom. Major reviews of the literature on reading, mathematics, science, and learning in general by the National Research Council summarize much of the data. Ongoing studies are contributing to this understanding.

One of the more promising approaches to improving instruction involves the use of systematic and frequent data to inform teachers and students about how well students are learning the material and strategies they are expected to be learning. Substantially improving student performance—bringing almost all students to *challenging* standards of achievement, whether at the 2nd grade or community college level— appears to require that teachers have the data, skills, and opportunities necessary for continuously improving their instruction. As many researchers argue, systems of formative assessment, where teachers regularly identify and respond to students' changing needs, can lead to very substantial gains in student performance.

In the past three years, the idea of using data to help improve instruction has caught on like wildfire in the United States. Unfortunately, many schools and districts do not appreciate the complexity of the process: Teachers must have effective and easy-to-use measurement instruments, they must have the knowledge to interpret the instruments, and then they must understand how to alter their instruction to respond to the diagnostic information the instruments provide. In many districts, none of the steps is successfully implemented.

- **Deliberately support experimentation in public school practices, choice, governance, and use of technology.** The theory and practice of standards-based reform does not directly address the issues of stimulating innovation within the public system, or of safety valves for parents and students who would like an alternative to the standard public schools.

Two significant strategies address these issues. The first is the creation of charter schools and the development of small secondary schools in areas where they serve as an alternative to traditional large schools. Both charter and small schools typically offer choices to students, and stem from the widely held perception that many schools (particularly secondary schools) are too bureaucratized and impersonal to do a good job in teaching most students, especially those needing the most help.

Potentially, the two types of schools both provide the opportunity for competition in ideas and practice to the traditional systems and serve as incubators for new strategies. Though charters, on average, look a lot like regular public schools and have similar effects on student achievement, there are exceptions. In my view, the most important of the innovations that some charters have used has been to extend the time of schooling by significant amounts. Of course, the time has to be used well. The Knowledge Is Power Program, or KIPP, for example, extends time by roughly 60 percent, and is realizing striking and powerful results on achievement working with poor and minority children across the country. The widespread use of such interventions would greatly enhance our chances of closing achievement gaps.

The other strategy involves the use of technology. The private sector began to realize productivity gains from technology 10 to 15 years ago. At first, technology improved only the work rate. Later, it spurred changes in the nature of the work itself. The use of technology by school systems and schools lags behind the private sector by about a decade. By that calculation, schools, which have already realized some gains in efficiency from technology in their central offices and in certain aspects of instruction, should be just about ready to realize productivity gains from using technology to actually change some of their work processes.

One of the more important recent advances has been in the way central-office, school, and student-level data are gathered, organized, delivered, and used. New data systems make it possible in large districts to track the allocation of resources, as well as student outcomes, on a real-time basis, and to make the data available throughout the schools. It is in the direct service of teaching and learning, however, that the most important advances are being seen.

State standards-based reforms are here to stay. During the last decade, achievement scores in many states, and averaged across the United States, have increased, with African-American and Hispanic students generally gaining one to two grade levels in mathematics and reading. But the states may be ready to enter a second stage of the standards movement, one based on a strategy of continuous improvement, leavened by new knowledge, practice, and innovation from research, technology, and charter schools.

Our first step in that direction must be to fix the performance-accountability system, for in its present form it jeopardizes the standards movement, and will surely impede other important forms of progress. Our next step must be to act on the realization that improved student achievement is a function of improving content (curriculum and instruction), motivation (of students and adults), and time (for students and for reforms to succeed).

# Echoing Their Ancestors, Women Lead School Districts in the United States

Margaret Grogan

*Women have been involved in leadership activities throughout the history of the United States. Not always called leadership, their capacities to deal with difficult situations, and to manage enterprises have earned them the reputation of being strong and resilient, capable of great initiative. This article draws briefly on this history to situate a discussion of how women are shaping the most powerful position in U.S. education— the superintendency. Using published findings from the AASA (2003) national survey of women superintendents and central office administrators, conducted by Margaret Grogan and Cryss Brunner, the article argues that women are still seen as somewhat of an anomaly in the position, and that a collaborative effort must be made by all those involved to bring about real change.*

U.S. women have a history of leading in ways that have not always been labeled "leadership." The women who were instrumental in managing their families and property while their men folk went to war or while their husbands and fathers learned how to govern the country are excellent examples of this. So too, are the women who accompanied husbands and family members on their early expeditions out West, rebuilding a home life and finding the strength to keep going in times of great economic adversity. And the African-American women who fought to bring themselves and their families out of slavery showed that leadership was a private, domestic enterprise as well as a highly risky public one. The United States is founded on stories of white women and women of color whose work to manage a home and family affairs has never been described as leadership, though it was crucial to the survival and success of all. . . .

Like the educational leaders of today, early North American women managed human and material resources so that the family enterprise could be successful. This kind of leadership is not about the hero who risks all in the name of some ideal. It is a much more down-to-earth, messy business that involves navigating constantly changing circumstances and dealing with external forces over which individuals have little control.

*What are your thoughts on the question of why school leadership has ignored women?*

Why then, has school and district leadership been so little associated with women throughout U.S history? In her seminal work on women in the superintendency, Jackie Blount, 1998, explains how teaching became women's work and school administration men's. She shows that men took control of the more highly valued and highly paid work over time and that the social and political structures have combined to keep the gendered divisions ever since. As she points out, the superintendency is a key position to study because "[A]n important component of the effort to establish control of schools has occurred in contesting the definition of this position" (p. 2). Blount writes of Ella Flagg Young, superintendent of Chicago's public schools in the early twentieth century who believed that women were destined to become superintendents in every district. Young thought that a gender shift would be possible if the relationships in schooling changed and if the purposes of schooling were re-evaluated. A re-configuration of power was necessary. Not only should administrators give up some of their power but teachers should have more to begin with.

This process was to be more than merely "giving input" or "having a voice," which are little more than symbolic gestures, but rather involved having real power. This was to be part of a holistic social system with students and other members of the school community also engaged in meaningful democratic process (Blount, 1998, p. 168).

How far have we come towards realizing Young's vision? The following section relates some of the current views of women in the superintendency and of women in the central office. There are signs of progress, but when we juxtapose Grogan and Brunner's (2005, in press) findings against the stories of early U.S. women leading and managing as a matter of course, we realize that there are still powerful forces at work maintaining a gendered notion of leadership.

## LEADERSHIP IN THE SUPERINTENDENCY

The superintendency is the name given to the executive level position at the top of the educational hierarchy in the United States. Public school superintendents are typically appointed by a school board of five or more lay individuals who are the elected[1] representatives of the school community known as a school district. As a research topic, women in the U.S. superintendency has only been investigated for the past 20 years or so. Several fairly recent studies make up the body of information that researchers commonly draw upon (see Beekley, 1996, 1999; Bell, 1995; Blount, 1998, 1999; Brunner, 1998a, 1998b, 1999, 2000a, 2000b; Chase, 1995; Chase & Bell, 1990; Grogan, 1999, 2000a, 2000b, 2001; Grogan & Smith, 1998; Kamler & Shakeshaft, 1999; Marietti & Stout, 1994; Mendez-Morse, 1999; Ortiz, 1999; Ortiz & Ortiz, 1995; Pavan, 1999; Scherr, 1995; Sherman & Repa, 1994; Skrla, Reyes, Scheurich, 2000; Tallerico, 2000; Tallerico & Burstyn, 1996; Wesson & Grady, 1994; and others).

Until the AASA study (2003) conducted by Grogan and Brunner, there had been no comprehensive national studies of women in the superintendency. As for women central office administrators, much less is known—very few studies have been done of women in these positions. Further, little research has been conducted about women of color in both positions, and even when studies are done, because women of colour in leadership positions are rare, very few voices are heard (see Alston, 1999, 2000; Brunner & Peyton-Claire, 2000; Enomoto, Gardiner, & Grogan, 2000; Grogan, 1996; Gardiner, Enomoto & Grogan, 2000; Jackson 1999; Kalbus, 2000; Mendez-Morse, 2000, 2004; Nozaki, 2000; Ortiz, 1982, 2000; Ortiz & Ortiz, 1995; Simms, 2000).

To get a current glimpse of women in the superintendency, this article will discuss selected findings from reports of the AASA survey (Brunner, Grogan, & Prince 2003; Grogan & Brunner, 2005; in press) including comparisons between the 2003 survey and the 2000 survey of the general population of superintendents (Glass, Brunner & Björk, 2000). Gradually, research is building a comprehensive portrait of a group of modern women who are educational leaders in very public, risky settings. Although their forebears were not often (if ever) described as leaders, these superintendents are recognized as such. Are their activities and skills today very different from those of remarkable women in the past?

*What are possible barriers for women entering educational system leadership?*

One important statistic to emerge from this survey is that women now lead 18 percent of all public school districts in the United States (Grogan & Brunner, 2005). Ten years ago a mere 7 percent of districts nationwide were headed by women superintendents (Montenegro, 1993). But it is important to consider that although the numbers of women in the superintendency have more than doubled over the past ten years, they are still woefully small in light of the facts that women comprise 51 percent of the general population, 52 percent of elementary principals, 83 percent of teachers in elementary settings (Shakeshaft, 1999), 57 percent of central office administrators and 33 percent of assistant/associate/deputy/area /superintendencies (Hodgkinson & Montenegro, 1999). So, relatively few women are, in a sense, like the early pioneer women. They are finding their own ways to lead educational systems, and to manage all the unpredictable circumstances they are faced with in these turbulent times—even in large districts.

The survey revealed that the proportion of women serving in large, medium and small districts across the United States is very similar to the proportion of men serving in the same size districts (Grogan & Brunner, 2005). Of course, since 82 percent of districts are still headed by men, more men than women head up the largest districts, but women are there too. Women are in large districts, urban districts, suburban districts and rural districts. They are demonstrating that they can manage operations that are staffed by many as well as by few. They serve highly diverse communities and homogeneous ones dotted throughout the United States in every state and region. But women superintendents are not necessarily doing everything the same way as their male counterparts.

# WOMEN LEADERS SHAPING THE ROLE

One common thread between early North American women's activities and those of women superintendents today is their focus on the well-being of children and families. Most women superintendents have been elementary principals (Grogan & Brunner, 2005). They bring a strong interest in educating the whole child and in looking out for those most at-risk. Women ranked programmes for children-at-risk as significantly more important than men did (Grogan & Brunner, in press).

Tapping into the community is seen as important to women superintendents. Grogan and Brunner (in press) found that more women than men sought citizen participation very frequently. It was clear that all superintendents valued participation in decision-making, but women regularly invited it. For example, information from district administrators, school board members, fellow superintendents and teachers was important to all superintendents. However, women valued it more highly than men, and women were much more likely to include teachers in the groups giving input. Women appear to be situating their leadership efforts within the larger community.

Women view the importance of building learning communities through the instructional expertise they bring to the position. When comparing the results of the two most recent surveys of superintendents, both men and women believed that improving curriculum and instruction, knowledge of teaching and learning, and knowledge of curriculum are considered to be strengths for women (Grogan & Brunner, in press). More women than men also labeled the changing curriculum as high priorities for the pre-service and in-service of superintendents (Grogan & Brunner, in press).

Given the recent reform movement in the United States prompted largely by the *No Child Left Behind* Act (2001), there is a much greater emphasis on curriculum and testing issues, even at the level of superintendent of schools, than there has been in the past. The superintendent's role has not always been thought of as being directly involved in instruction. (See Brunner, Grogan & Björk, 2002, for a fuller discussion of the evolution of the role of the superintendent.) Grogan and Brunner's findings (in press) show that women are bringing to the superintendency a strong emphasis on learning and creating communities of learners.

When the 2003 study of women superintendents' perception of their board's primary expectations is compared with the perceptions of male and female superintendents reported in the 2000 study, some revealing differences are found. Both groups chose educational leader as their top choice, but significantly more women in both studies felt it to be the primary expectation. The facts are that a significant number of women superintendents have backgrounds in curriculum and instruction, most women have spent more years in the classroom before entering administration, and most place a high premium on continuing education for themselves (Grogan & Brunner, 2005). Women see themselves as educational leaders perhaps because they enjoy teaching, and administration gives them an opportunity to foster learning on a greater scale.

A small but growing number of women superintendents are associated with reform initiatives—particularly women of colour (Grogan & Brunner, 2005). They are seeing themselves as change agents who have the capacity to turn around districts where students are struggling. All superintendents must focus today on the achievement gap and find ways to keep students in schools, but it is notable that women do not shy away from entering the political fray to transform their districts.

It is too early to tell whether or not the current context of heightened attention to student academic achievement is responsible for the surge in the numbers of women in the superintendency. To be sure, women have been socialized into administrative positions associated with curriculum and instruction, and women have been encouraged to build communities of support for themselves from earlier times of being isolated and on the margins of leadership. In teaching longer and remaining in the arena of children and families, women view educational leadership as an extension of classroom work. Thus, at the risk of essentializing women, these may be some explanations for why more women are obtaining superintendencies now than in the past, and for why many women currently express interest in serving in the role.

Not only do women appear to be gaining a stronger grasp on the highest educational position in the United States, but they also appear to be finding ways to bring to the position skills and expertise more typically associated with women—keeping instruction at the forefront and developing relationships with school and wider community members that can help foster the academic and social growth of the student. It is evident from the results of the surveys, that women and men superintendents are different enough in their responses to questions surrounding the role that we might expect women educational leaders to evolve further in the future. And we might expect that women educators will view the position as an attractive opportunity to make a difference for children and their families.

As mentioned earlier, 40 percent of the central office participants in the 2003 study expressed interest in pursuing the position (Grogan & Brunner, 2005). This means that 60 percent did not. It is not known how many central office men aspire to the superintendency. Since it is a highly stressful position associated with exaggeratedly long hours and relatively low compensation, (Grogan & Brunner, 2005), it is possible that the numbers of men aspiring to the superintendency are similar to the numbers of women. More important, the recent survey dispels the myth that women do not want the position.

But for women, there are detractors. Few receive the necessary mentoring, even fewer women of colour are encouraged to pursue the job, and the pressures of combining family responsibilities with administrative ones take their toll on marriages and career opportunities (Grogan & Brunner, 2005). Very few women educators serve yet in districts headed by women (Brunner, Grogan &

*Are there any cautions about the ways women are shaping the role of school leader?*

Prince, 2003). This means that for women considering the position, there are few role models and few opportunities to even discuss the possibility.

## CONCLUSION

It would be premature to predict the kind of impact on the superintendency that will be made by the growing presence of women in the position. Currently, the weight of the discourse of educational leadership is much stronger than the influence of the relatively few women shaping the role in ways indicated by the survey. What is important though, is the value of the presence of women in and of itself. Even if women cannot immediately change the way superintending has been done in the past, their public declaration of interest in the position, and their increasing success in gaining the position will have a powerful effect on the next generation of women educators. Once it becomes commonplace to see women as executive leaders in education, they can settle into the job and determine priorities for themselves.

There are indications that Ella Flagg Young's vision resonates with contemporary U.S. women educators. The results of the 2003 study certainly suggest that the superintendency is more closely associated with learning and teaching than it has been since the very early conception of the position as teacher-scholar (Callahan, 1966). Increasingly, superintendents are being described as instructional leaders (Petersen & Barnett, 2003). In addition, there is an emphasis on the need for more democratic processes (Kowalski, 2003) allowing superintendents to manage the politics of serving diverse communities. These trends echo Young's hope for more integration of administration with the business of the classroom.

However, until there is a more equitable distribution of women in the highest levels of educational leadership, we are sending a message that says women's leadership is still not much valued. Power resides in the system structures and practices that have gone unquestioned for too long. Researching and writing about women in leadership helps to draw attention to the power imbalance, but it is doubtful that research alone has much impact on the discourse of educational leadership. Change will only come about if the battle is fought on many fronts.

First we need to think of women as having always demonstrated the skills that are associated with leadership of school systems—like managing human and material resources to achieve collective goals, taking initiative, fighting contentious battles in public as well as in private, taking risks for the welfare of children and families, and dealing with uncertainty on a daily basis. Having done the reading that formed the basis of the beginning of this article, I am more convinced than ever that there is a false sense of women's and men's activities as somehow socializing them differently to notions of leadership. While it might have been true, until recently, that women were not military generals, business magnates or politicians, the kind of leadership that educational systems need is not learned in those settings. It is learned in studying the business of education and in honing the skills described above—skills as much associated with women's activities as with men's.

Some hold that U.S. women are already seen as leaders, but the dearth of women not only in the superintendency but also in all politically charged, public positions belies the fact. Thus all educators, researchers and practitioners alike must take the situation to heart. The following eight recommendations grow out of a firm belief that it will take a collaborative effort to bring about real change—researchers working with practitioners, women working with men, white educators working with educators of color.

Some of these recommendations emerge from the results of the recent surveys that are echoes of past research. Some of the recommendations have formed as a consequence of addressing many groups of women superintendents and other aspiring women leaders across the country. They are not the only ideas, but they would serve as a good start.

*What issues arise for groups who attempt to implement these recommendations?*

To address the striking imbalance in the numbers of women and men in the highest position of educational leadership: (1) state and federal agencies and foundations must fund more research on the topic; (2) women and men researchers need to take the topic more seriously and bring renewed critical perspectives and energy to it; (3) women in positions of leadership must talk about the joy they derive from their work; (4) women and men in positions of power in educational systems must deliberately mentor more women and especially more women of color; (5) pre-service women teachers must be directed towards leadership as a way to remain close to teaching and learning; (6) women leaders must talk about and think creatively with other women of ways to couple family responsibilities with administration; (7) compensation for superintendents must increase to attract the highly qualified women central office administrators who are already relatively well paid; and (8) gender power differentials in educational administration must be acknowledged.

In the interests of the next generation of young women not only in the United States but in many other countries, the daughters, nieces and cousins of the men who remain in control of educational leadership we must make this concerted effort, men and women together, white and of color around the globe.

## NOTE

1.  There are some instances where the school board is appointed by the mayor or the county councillor and others in which the superintendent is elected.

## REFERENCES

Alston, J. A. (1999). Climbing hills and mountains: Black females making it to the superintendency. In C. C. Brunner (Ed.), *Sacred Dreams: Women and the superintendency*. New York: State University of New York Press.

Alston, J. A. (2000). Missing from action: Where are the Black female school superintendents? *Urban Education, 35 (5),* 525–531.

Beekley, C. (1996). *Gender, Expectations and Job Satisfaction: Why women exit the public school superintendency.* Paper presented at the annual meeting of the American Educational Research Association, New York.

Beekley, C. (1999). Dancing in red shoes: Why women leave the superintendency. In C. C. Brunner (Ed.), *Sacred Dreams: Women and the superintendency.* Albany, NY: State University of New York Press.

Bell, C. S. (1995). "If I weren't involved in schools, I might be radical": Gender consciousness in context. In M. Dunlap & P. A. Schmuck (Eds.), *Women Leading in Education,* (pp. 288–312). Albany, NY: State University of New York Press.

Blount, J. (1998). *Destined to Rule the World: Women and the superintendency, 1873-1995.* Albany, NY: State University of New York Press.

Blount, J. (1999). "Turning out the ladies": Elected women superintendents and the push for the appointive system, 1900–1935. In C. C. Brunner (Ed.), *Sacred Dreams: Women and the superintendency,* (pp. 9–28). Albany, NY: State University of New York Press.

Brunner, C. C. (1998a). Can power support an ethic of care? An examination of the professional practices of women superintendents. *Journal for a Just and Caring Education, 4 (2),* 142–175.

Brunner, C. C. (1998b). Women superintendents: Strategies for success. *The Journal of Educational Administration, 36 (2),* 160–182.

Brunner, C. C. (1999). *Sacred Dreams: Women and the superintendency.* New York: State University of New York Press.

Brunner, C. C. (2000a). *Principles of Power: Women superintendents and the riddle of the heart.* Albany, NY: State University of New York Press.

Brunner, C. C. (2000b). Unsettled moments in settled discourse: Women superintendents' experiences of inequality. *Educational Administration Quarterly, 36 (1),* 76–116.

Brunner, C. C. (2003). Invisible, limited, and emerging discourse: Research practices that restrict and/or increase access for women and persons of color to the superintendency. *Journal of School Leadership, 13 (4),* 428–450.

Brunner, C. C., & Peyton-Claire, L. (2000). Seeking representation: Supporting Black female graduate students who aspire to the superintendency. *Urban Education, 35 (5),* 532–548.

Brunner, C., Grogan, M. & Björk, L. (2002). Shifts in the discourse defining the superintendency: Historical and current foundations of the position. In Murphy, J. (Ed.), *The Educational Leadership Challenge: Redefining leadership for the 21st century* (pp. 211–238). Chicago: National Society for the Study of Education.

Brunner, C. C., Grogan, M. & Prince, C. (2003, April). *AASA National Survey of Women in the Superintendency and Central Office: Preliminary*

*Results*. Paper presented at the annual conference of the American Educational Research Association, Chicago, IL.

Callahan, R. E. (1966). *The Superintendent of Schools: A historical analysis*. (ERIC Document Reproduction Service No. ED0104 410)

Chase, S., & Bell, C. (1990). Ideology, discourse, and gender: How gatekeepers talk about women school superintendents. *Social Problems, 37 (2)*, 163–177.

Chase, S. (1995). *Ambiguous Empowerment: The work narratives of women school superintendents*. Amherst, MA: University of Massachusetts Press.

Enomoto, E. K., Gardiner, M. E., & Grogan, M. (2000). Notes to Athene: Mentoring relationships for women of color. *Urban Education, 35 (5)*, 567–583.

Floyd, J. (2002). *The Pioneer Woman*. Columbia, MO: The University of Missouri Press.

Gardiner, M., Enomoto, E., & Grogan, M. (2000). *Coloring outside the Lines, Mentoring women into educational leadership*. Albany, NY: Suny Press.

George, R. Marangoly (1996). *The Politics of Home: Postcolonial relocations and twentieth century fiction*. Cambridge: Cambridge University Press.

Glass, T. E., Björk, L. & Brunner, C. C. (2000). *The Study of the American School Superintendency, 2000*. Arlington, VA: American Association of School Administrators.

Gould, V. Meacham (1998). *Chained to the Rock of Adversity: To be free, black and female in the old south*. Athens, GA: The University of Georgia Press.

Grogan, M. & Blackmon, M. (2001). A superintendent's approach to coalition building: Working with diversity to garner support for educational initiatives. Brunner C. & Björk, L. (Eds.), *The New Superintendency* (pp. 95–113). Amsterdam: JAI Press.

Grogan, M. & Brunner, C. C. (in press). Women superintendents and role conceptions: (Un)Troubling the norms. In L. Björk, & T. J. Kowalski (Eds.), *School District Superintendents: Role Expectations, Professional Preparation, Development and Licensing*. Thousand Oaks, CA: Corwin Press.

Grogan, M. & Brunner, C. (2005, February). Women leading systems. *The School Administrator, 62 (2)*, 46–50.

Grogan, M. & Smith, F. (1998). A feminist perspective of women superintendents' approaches to moral dilemmas. *Just and Caring Education 4 (2)*, 176–192. (Reprinted in *Values and educational leadership*, pp. 273–288, by P. Begley, Ed., 1999, Albany, NY: Suny Press).

Grogan, M. (1996). *Voices of Women Aspiring to the Superintendency*. New York: State University of New York Press.

Grogan, M. (1999). A feminist poststructuralist account of collaboration: A model for the superintendency. In C. C. Brunner (Ed.), *Sacred Dreams: Women and the superintendency*. New York: State University of New York Press.

Grogan, M. (2000a). The short tenure of a woman superintendent: A clash of gender and politics. *Journal of School Leadership, 10 (2)*, 104–130.

Grogan, M. (2000b). A Black woman superintendent tells. *Urban Education, 35 (5)*, 597–602.

Hodgkinson, H. & Montenegro, X. (1999). *The U.S. School Superintendent: The invisible CEO*. Washington, D.C.: Institute for Educational Leadership.

Jackson, B. L. (1999). Getting inside history—against all odds: African American women school superintendents. In C. C. Brunner (Ed.), *Sacred Dreams: Women and the superintendency*. New York: State University of New York Press.

Kalbus, J. C. (2000). Path to the superintendency. *Urban Education, 35 (5)*, 549–556.

Kamler, E., & Shakeshaft, C. (1999). The role of the search consultant in the career paths of women superintendents. In C. C. Brunner (Ed.), *Sacred dreams: Women and the superintendency*, (pp. 51–62). Albany, NY: State University of New York Press.

Kowalski, T. J. (2003, April). *The Superintendent as Communicator*. Paper presented at the annual meeting of the American Educational Research Association, Chicago, IL.

Marietti, M., & Stout, R. (1994). School boards that hire female superintendents. *Urban Education, 8 (4)*, 383–397.

Méndez-Morse, S. E. (1999). Re-definition of self: Mexican American women becoming superintendents. In C. C. Brunner (Ed.), *Sacred Dreams: Women and the superintendency*. New York: State University of New York Press.

Méndez-Morse, S. E. (2000). Claiming forgotten leadership. *Urban Education, 35 (5)*, 584–595.

Méndez-Morse, S. E. (2004). Constructing mentors: Latina educational leaders role models and mentors. *Educational Administration Quarterly, 40 (4)*.

Montenegro, X. (1993). *Women and Racial Minority Representation in School Administration*. Arlington, VA: American Association of School Administrators.

Nozaki, Y. (2000). Feminist theory and the media representation of a woman-of-color superintendent: Is the world ready for *Cyborgs? Urban Education, 35 (5)*, 616–629.

Ortiz, F. I. (1982). *Career Patterns in Education: Women, men and minorities in public school administration*. New York: Prager.

Ortiz, F. I. (1999). Seeking and selecting Hispanic female superintendents. In C. C. Brunner (Ed.), *Sacred Dreams: Women and the superintendency*. New York: State University of New York Press.

Ortiz, F. I. (2000). Who controls succession in the superintendency: A minority perspective. *Urban Education, 35 (5)*, 557–566.

Ortiz, F. I., & Ortiz, D. J. (1995). How gender and ethnicity interact in the practice of educational administration: The case of Hispanic female superintendents. In R. Donmoyer, M. Imber, and J. Scheurich (Eds.), *The Knowledge Base in Educational Administration: Multiple perspectives.* Albany, NY: State University of New York Press.

Pavan, B. N. (1999). The first years: What should a female superintendent know beforehand? In C. C. Brunner (Ed.), *Sacred Dreams: Women and the superintendency,* (pp. 105–124). Albany, NY: State University of New York Press.

Petersen, G. & Barnett, B. (2003, April). *The Superintendent as Instructional Leader: Evolution, future conceptualizations and implications for practice and preparation.* Paper presented the Annual Meeting of the American Educational Research Association, Chicago, IL.

Roberts, C. (2004). *Founding Mothers.* New York: Harper Collins Publishers Inc.

Scherr, M. W. (1995). The glass ceiling reconsidered: Views from below. In M. Dunlap & P. A. Schmuck (Eds.), *Women Leading in Education,* (pp. 313–323). Albany, NY: State University of New York Press.

Shakeshaft, C. (1999). The struggle to create a more gender-inclusive profession. In J. Murphy & K. Seashore-Louis (Eds.), *Handbook of Research on Educational Administration, 2^{nd} ed.,* (pp. 99–118). San Francisco: Jossey-Bass.

Sherman, D., & Repa, T. (1994). Women at the top: The experiences of two superintendents. *Equity and Choice, 10 (2),* 59–64.

Simms, M. (2000). Impressions of leadership through a Native woman's eyes. *Urban Education, 35 (5),* 637–644.

Skrla, L., Reyes, P., & Scheurich, J. J. (2000). Sexism, silence, and solutions: Women superintendents speak up and speak out. *Educational Administration Quarterly, 36 (1),* 19–43.

Tallerico, M. (2000). Gaining access to the superintendency: Headhunting, gender, and color. *Educational Administration Quarterly, 36 (1),* 18–43.

Tallerico, M., & Burstyn, J. N. (1996). Retaining women in the superintendency: The location matters. *Educational Administration Quarterly, 32,* 642–664.

Wesson, L., & Grady, M. (1994). An analysis of women urban superintendents: A national study. *Urban Education, 8 (4),* 412–424.

# ARTICLE 10.4

# Educational Leaders in a Globalising World: A New Set of Priorities?

Mike Bottery

## INTRODUCTION—WHAT THIS PAPER IS *NOT* ARGUING

It is perhaps best to begin by stating what this article is *not* arguing. It is not arguing that the global level is the only one of which educational leaders need to take cognisance. There are clearly many other levels which impact upon educational thought and practice, and of which educational leadership needs to be aware. There are, for instance, those who argue that the critical level at which most thought and practice is determined is the cultural level (Huntington, 1998; Harrison & Huntington, 2000). For such critics, there are a number of distinctive world cultures, transcending individual nation states (Asian, European, African, Arabic) which set the context within which most thinking is done, and which frame the way in which concepts are understood, leading to assertions by some (e.g. Nisbett, 2003), that, for instance, Asian and western individuals actually exhibit profound cognitive differences.

Whilst such a thesis may be persuasive, one of its problems lies in that most 'Asians' and 'westerners' would want to assert a more finely grained distinctiveness, based on nationality, religion or ethnic grouping. There do indeed seem to be as many differences between the French, the Spanish and the English, as there are between the Japanese, the Chinese and the Koreans. Moreover, it is clearly the case that most educational professionals work within national educational contexts, and the nation state has historically, framed the nature, purposes and structure of much educational practice (see Green, 1998). Moreover, despite pronouncements by writers like Ohmae (1996) that influence at the level of the nation state is dead, this is generally far from the truth. Ribbins and Zhang (2005) have shown how the various components of Chinese culture ensure that educational leadership looks very different there from its counterpart in the UK, even when they have governments with apparently similar economic policies.

Yet even the national focus may be too large: there has been a considerable retreat over the past decade from beliefs that big pictures can fully explain what is going on at the institutional level. Generalisations derived from large-scale surveys of best educational practice, then, are insufficient to engineer good practice into the individual institutional level. The local context needs to be fully appreciated, and this includes not only local culture and material conditions, but the personalities of those involved in any practice.

## THE NEED FOR MACRO-LEVEL ANALYSIS

*What does globalization mean, and why is it important for educational leaders?*

None of these foci is wrong; none should be ignored. Each demands that its nature and functioning be appreciated, as well as how it affects levels below it and how it mediates the effects of those above. Yet it is time to add a further level of context to an understanding of educational practice, and that is the global level. Thus, seeing the Earth from space in the middle of the twentieth century was a seminal moment for the human race, for until that moment, people had talked of the concerns of all humanity, had argued the concerns of one earth, but no one had actually *seen* this picture of global wholeness, unity and beauty. Most visions, indeed, were locked into and framed by the concerns of nation states. Viewing the earth from space brought home how tiny and transitory the human presence is, how fragile is the ecosystem we inhabit. 'Globalisation', as a concept, is, then, intimately connected with the way we view our place and meaning on this planet. However, it is more than this, for it also describes *processes* which steer the policies of nation states which directly impact upon their educational institutions. A globalising world is now the context within which humanity lives and works, and educational leaders need to understand the challenges that originate at this level, for failing to do so renders them powerless to respond. . . .

[In] the summer of 2005, there were two major issues on the agenda of the G8 Summit. One was debt relief, the other was global warming. In both cases, such was the importance and power of the US, that neither was felt to be resolvable without its commitment. If globalisation is measured in terms of power and reach, then consider that the US spends more on military expenditure than the next eight countries *combined* (Nye, 2002). Johnson (2004) points out that of the 189 countries registered with the UN in 2002, 153 have a US military presence in their territory. In terms of economic power, the US has a 27% share of world product, equal to the next three largest economic powers, again combined. Finally, in a world where economic power is heavily dependent upon a facility in IT, the US contains one-half of all Internet users. Technological and economic globalisations may be forces in their own right, but they have intimate connections with such American globalisation.

Such power makes its weaknesses cause for global concern as well. Klare (2005) argues that its Achilles' heel lies in its dependency upon foreign imports of oil, a dependency which will increase as its own reserves decrease, when the global reserve of oil is now decreasing (a reserve increasingly competed for by growing economies like those of China and India). Crucially as well, the location of these reserves poses global problems, as the largest oil reserves are to be found in Saudi Arabia, a country with a youthful population, an unemployment rate of over 30%, and ruled by a family which sustains over 7000 'princes', whilst watching the average income of the rest of its population decline from $28,600 in 1981 to $6800 in 2001. It is little wonder, then, that the US has become militarily embroiled in this area, and looks likely to continue to do so, with all of the consequences of such involvement. This dilemma—of increasing competition in a politically volatile area for decreasing energy supplies—is one which most other developed countries are going to have to deal with as well.

What are the implications of this for educators? US economic influence and values penetrate the workings of even the most distant nation states, and affect their functioning, and through this the aims and functioning of their educational organisations. At the same time, US military intervention around the globe produce outcomes difficult to predict, but which are likely to raise tensions wherever they occur. Yet one should not forget US soft power, for the influence of its food (McDonaldisation), its fashion (jeans, sweatshirts and trainers), its films (with subliminal messages of the triumph of the individual over the system, and of personal responsibility), and its political values (of democracy and free markets), exerts enormous effects upon other cultures. Some of these are enthusiastically adopted, others just as aggressively resisted. Educational leaders everywhere will be confronted by, and need to understand and be able to respond to, their effects upon local identity, culture and educational communities. . . .

[Different] types of globalisation interact and influence one another in diverse ways, producing a complex and difficult world. They are likely to generate the following global realities for those living into the twenty-first century:

- the effects of neo-liberal economic strategies
- the effects of ageing populations
- a dispersal of state power
- the problems and possibilities of advanced technology
- greater cultural variety, and greater commodification
- issues of a degrading environment
- the hard and soft power of the US—and reactions
- consequences of increasing energy shortages
- issues of a global language.

For many public-sector educational leaders, such global realities, despite their mediation by lower levels of context, seem to result in heightened tensions in their work. Five in particular seem to stand out:

1. Attempts to satisfy the greater demands of both clients and governments for an improved service are likely to clash with demands to reduce expenditure and to increase efficiencies.
2. Attempts to respond to nation state needs to strengthen its legitimacy as the sole provider of citizenship may conflict with claims by sub-national groups, and supra-national organisations for more 'nested' forms of citizenship.

3.  The pressure to use private-sector concepts and practices, primarily based around questions of efficiency, economy and profit, will likely conflict with public-sector values and practices, based more around values of equity and care.

4.  Educational leaders will continue to experience governmental control and steerage of their activities; yet will also find that they are being asked to be more flexible and creative in developing institutional and pedagogical strategies.

5.  The same tension will be seen with respect to trust, as governments see the need for enhanced autonomy and creativity, yet feel unwilling or unable to abandon more directive policies which result in low-trust cultures of targets and performativity.

*What is the relationship between public education and "public good"?*

Such tensions are generated by contradictory movements: on the one hand, movements towards decentralisation, flexibility and empowerment, and on the other, towards centralisation and control, which result, paradoxically, in increases in both the fragmentation *and* the control of professional work. Yet there are other effects upon their work, particularly in terms of the movement of professional values. This is particularly true in terms of the invasion of the privatising discourse of economic activity into the discourse and activities of education. When education is infiltrated by this discourse, it is in danger of becoming no more than a private consumable item, a positional good, in which self-interest, and 'consumerism' as the model for living (Bottery, 2004), come to dominate. Such movement almost inevitably erodes the concept of a public good, 'a sense of social and fraternal responsibility for others' (Grace, 1994, p. 214), upon which any inclusive global citizenship would be built. Without such an understanding, we are reduced in the relationships we can enter, and our potentiality as human beings is diminished. The championing of personal, institutional or national self-interest not only prevents concerns with structural inequalities, but may actually *promote* them, for this is one more way of securing competitive advantage. As Barber (1996, p. 243) argued, 'Consumers speak the elementary rhetoric of "me", citizens invent the common language of "we"'. The need for educational leaders to understand and resist such developments could not be stronger at the present time, as there is evidence that not only do policy-makers see education in such terms, but so, increasingly it seems, do many public-sector professionals. Bottery (1998) for instance, found that as teachers and nurses in the UK worked in more competitive and more business-oriented organisations, so their views of professionalism were increasingly defined in terms of loyalty and competitive advantage to the institution they worked within, rather than to some greater public or communal good. Moreover, in the US, Australia and the UK, Slaughter and Leslie (1998) found that as universities were driven by reduced governmental funding to seek other revenue streams, administrators and senior academics increasingly favoured (or tolerated) the practices and values of entrepreneurial individuals, who ceased to support traditional university values of open enquiry and a community of scholars.

As a global competitive, economic framing of activity increasingly influences and infiltrates that of educational activity, so it then comes to challenge and then to change professional values. This process has not happened overnight; it has happened over months and years, mostly in subtle and imperceptible ways, so that for individuals, the change to practice comes to be seen as so natural that it may be unnoticed. As Fergusson (1994, p. 213) suggested, an acculturation then takes place during which educators come 'to live and be imbued by the logic of the new roles, new tasks, new functions . . . in the end [they] absorb partial re-definitions of their professional lives, first inhabiting them, eventually becoming them'. And when this happens, Lukes' (1986, p. 24) disturbing vision of power becomes a reality, for now individuals are unable to develop a critique of existing conditions because 'their perceptions, cognitions, and preferences' are shaped 'in such a way that they accept their role in the existing order of things, either because they can see no alternative to it, or because they see it as natural and unchangeable'. What kinds of response can educational leaders make?

*What does the author mean by "ecological leadership"?*

# NEW LEADERSHIP REQUIREMENTS

## (i) An 'Ecological' Leadership

In 2003, the UK National College for School Leadership (NCSL) formally recognised the need for educational leaders to more greatly appreciate the context within which they worked (NCSL, 2003). It was, however, clear that the context they were thinking of was reasonably local. Similarly, Fullan (2004) argued that effective educational leaders need to attend to issues beyond their own institution, yet his focus once again was upon the local and regional. There is much to be said for such exhortations, yet appreciation of context cannot remain at the local or even the national level, for if important effects upon people's lives originate at the global level, then an appreciation of this level—and an understanding of the impact of these forces upon them—has to be a critical part of an educator's role. A first requirement, then, is a greater 'ecological' role in providing others with an understanding of the world in which they live. When people find that the age at which they can retire is receding, yet 'greedy' organisations seem to want more and more from them in both intellectual and emotional terms during this expanded working life; when they have to worry about freak weather conditions and skin cancers more than ever before; when their jobs are relocated to the other side of the world or the skills underpinning them are no longer valued; when governments legislate on more and more, and yet at the same time seem to withdraw support from the individual; when high streets seem to be increasingly carbon copies of each other, as the local and different is leached out; if educators do not help them to understand these phenomena by explaining the global context and causes of such change, who else will? If educators do not provide this, who will provide such understanding?

However, such an understanding cannot just be an education in accommodation through the honing of employment skills and self-preservation techniques for individuals of the developed world. Whatever the theoretical benefits of the current pre-eminent global economic model, in practice it has not only exacerbated differences between rich and poor, but has been manipulated by the already powerful to benefit them at the expense of the world's poor. An education in such issues must, then, also be one of assimilation to other models of living. Its understanding must be part of an expanding moral circle of concern (Singer, 1981), where we move from an ethical concern for those close to us, through to concerns for the communities we live in, on to the societal level, and from there to a global conception of all humanity. Singer would ask us not to stop there, and to include within our ethical concerns other species as well. The global level encompasses this, for it recognises that the life-styles and practices of the rich and powerful of the developed world do have consequences, not only for other human beings, but for the other inhabitants of the planet as well. Economic discourse needs to be understood *within* a moral discourse of equity, justice and community. Perhaps, for some, this does come back to self-interest, for there must be concern that what the developed world is experiencing at the moment is in part a backlash for previous behaviours: that the motivation for at least some terrorist outrages is in part a response to the structured impoverishment of the underdeveloped world; and heightened concerns over the environment are at least in part a product of the developed world's patterns of consumption. An education for a more just and equitable world would not simply help to create more justice and more equity: it would also create a safer and healthier world as well.

## (ii) Understanding the Context of Professional Work

Such a changing global world, then, has important effects upon individual lives: it also has had important effects upon the way in which educational professionals have been viewed by the larger public. Over the last 50 years, conceptions of professional work have changed from ones based upon high-trust, peer-based accountability, mystique and autonomy to a low-trust model involving extensive external quantitative accountability, with increasingly limited discretion. From being viewed as an altruistic group deserving considerable trust and autonomy, much literature has suggested that professional educators amount to no more than a self-serving group: Marquand (1997, p. 141) suggests that neo-liberal critiques have portrayed professionals as no more than 'market distorting cabals of rent seekers, engaged in a collaborative conspiracy to force the price of their service above their true market'. 'Third way' governments have largely accepted such assumptions, at the same time intensifying an 'audit explosion' (Power, 1994, p. 38) of professional work, which has stressed its

*Why does the author consider external quantitative accountability as a "low-trust" model?*

measurement by external quantitative measures. This has resulted in a form of administrative control under which professionals have ceased to be 'on top', and have instead increasingly been reduced to a group 'on tap' to managerial requirements (Pollitt, 1992). In the process, the values of economy, efficiency and effectiveness have trumped long-standing professional values. Those who continue to uphold the pursuit of truth as a primary value, Parker (2001) argues, are in danger of becoming no more than 'court jesters', living out their professional lives in 'noisy, but largely ineffectual' manner, whilst the 'real' work of the institution is carried out by the more managerially inclined. A vital role for educational leaders, then, is to recognise and understand such changes, realise their implications, and to reflect upon what educators need to do in order to usefully respond.

## (iii) Changing the Accountability Context

A further requirement lies in responding to the manner in which professional work is largely measured. External, quantitative low-trust forms of accountability based upon private-sector strategies of 'exit' rather than of public-sector values of 'voice', linked to systems of targets and performativity, have generated poor morale in the teaching profession across a number of countries (Hargreaves, 2003). They are also a critical element in the decline in trust by professionals of policy-makers, leading to an unhealthy and unproductive antagonism which exacerbates the situation, leading to a vicious circle in which policy-makers then view such professional antipathy with a reciprocal distrust, leading to further micro-managed forms of accountability. As a consequence, they are likely to have been major contributory factors in previously mentioned problems of retention and recruitment at leadership levels across the western world.

Such forms of accountability, however, do not just depress morale. Because they tend to measure the observable and quantifiable, they also fail to reflect or measure other aspects of professional practice which contribute to educational success. Educational leaders therefore need to work towards developing proactive and reflexive forms of accountability, ones which are not simply of the form which are 'done' to them, but to whose definition and scope they contribute. Educational leaders not only need to be conversant with the origins and meanings of 'professionalism', but also with the origins, meanings and manifestations of forms of accountability, recognising the need to work towards kinds which demonstrate how neglected aspects of practice may be essential to rich conceptions of both successful education and professionalism.

There are certainly those who are pessimistic about the realisation of such change. Jary (2001), for instance, believes that the forces driving audit will sustain the preeminence of current quantitative forms. Yet there are others, like Misztal (2001), who point out that some of these global forces actually work towards such an outcome. To be successful in the knowledge economy, organisations need to generate greater creativity, teamwork and problem-solving, which not only entail more extensive sharing of information within flatter organisational forms, but also sit more comfortably with richer forms of accountability.

Such optimism and pessimism are reflected in the educational practices of different countries. The optimism seems to be supported by recent pronouncements by the New Labour government in the UK. One major official publication for primary schools, *Excellence and enjoyment*, explicitly argued that 'We need to support heads in developing professional self-confidence so that they do not focus on 'complying' with the National Curriculum or the Primary Strategy, but on actively shaping both, to meet their own children's needs and improve their outcomes' (DfES, 2003, p. 58).

Similar flexibility has appeared for the UK secondary sector with proposals for a condensed Key Stage 3 (QCA, 2004). These seem to cohere with the espousal of a more flexible and creative school leadership, and perhaps also with a greater mixture of accountability forms.

On the other hand, the impact of the 'No Child Left Behind' (NCLB) legislation in the US which came into effect in 2002 seems to have had precisely the opposite effect. Reversing the movement towards richer forms of teaching, evaluation and accountability instruments, NCLB has mandated at federal level a series of targets for children to achieve, based on standardised tests, but with no extra finance to schools currently doing poorly, and taking no account of value added. The result is that in a country where only about 10% of school finances is provided centrally, massive differences in financing are preventing achievement of satisfactory grades in precisely those schools it was supposed to help lever up. Even worse, it has led in many cases to a return to teaching focused on the tests, to limiting curricula, to poor attendance and increased drop-out rates, which in some cases have been encouraged by schools in order to boost the numbers who can achieve the required standards (see Meier *et al.*, 2004). The accountability context is massively important.

*Do you agree that one of the problems with lack of achievement under NCLB is massive differences in financing?*

## (iv) Building Trust, Building Communities

Power (1997, pp. 145–146) argues that governmental change will only occur when a government is 'capable of knowing when to trust, and when to demand an audited account'. This issue of trust is a critical one, not just for reasons of morale and accountability, but because it frames the manner of relationships, and different levels of trust seem to generate different kinds of relationship (Bottery, 2004). Thus, the lowest level of trust, a *calculative* form in which the parties involved in a relationship do little more than perform mathematical-type calculations on the degree to which the other can be trusted. This level is normally that at which external quantitative accountability is generated. Educational leaders need to build beyond this. *Role* trust is a richer, more traditional form, being the normative assertion that an education into and practice of a set of professional values, is a guarantee of good practice. In current conditions this is not going to be sufficient. It will need to be supplemented by a form of *practice* trust, in which claims are confirmed or disconfirmed by evidence.

Such evidential bases for practice lead into the realisation that there are different foundations for trust. A first foundation area for trust is an agreement over values and value priorities: not an easy area when educators and governments may come at the same issue with very different concerns. A second foundation area is based upon a perception of integrity—that people will do what they say they will do. The third foundation area of trust is based upon perceptions of job competence. Educational leaders need to recognise these foundational differences, and how they require different responses if support for practice is to be built.

Finally, in a world where the predominant global discourse is economic and privatising in nature, an invigorated professional role will not be generated solely by pursuing such issues with governments and policy-makers. As important will be the building of trust with the educational stakeholders of local communities. This will involve a number of different activities. A first will be in helping others better understand the ecology of forces which surround, steer and constrain their current existences. Such education could lead to the building of bridges through a sharing of similar concerns. A second stems from the first, a greater education of these others in the nature, purpose and constraints of professional work. In doing so, not only is a better understanding of their own practice provided, but so also is a richer accountability. A third is also closely linked to these two, for any account of professional practice is likely to be more respected, more trusted, when there is a strong evidential base for such practice. This must mean a commitment to research performed upon their own practice. The final act of trust begins, underpins and stems from these other activities—the recognition that these others, normally described as clients, have valuable and significant input, not only into the educational process, but also into an understanding of such global processes. Through such professional humility, educational communities are more likely to be built.

## CONCLUSION

This article has suggested that the global context needs to be understood by educational leaders, not just to help others understand and mediate such effects, but because it impacts upon the work of themselves and of their profession.

In this globalising world, then, perhaps it is time for a change to the nature and role of educational leaders. This begins with an acceptance of their role in educating others as to the nature of the globalisation phenomena described in this article. But their role needs to be one of critique, for many of these forces are not descriptive but prescriptive, reflecting particular interests and particular accumulations of power. Through their discourses they mould consciousnesses away from notions of public sectors and public goods, and away from the striving for a fairer and more just world, towards values and ways of living which are narrower, meaner and spiritually more impoverished. To recognise such movements, yet fail to voice such concerns, and fail to help others to understand and voice such concerns, is to tacitly condone them. It is also to accept an emasculation of the professional role. Perhaps it is time for educational leaders to recognise that in this globalised world neutrality in such matters is not an option. Living in a politicised world, educational leaders will have to learn to live and lead within it.

# NOTE

1. This paper is a slightly amended version of a keynote address given at the Belmas Annual Conference, 23–25 September, 2005, at Kent's Hill Park Conference and Training Centre, Milton Keynes, England.

# REFERENCES

Barber, B. (1996) *Jihad V. McWorld* (New York, Ballantine Books).

Bottery, M. (1998) *Professionals and policy* (London, Continuum).

Bottery, M. (2004) *The challenges of educational leadership* (London, Paul Chapman).

Boulding, J. (1968) The economics of the coming spaceship earth, in: M. Allenby (Ed.) *Thinking green: an anthropology of essential ecological writing* (London, Barrie and Jenkins), 133–138.

Chua, N. (2003) *World on fire* (London, William Heinemann).

Crystal, D. (2003) *English as a global language* (Cambridge, Cambridge University Press).

DfES (2003) *Every child matters* (London, DfES).

Dychtwald, K. (1999) *Age power* (New York, Tarcher Putnam).

Fagan, B. (2005) *The long summer: how climate changed civilization* (London, Granta).

Ferguson, R. (1994) Managerialism in education, in: J. Clarke, A. Cochrane & E. McLaughlin (Eds) *Managing social policy* (London, Sage), 93–114.

Fukuyama, F. (1991) *The end of history and the last man* (London, Penguin).

Fullan, M. (2004) *The moral imperatives of school leadership* (London, Sage).

Gittings, J. (2005) *The changing face of China* (Oxford, Oxford University Press).

'Global aging' (2005, February 8) *BusinessWeek*.

Grace, G. (1994) Education is a public good: on the need to resist the domination of economic science, in: D. Bridges & T. McClaughlin (Eds) *Education and the marketplace* (London, Falmer), 126–138.

Green, A. (1998) *Education, gobalization and the nation state* (London, Macmillan).

Gronn, P. (2003) *The new work of educational leaders* (London, Paul Chapman).

Hargreaves, A. (2003) *Teaching in the knowledge society* (Milton Keynes, Open University Press).

Harrison, L. & Huntingdon, P. (Eds) (2000) *Culture matters* (New York, Basic Books).

Harvey, D. (1989) *The condition of post modernity* (Oxford, Blackwell).

Heater, D. (2004) *A history of citizenship education* (London, Routledge).

Huntingdon, S. (2004) *Who are we? America's great debate* (New York, Free Press).

Jary, D. (2001) Aspects of the 'audit society', in: M. Dent & S. Whitehead (Eds) *Managing professional identities* (London, Routledge), 38–60.

Johnson, C. (2004) *The sorrows of empire* (New York, Metropolitan Books).

Klare, M. (2005) *Blood and oil* (London, Penguin).

Laabs, J. (1996) Downshifters: workers are scaling back, *Personnel Journal*, 75(3), 62–76.

Laing, R. D. (1975) *Knots* (Harmondsworth, Penguin).

Lukes, S. (1986) *Power* (Oxford, Oxford University Press).

Lynas, M. (2005) *High tide* (London, Harper Perennial).

Marquand, D. (1997) Professionalism and politics, in: J. Broadbent, M. Dietrich & J. Roberts (Eds) *The end of the professions?* (London, Routledge), 140–147.

Meier, D., Kohn, A., Darling Hammond, L., Sizer, T. & Wood, G. (2004) *Many children left behind* (Boston, MA, Beacon Press).

Misztal, B. A. (2001) Trusting the professional, in: M. Dent & S. Whitehead (Eds) *Managing professional identities* (London, Routledge), 19–37.

National College for School Leadership (NCSL) (2003) *Annual review of research* 2002–3 (Nottingham, NCSL).

Nisbett, R. (2003) *The geography of thought* (London, Nicholas Brearley).

Nye, J. (2002) *The paradox of American power* (Oxford, Oxford University Press).

Ohmae, K. (1996) *The end of the nation state* (New York, Free Press).

Parker, M. (2001) The romance of lonely dissent, in: M. Dent & S. Whitehead (Eds) *Managing professional identities* (London, Routledge), 138–156.

Pollitt, C. (1992) *Managerialism and the public services* (2nd edn) (Oxford, Basil Blackwell).

Power, M. (1994) *The audit explosion* (London, Demos).

QCA (2004) *A condensed key stage 3: designing a flexible curriculum* (London, QCA).

Reich, R. (2004) *The destruction of public higher education in America, and how the UK can avoid the same fate* (London, Higher Education Policy Institute).

Ribbins, P. & Zhang, J. (unpublished) *Culture, societal culture and school leadership—a study of selected head teachers in rural China.*

Ritzer, G. (1993) *The McDonaldization of society* (London, Sage).

Ritzer, G. (2003) *The globalization of nothing* (London, Sage).

Singer, P. (1981) *The expanding circle* (Oxford, Oxford University Press).

Slaughter, S. & Leslie, L. (2004) *Academic capitalism* (Baltimore, MD, John Hopkins University Press).

Stiglitz, J. (2002) *Globalization and its discontents* (London, Penguin).

Watters, M. (1995) *Globalization* (London, Routledge).

# ISSUE SUMMARY

S everal themes emerge in the readings selected for this issue of forecasting the future of education organizations: use of trend data, broader goals, continuous improvement, attention to global forces, gender-neutral leadership, partnering. But there are many more themes that could have been chosen for this section. The choice was subjective and merely points to the fact that we are in an age of hyperchange and the educational organization of the future is likely to be reshaped frequently and rapidly.

Gone are the days when a school or institution could count on being able to offer a standard curriculum and traditional programs to a steady stream of students and their parents. Gone too are the days when communication was top-down, in the form of memos delivered to faculty and staff in their inner-office mail boxes. And long gone is the notion that accountability measures are locally determined. At the broadest level, what is gone is the security of leaders who know where they are headed because they have sensible long-range plans and a captive audience.

The reality that education institutions are in constant flux has direct implication for leaders. What leaders knew in the past does not necessarily shape what will happen in the future. Instead, the dazzling pace of change brings with it unimagined new directions. The wise leader's response will be:

> Rather than talk about change, then, let's focus our energies on developing descriptions of the system we need to help create an even more effective future for our schools and our students. It's one of the most uplifting things we could ever do and will become a part of our legacy. (Marx, 2006, p. 7)

What does all of this bode for the future of educational leadership? In many ways, leadership will continue to be about culture, strategy, process, and ideas. Clear thinking, seeing the patterns, discerning good-better-best, and making wise decisions will continue to be the building blocks of good leadership. What is most likely to change for education organizations and their leaders is that knowing won't be as important as learning.

At this point the devil's advocate would be prompted to ask, who has time to spend scanning the environment when there are accountability reports to issue to parents, when teacher performance reviews are due, when the school board has called an emergency meeting on school safety—these are the orders of the day. Neither skepticism about the future nor romanticizing about the past is a valid alternative. Leaders must become future-oriented because that is the responsible way for their work to reflect their principles.

Legacy-building must start now—during America's perfect storm. Leaders need to take a positive attitude about the future, keep a clear sense of purpose, and maintain a calm but courageous stance in order to ride out the storm.

# ISSUE HIGHLIGHTS

- Use of trend data is essential as leaders plan ahead.
- Connected leadership in terms of cross-disciplines and inclusion of diverse groups of people is vital for a successful future.
- Designing the systems needed to create a more effective future should be a major focus of education leaders.
- District and state goals for content and skills should be broader, with more challenging standards.
- School finance systems should give students adequate opportunities to reach performance.
- A continuous improvement approach to internal processes at all levels of schooling is necessary for future success.
- A nongendered approach to leadership will become the norm in America's school systems; more women will have leadership roles at higher levels.
- Women superintendents and higher education leaders will likely keep instruction and development of broad partnerships at the forefront.
- Forces occurring at the global level will have greater impact on the work of educational leaders.
- Leaders will adopt an ecological role as they frame the worldwide implication of issues.
- The differences between leading and managing will become even more significant.
- Leaders need to take a more proactive role in developing reflexive forms of accountability that are more in keeping with the knowledge economy.

# CRITICAL THINKING

In the future, will schools and institutions be able to engage more fully with the knowledge economy or will they observe it? Will education leaders lead by connecting or by watching?

Some experts believe that organizations of the future will be defined by generative capabilities—innovation, knowledge-creation, and close connection to networks and partners. These will be foundational drivers of any organization that functions within the knowledge economy, according to Saint-Onge and Armstrong in their work, *The Conductive Organization: Building Beyond Sustainability.* On the landing page of their Web site, Saint-Onge and Armstrong distill organizational conductivity to a singular capability: "to effectively transmit quality knowledge throughout the organization as well as with and between customers and employees." Clearly this calls for flexible internal structures and self-initiated learning.

It's interesting that a similar cluster of capabilities often defines educational organizations—learning, collaborating, and strategy making. But here's the conundrum: Will schools and institutions be capable of contributing to innovation and knowledge-creation, and will they have a credible role in networking? Or will they simply observe these capabilities in business and other organizations but continue to rely on memory and past reforms for how to educate?

To explore whether schools and institutions will be conductive organizations in the future, compare ideas in the readings for this issue with the principles of the conductive organization:

- Leadership is a capability that must be encouraged and nurtured within all employees, not just the few who sit at the top of the organization chart.
- The ability to configure and reconfigure processes and capabilities, to continually calibrate to the customer, is central to the leadership agenda today.
- Leadership's responsibility is to ensure that systems and structures are in place to enable members of a value-creation network to collaborate, learn, share knowledge, and execute their responsibilities.
- Employees must assume responsibility for knowledge exchange as a key part of their learning and capability development as part of the way they do their work.
- New technologies impacting on human communication drive new organizing principles and structures.
- High-quality relationships support core values.
- High-performing organizations know how to build and maintain the relationships that are the conduits for knowledge flow, leveraging capabilities, and strategy-making processes.
- Performance gives freedom to be who we want to be, to express our collective greatness as individuals, to actualize our full potential, and to realize our destiny.
- Strategy making is an action verb as opposed to a noun or an object. It's an embedded process as opposed to a finite set of activities in a defined time cycle. (Adapted from www.conductiveorg.com)

## ADDITIONAL READING RESOURCES

Jeff Faux, *The Global Class War*. John Wiley & Sons, 2006.

Koret Task Force on K-12 Education, *Our Schools and Our Future: Are We Still at Risk?* Hoover Institution, Stanford University, 2003.

Gary Marx, *Sixteen Trends . . . Their Profound Impact on Our Future*. Educational Research Service, 2006.

The National Center for Public Policy and Higher Education, *Income of U.S. Workforce Projected to Decline if Education Doesn't Improve*. Policy Alert, Author, November, 2005.

Hubert Saint-Onge and Charles Armstrong, *The Conductive Organization: Building Beyond Sustainability*. Elsevier, 2004.

Edie Weiner and Arnold Brown, *FutureThink*. Pearson Education/Prentice Hall, 2005.

For more information on the future of educational organizations, check these sites:

The Conductive Organization www.conductiveorg.com
The Conference Board www.conference-board.org
The Futurist Journal www.futurist.com
Forces that Can Change America's Future www.centerforpubliceducation. org/site/c.kjJXJ5MPIwE/b.2511445/k.A4D/Forces_that_can_change_ Americas_future.htm

# CONTRIBUTORS TO THIS VOLUME

## EDITOR

**JOYCE HUTH MUNRO**, Ph.D., is the dean of the School of Graduate Studies at Chestnut Hill College in Philadelphia. In addition to K–12 and higher education experience, she has worked for professional associations in issues of teacher quality, standards, and accountability. Dr. Munro has published articles on professional development and leadership. Her current interest is helping professionals in educational institutions become systems thinkers. Dr. Munro holds graduate degrees from the University of South Carolina and Vanderbilt University.

## AUTHORS

**RUSSELL ACKOFF** is author of books on management and systems thinking. He is Anheuser-Busch Professor Emeritus of Management Science at The Wharton School and a former president of both the Operations Research Society of America and the Society for General Systems Research.

**JACOB E. ADAMS, Jr**. is research associate professor of Public Affairs at Stanford University.

**JEFF ARCHER** is an associate editor for *Education Week*. His beats are school leadership, with an emphasis on the business community's role in education policy.

**MIKE BOTTERY** is director of Research Degrees, Centre for Educational Studies, University of Hull. He is author of *Challenges of Educational Leadership*, published by Sage.

**NELDA CAMBRON-McCABE** is a professor of educational leadership at Miami University in Miami, Ohio. She is coauthor, along with Luvern Cunningham, James Harvey, and Robert Koff, of *The Superintendent's Fieldbook: A Guide for Leaders of Learning.*

**COMMISSION ON NO CHILD LEFT BEHIND** is a bipartisan, independent effort dedicated to improving NCLB.

**LUVERN L. CUNNINGHAM** is an emeritus professor and former dean of the College of Education at Ohio State University. She is coauthor, along with Nelda Cambron-McCabe, James Harvey, and Robert Koff, of *The Superintendent's Fieldbook: A Guide for Leaders of Learning.*

**EDWIN C. DARDEN** is an attorney and the director of education policy for Appleseed, a national organization focusing on K–12 education law, policy, and social justice.

**WILFRED H. DRATH** is a senior fellow and director of the New Lenses Initiative at the Center for Creative Leadership in Greensboro, North Carolina.

**PETER K. EISINGER** is a professor in the College of Urban, Labor and Metropolitan Affairs at Wayne State University. He serves as the director of the State Policy Center at the university.

**SUSAN P. EISNER** is a professor of Management at Ramapo College, New Jersey, and consultant with senior practitioner experience in national ventures of major organizations including a leading television station, a prominent health care foundation, a presidential campaign, a public interest group, and a national political party.

**DEAN FINK** is an international education consultant in Ontario, Canada. He is coauthor of *Sustainable Leadership*.

**MICHAEL FULLAN** is professor emeritus and former dean, Ontario Institute for Studies in Education, University of Toronto. He is currently special advisor to the premier and minister of education in Ontario. Among his books are *Leading in a Culture of Change, Turnaround Leadership,* and *Leadership and Sustainability: Systems Thinkers in Action.*

**DANIEL GOLEMAN** is codirector of the Consortium for Research on Emotional Intelligence in Organizations at Rutgers University. His latest book is *Social Intelligence: The New Science of Human Relationships* (Bantam, 2006).

**MARGARET GROGAN** is professor and chair, Department of Educational Leadership and Policy Analysis, University of Missouri–Columbia.

**HOWARD M. GUTTMAN** is the principal of Guttman Development Strategies, Inc., a management consulting firm specializing in executive development, management development, and organization development. His corporate experience includes Johnson & Johnson and Automatic Data Processing.

**ANDY HARGREAVES** is the Thomas More Brennan Chair of Education at the Lynch School of Education, Boston College. He is author of *Teaching in the Knowledge Society: Education in the Age of Insecurity* and *Sustainable Leadership*.

**FREDERICK M. HESS** is director of Education Policy Studies and a resident scholar at the American Enterprise Institute.

**PAUL T. HILL** is the John and Marie Corbally Professor at the University of Washington's Daniel J. Evans School of Public Affairs and a director of the Center on Reinventing Public Education.

**RICHARD C. HULA** is a professor and chair of the Department of Political Science at Michigan State University.

**BRIAN JACOB** is assistant professor of Public Policy at the John F. Kennedy School of Government, Harvard University, and a faculty research fellow with the National Bureau of Economic Research.

**RALPH JACOBSON** is a principal of The Leader's Toolbox, author of *Leading for a Change: How to Master the Five Challenges Faced by Every Leader,* and faculty member at the Physician's Leadership College, University of St. Thomas.

**BARRY C. JENTZ** is an organizational consultant to public and private schools, corporations, and private firms and a lecturer in the Graduate School of Education, Harvard University.

**CRAIG D. JERALD** is president of Break the Curve Consulting, located in Washington, D.C. Jerald was previously a principal partner at the Education Trust, an advocacy and research organization, and a senior editor at *Education Week.*

**DEL JONES** is a reporter for *USA Today.*

**PAUL KELLEHER** is the Murchison Distinguished Professor of Education and Chair of the Education Department at Trinity University.

**MARY BETH KLOTZ** is a school psychologist and the director of IDEA Projects and Technical Assistance for the National Association of School Psychologists.

**LARS LEFGREN** is assistant professor of Economics, Brigham Young University.

**RICHARD LEPSINGER** is president of OnPoint Consulting and has over 20 years experience as a human resource consultant and executive. He is coauthor (with Gary Yukl) of several books as well as author of articles on leadership.

**MARYA LEVENSON** is the Levitan Director of Teacher Education and a Professor of education at Brandeis University.

**ROBERT L. LINN** is codirector of the National Center for Research on Evaluation, Standards, and Student Testing and former president of the American Educational Research Association and the National Council on Measurement in Education.

**ANDREW LONGMAN** is a partner and vice president of marketing at Kepner-Tregoe. He is responsible for the worldwide promotion of the company's brand and consultants. Longman is coauthor of *The Rational Project Manager: A Thinking Team's Guide to Getting Work Done.*

**MICHAEL C. MANKINS** is a managing partner of Marakon Associates, a strategy and management consulting firm. Based in San Francisco, he advises business leaders on strategic and organizational initiatives to drive performance and long-term value growth. Mankins holds an MBA from The Wharton School of the University of Pennsylvania.

**KIM MARSHALL** is a leadership coach for new principals in New York City and Newark, New Jersey. He publishes *The Marshall Memo*, a weekly digest of ideas and research on K–12 education.

**GARY MARX** is president of the Center for Public Outreach in Vienna, Virginia.

**JEROME T. MURPHY** is Harold Howe II Professor of Education and dean emeritus, Graduate School of Education, Harvard University.

**GARY L. NEILSON** is a senior vice president based in Booz Allen Hamilton's Chicago office. He is a member of Booz Allen's Board of Directors and Operating Council and holds an MBA in finance from Columbia University.

**NEL NODDINGS** is Lee L. Jacks Professor of Education, Emerita, at Stanford University. Among her best known books are *Caring* and *The Challenge to Care in Schools*. Her most recent book is *Critical Lessons: What Our Schools Should Teach* by Cambridge University.

**BRUCE A. PASTERNACK** is president and chief executive officer of Special Olympics, Inc., and a former senior vice president at Booz Allen Hamilton. He has coauthored two business books, *The Centerless Corporation* and *Results*. Pasternack has also authored articles in *Harvard Business Review* and *Strategy+Business*.

**JAMES W. PELLEGRINO** is distinguished professor in Psychology and Education at the University of Illinois at Chicago.

**ANDREW J. ROTHERHAM** is cofounder and codirector of Education Sector.

**RICHARD ROTHSTEIN** is a research associate at the Economic Policy Institute and author of *Class and Schools: Using Social, Economic and Educational Reform to Close the Black-White Achievement Gap*.

**ROBERT W. ROWDEN** is associate professor of management in the Stetson School of Business and Economics at Mercer University in Georgia. His research is in workplace learning and human resources.

**PHILLIP C. SCHLECHTY** is founder and CEO of the Schlechty Center for Leadership in School Reform. He is author of *Creating Great Schools: Six Critical Systems at the Heart of Educational Innovation, Inventing Better Schools: An Action Plan for Educational Reform,* and *Shaking Up the Schoolhouse: How to Support and Sustain Educational Innovation*.

**JUDD SILLS** is a project manager and certified diversity facilitator for Southern California Edison.

**MARSHALL S. SMITH** is the program director for education at the William and Flora Hewlett Foundation. Previously he was the Undersecretary of Education in the Clinton administration.

**JAMES P. SPILLANE** is professor of education and social policy and a faculty fellow at the Institute for Policy Research, Northwestern University. Spillane is principal investigator of the Distributed Leadership Study.

**RICHARD STEELE** heads the Global Diversity Initiative of Marakon Associates. He has been published in *Harvard Business Review, Harvard Management Update, MIT Sloan Management Review*, and *The Financial Times.*

**KAREN E. VAN NUYS** is a principal with Booz Allen Hamilton, a consulting firm that provides services in strategy, operations, organization and change, and information technology for government and commercial clients.

**JOHN VOGELSANG** is associate director of the Support Center for Nonprofit Management in New York. He has published articles and monographs on organization development and leadership issues. He also serves on the editorial board of the OD Practitioner.

**GARY YUKL** is a professor of management in the School of Business at the University at Albany, State University of New York, and the author of books on organizational leadership. His areas of research are leadership, power and influence, and managerial skills.

# CREDITS

# INDEX